HOLDER!

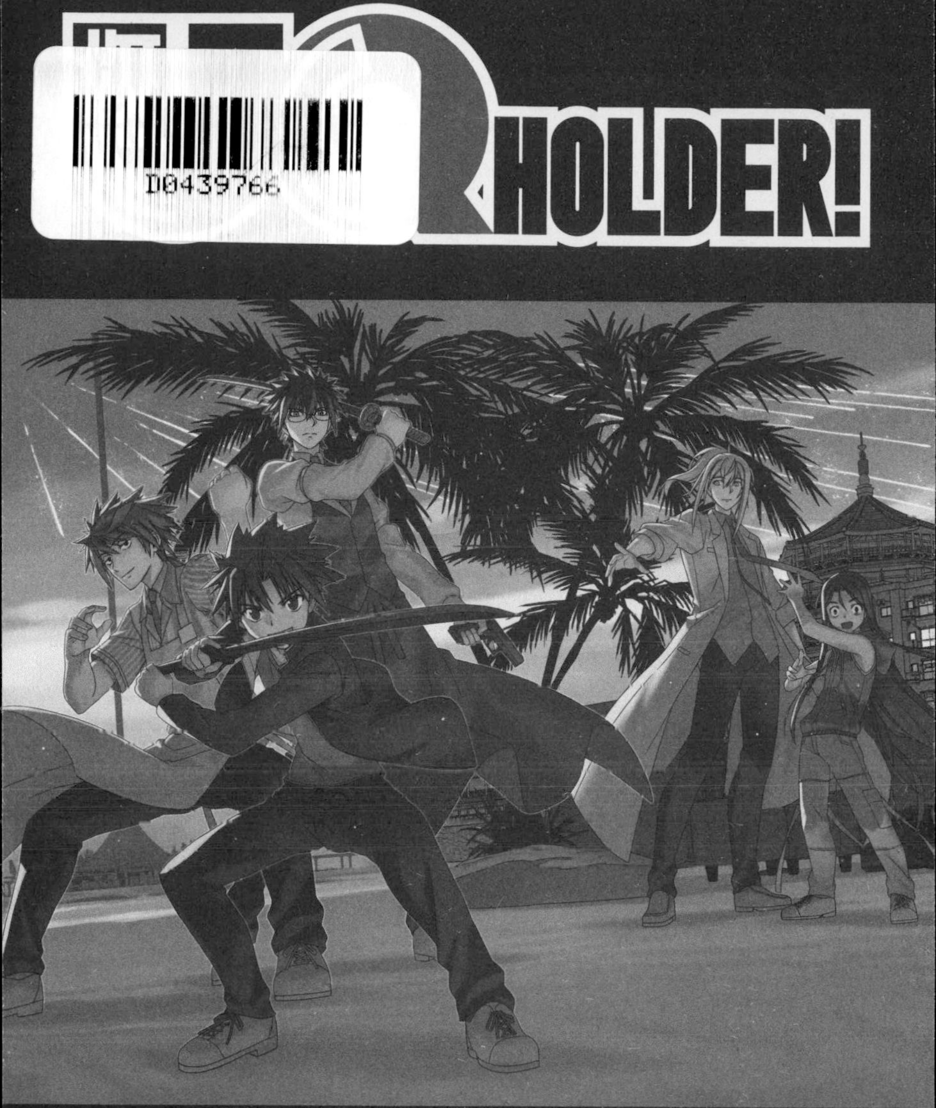

CONTENTS

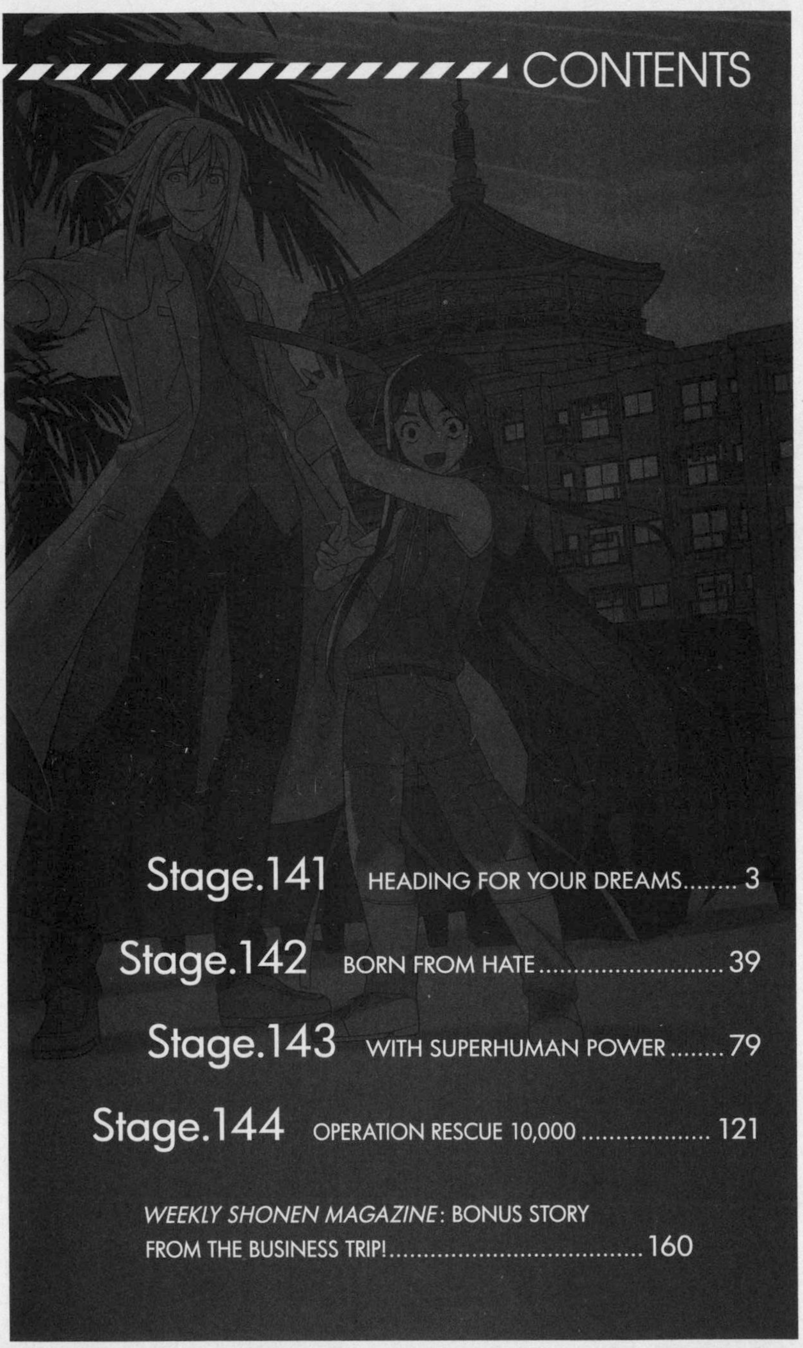

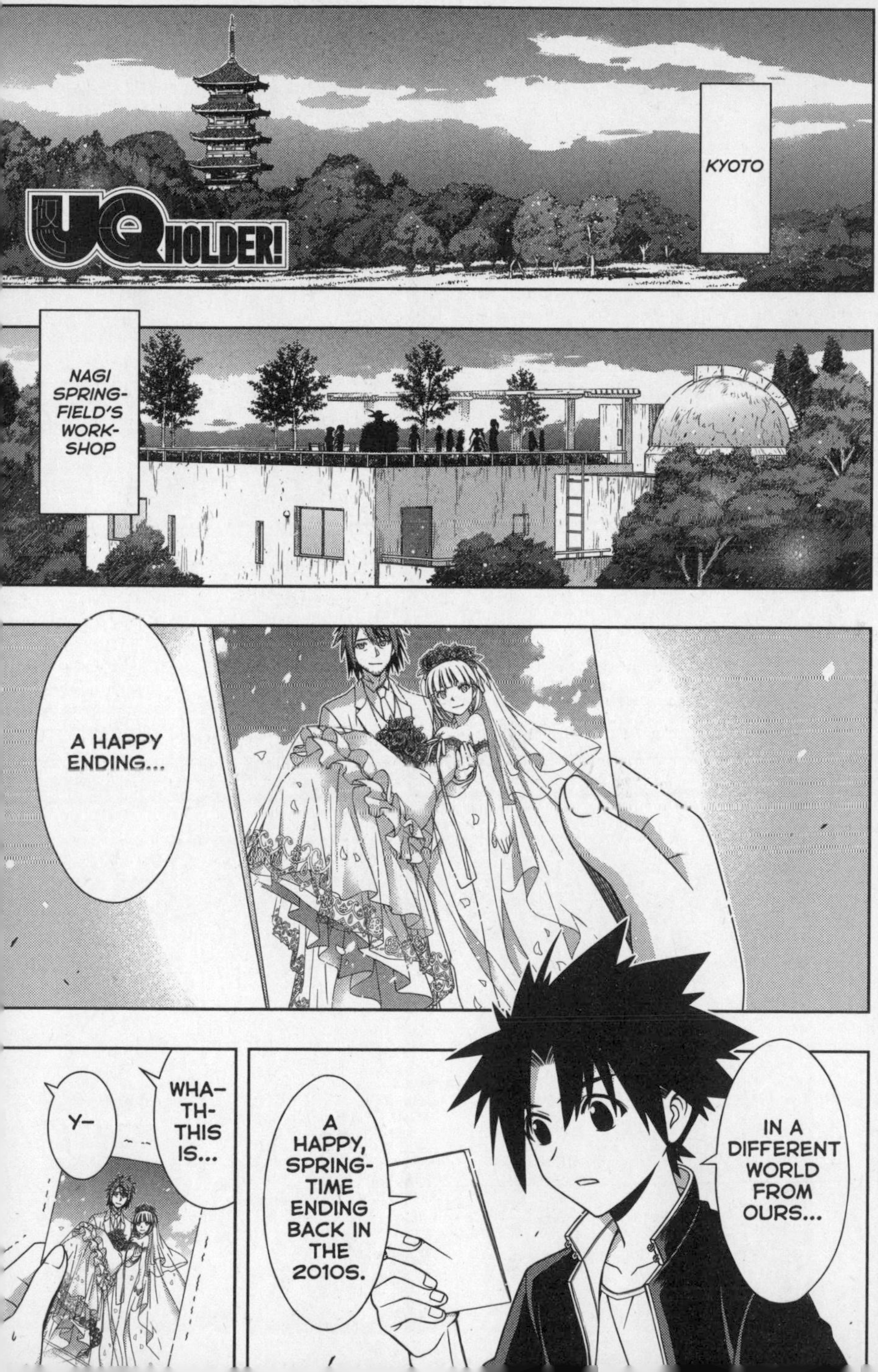
KYOTO
UQ HOLDER!
NAGI SPRING-FIELD'S WORK-SHOP
A HAPPY ENDING...
IN A DIFFERENT WORLD FROM OURS...
A HAPPY, SPRING-TIME ENDING BACK IN THE 2010S.
WHA- TH- THIS IS...
Y-

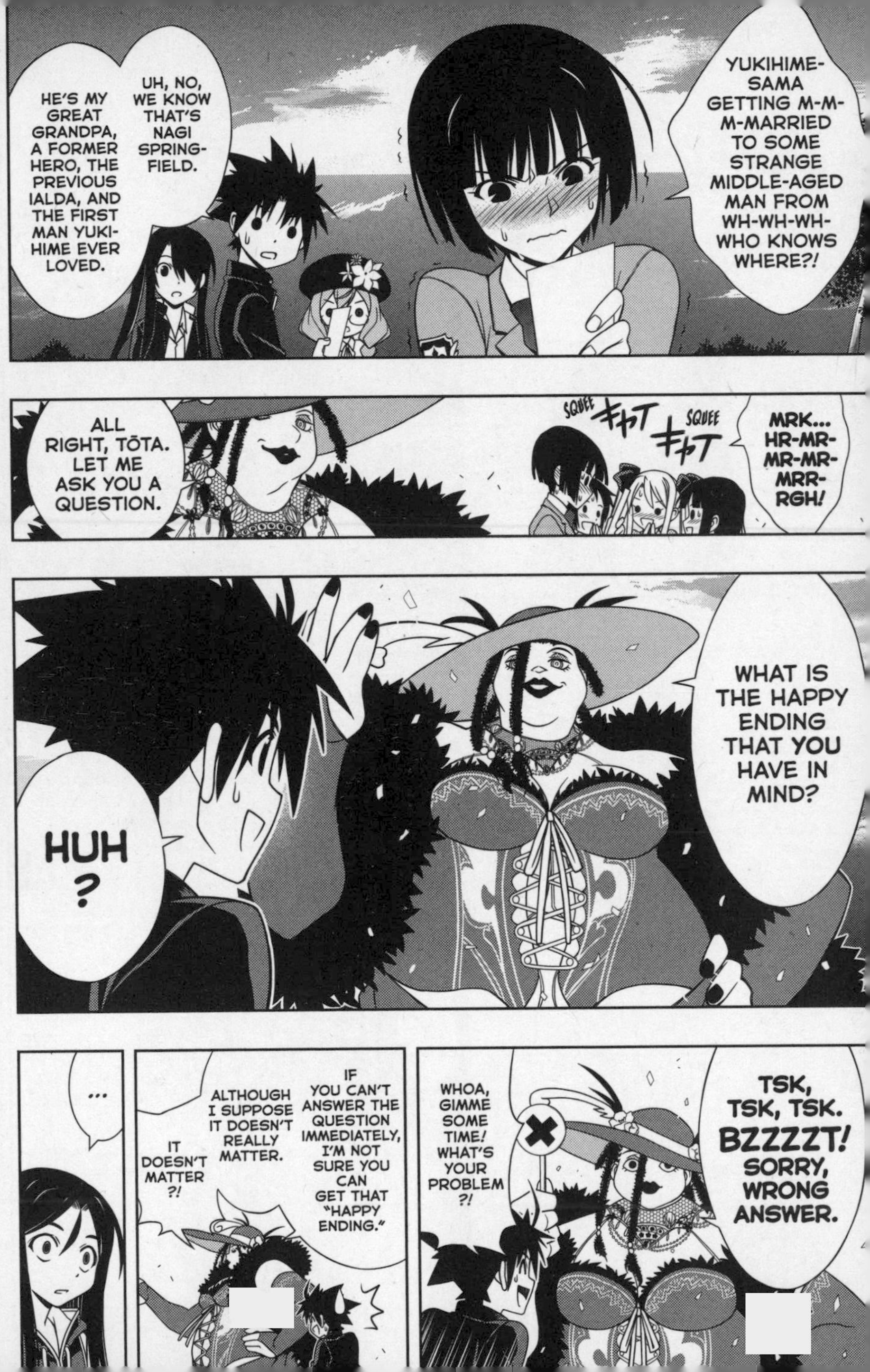
YUKIHIME-SAMA GETTING M-M-M-MARRIED TO SOME STRANGE MIDDLE-AGED MAN FROM WH-WH-WH-WHO KNOWS WHERE?!
UH, NO, WE KNOW THAT'S NAGI SPRINGFIELD.
HE'S MY GREAT GRANDPA, A FORMER HERO, THE PREVIOUS IALDA, AND THE FIRST MAN YUKIHIME EVER LOVED.
MRK... HR-MR-MR-MR-MRR-RGH!
SQUEE
キャア
SQUEE
キャア
ALL RIGHT, TŌTA. LET ME ASK YOU A QUESTION.
WHAT IS THE HAPPY ENDING THAT YOU HAVE IN MIND?
HUH ?
TSK, TSK, TSK. BZZZZT! SORRY, WRONG ANSWER.
WHOA, GIMME SOME TIME! WHAT'S YOUR PROBLEM ?!
IF YOU CAN'T ANSWER THE QUESTION IMMEDIATELY, I'M NOT SURE YOU CAN GET THAT "HAPPY ENDING."
ALTHOUGH I SUPPOSE IT DOESN'T REALLY MATTER.
IT DOESN'T MATTER ?!
...

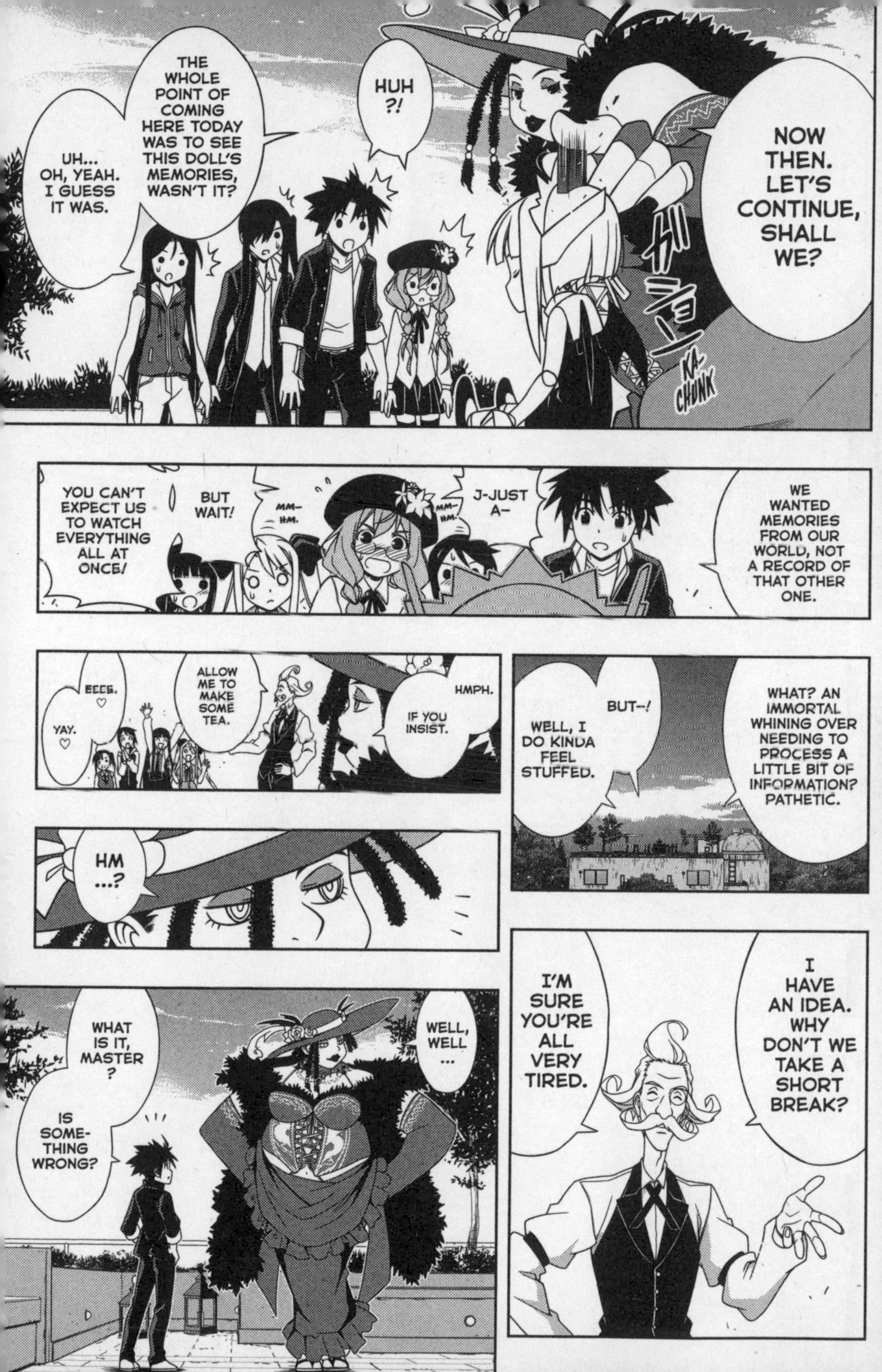
NOW THEN. LET'S CONTINUE, SHALL WE?
KA-CHUNK
HUH ?!
THE WHOLE POINT OF COMING HERE TODAY WAS TO SEE THIS DOLL'S MEMORIES, WASN'T IT?
UH... OH, YEAH. I GUESS IT WAS.
WE WANTED MEMORIES FROM OUR WORLD, NOT A RECORD OF THAT OTHER ONE.
J-JUST A-
MM-HM.
MM-HM.
BUT WAIT!
YOU CAN'T EXPECT US TO WATCH EVERYTHING ALL AT ONCE!
WHAT? AN IMMORTAL WHINING OVER NEEDING TO PROCESS A LITTLE BIT OF INFORMATION? PATHETIC.
BUT-!
WELL, I DO KINDA FEEL STUFFED.
HMPH.
IF YOU INSIST.
ALLOW ME TO MAKE SOME TEA.
EEEE. ♡
YAY. ♡
HM ...?
I HAVE AN IDEA. WHY DON'T WE TAKE A SHORT BREAK?
I'M SURE YOU'RE ALL VERY TIRED.
WELL, WELL ...
WHAT IS IT, MASTER ?
IS SOMETHING WRONG?

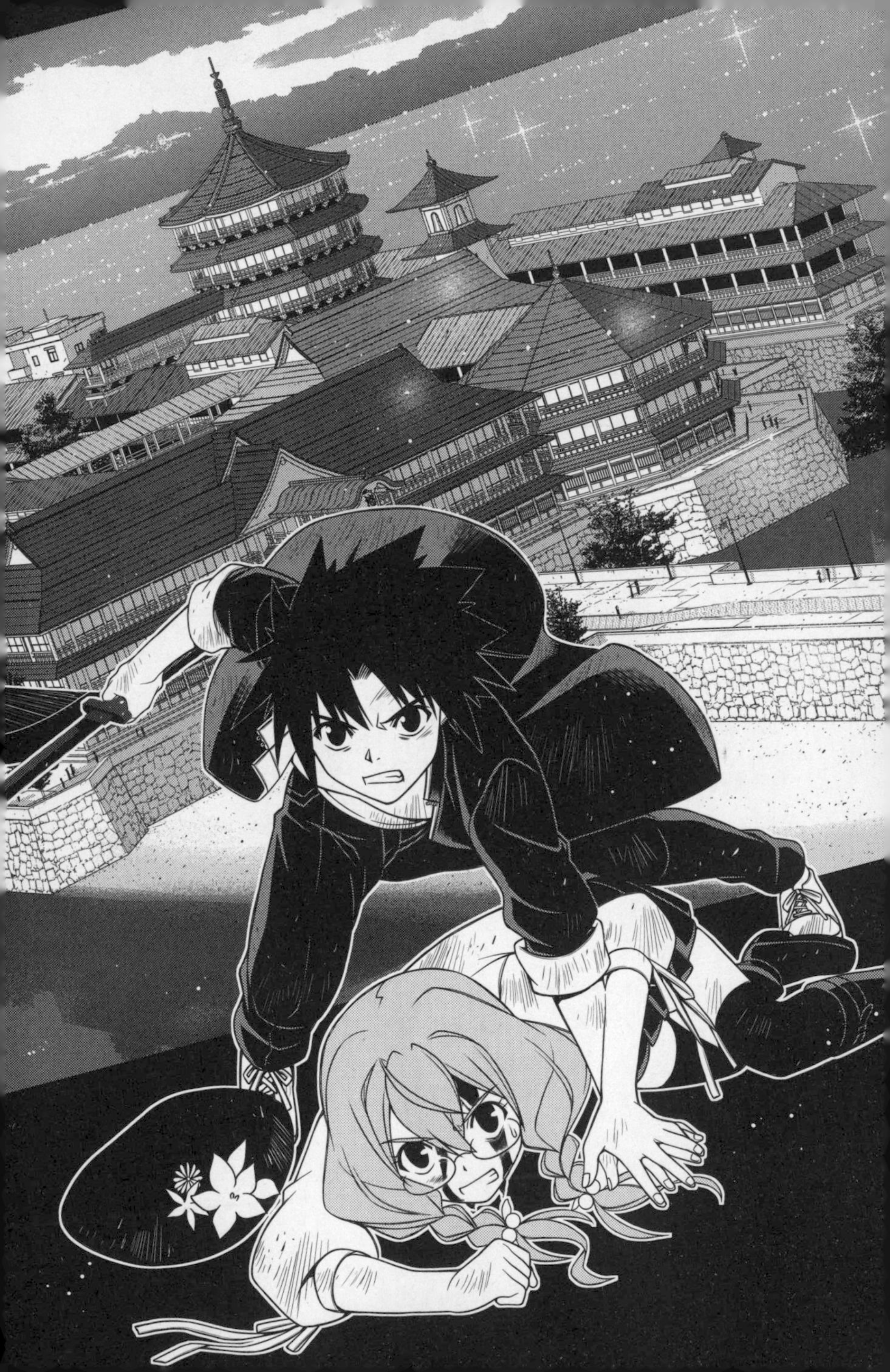

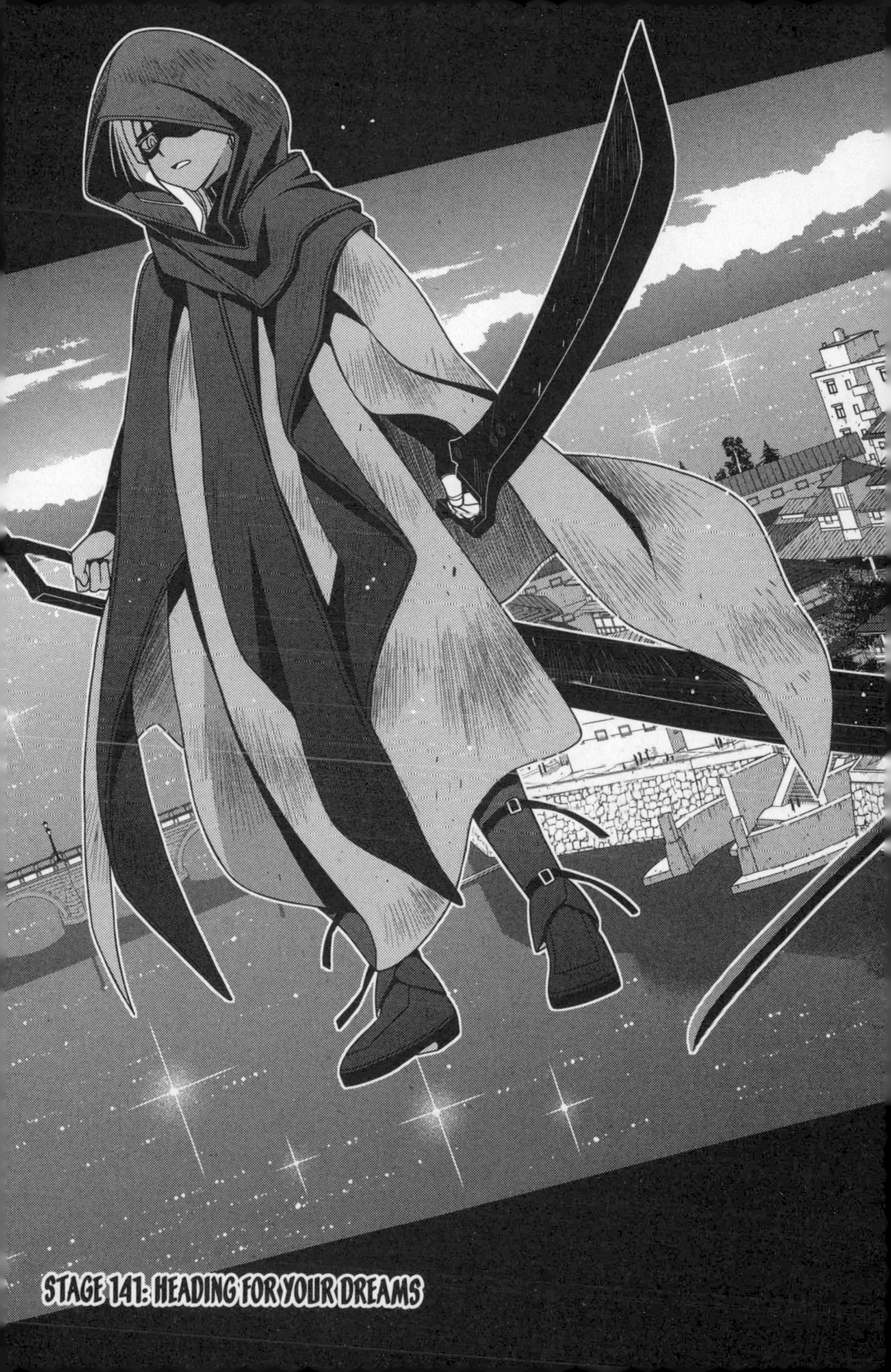
STAGE 141: HEADING FOR YOUR DREAMS

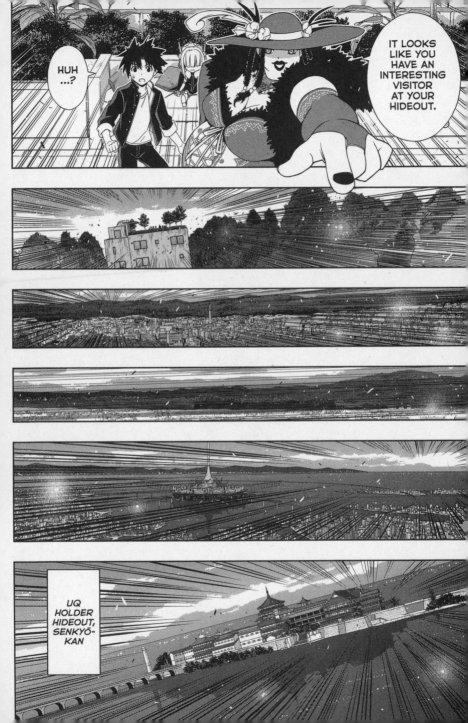

HUH ....?

IT LOOKS LIKE YOU HAVE AN INTERESTING VISITOR AT YOUR HIDEOUT.

UQ HOLDER HIDEOUT, SENKYŌ-KAN

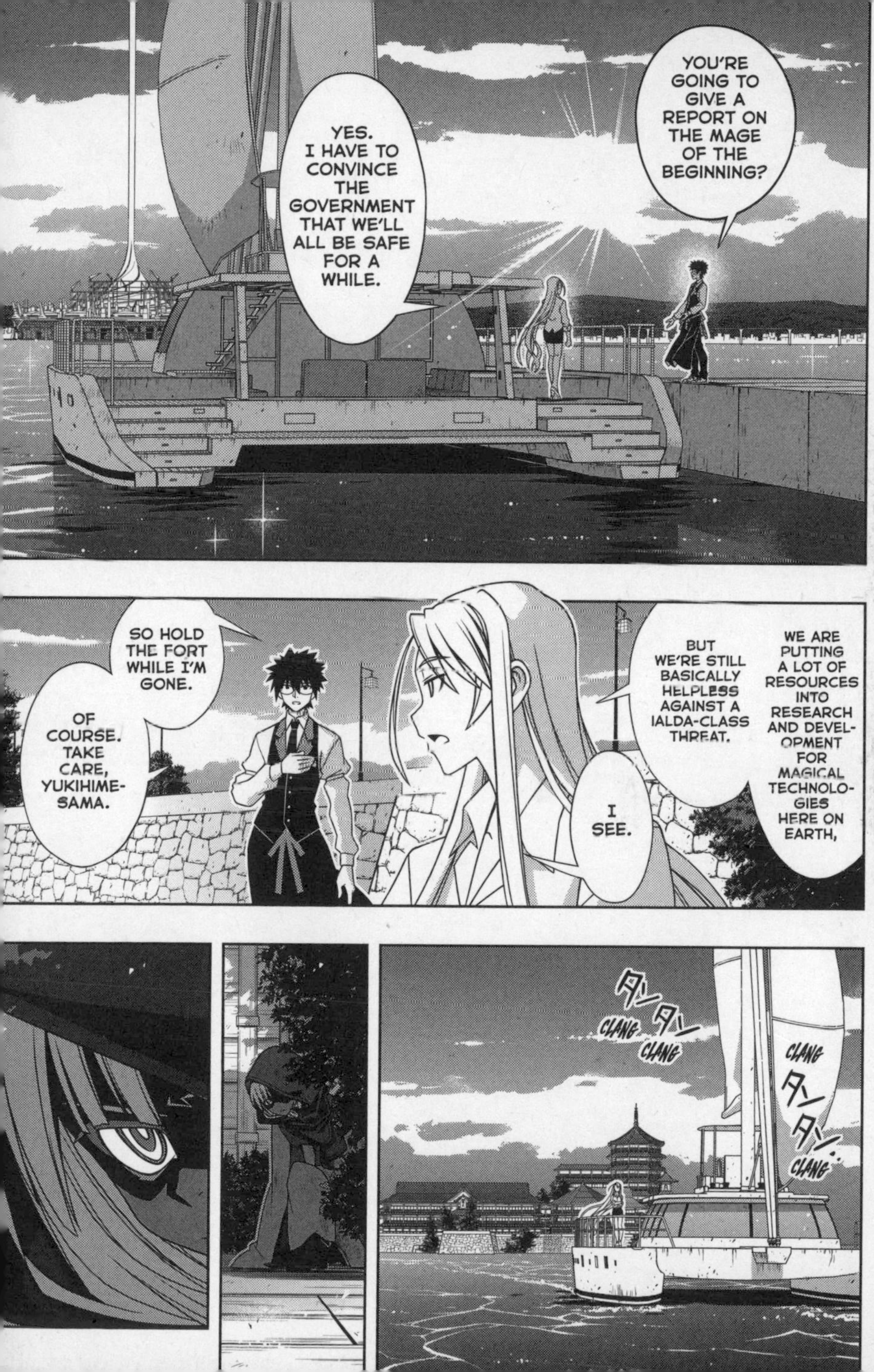
YOU'RE GOING TO GIVE A REPORT ON THE MAGE OF THE BEGINNING?
YES. I HAVE TO CONVINCE THE GOVERNMENT THAT WE'LL ALL BE SAFE FOR A WHILE.
WE ARE PUTTING A LOT OF RESOURCES INTO RESEARCH AND DEVEL-OPMENT FOR MAGICAL TECHNOLO-GIES HERE ON EARTH,
BUT WE'RE STILL BASICALLY HELPLESS AGAINST A IALDA-CLASS THREAT.
I SEE.
SO HOLD THE FORT WHILE I'M GONE.
OF COURSE. TAKE CARE, YUKIHIME-SAMA.
CLANG タン
タン... CLANG
タン CLANG
タン CLANG

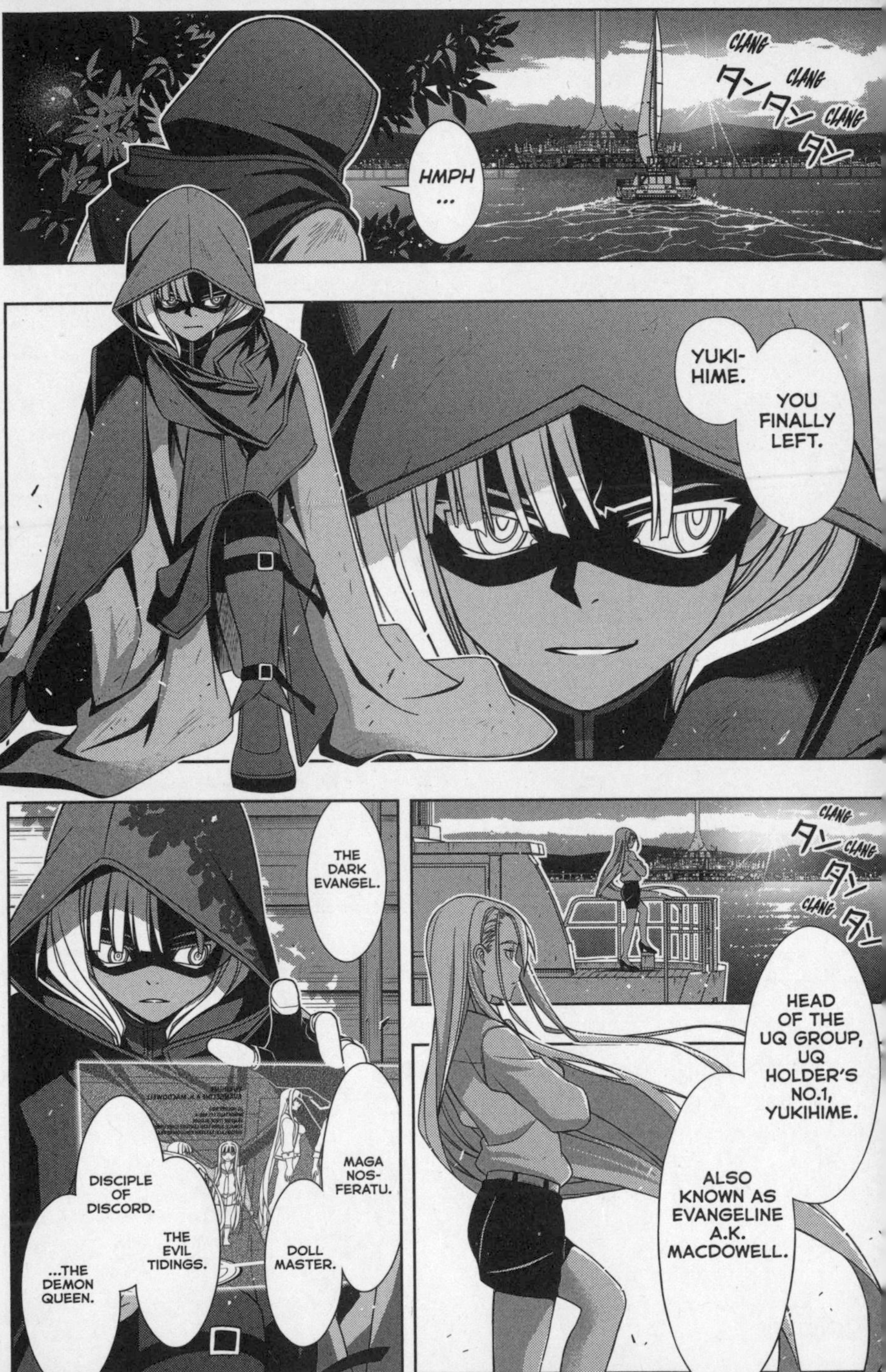
CLANG
タン
CLANG
タン
CLANG
タン
HMPH ...
YUKI-HIME.
YOU FINALLY LEFT.
CLANG
タン
CLANG
タン
CLANG
タン
HEAD OF THE UQ GROUP, UQ HOLDER'S NO.1, YUKIHIME.
ALSO KNOWN AS EVANGELINE A.K. MACDOWELL.
THE DARK EVANGEL.
MAGA NOS-FERATU.
DOLL MASTER.
THE EVIL TIDINGS.
DISCIPLE OF DISCORD.
...THE DEMON QUEEN.

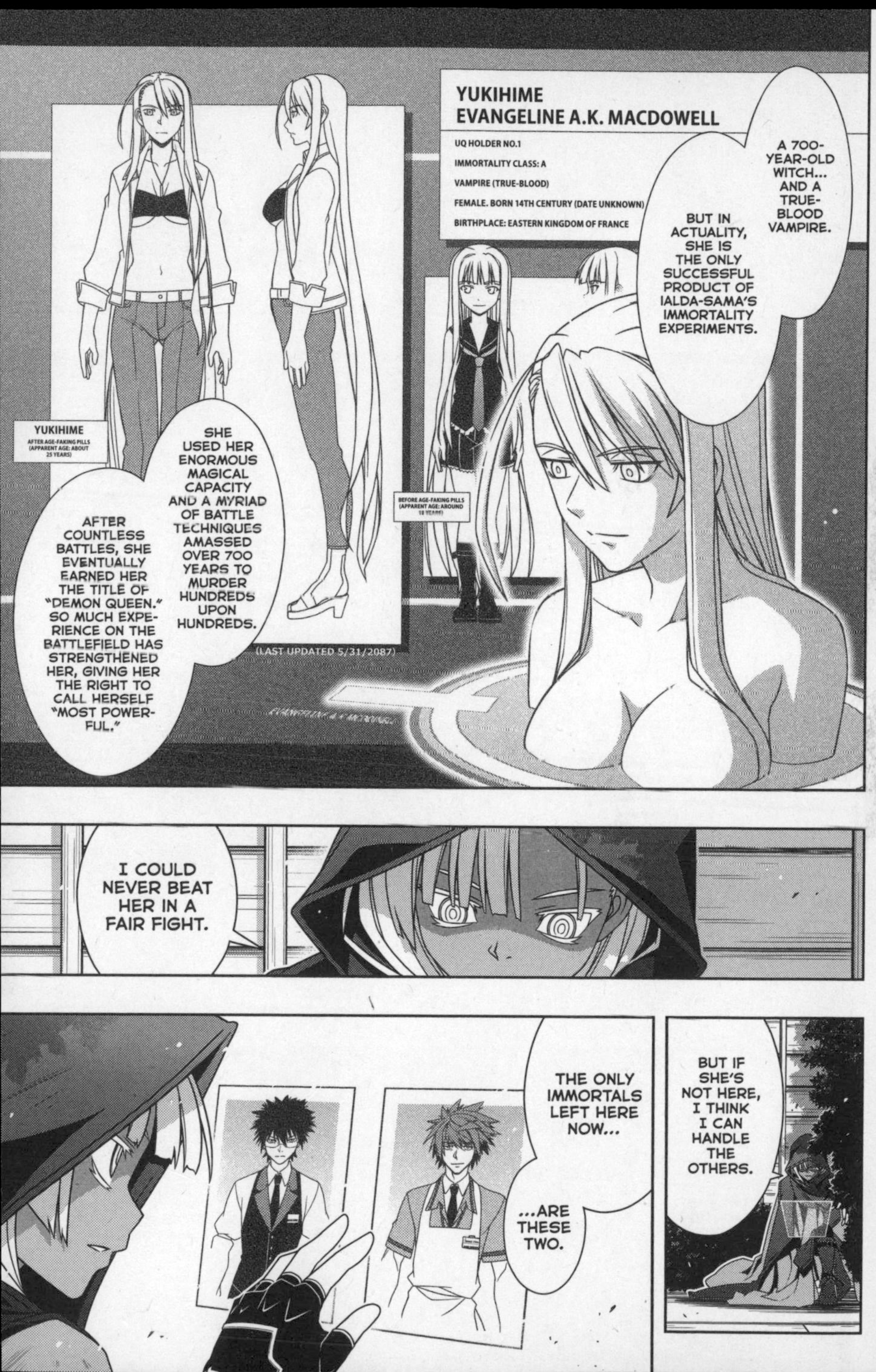
A 700-YEAR-OLD WITCH... AND A TRUE-BLOOD VAMPIRE.
BUT IN ACTUALITY, SHE IS THE ONLY SUCCESSFUL PRODUCT OF IALDA-SAMA'S IMMORTALITY EXPERIMENTS.
YUKIHIME
EVANGELINE A.K. MACDOWELL
UQ HOLDER NO.1
IMMORTALITY CLASS: A
VAMPIRE (TRUE-BLOOD)
FEMALE. BORN 14TH CENTURY (DATE UNKNOWN)
BIRTHPLACE: EASTERN KINGDOM OF FRANCE
BEFORE AGE-FAKING PILLS (APPARENT AGE: AROUND 18 YEARS)
YUKIHIME
AFTER AGE-FAKING PILLS (APPARENT AGE: ABOUT 25 YEARS)
(LAST UPDATED 5/31/2087)
SHE USED HER ENORMOUS MAGICAL CAPACITY AND A MYRIAD OF BATTLE TECHNIQUES AMASSED OVER 700 YEARS TO MURDER HUNDREDS UPON HUNDREDS.
AFTER COUNTLESS BATTLES, SHE EVENTUALLY EARNED HER THE TITLE OF "DEMON QUEEN." SO MUCH EXPERIENCE ON THE BATTLEFIELD HAS STRENGTHENED HER, GIVING HER THE RIGHT TO CALL HERSELF "MOST POWERFUL."
I COULD NEVER BEAT HER IN A FAIR FIGHT.
BUT IF SHE'S NOT HERE, I THINK I CAN HANDLE THE OTHERS.
THE ONLY IMMORTALS LEFT HERE NOW...
...ARE THESE TWO.

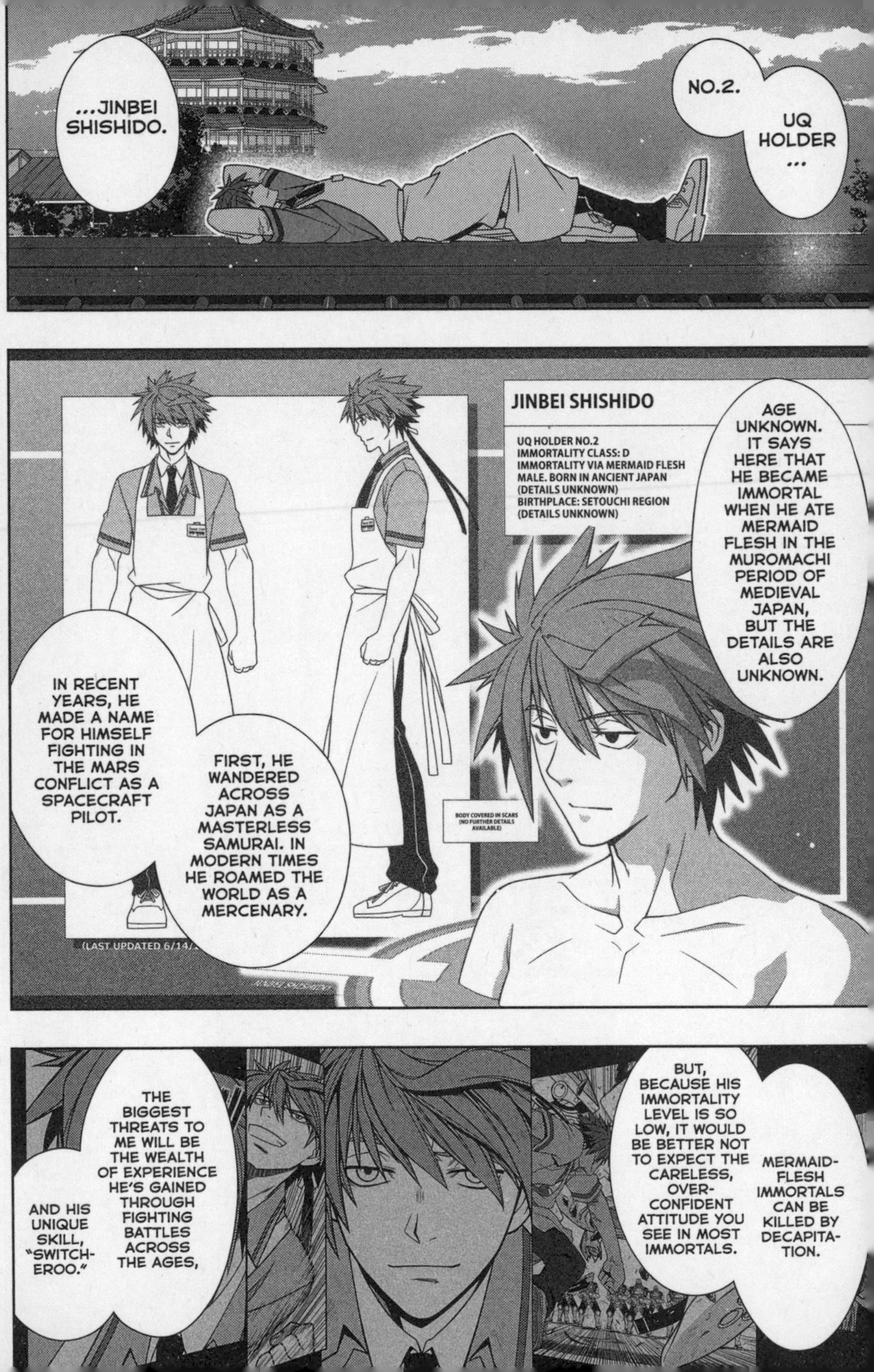
NO.2.
UQ HOLDER ...
...JINBEI SHISHIDO.
JINBEI SHISHIDO
UQ HOLDER NO.2
IMMORTALITY CLASS: D
IMMORTALITY VIA MERMAID FLESH
MALE. BORN IN ANCIENT JAPAN (DETAILS UNKNOWN)
BIRTHPLACE: SETOUCHI REGION (DETAILS UNKNOWN)
AGE UNKNOWN. IT SAYS HERE THAT HE BECAME IMMORTAL WHEN HE ATE MERMAID FLESH IN THE MUROMACHI PERIOD OF MEDIEVAL JAPAN, BUT THE DETAILS ARE ALSO UNKNOWN.
BODY COVERED IN SCARS (NO FURTHER DETAILS AVAILABLE)
FIRST, HE WANDERED ACROSS JAPAN AS A MASTERLESS SAMURAI. IN MODERN TIMES HE ROAMED THE WORLD AS A MERCENARY.
IN RECENT YEARS, HE MADE A NAME FOR HIMSELF FIGHTING IN THE MARS CONFLICT AS A SPACECRAFT PILOT.
MERMAID-FLESH IMMORTALS CAN BE KILLED BY DECAPITATION.
BUT, BECAUSE HIS IMMORTALITY LEVEL IS SO LOW, IT WOULD BE BETTER NOT TO EXPECT THE CARELESS, OVER-CONFIDENT ATTITUDE YOU SEE IN MOST IMMORTALS.
THE BIGGEST THREATS TO ME WILL BE THE WEALTH OF EXPERIENCE HE'S GAINED THROUGH FIGHTING BATTLES ACROSS THE AGES,
AND HIS UNIQUE SKILL, "SWITCH-EROO."

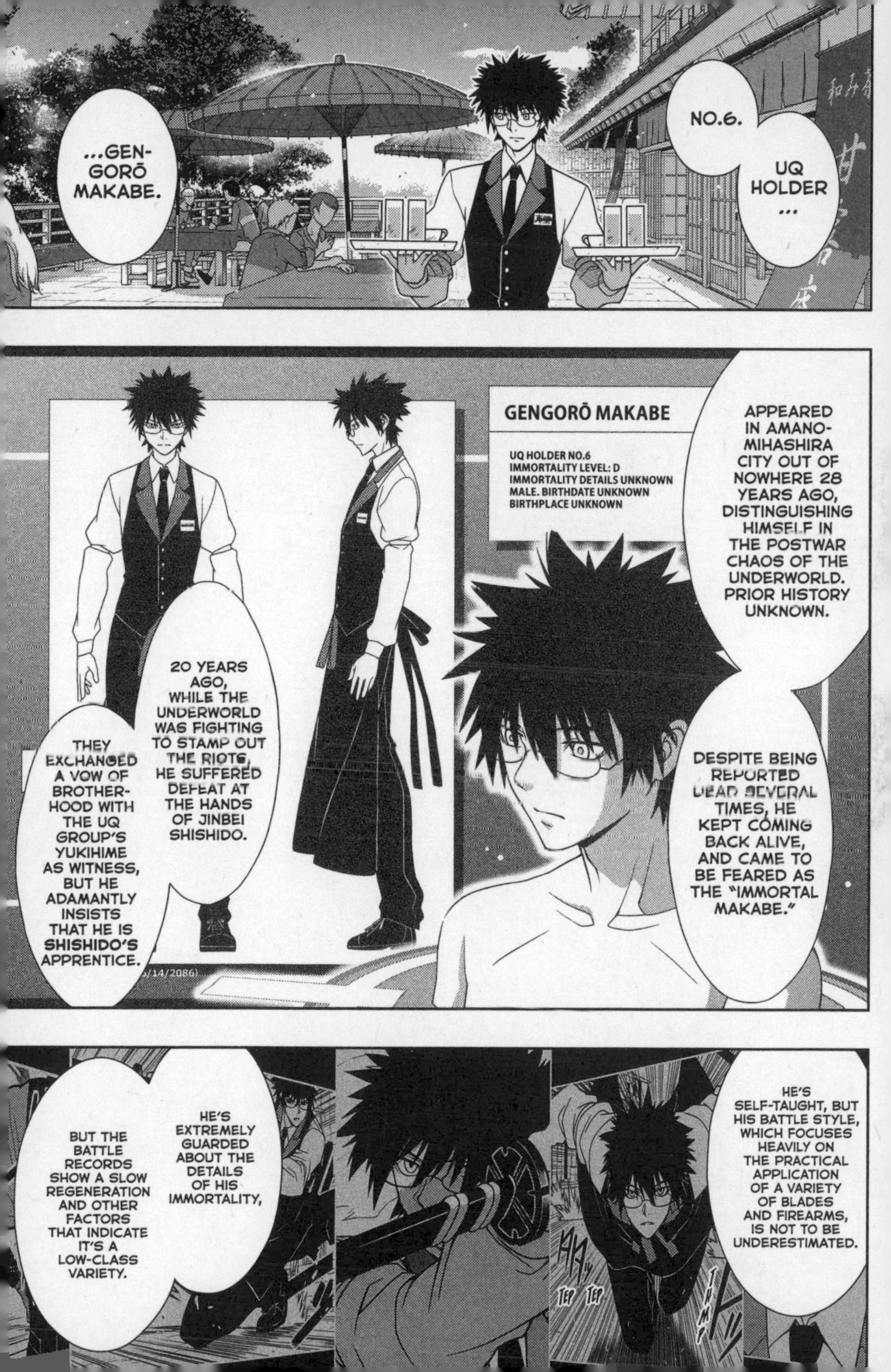
UQ HOLDER ...
NO.6.
...GEN-GORŌ MAKABE.
GENGORŌ MAKABE
UQ HOLDER NO.6
IMMORTALITY LEVEL: D
IMMORTALITY DETAILS UNKNOWN
MALE. BIRTHDATE UNKNOWN
BIRTHPLACE UNKNOWN
APPEARED IN AMANO-MIHASHIRA CITY OUT OF NOWHERE 28 YEARS AGO, DISTINGUISHING HIMSELF IN THE POSTWAR CHAOS OF THE UNDERWORLD. PRIOR HISTORY UNKNOWN.
DESPITE BEING REPORTED DEAD SEVERAL TIMES, HE KEPT COMING BACK ALIVE, AND CAME TO BE FEARED AS THE "IMMORTAL MAKABE."
20 YEARS AGO, WHILE THE UNDERWORLD WAS FIGHTING TO STAMP OUT THE RIOTS, HE SUFFERED DEFEAT AT THE HANDS OF JINBEI SHISHIDO.
THEY EXCHANGED A VOW OF BROTHER-HOOD WITH THE UQ GROUP'S YUKIHIME AS WITNESS, BUT HE ADAMANTLY INSISTS THAT HE IS SHISHIDO'S APPRENTICE.
HE'S SELF-TAUGHT, BUT HIS BATTLE STYLE, WHICH FOCUSES HEAVILY ON THE PRACTICAL APPLICATION OF A VARIETY OF BLADES AND FIREARMS, IS NOT TO BE UNDERESTIMATED.
TEP TEP
HE'S EXTREMELY GUARDED ABOUT THE DETAILS OF HIS IMMORTALITY,
BUT THE BATTLE RECORDS SHOW A SLOW REGENERATION AND OTHER FACTORS THAT INDICATE IT'S A LOW-CLASS VARIETY.

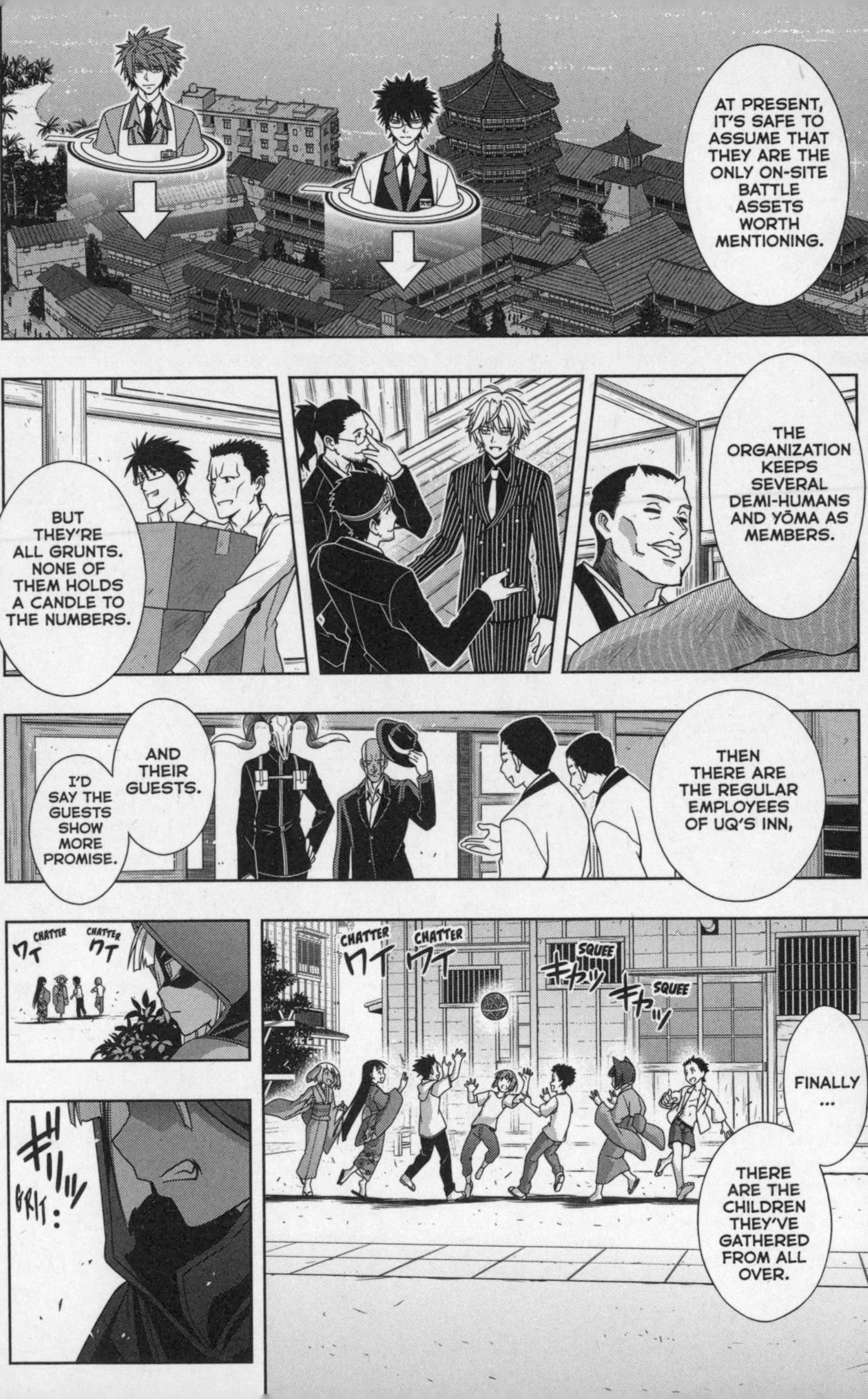
AT PRESENT, IT'S SAFE TO ASSUME THAT THEY ARE THE ONLY ON-SITE BATTLE ASSETS WORTH MENTIONING.
THE ORGANIZATION KEEPS SEVERAL DEMI-HUMANS AND YŌMA AS MEMBERS.
BUT THEY'RE ALL GRUNTS. NONE OF THEM HOLDS A CANDLE TO THE NUMBERS.
THEN THERE ARE THE REGULAR EMPLOYEES OF UQ'S INN,
AND THEIR GUESTS.
I'D SAY THE GUESTS SHOW MORE PROMISE.
CHATTER ワイ
CHATTER ワイ
SQUEE キャッ
SQUEE キャッ
FINALLY ...
THERE ARE THE CHILDREN THEY'VE GATHERED FROM ALL OVER.
CHATTER ワイ
CHATTER ワイ
ギリッ
GRIT

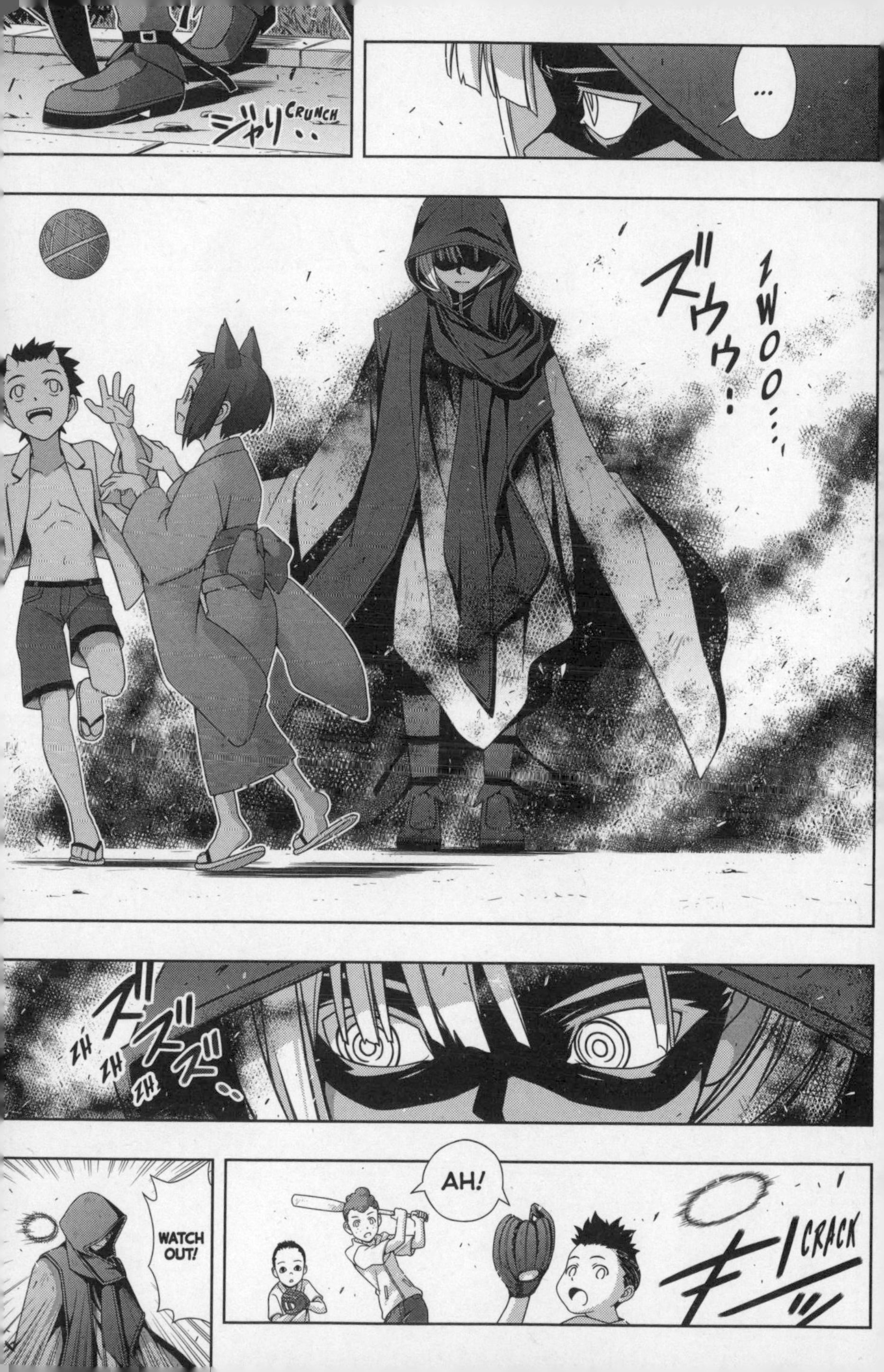
...
ジャり CRUNCH
ズウウ..
ZWOO...
ズズズズ..
ZH ZH ZH
AH!
キッ
CRACK
WATCH OUT!

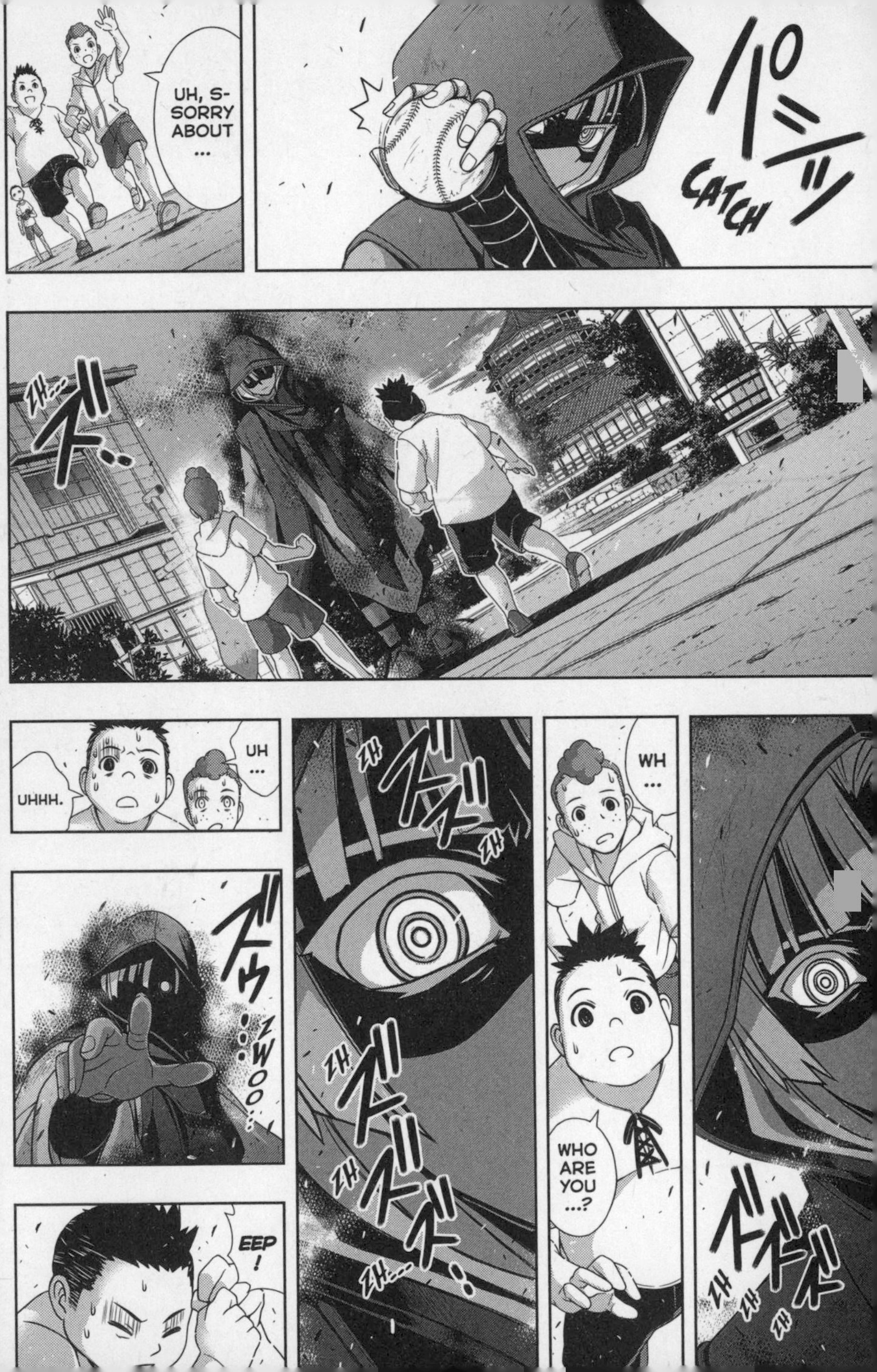
CATCH
UH, S-SORRY ABOUT ...
ZH...
ZH ZH ZH
WH ...
WHO ARE YOU ...?
ZH ZH ZH ZH...
UH ...
UHHH.
ZWOOO...
EEP!

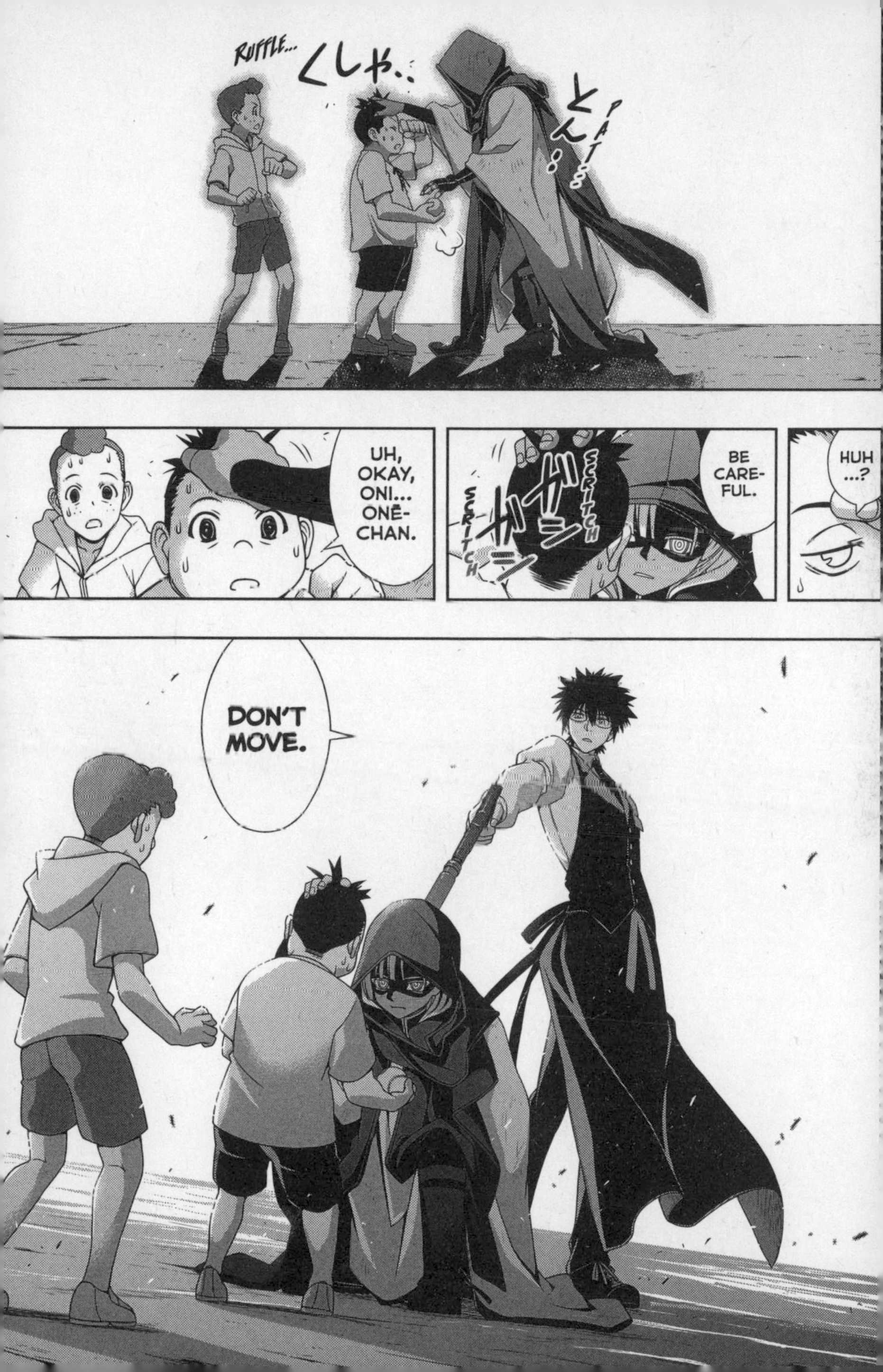
とん..
PAT..
くしゃ..
RUFFLE...
HUH ...?
BE CARE-FUL.
SCRITCH
SCRITCH
UH, OKAY, ONI... ONĒ-CHAN.
DON'T MOVE.

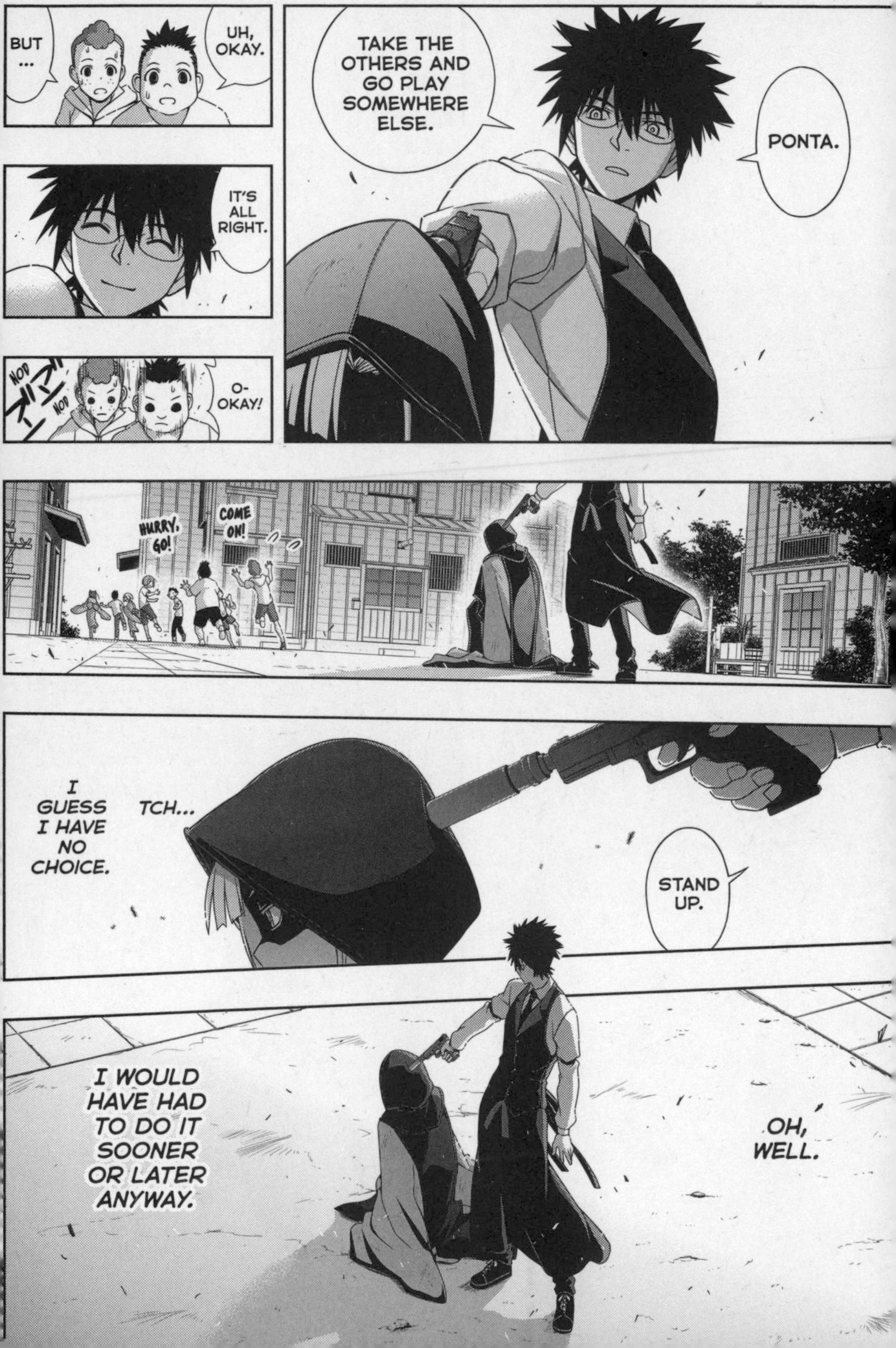
PONTA.
TAKE THE OTHERS AND GO PLAY SOMEWHERE ELSE.
UH, OKAY.
BUT ...
IT'S ALL RIGHT.
O-OKAY!
NOD NOD
COME ON!
HURRY, GO!
STAND UP.
TCH...
I GUESS I HAVE NO CHOICE.
OH, WELL.
I WOULD HAVE HAD TO DO IT SOONER OR LATER ANYWAY.

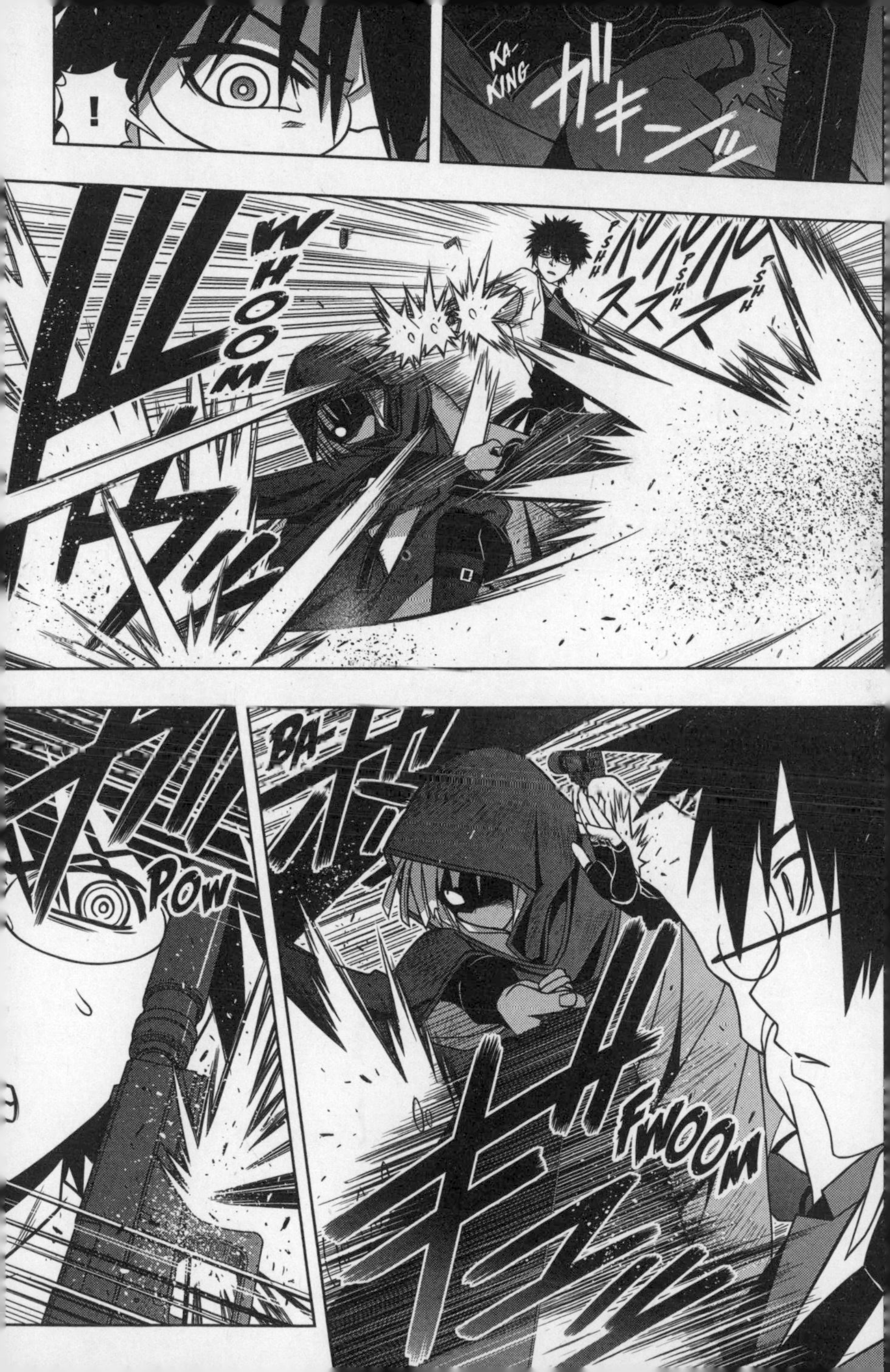
KA-KING
!
PSHH
PSHH
PSHH
WHOOOM
BA-
POW
FWOOM

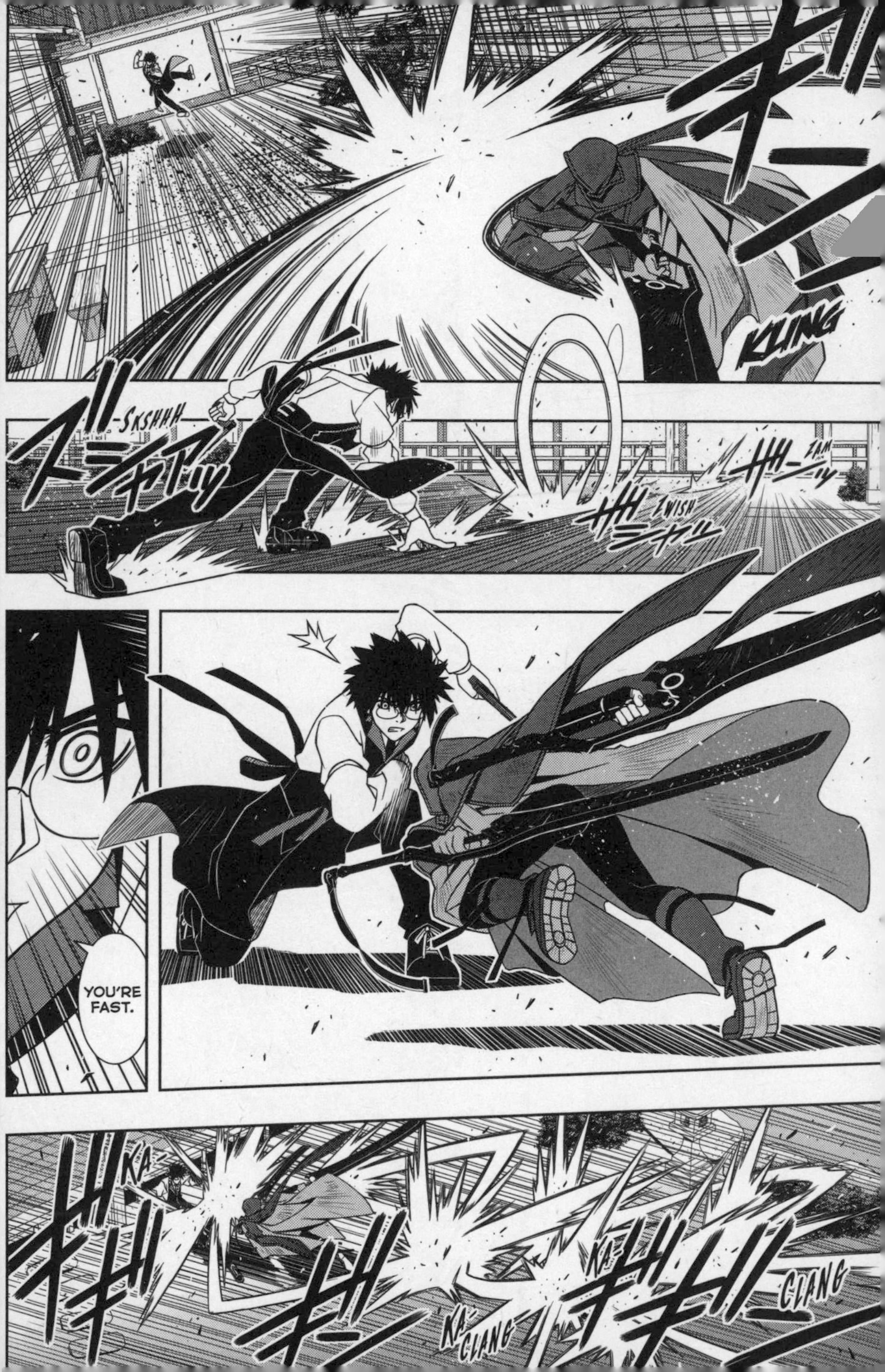

KLING
ZAM
ZWISH
SKSHHH
YOU'RE FAST.
CLANG
KA-
KA-CLANG
KA-

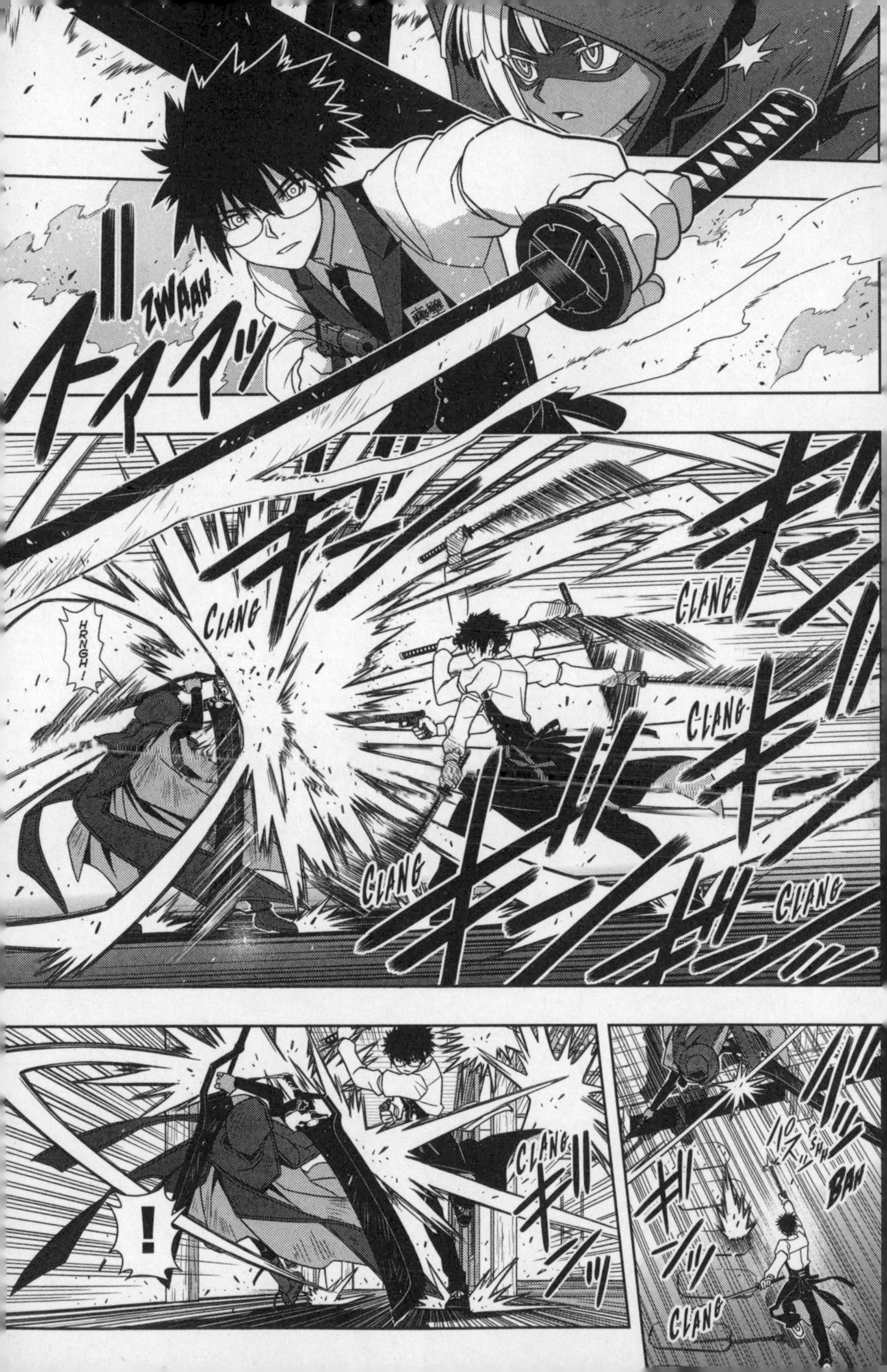
ZWAAH
CLANG
CLANG
CLANG
CLANG
CLANG
HRNGH!
P'SHH
BAN
CLANG
CLANG
!

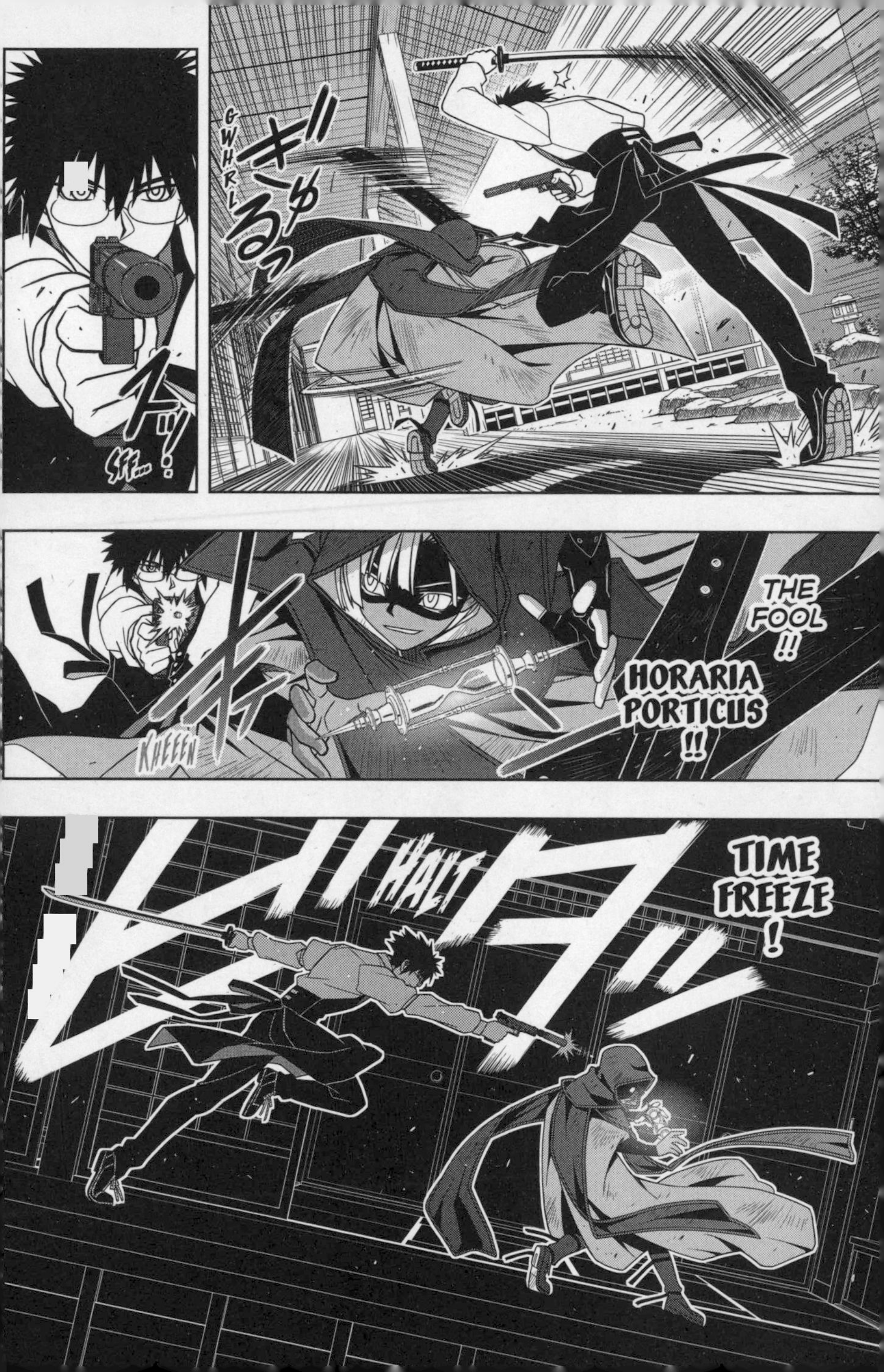
GWHRL
SFFF...
THE FOOL!!
HORARIA PORTICUS!!
KHEEEN
TIME FREEZE!
HALT

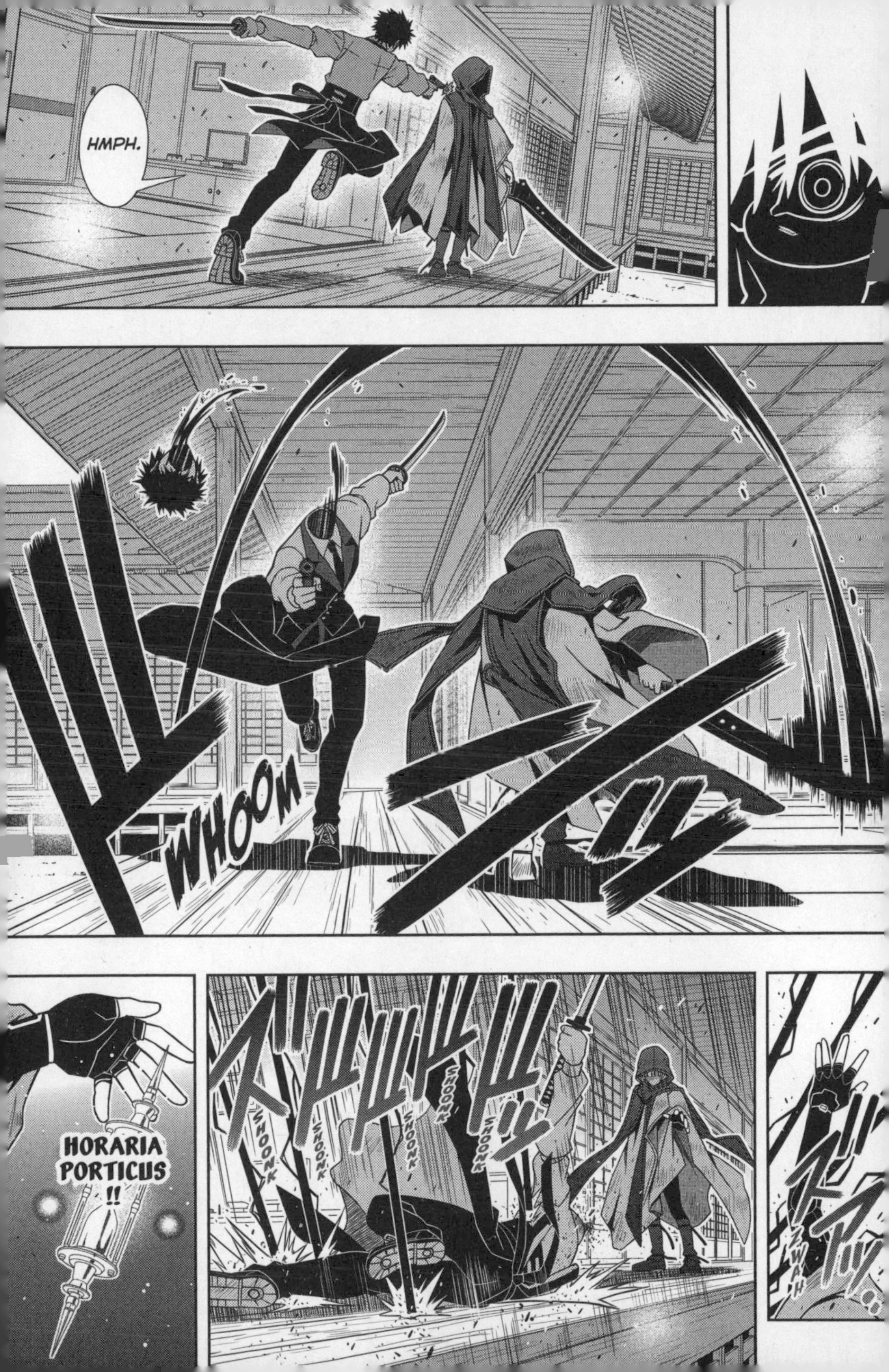
HMPH.
WHOOM
ZWAH
SHOONK
SHOONK
SHOONK
SHOONK
SHOONK
HORARIA PORTICUS !!

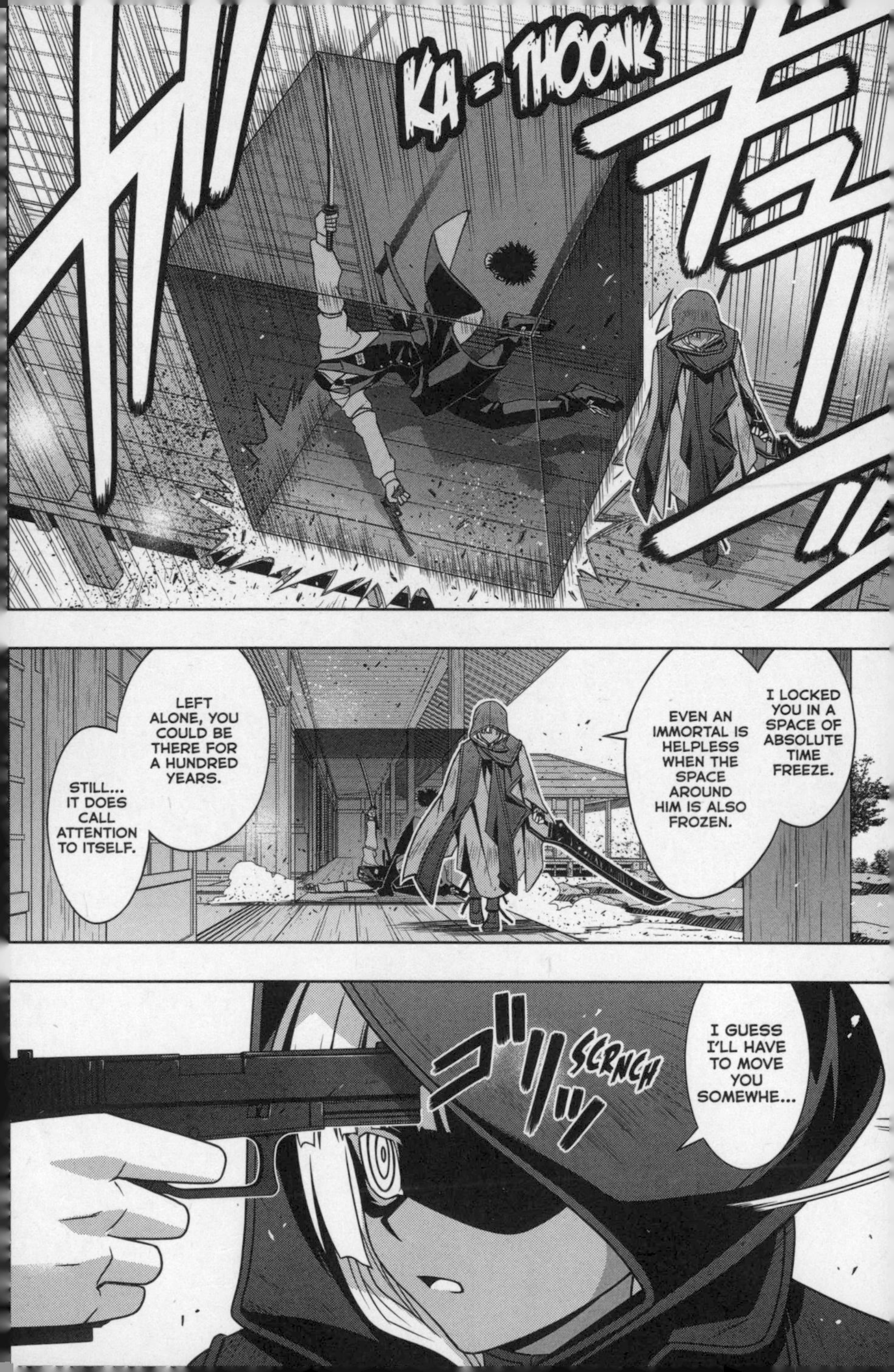
KA-THOONK
I LOCKED YOU IN A SPACE OF ABSOLUTE TIME FREEZE.
EVEN AN IMMORTAL IS HELPLESS WHEN THE SPACE AROUND HIM IS ALSO FROZEN.
LEFT ALONE, YOU COULD BE THERE FOR A HUNDRED YEARS.
STILL... IT DOES CALL ATTENTION TO ITSELF.
I GUESS I'LL HAVE TO MOVE YOU SOMEWHE...
SCRNCH

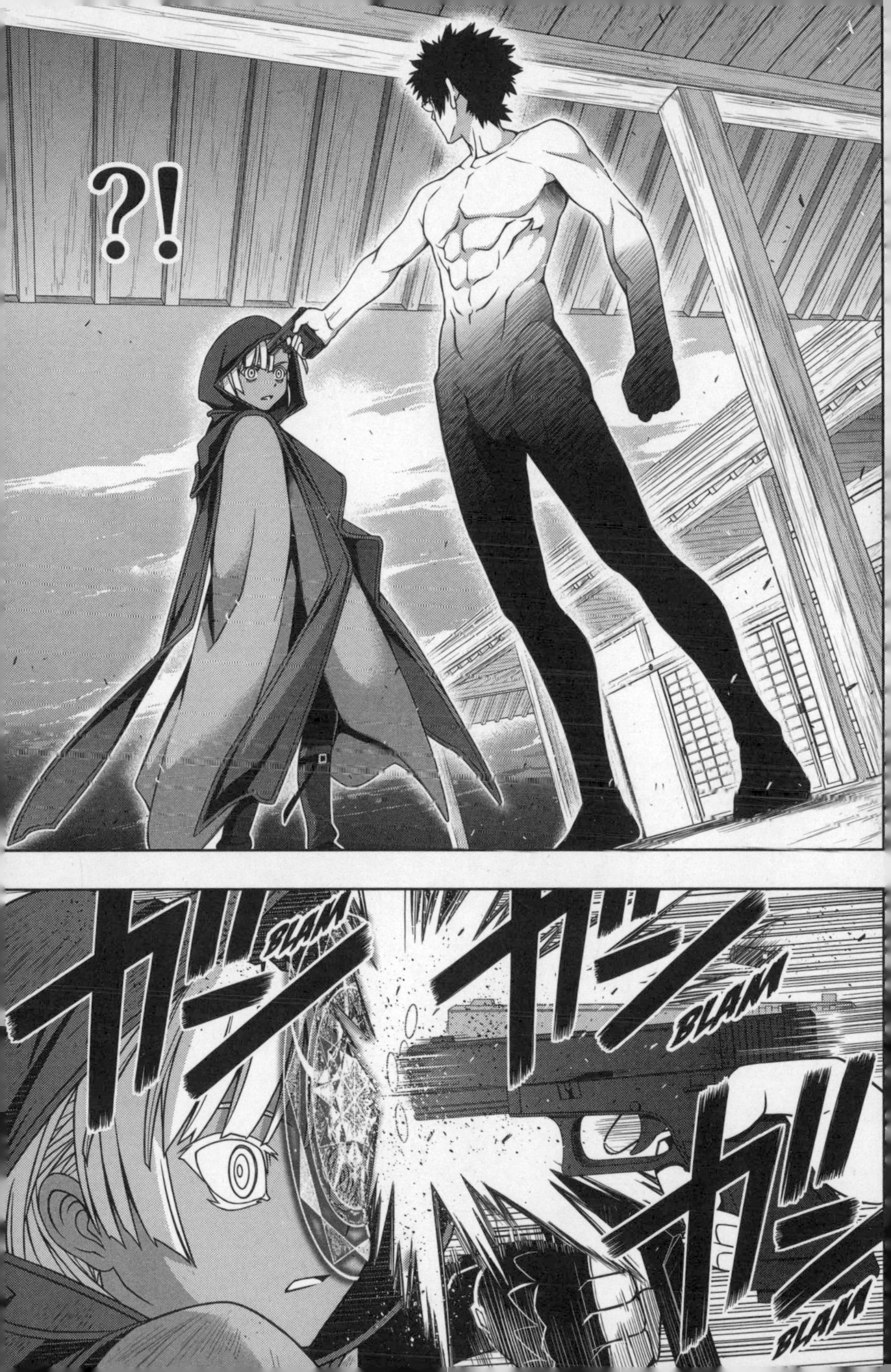
?!
BLAM
BLAM
BLAM
BLAM

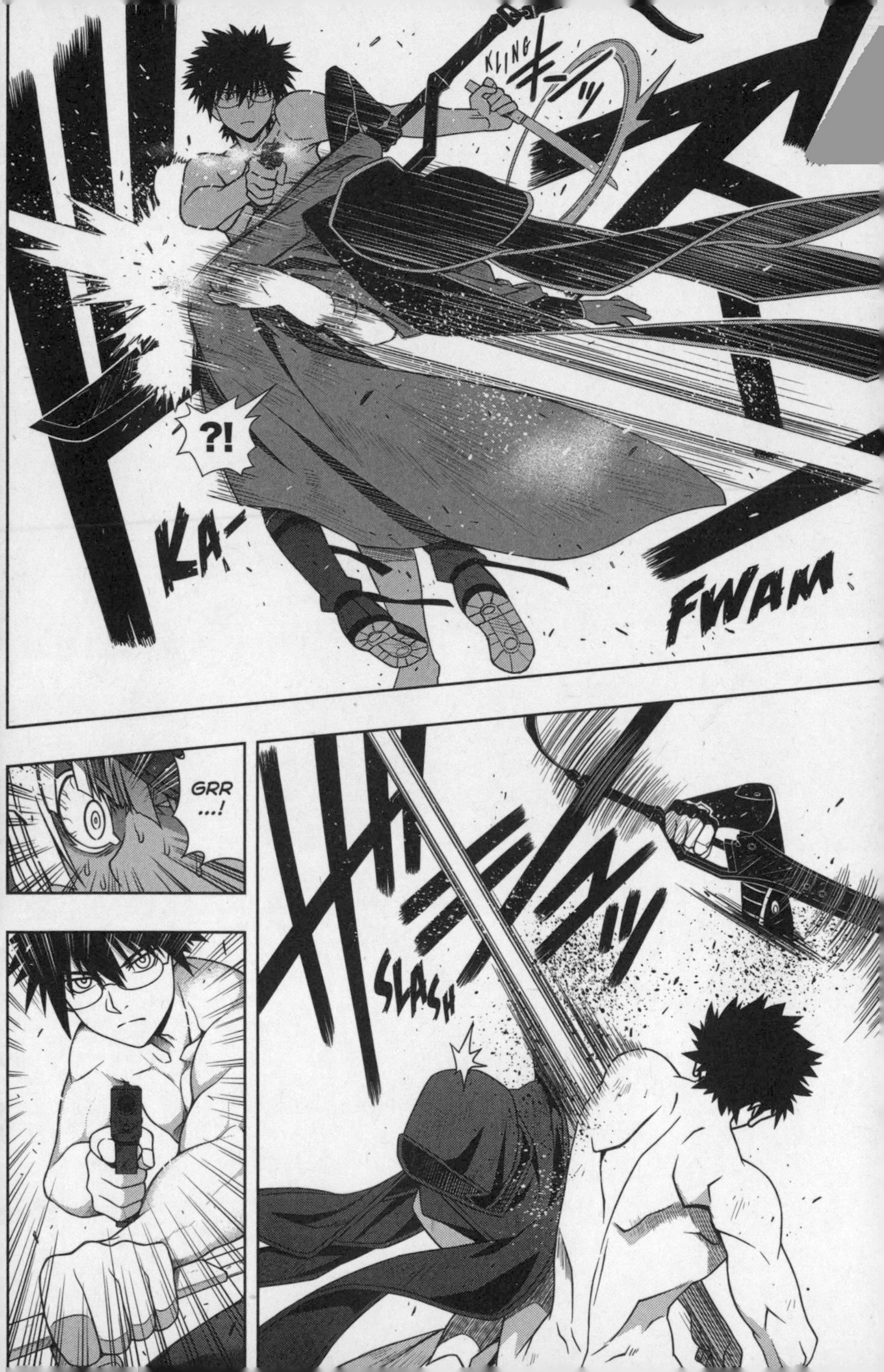
KLING
?!
KA-
FWAM
SLASH
GRR
...!

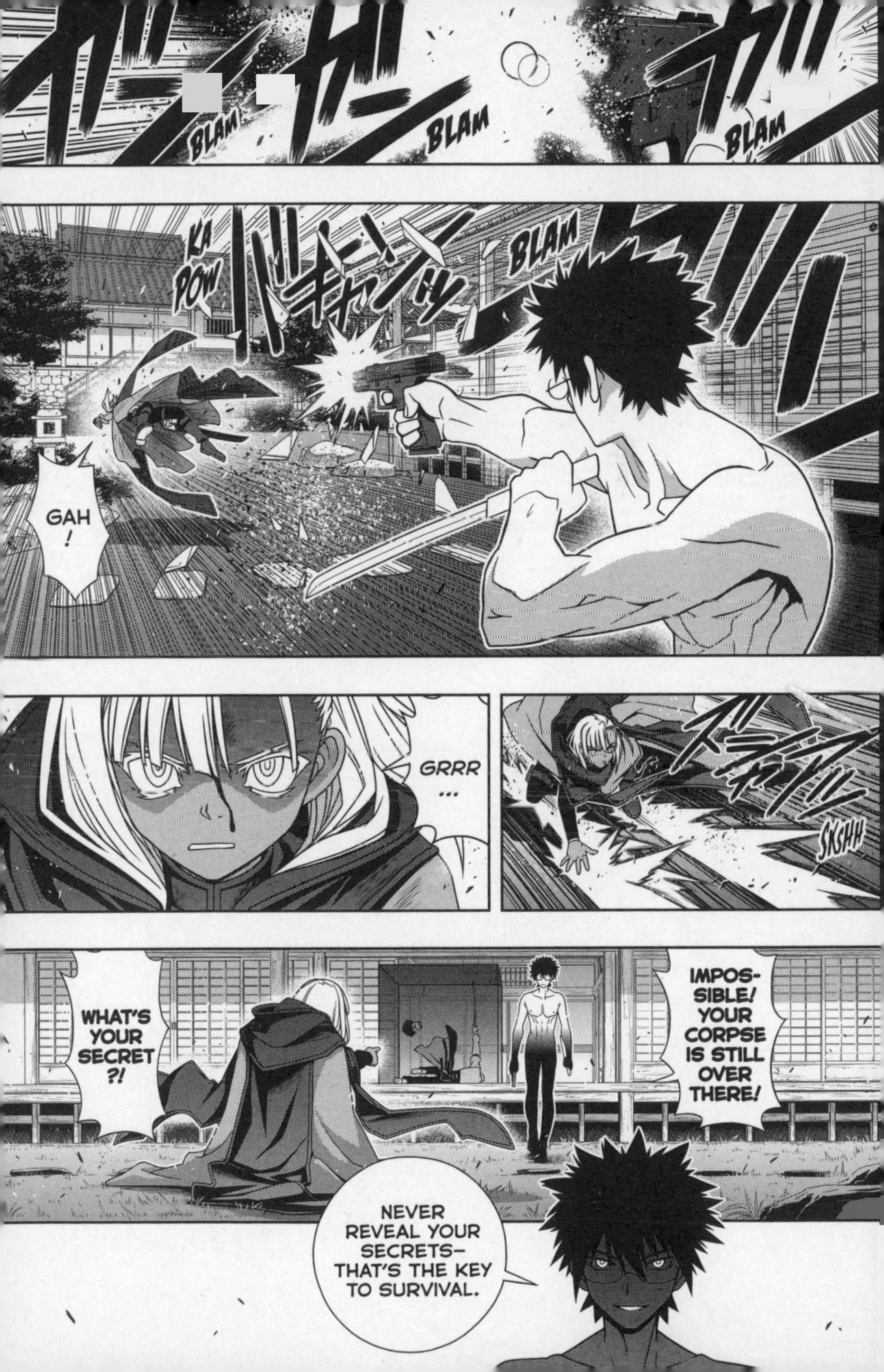

BLAM
BLAM
BLAM
KA POW
BLAM
GAH!
SKSHH
GRRR...
IMPOSSIBLE! YOUR CORPSE IS STILL OVER THERE!
WHAT'S YOUR SECRET?!
NEVER REVEAL YOUR SECRETS— THAT'S THE KEY TO SURVIVAL.

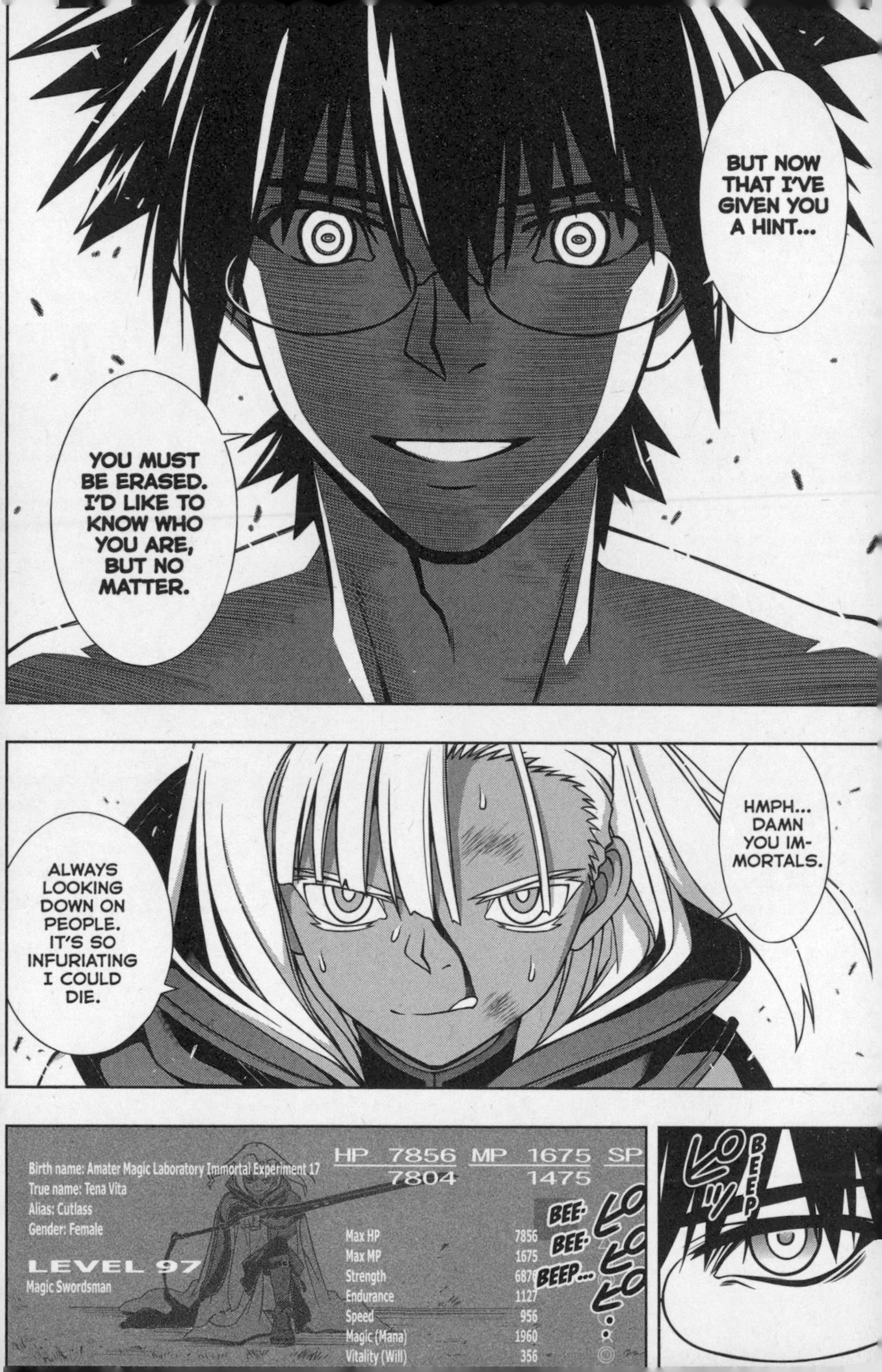
BUT NOW THAT I'VE GIVEN YOU A HINT...
YOU MUST BE ERASED. I'D LIKE TO KNOW WHO YOU ARE, BUT NO MATTER.
HMPH... DAMN YOU IM-MORTALS.
ALWAYS LOOKING DOWN ON PEOPLE. IT'S SO INFURIATING I COULD DIE.
BEEP
HP 7856 MP 1675 SP
7804 1475
Birth name: Amater Magic Laboratory Immortal Experiment 17
True name: Tena Vita
Alias: Cutlass
Gender: Female
LEVEL 97
Magic Swordsman
Max HP 7856
Max MP 1675
Strength 687
Endurance 1127
Speed 956
Magic (Mana) 1960
Vitality (Will) 356
BEE- BEE- BEEP...

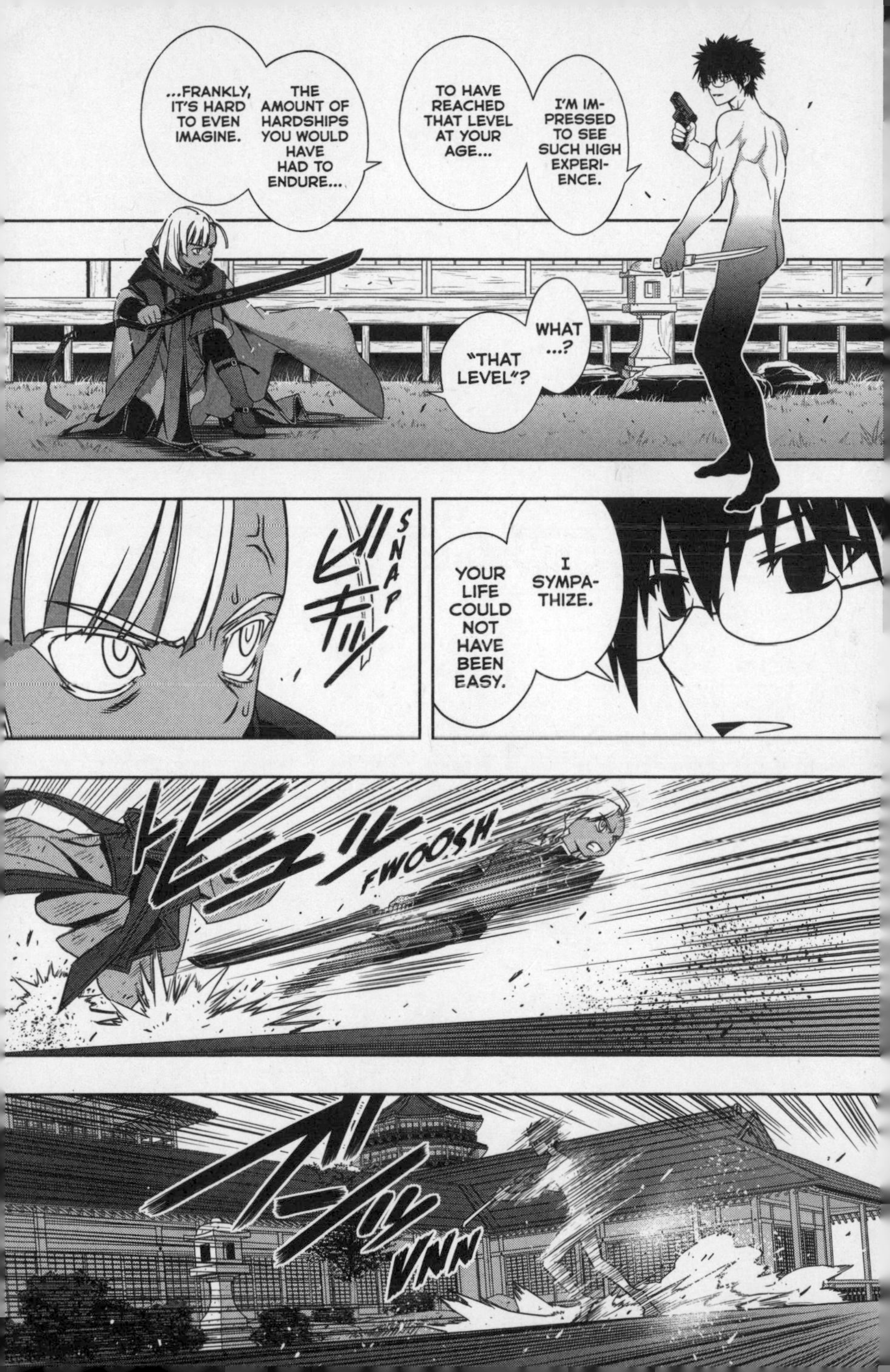

I'M IMPRESSED TO SEE SUCH HIGH EXPERIENCE.
TO HAVE REACHED THAT LEVEL AT YOUR AGE...
THE AMOUNT OF HARDSHIPS YOU WOULD HAVE HAD TO ENDURE...
...FRANKLY, IT'S HARD TO EVEN IMAGINE.
WHAT ...?
"THAT LEVEL"?
I SYMPATHIZE.
YOUR LIFE COULD NOT HAVE BEEN EASY.
SNAP
FWOOSH
VNN

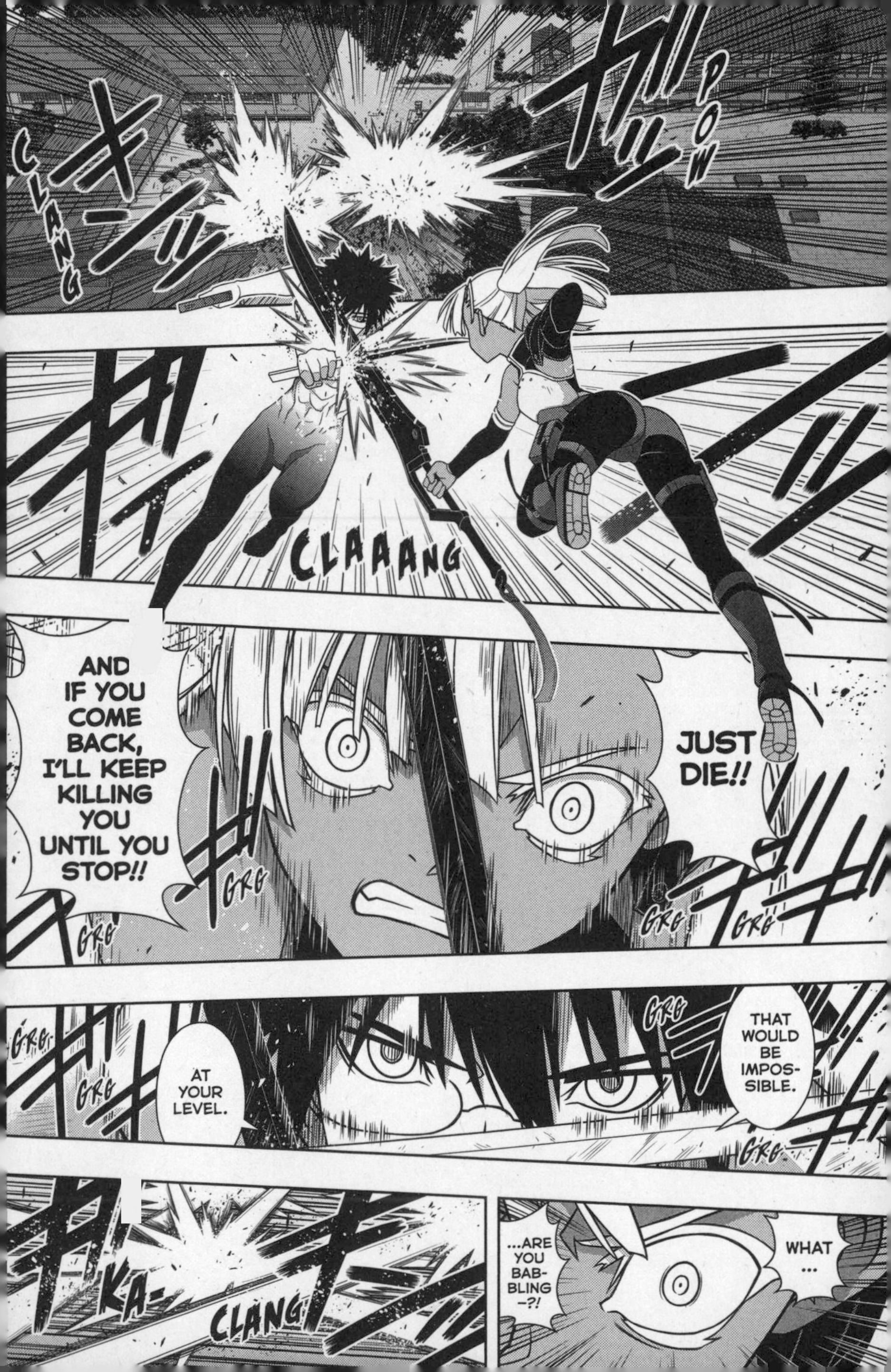
POW
CLANG
CLAAANG
JUST DIE!!
GRG
GRG
AND IF YOU COME BACK, I'LL KEEP KILLING YOU UNTIL YOU STOP!!
GRG
GRG
GRG
THAT WOULD BE IMPOSSIBLE.
GRG
AT YOUR LEVEL.
GRG
GRG
WHAT...
...ARE YOU BABBLING—?!
KA-CLANG

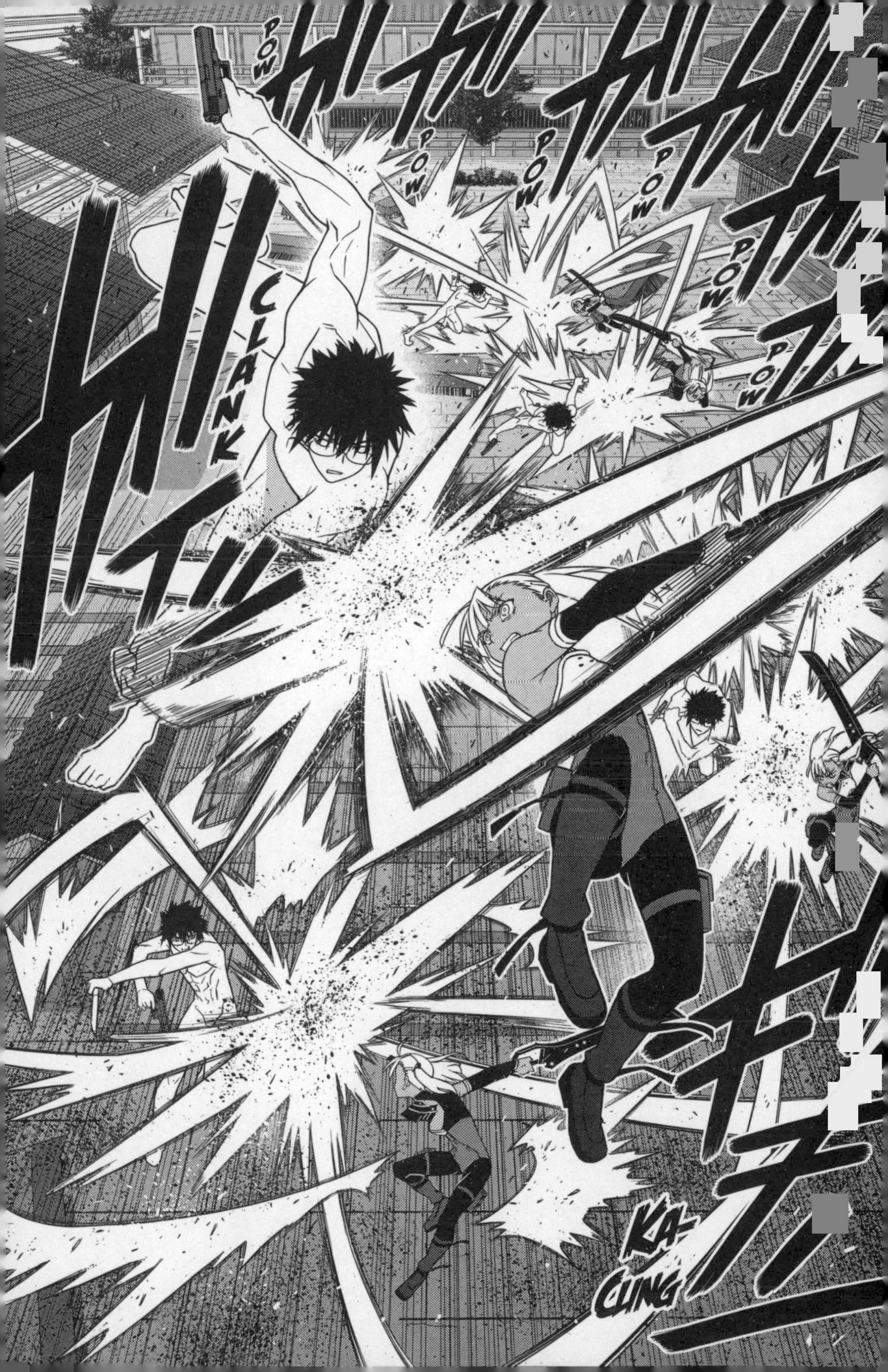
POW
POW
POW
POW
POW
POW
CLANK
KA-CLING

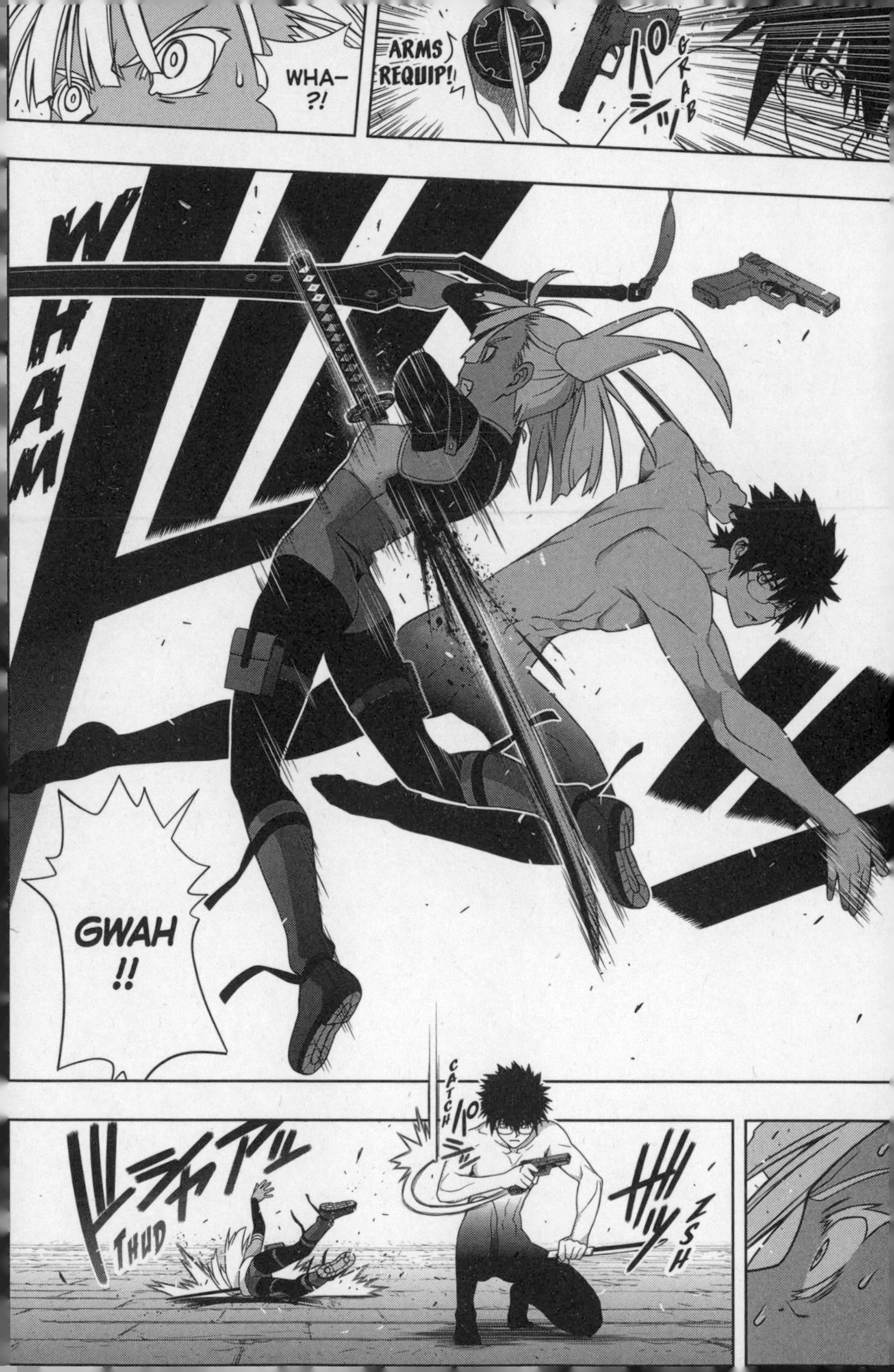

ARMS REQUIP!
GRAB
WHA-?!
WHAM
GWAH !!
CATCH
ZSH
ドシャアッ
THUD

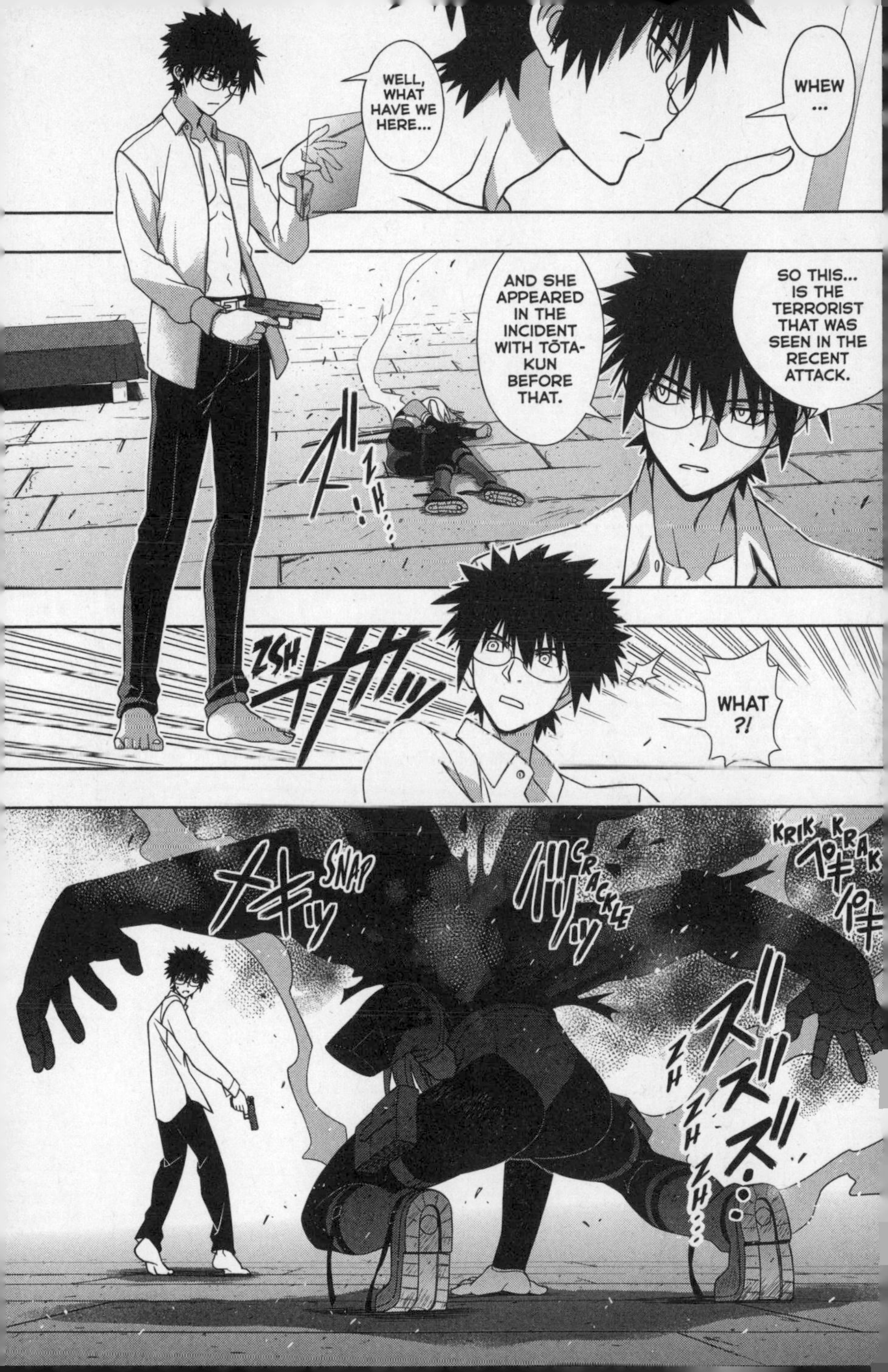
WHEW ...
WELL, WHAT HAVE WE HERE...
SO THIS... IS THE TERRORIST THAT WAS SEEN IN THE RECENT ATTACK.
AND SHE APPEARED IN THE INCIDENT WITH TŌTA-KUN BEFORE THAT.
ZH!...
WHAT ?!
ZSH
KRIK KRAK
ZH ZH ZH...
CRACKLE
SNAP

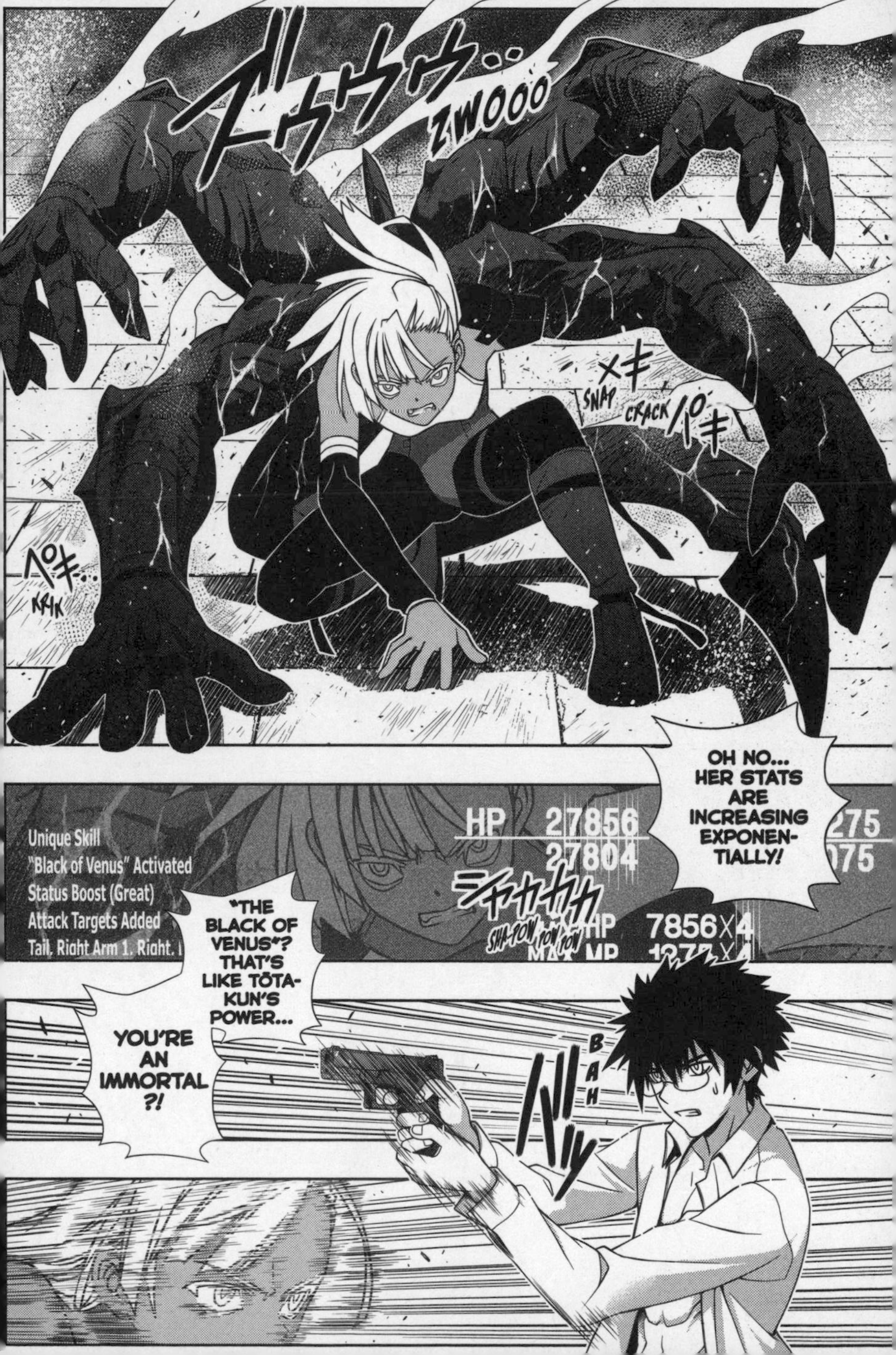

ズウウウ..
ZWOOO
メキ
SNAP
パキ
CRACK
ペキ...
KRIK
OH NO... HER STATS ARE INCREASING EXPONEN-TIALLY!
HP 27856
27804
275
075
Unique Skill
"Black of Venus" Activated
Status Boost (Great)
Attack Targets Added
Tail, Right Arm 1, Right.
シャカカカ
SHA-TON TON TON
HP 7856×4
"THE BLACK OF VENUS"? THAT'S LIKE TŌTA-KUN'S POWER...
バッ
BAH
YOU'RE AN IMMORTAL?!

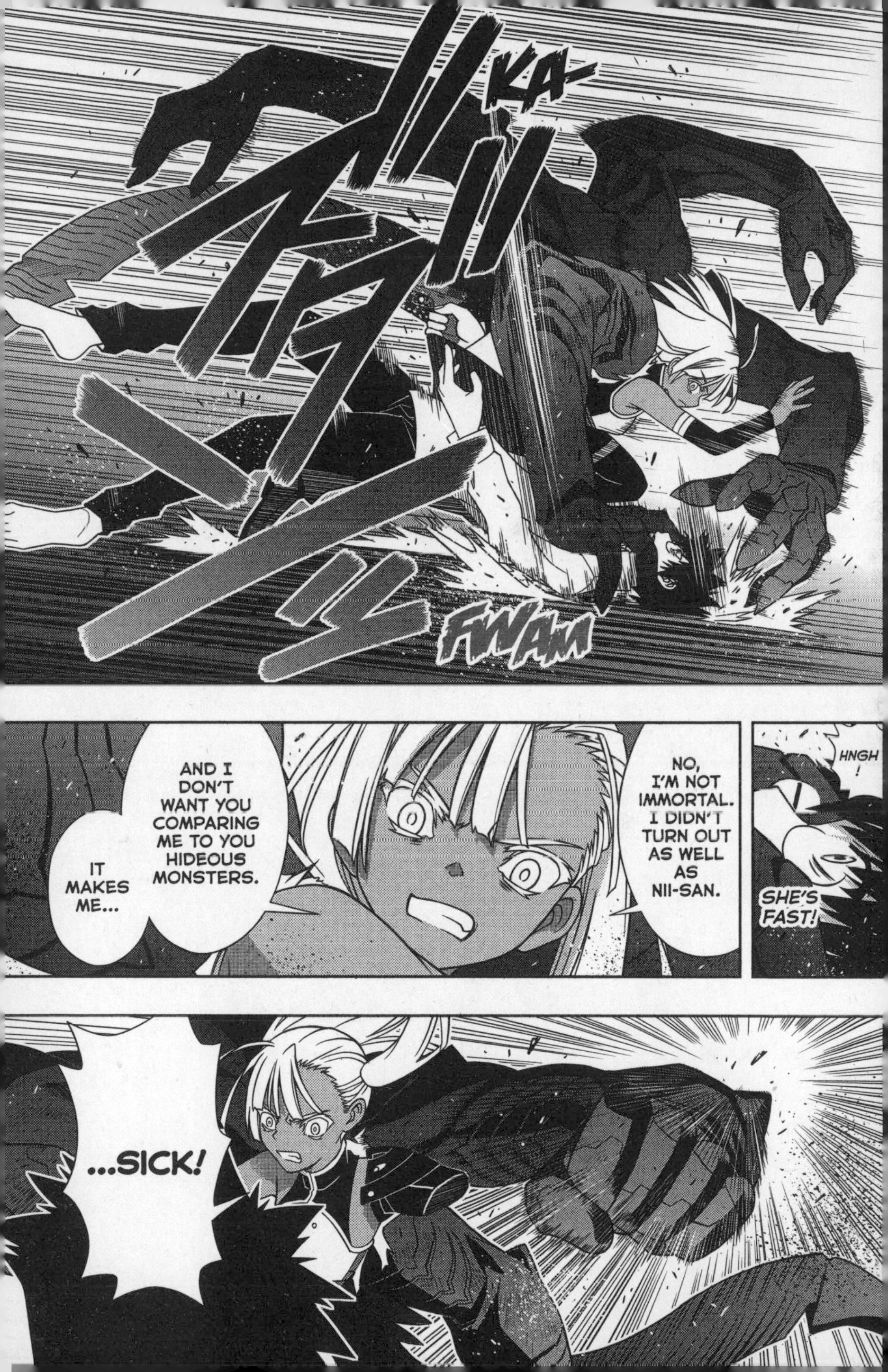
KA-
FWAM
HNGH!
SHE'S FAST!
NO, I'M NOT IMMORTAL. I DIDN'T TURN OUT AS WELL AS NII-SAN.
AND I DON'T WANT YOU COMPARING ME TO YOU HIDEOUS MONSTERS.
IT MAKES ME...
...SICK!

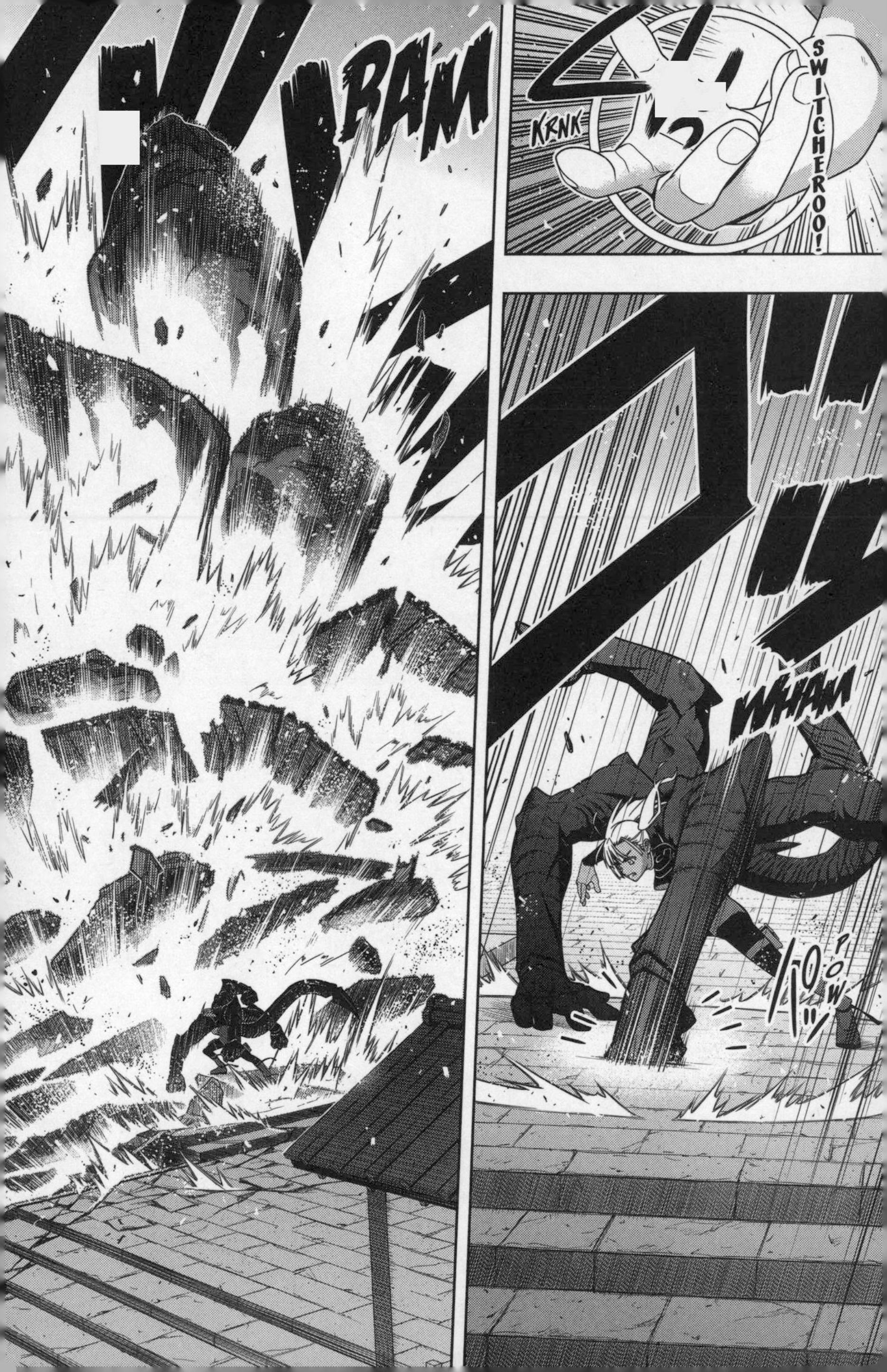
SWITCHEROO!
KRNK
WHAM
POW!!
BAM

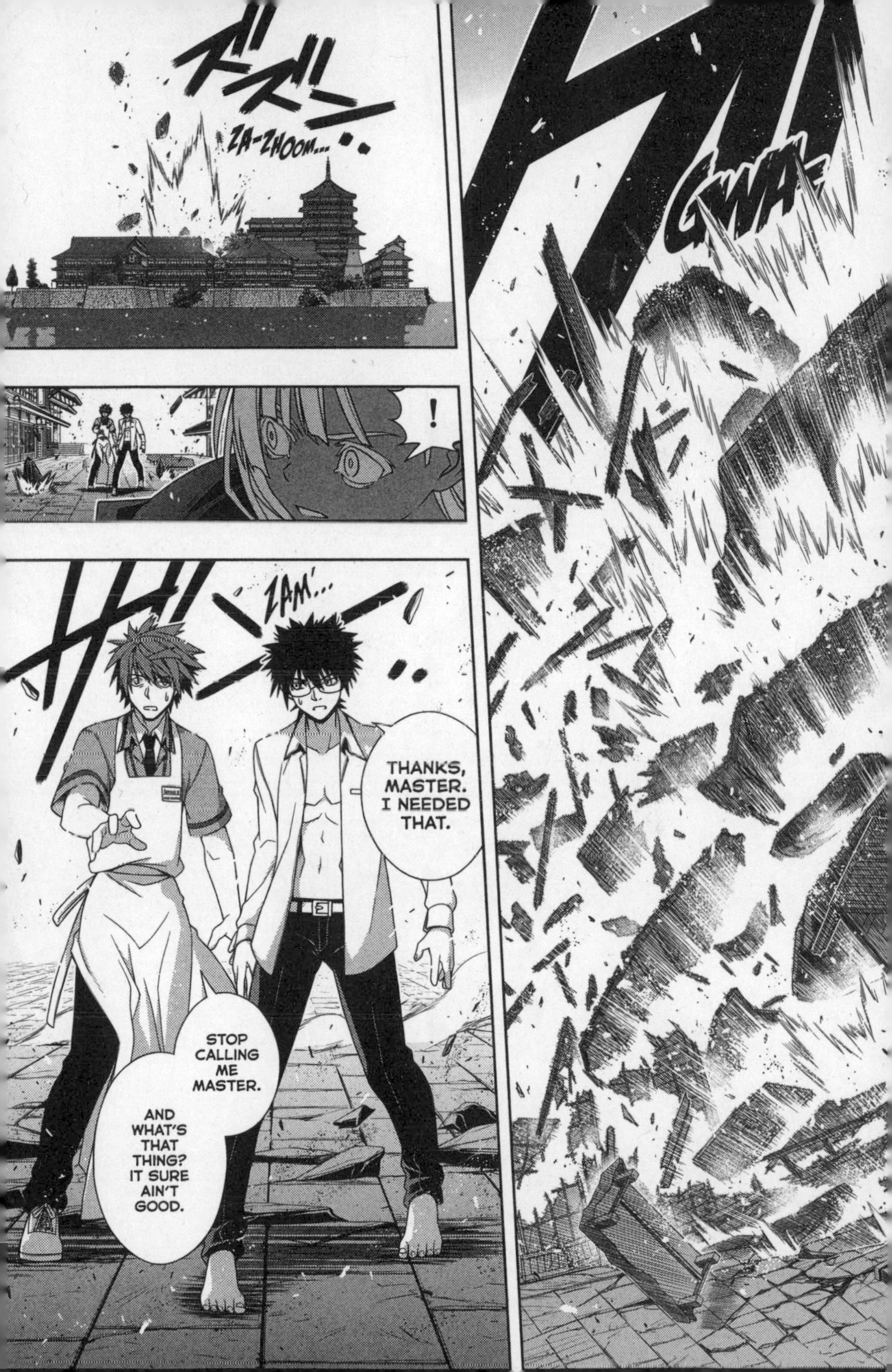
GWA
ZA-ZHOOM...
!
ZAM'...
THANKS, MASTER. I NEEDED THAT.
STOP CALLING ME MASTER.
AND WHAT'S THAT THING? IT SURE AIN'T GOOD.

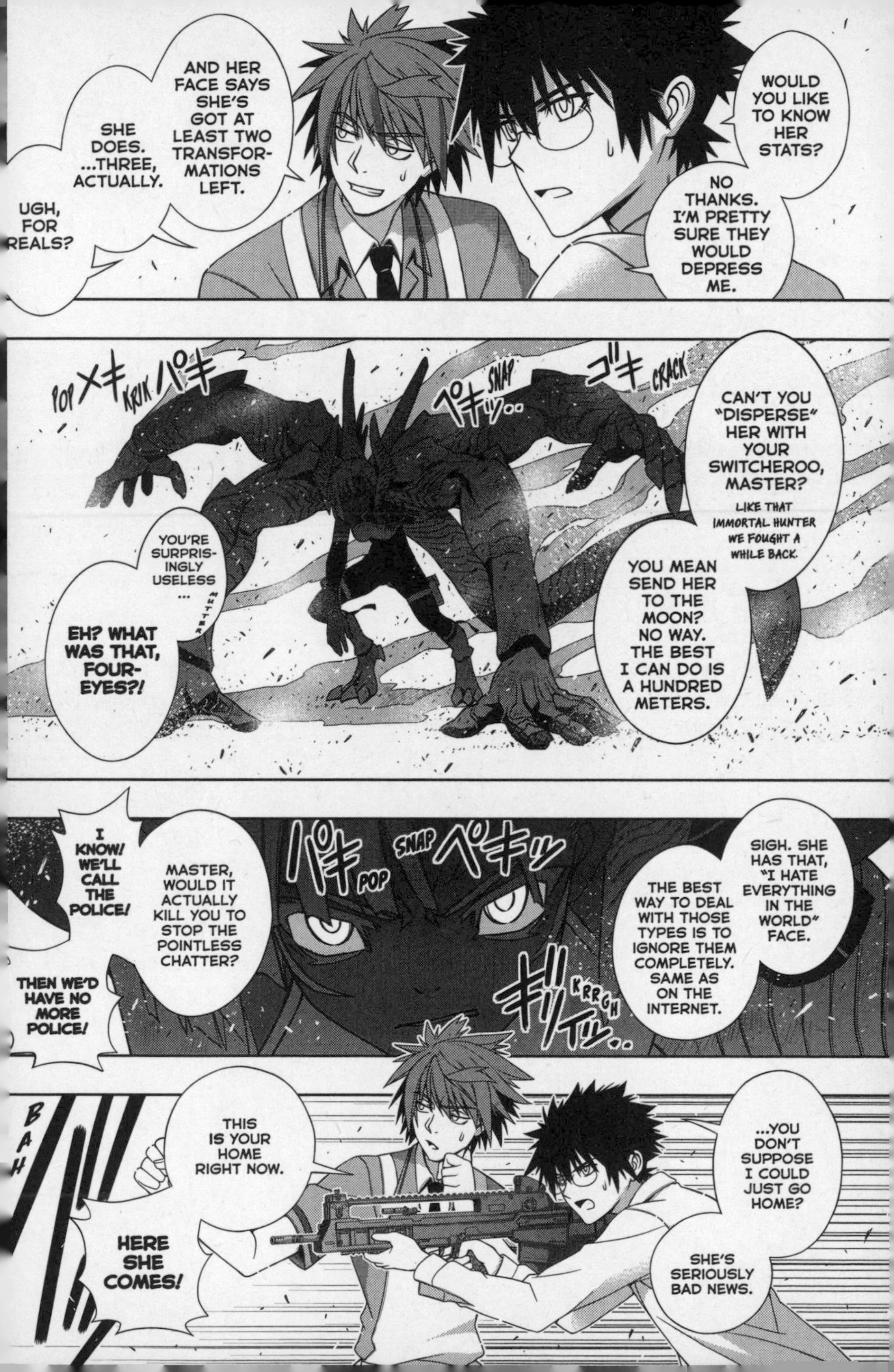
WOULD YOU LIKE TO KNOW HER STATS?
NO THANKS. I'M PRETTY SURE THEY WOULD DEPRESS ME.
AND HER FACE SAYS SHE'S GOT AT LEAST TWO TRANSFORMATIONS LEFT.
SHE DOES. ...THREE, ACTUALLY.
UGH, FOR REALS?
ゴキ CRACK
ペキッ.. SNAP
パキ KRIK
メキ POP
CAN'T YOU "DISPERSE" HER WITH YOUR SWITCHEROO, MASTER?
LIKE THAT IMMORTAL HUNTER WE FOUGHT A WHILE BACK.
YOU MEAN SEND HER TO THE MOON? NO WAY. THE BEST I CAN DO IS A HUNDRED METERS.
YOU'RE SURPRISINGLY USELESS...
MUTTER
EH? WHAT WAS THAT, FOUR-EYES?!
SIGH. SHE HAS THAT, "I HATE EVERYTHING IN THE WORLD" FACE.
THE BEST WAY TO DEAL WITH THOSE TYPES IS TO IGNORE THEM COMPLETELY. SAME AS ON THE INTERNET.
ペキッ SNAP
パキ POP
ギリィッ.. KRRGH
MASTER, WOULD IT ACTUALLY KILL YOU TO STOP THE POINTLESS CHATTER?
I KNOW! WE'LL CALL THE POLICE!
THEN WE'D HAVE NO MORE POLICE!
...YOU DON'T SUPPOSE I COULD JUST GO HOME?
SHE'S SERIOUSLY BAD NEWS.
THIS IS YOUR HOME RIGHT NOW.
HERE SHE COMES!
BAAH

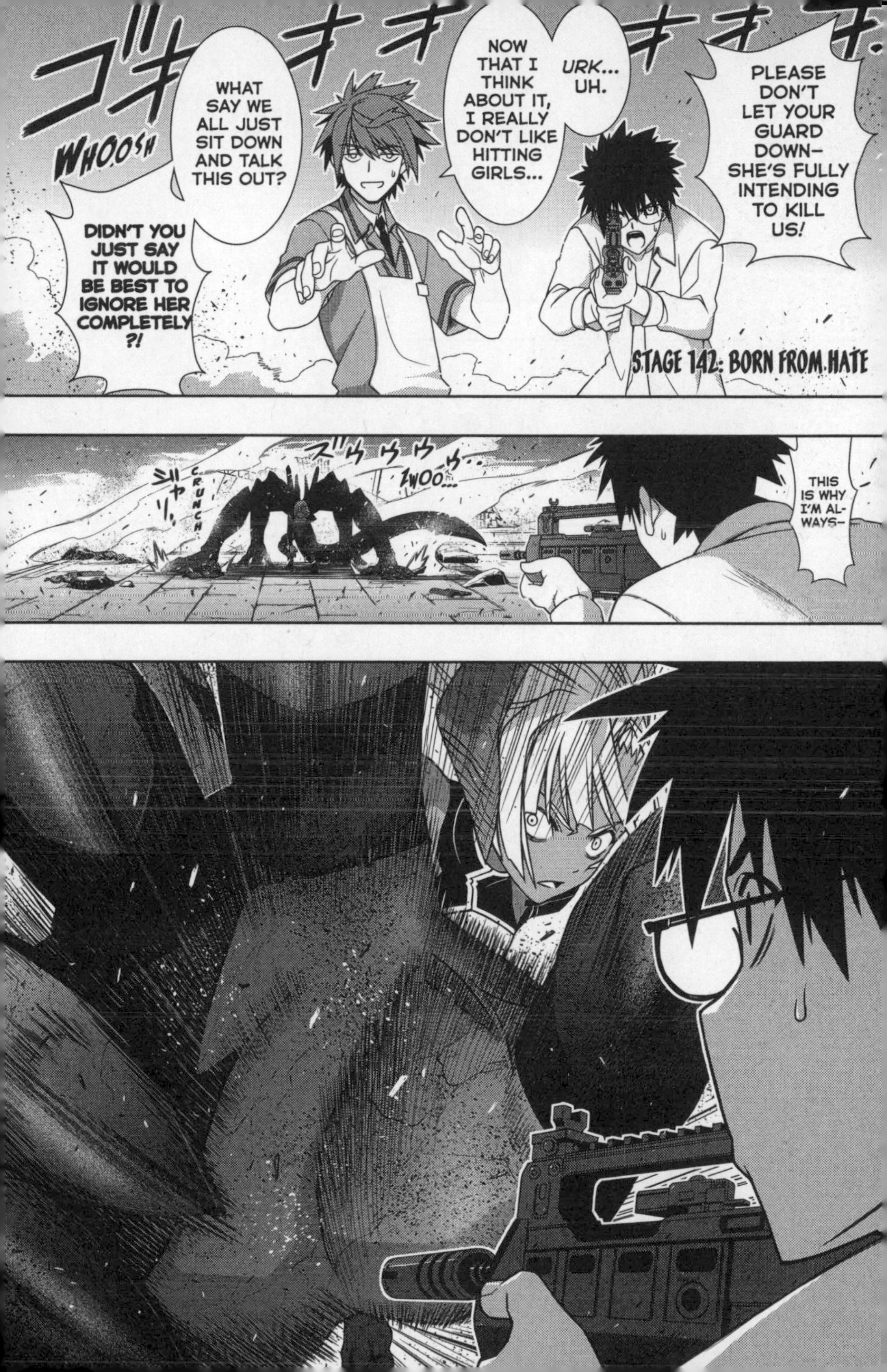
PLEASE DON'T LET YOUR GUARD DOWN—SHE'S FULLY INTENDING TO KILL US!
URK... UH.
NOW THAT I THINK ABOUT IT, I REALLY DON'T LIKE HITTING GIRLS...
WHAT SAY WE ALL JUST SIT DOWN AND TALK THIS OUT?
WHOOSH
DIDN'T YOU JUST SAY IT WOULD BE BEST TO IGNORE HER COMPLETELY?!
STAGE 142: BORN FROM HATE
THIS IS WHY I'M AL-WAYS—
WOO...
CRUNCH

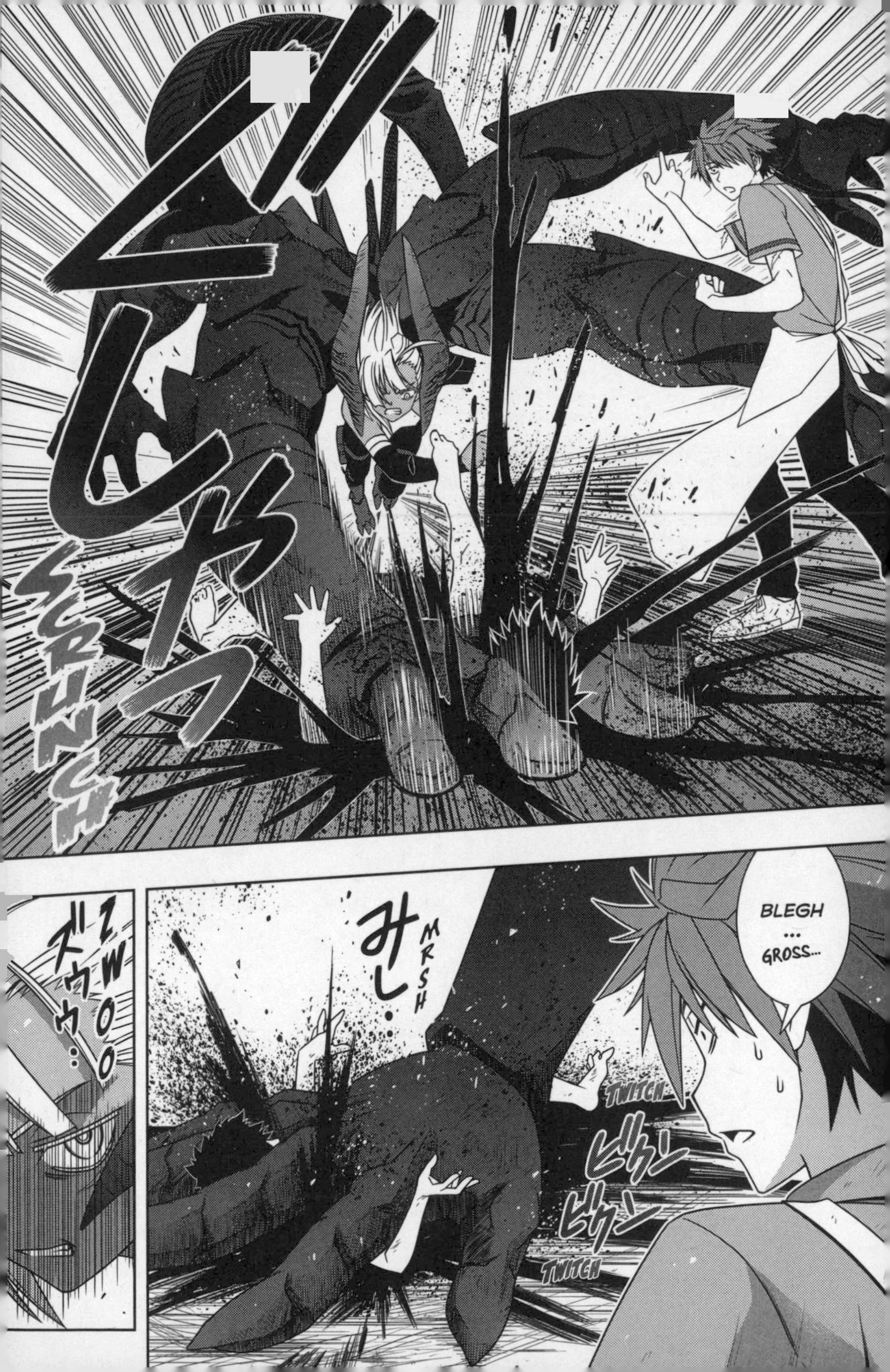
SCRUNCH
BLEGH ... GROSS...
みし
MRSH
TWITCH
ビクン
ビクン
TWITCH
ズウゥゥ..
ZWOOO

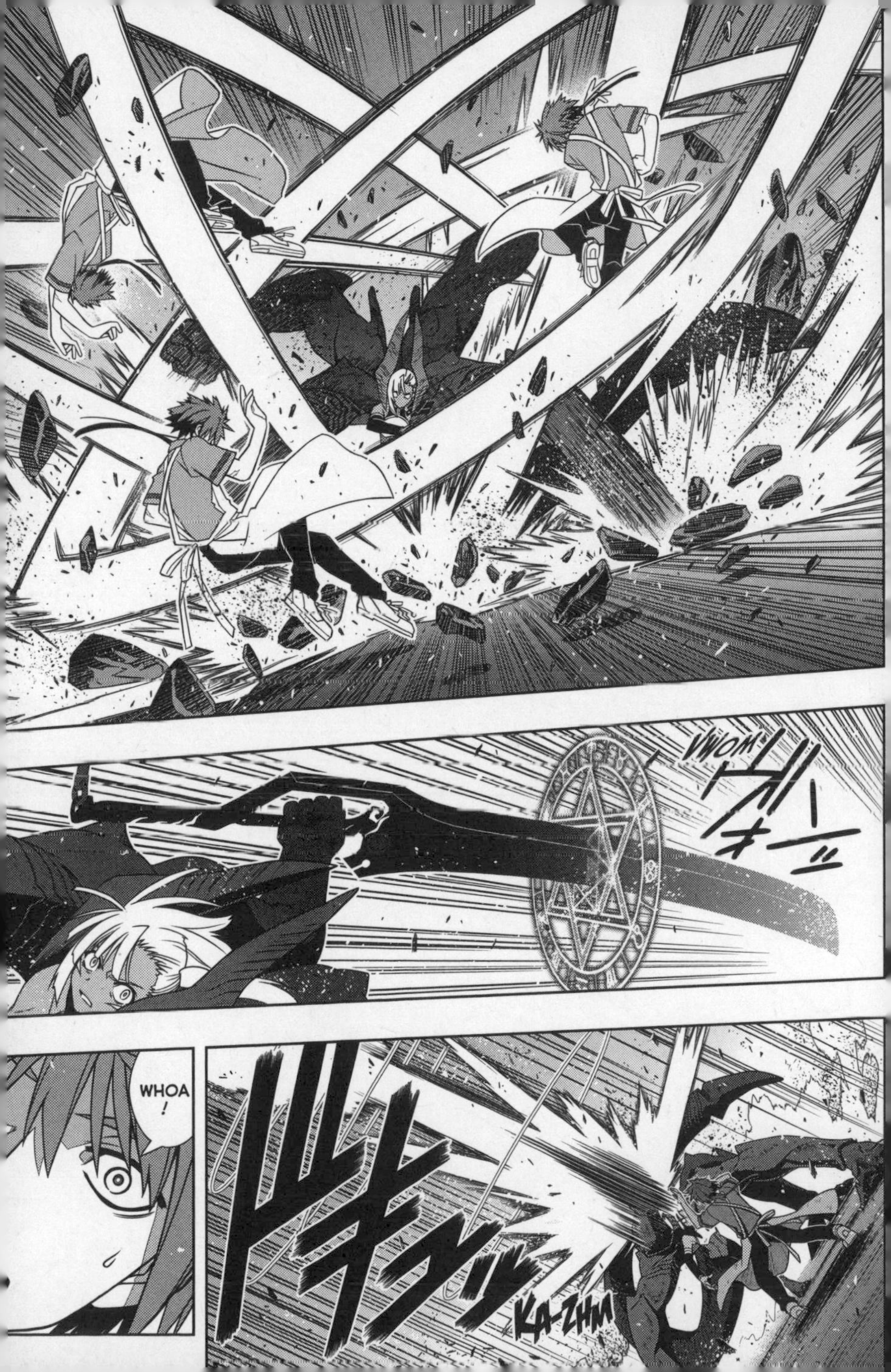
VWOM
KA-ZHM
WHOA!

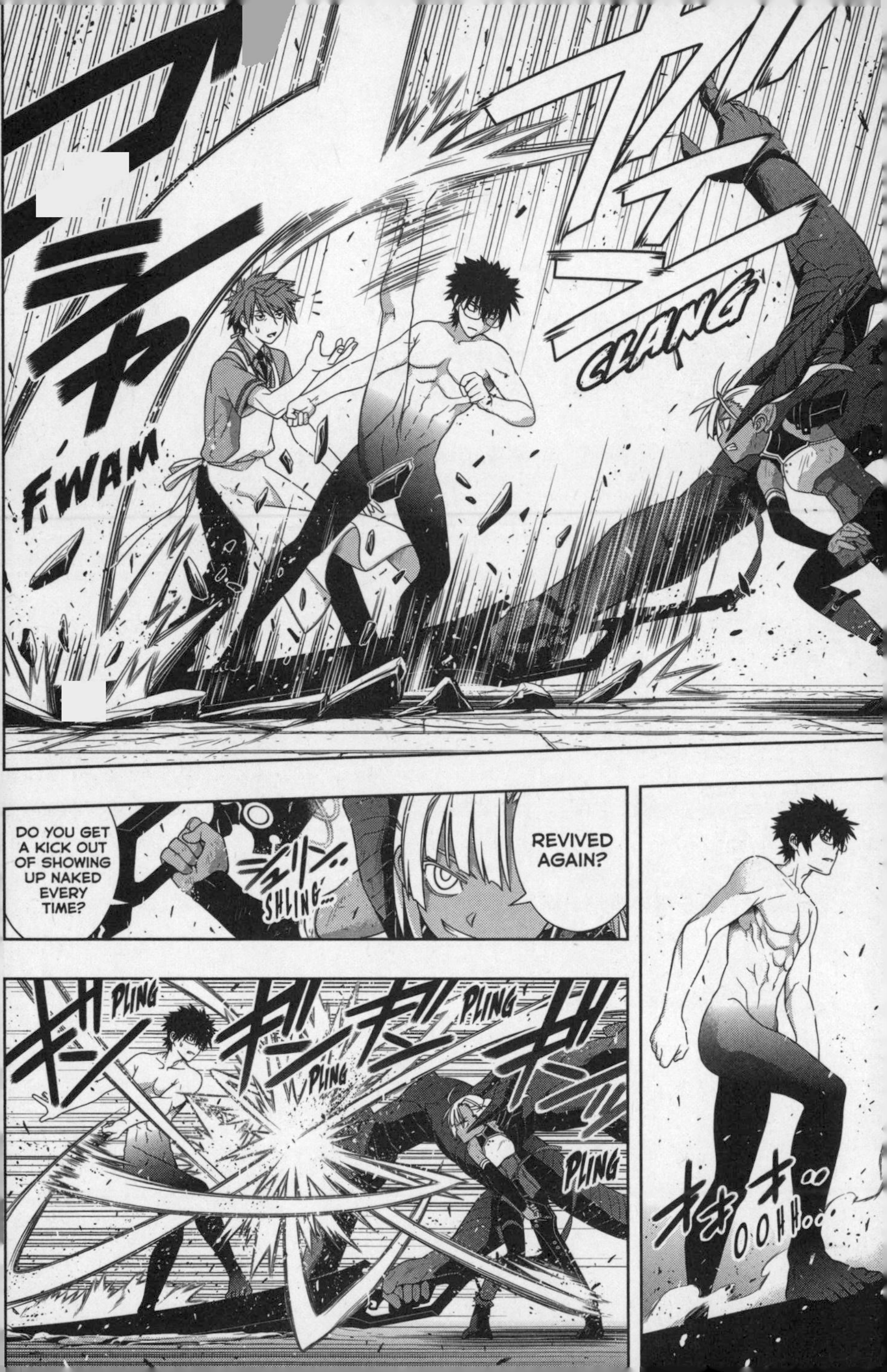
CLANG
FWAM
OOHH...
REVIVED AGAIN?
SHLING...
DO YOU GET A KICK OUT OF SHOWING UP NAKED EVERY TIME?
PLING
PLING
PLING
PLING

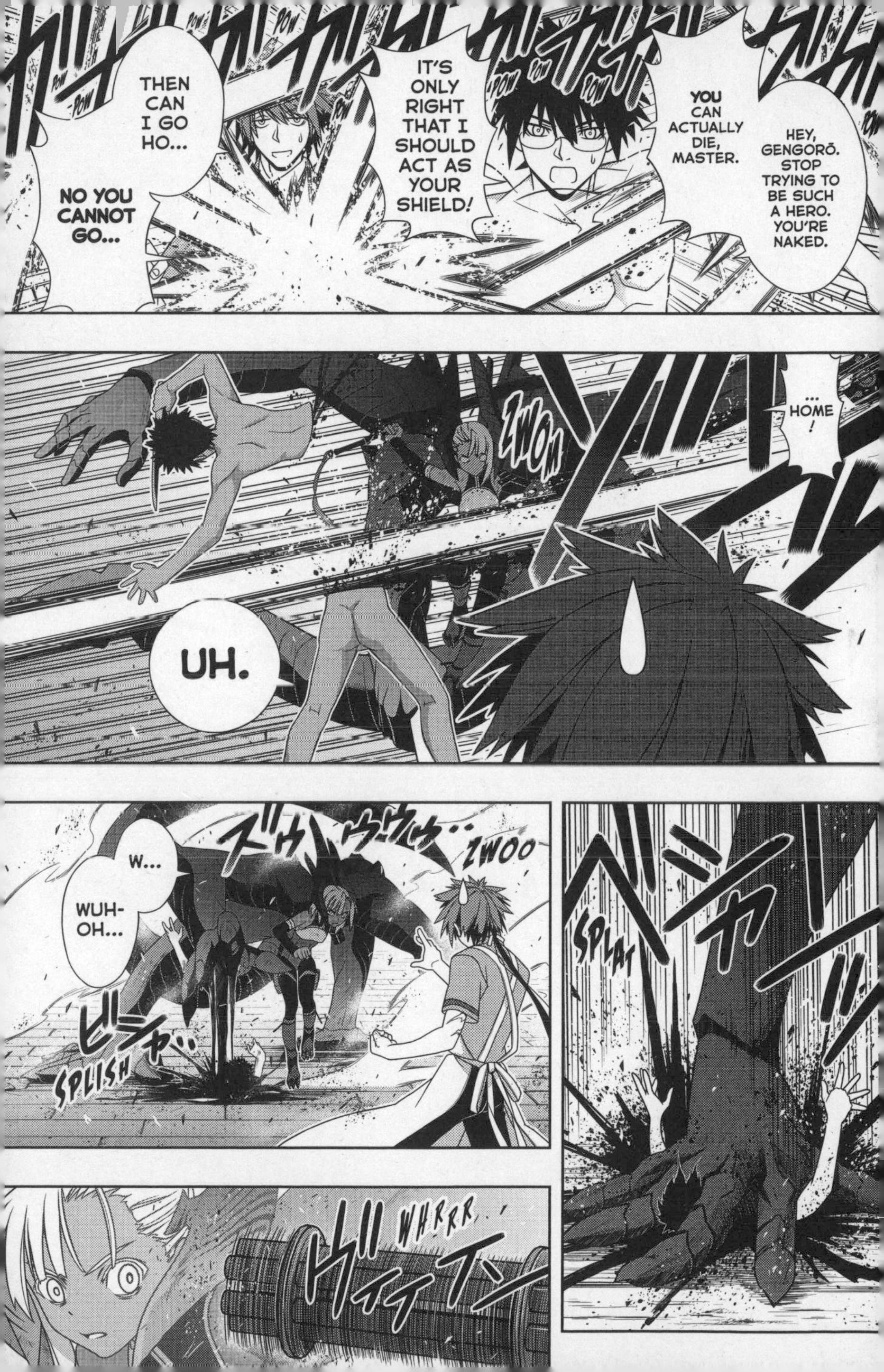
POW
HEY, GENGORŌ. STOP TRYING TO BE SUCH A HERO. YOU'RE NAKED.
YOU CAN ACTUALLY DIE, MASTER.
IT'S ONLY RIGHT THAT I SHOULD ACT AS YOUR SHIELD!
THEN CAN I GO HO...
NO YOU CANNOT GO...
...HOME!
ZWOM
UH.
SPLAT
ZWOO
W...
WUH-OH...
SPLISH
WHRRR

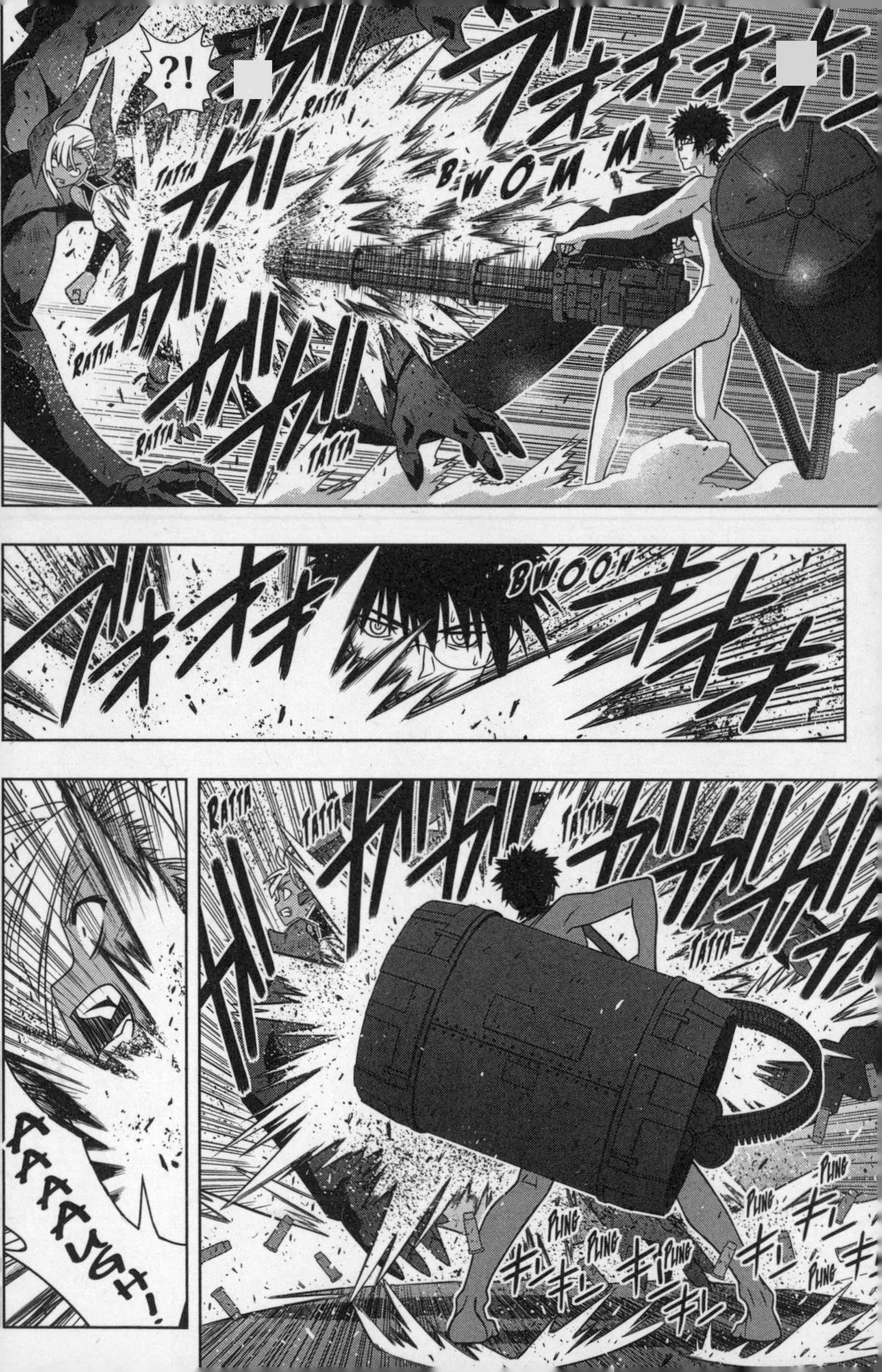
BWOMM
RATTA
?!
TATTA
RATTA
RATTA
TATTA
BWOOH
TATTA
TATTA
RATTA
TATTA
PLING
PLING
PLING
PLING
PLING
PLING
PLING
AAAAUGH!

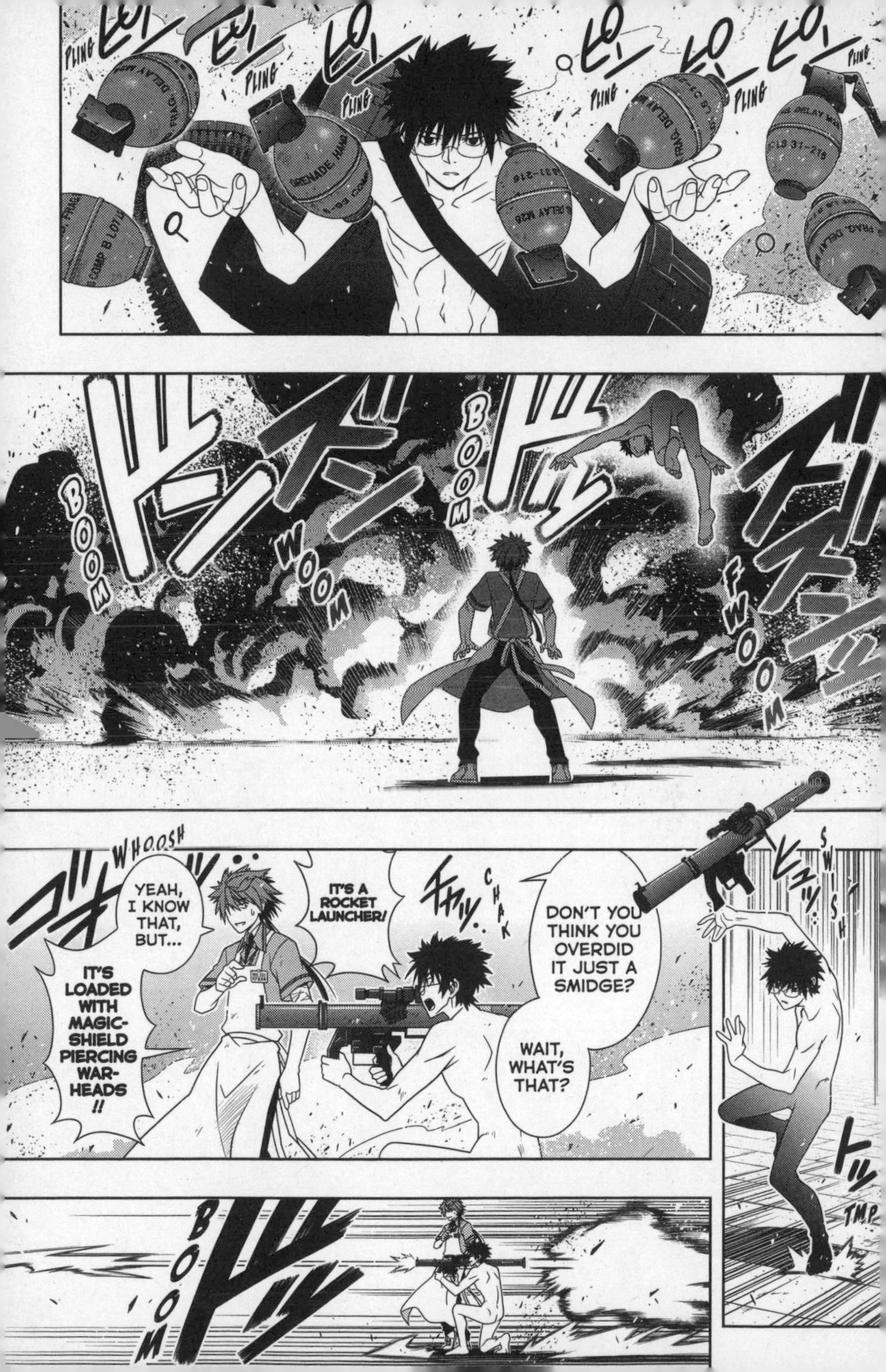
PLING
PLING
PLING
PLING
PLING
PLING
FWOOM
BOOM
WOOM
BOOM
SWISH
TMP
DON'T YOU THINK YOU OVERDID IT JUST A SMIDGE?
WAIT, WHAT'S THAT?
CHAK
IT'S A ROCKET LAUNCHER!
YEAH, I KNOW THAT, BUT...
IT'S LOADED WITH MAGIC-SHIELD PIERCING WAR-HEADS!!
WHOOSH
BOOM

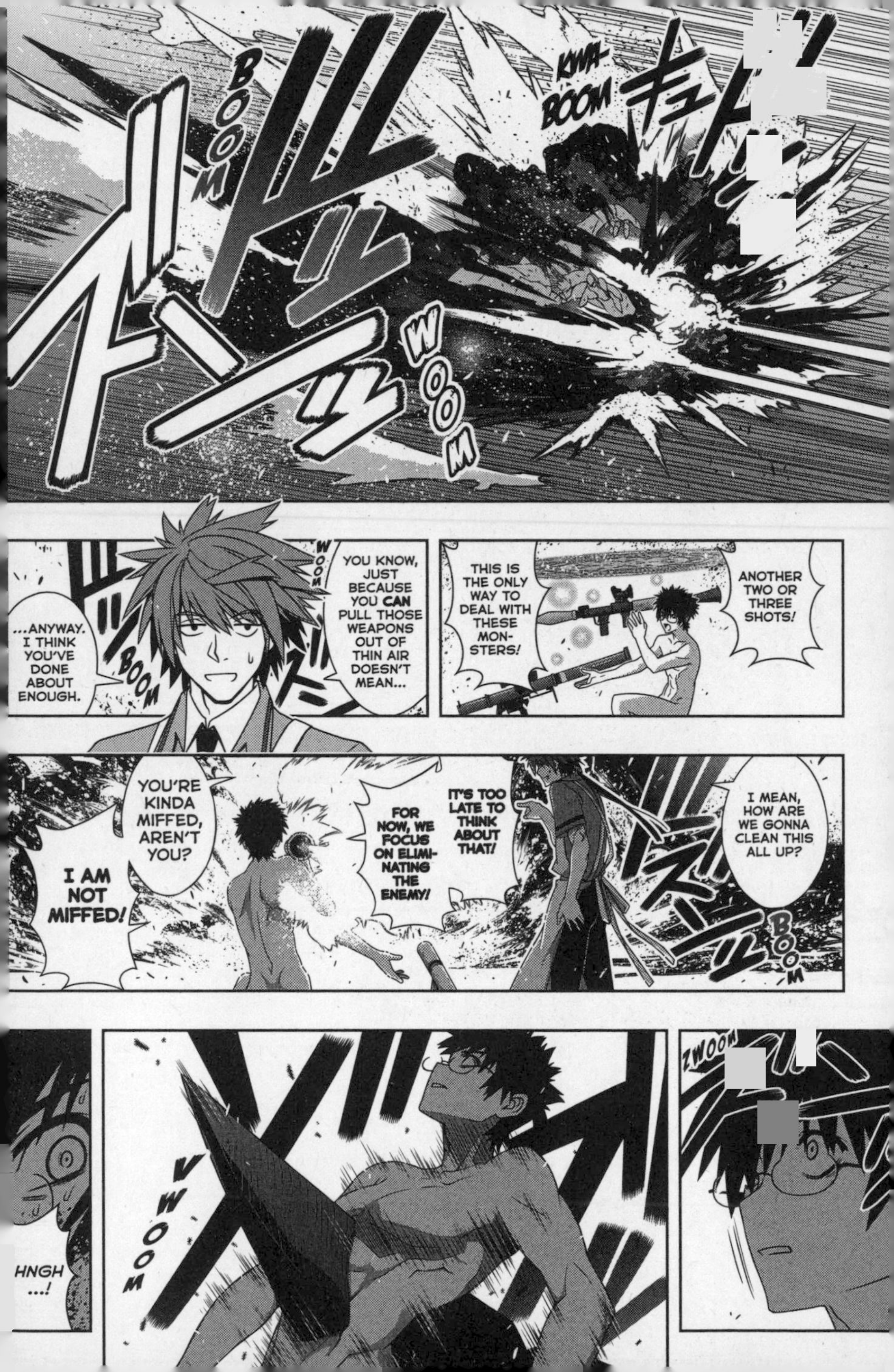
KWA-BOOM
BOOM
WOOM
ANOTHER TWO OR THREE SHOTS!
THIS IS THE ONLY WAY TO DEAL WITH THESE MONSTERS!
WOOM
YOU KNOW, JUST BECAUSE YOU CAN PULL THOSE WEAPONS OUT OF THIN AIR DOESN'T MEAN...
BOOM
...ANYWAY. I THINK YOU'VE DONE ABOUT ENOUGH.
BOOM
I MEAN, HOW ARE WE GONNA CLEAN THIS ALL UP?
IT'S TOO LATE TO THINK ABOUT THAT!
FOR NOW, WE FOCUS ON ELIMINATING THE ENEMY!
YOU'RE KINDA MIFFED, AREN'T YOU?
I AM NOT MIFFED!
ZWOOM
VWOOM
HNGH ...!

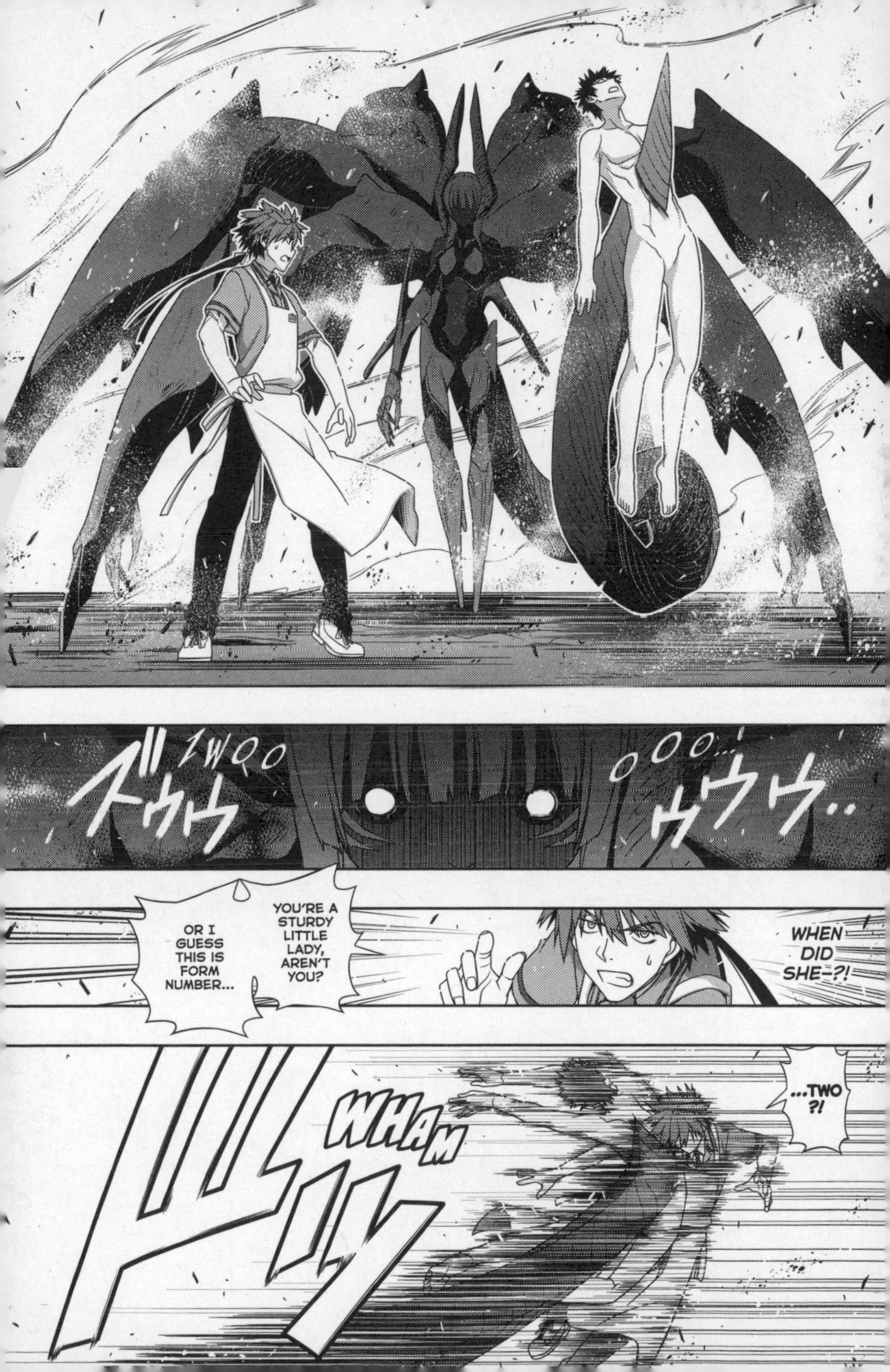
ZWOO
OOO...!
WHEN DID SHE–?!
YOU'RE A STURDY LITTLE LADY, AREN'T YOU?
OR I GUESS THIS IS FORM NUMBER...
...TWO ?!
WHAM

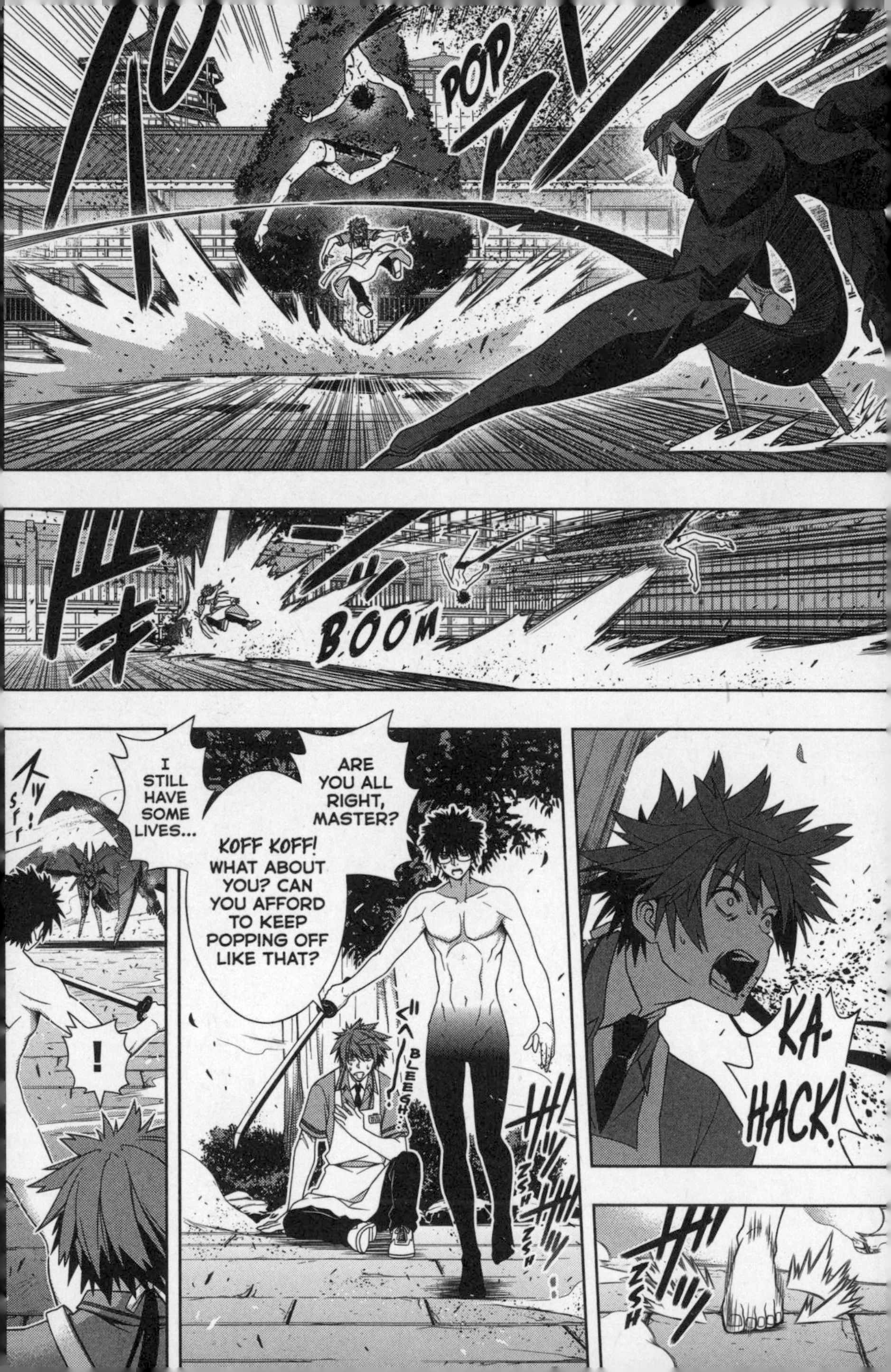
POP
BOOM
KA-HACK!
ZSH
ARE YOU ALL RIGHT, MASTER?
I STILL HAVE SOME LIVES...
KOFF KOFF! WHAT ABOUT YOU? CAN YOU AFFORD TO KEEP POPPING OFF LIKE THAT?
BLEESH...
ZSH
SFF
!

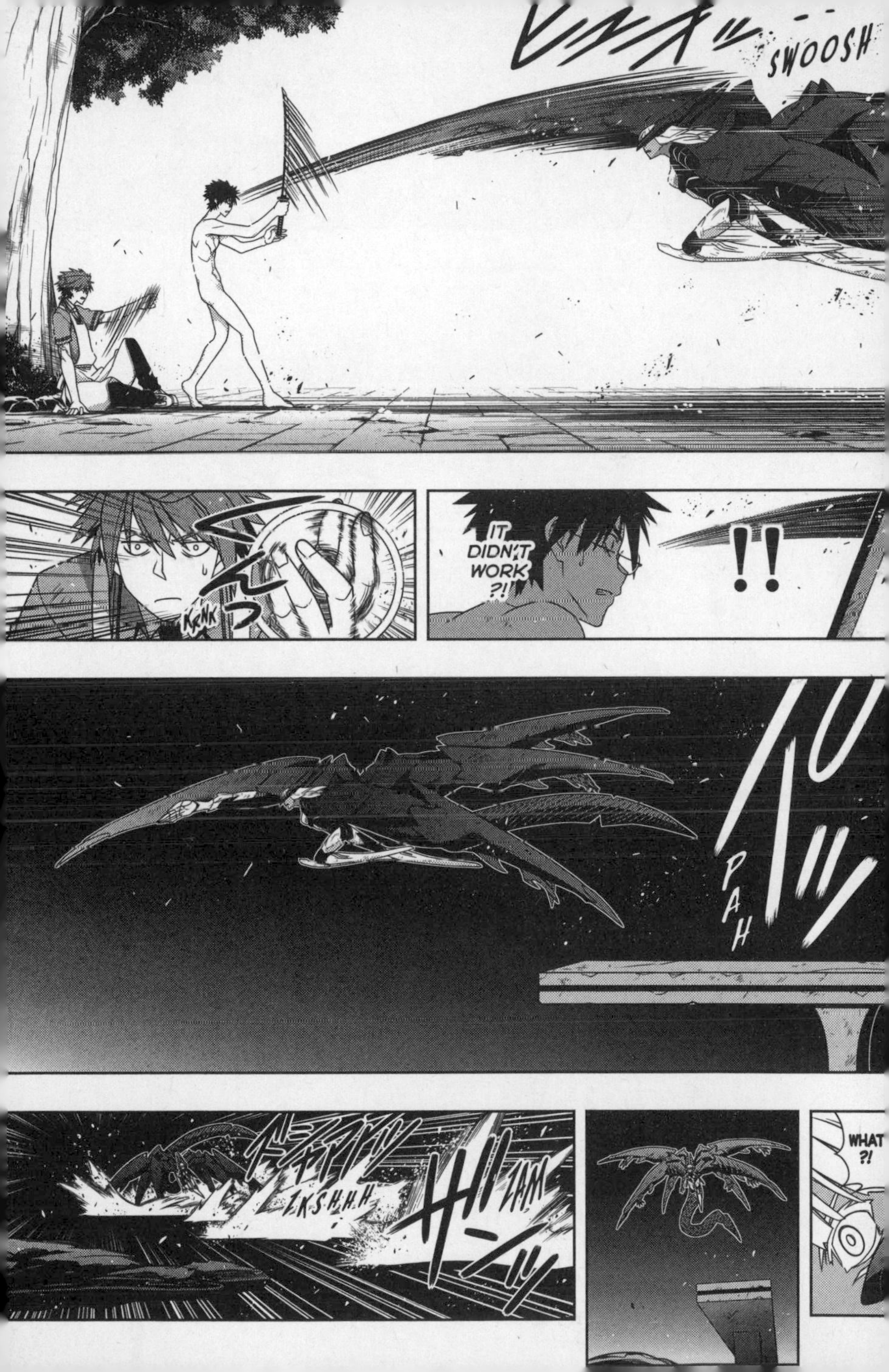
SWOOSH
IT DIDN'T WORK ?!
!!
KRNK
PAH
WHAT ?!
ZAM
KSHHH

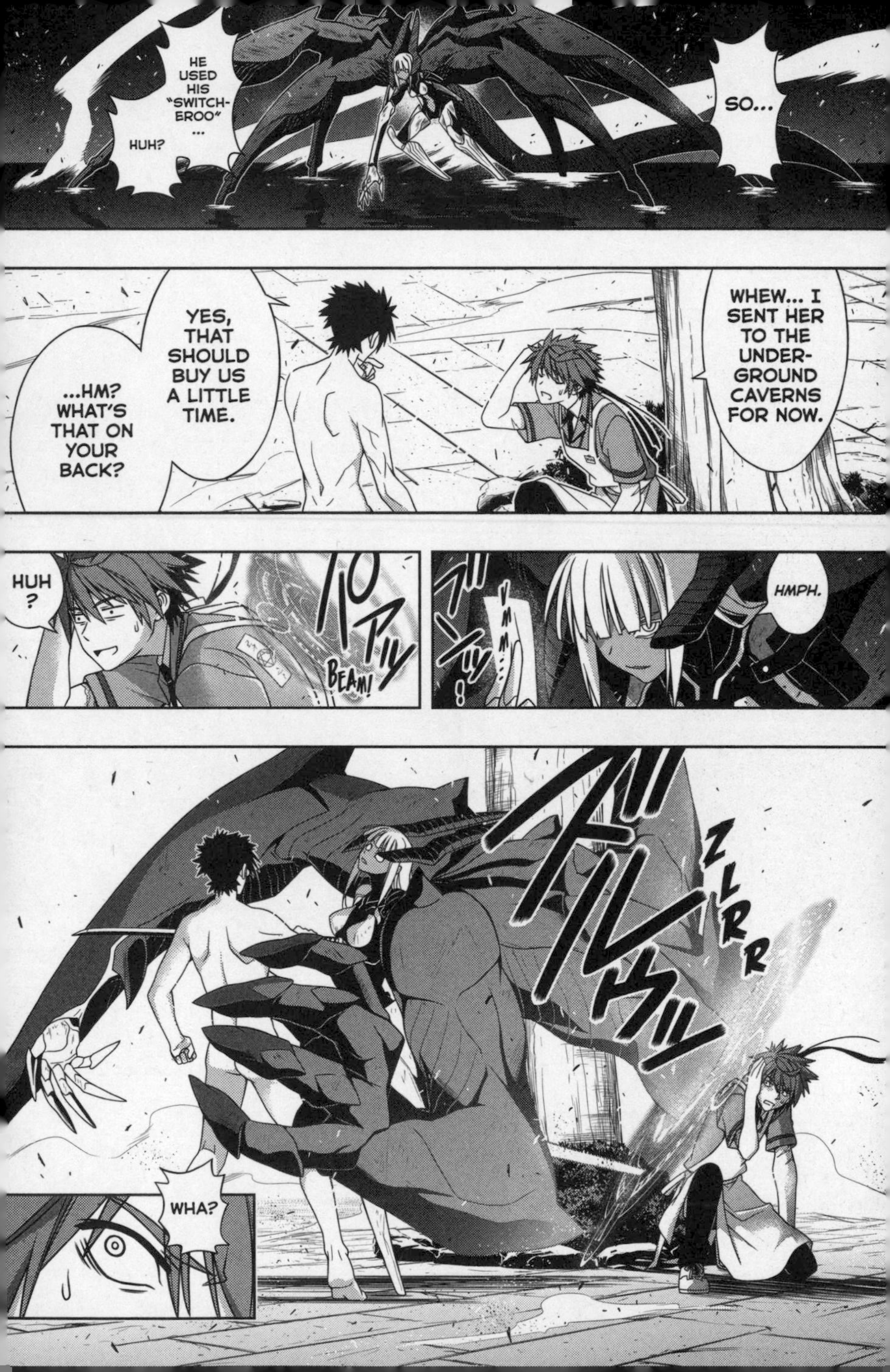
SO...
HE USED HIS "SWITCH-EROO"...
HUH?
WHEW... I SENT HER TO THE UNDER-GROUND CAVERNS FOR NOW.
YES, THAT SHOULD BUY US A LITTLE TIME.
...HM? WHAT'S THAT ON YOUR BACK?
HMPH.
VMMM...!
BEAM!
HUH?
ZLRRR
WHA?

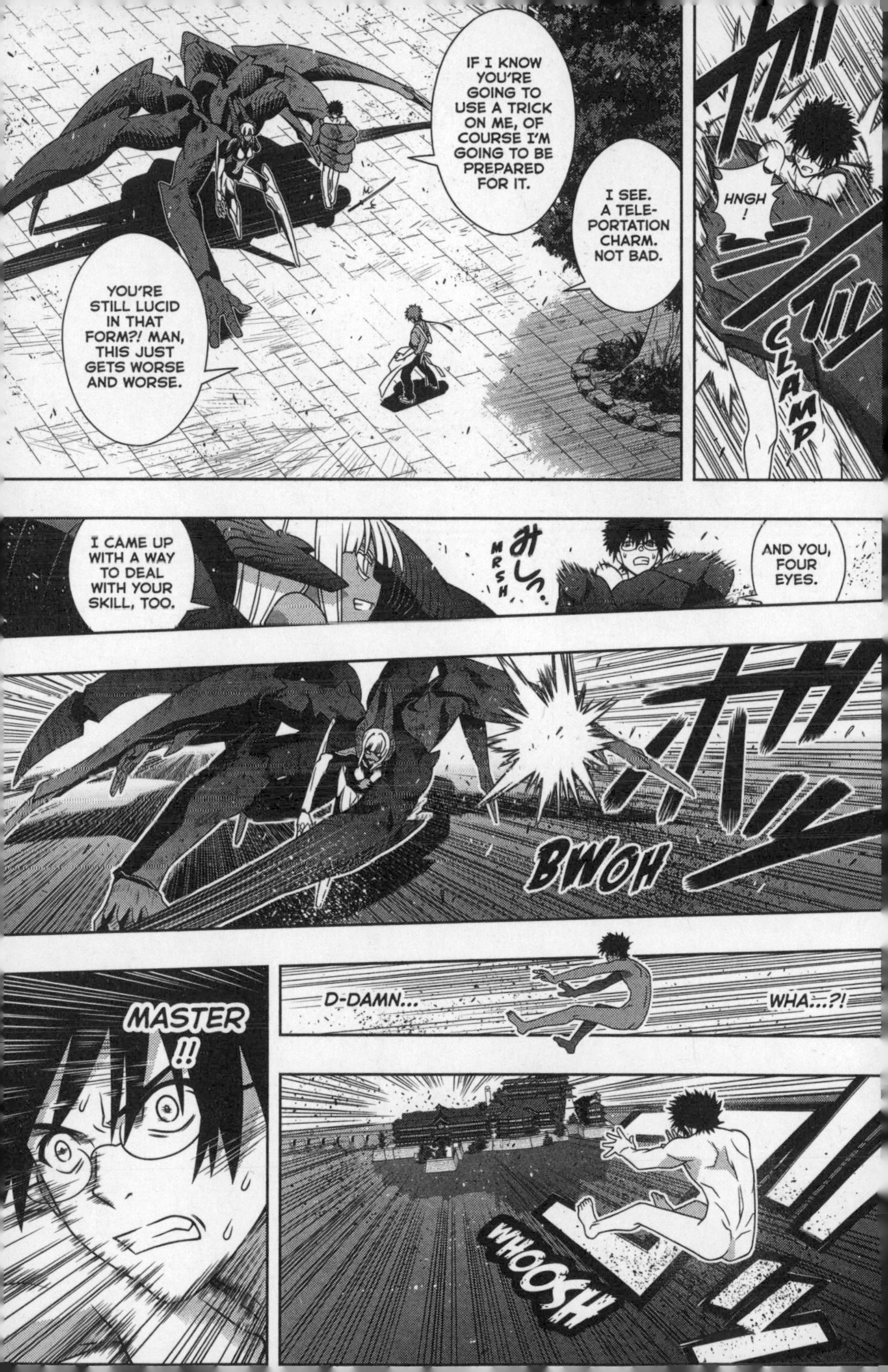
HNGH!
CLAMP
I SEE. A TELEPORTATION CHARM. NOT BAD.
IF I KNOW YOU'RE GOING TO USE A TRICK ON ME, OF COURSE I'M GOING TO BE PREPARED FOR IT.
YOU'RE STILL LUCID IN THAT FORM?! MAN, THIS JUST GETS WORSE AND WORSE.
AND YOU, FOUR EYES.
みしっ
MRSH
I CAME UP WITH A WAY TO DEAL WITH YOUR SKILL, TOO.
BWOH
WHA...?!
D-DAMN...
WHOOSH
MASTER!!

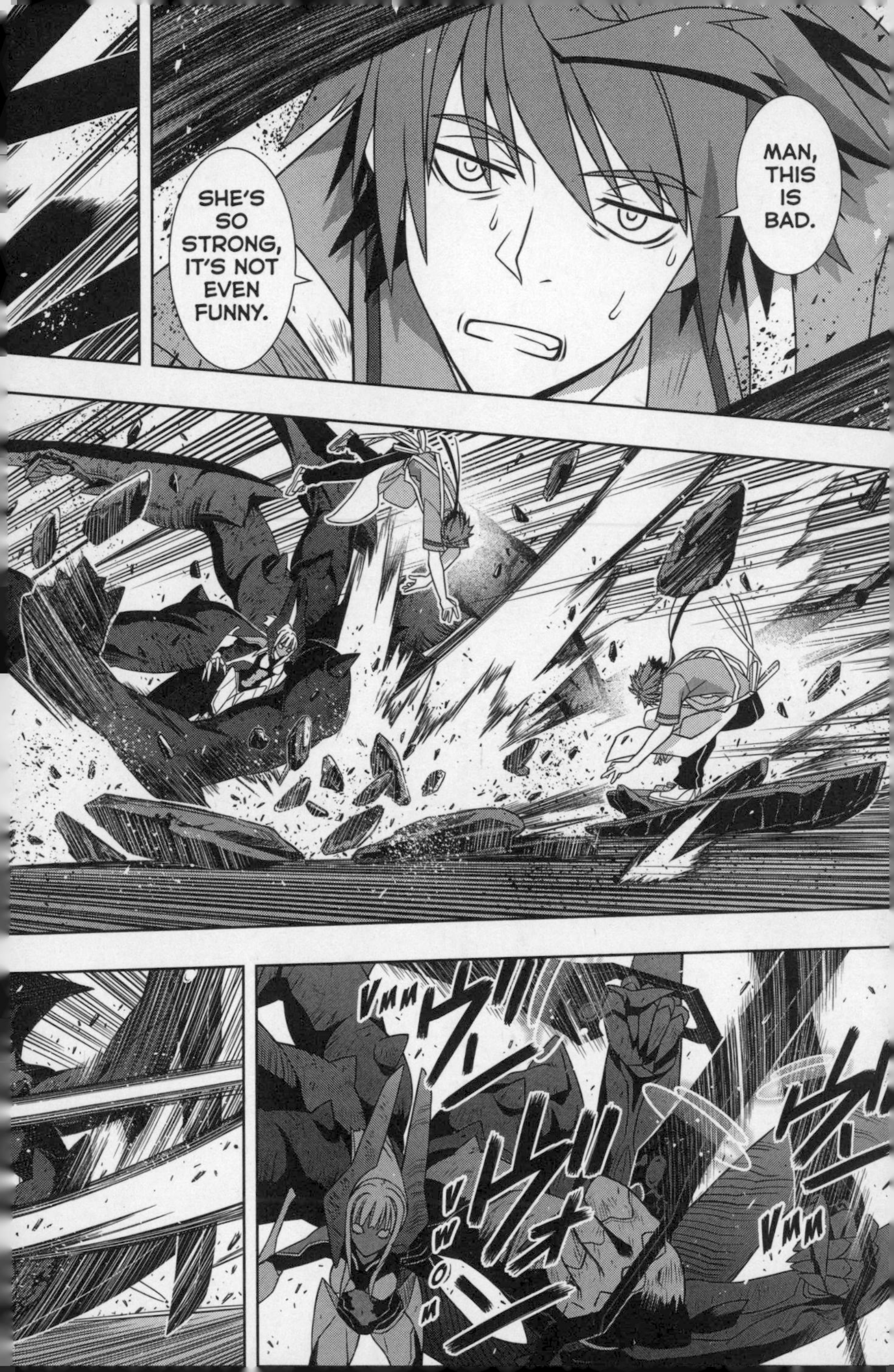
MAN, THIS IS BAD.
SHE'S SO STRONG, IT'S NOT EVEN FUNNY.
VMM
VMM
VWOM

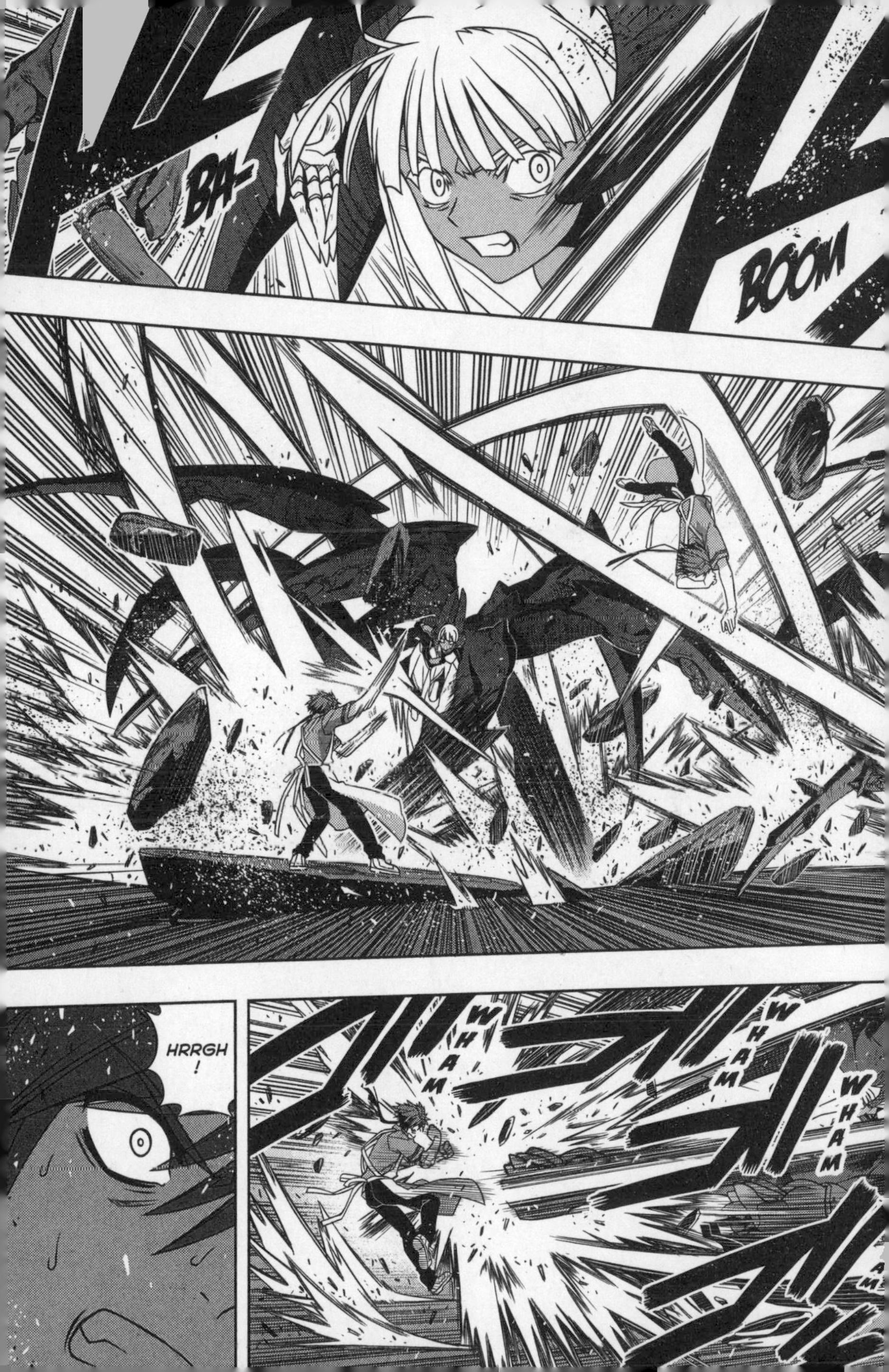
BOOM
BA-
HRRGH!
WHAM
WHAM
WHAM
WHAM

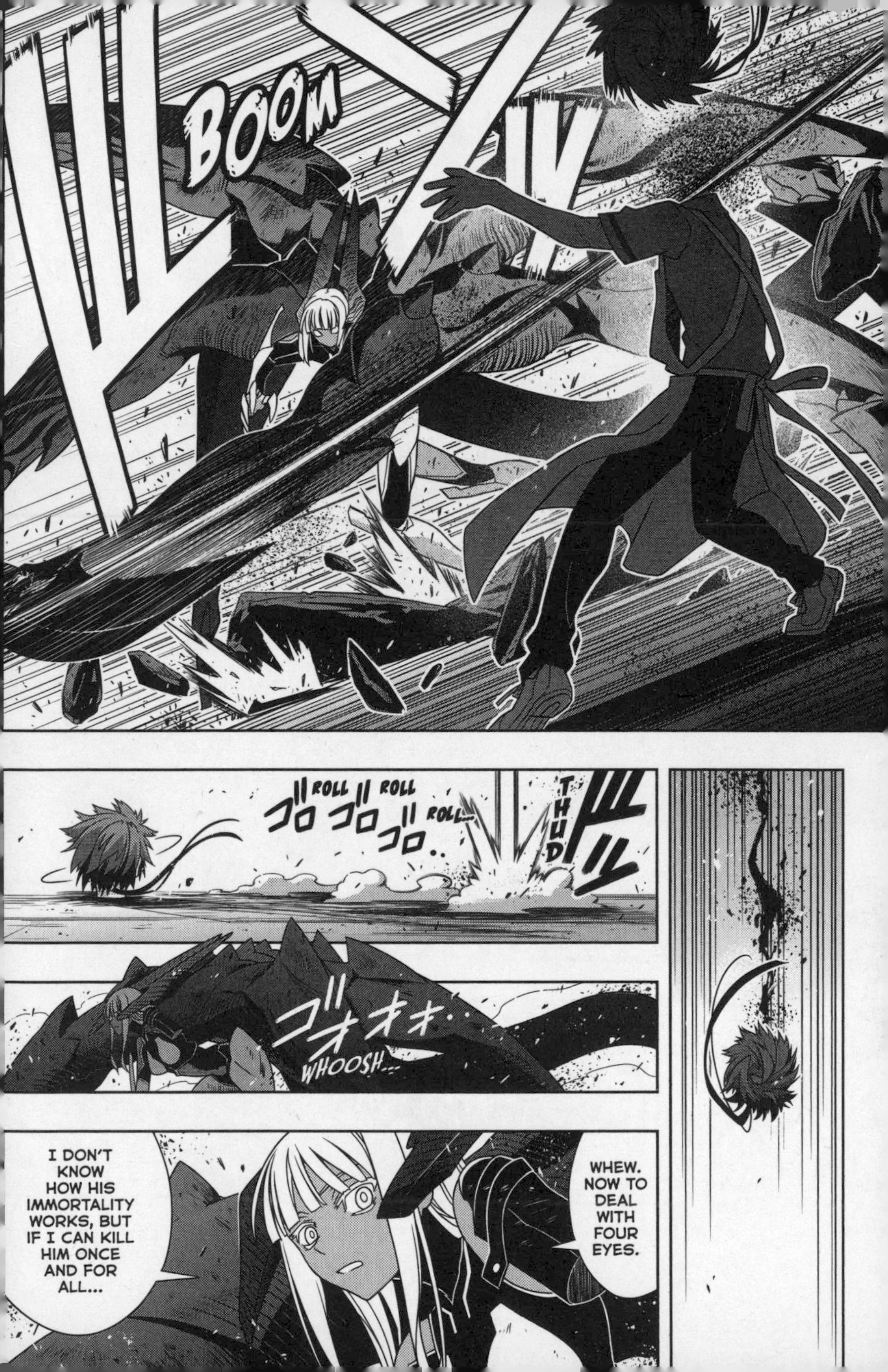

BOOM
THUD
ゴロ ROLL ゴロ ROLL ゴロ ROLL...
ゴオオオ WHOOSH...
WHEW. NOW TO DEAL WITH FOUR EYES.
I DON'T KNOW HOW HIS IMMORTALITY WORKS, BUT IF I CAN KILL HIM ONCE AND FOR ALL...

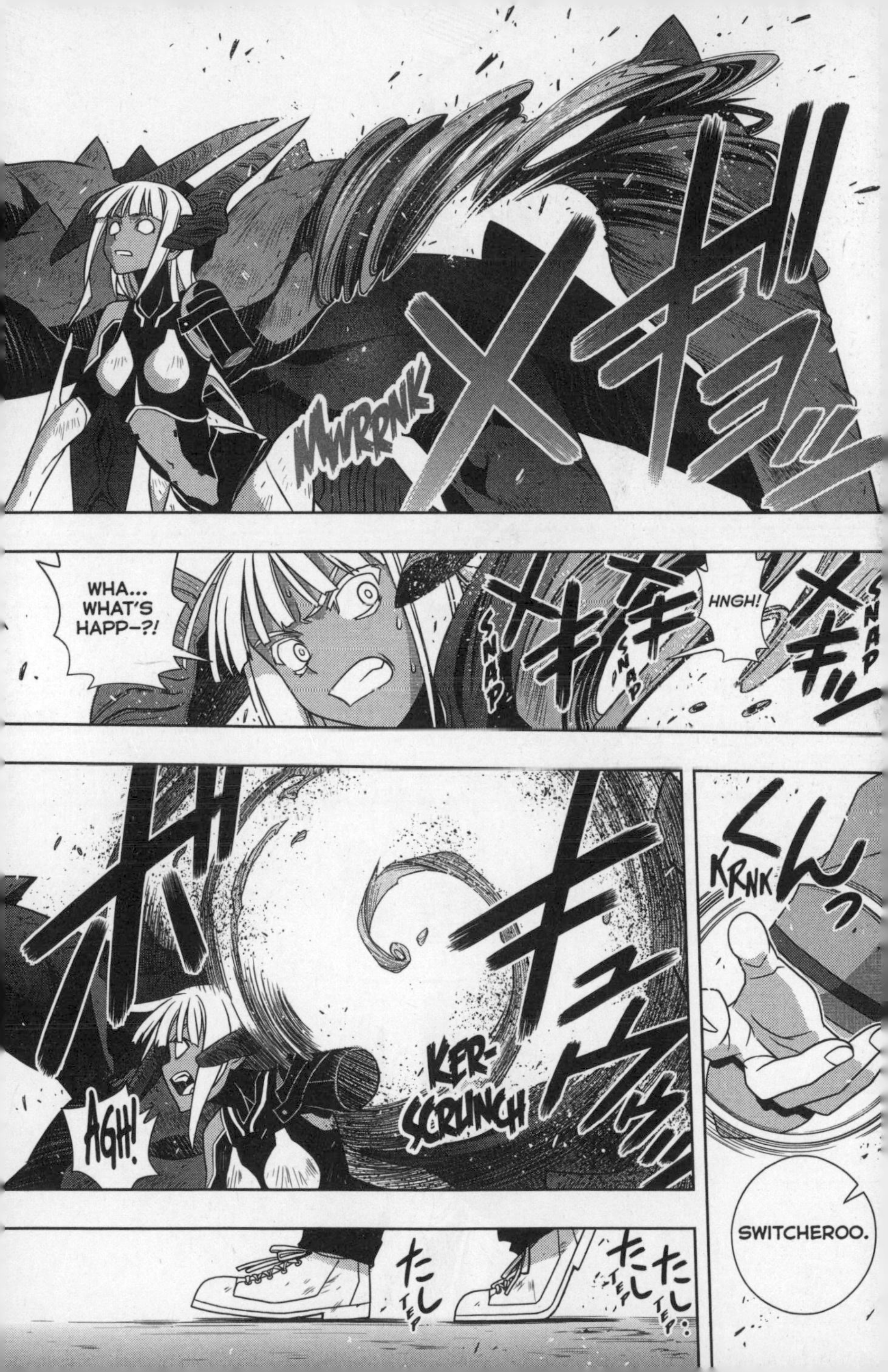
MWRRNK
SNAP
HNGH!
SNAP
SNAP
WHA... WHAT'S HAPP–?!
くんっ
KRNK
KER-SCRUNCH
AGH!
SWITCHEROO.
たし
TEP
たし
TEP
たし
TEP

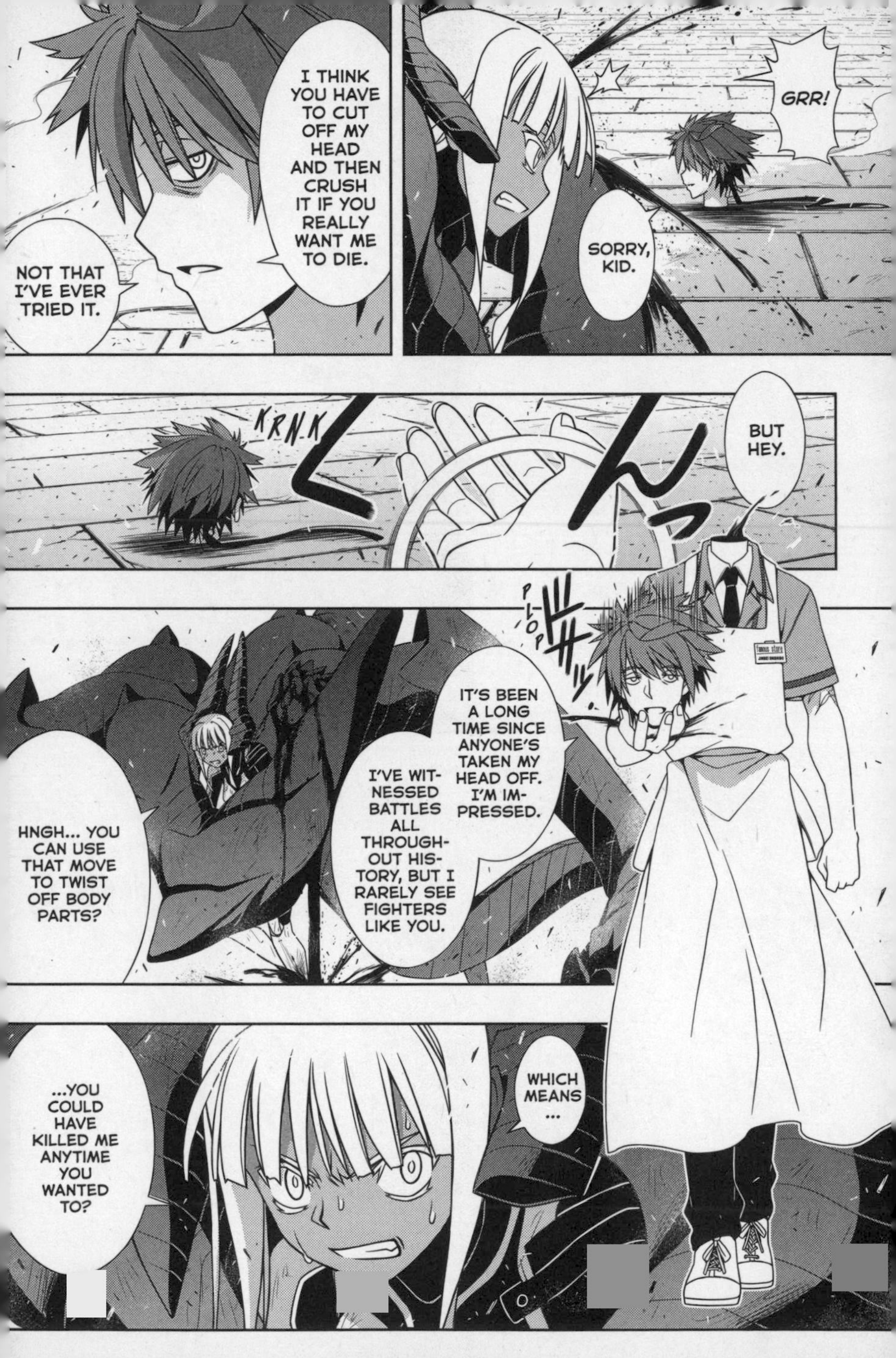
GRR!
SORRY, KID.
I THINK YOU HAVE TO CUT OFF MY HEAD AND THEN CRUSH IT IF YOU REALLY WANT ME TO DIE.
NOT THAT I'VE EVER TRIED IT.
BUT HEY.
KRNK
PLOP
IT'S BEEN A LONG TIME SINCE ANYONE'S TAKEN MY HEAD OFF. I'M IMPRESSED.
I'VE WITNESSED BATTLES ALL THROUGHOUT HISTORY, BUT I RARELY SEE FIGHTERS LIKE YOU.
HNGH... YOU CAN USE THAT MOVE TO TWIST OFF BODY PARTS?
WHICH MEANS ...
...YOU COULD HAVE KILLED ME ANYTIME YOU WANTED TO?

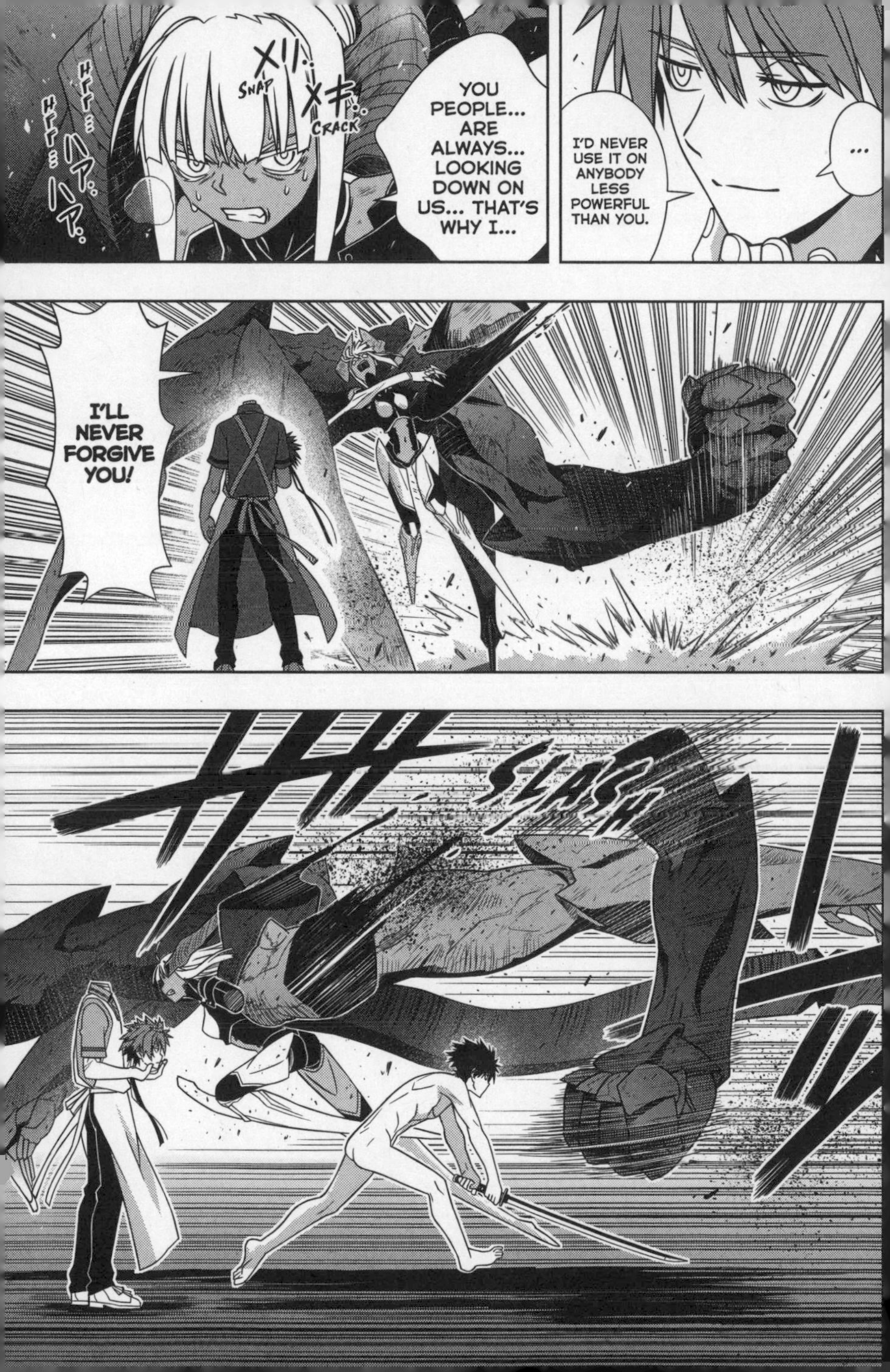
...
I'D NEVER USE IT ON ANYBODY LESS POWERFUL THAN YOU.
YOU PEOPLE... ARE ALWAYS... LOOKING DOWN ON US... THAT'S WHY I...
メリ…
SNAP
メギ…
CRACK
ハア…ハア…
Hrr... Hrr...
I'LL NEVER FORGIVE YOU!
ザザ
SLASH

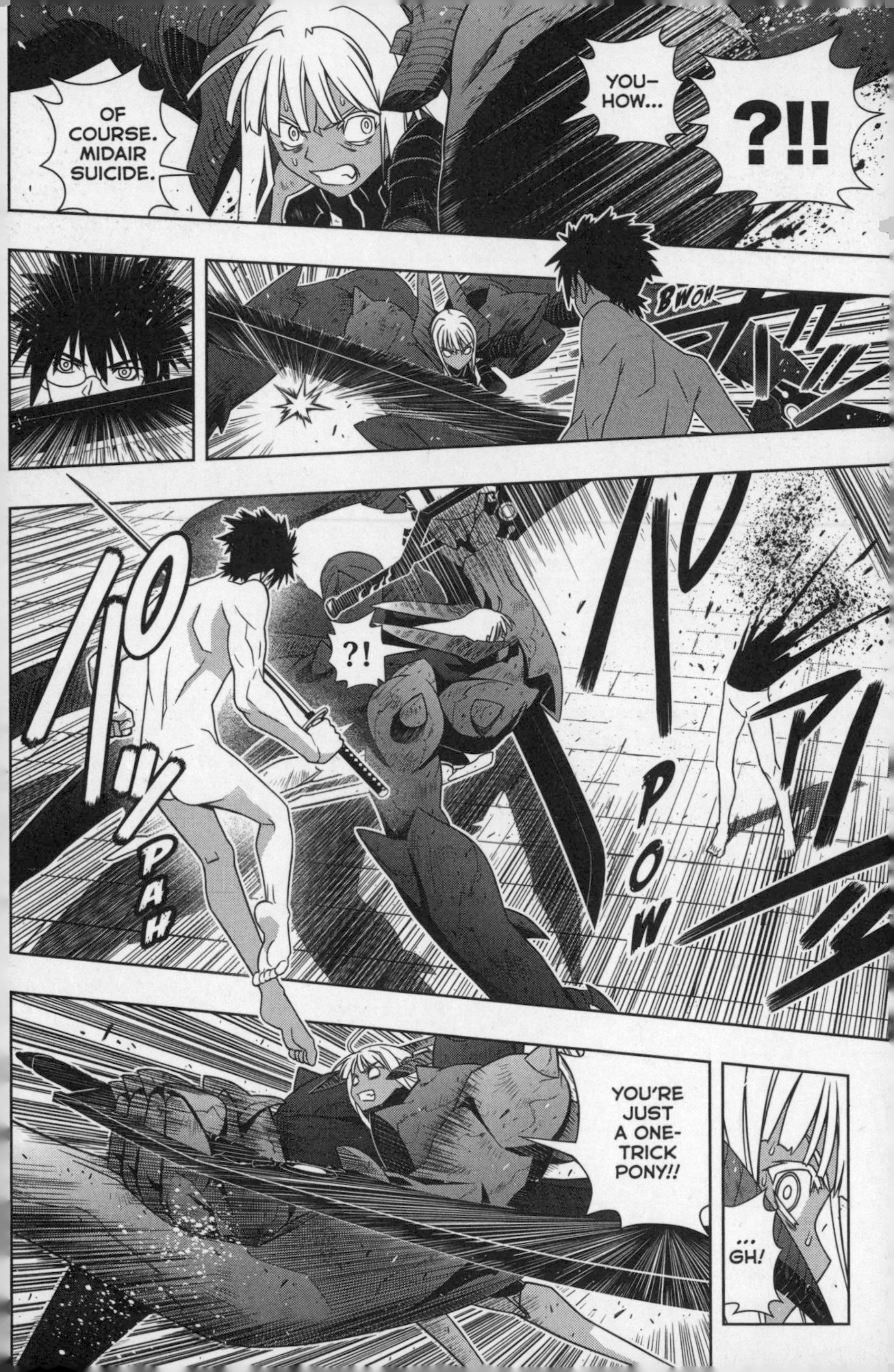
?!!
YOU— HOW...
OF COURSE. MIDAIR SUICIDE.
BWOH
POW
?!
PAH
...GH!
YOU'RE JUST A ONE-TRICK PONY!!

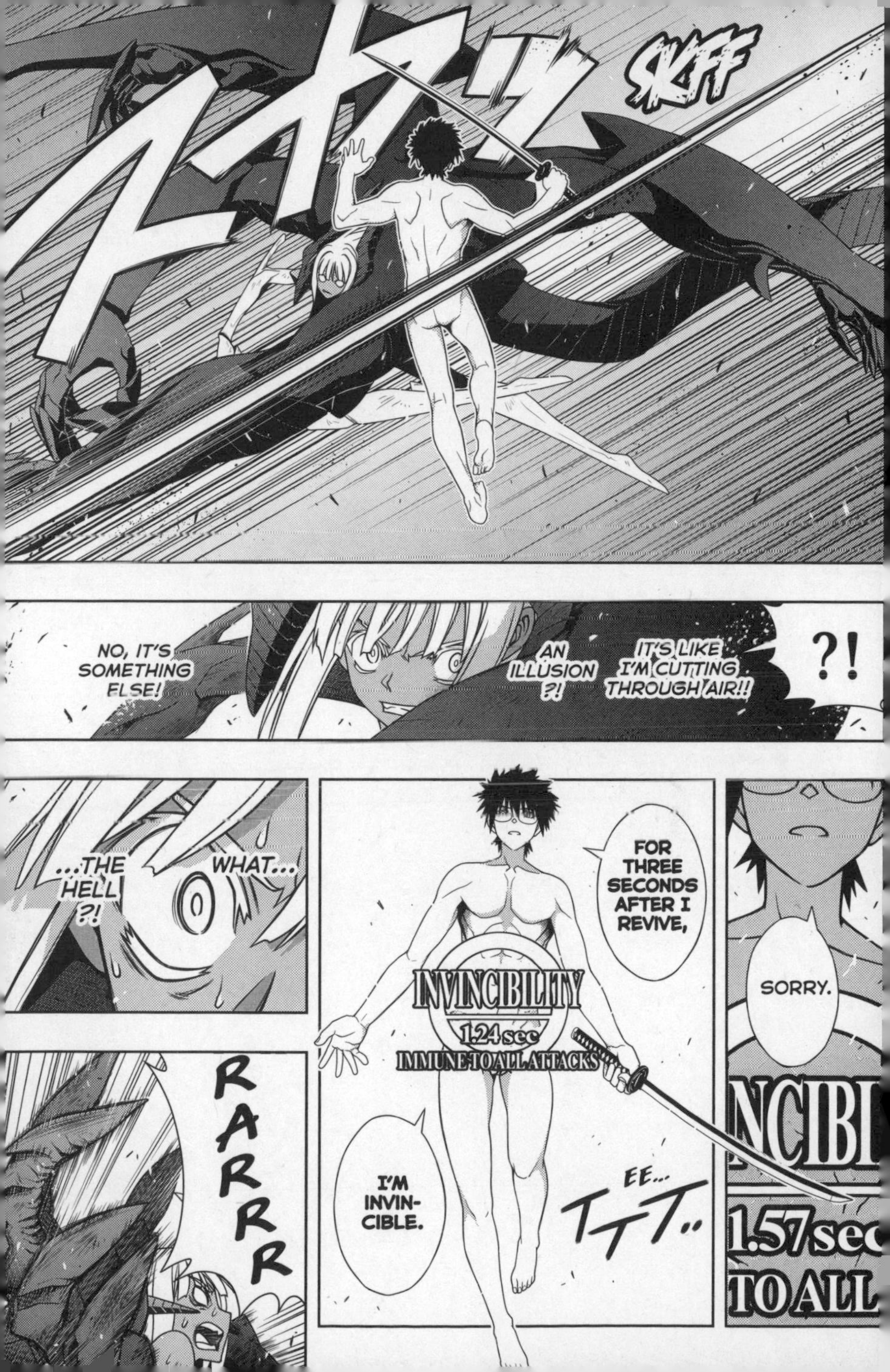
SKFF
?!
IT'S LIKE I'M CUTTING THROUGH AIR!!
AN ILLUSION ?!
NO, IT'S SOMETHING ELSE!
SORRY.
NCIBI
1.57 sec
TO ALL
FOR THREE SECONDS AFTER I REVIVE,
INVINCIBILITY
1.24 sec
IMMUNE TO ALL ATTACKS
I'M INVINCIBLE.
EE...
WHAT...
...THE HELL ?!
RARRR

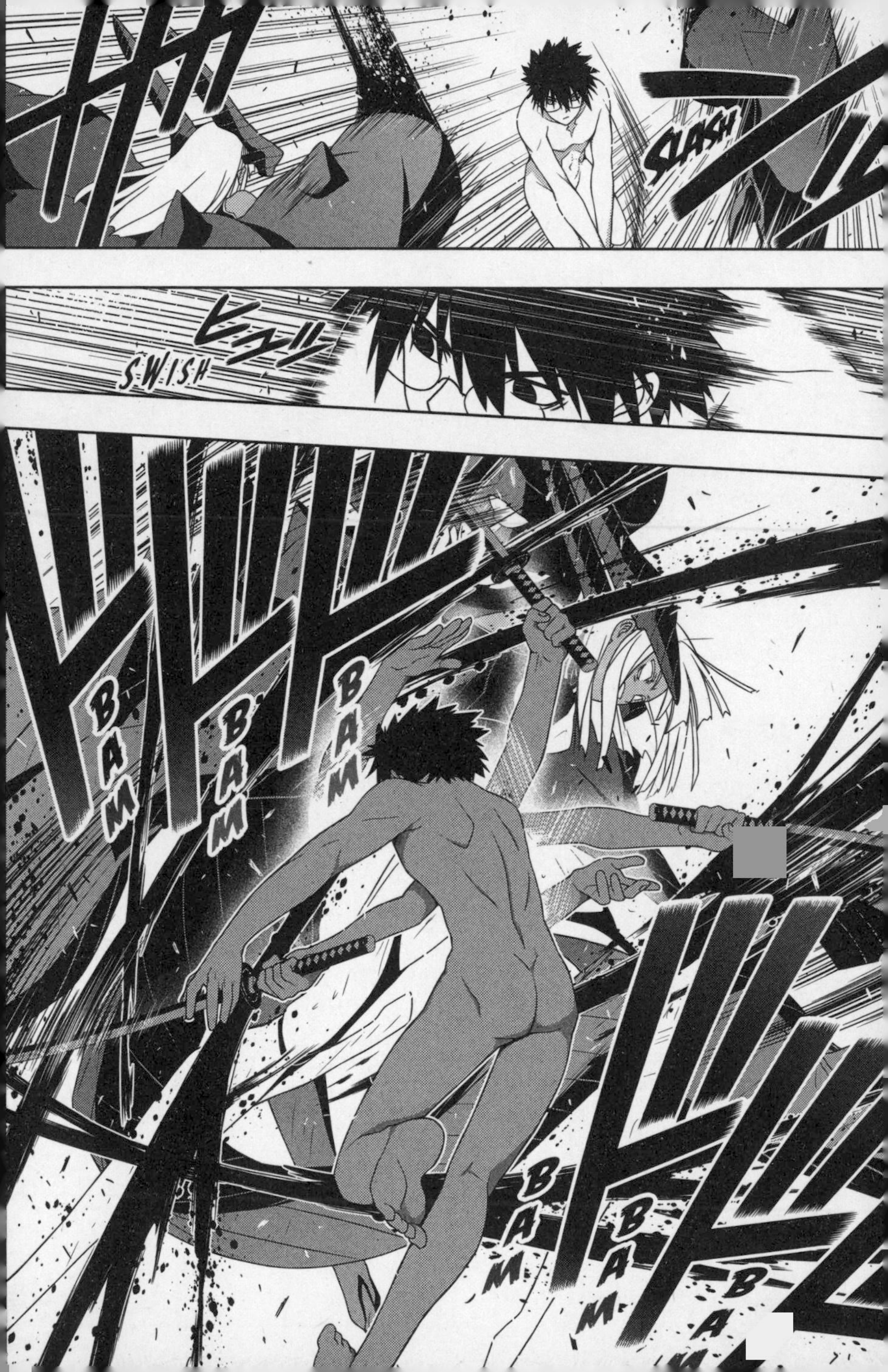
SLASH
SWISH
BAM
BAM
BAM
BAM
BAM
BAM

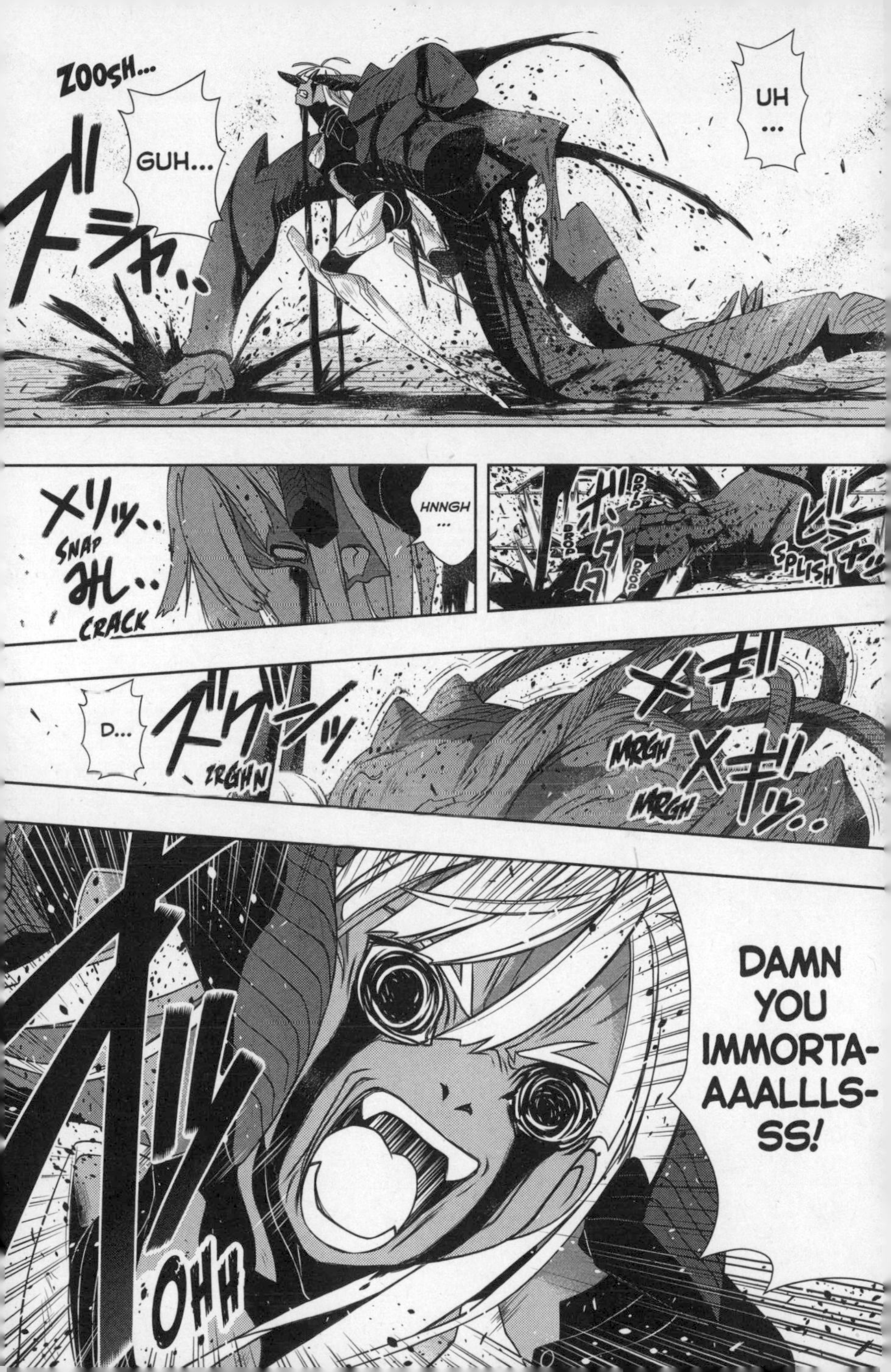
UH...
GUH...
ZOOSH...
DRIP
DROP
DROP
SPLISH
HNNGH...
SNAP
CRACK
NARGH
NARGH
ZRGHN
D...
DAMN YOU IMMORTA-AAALLLS-SS!
OHH

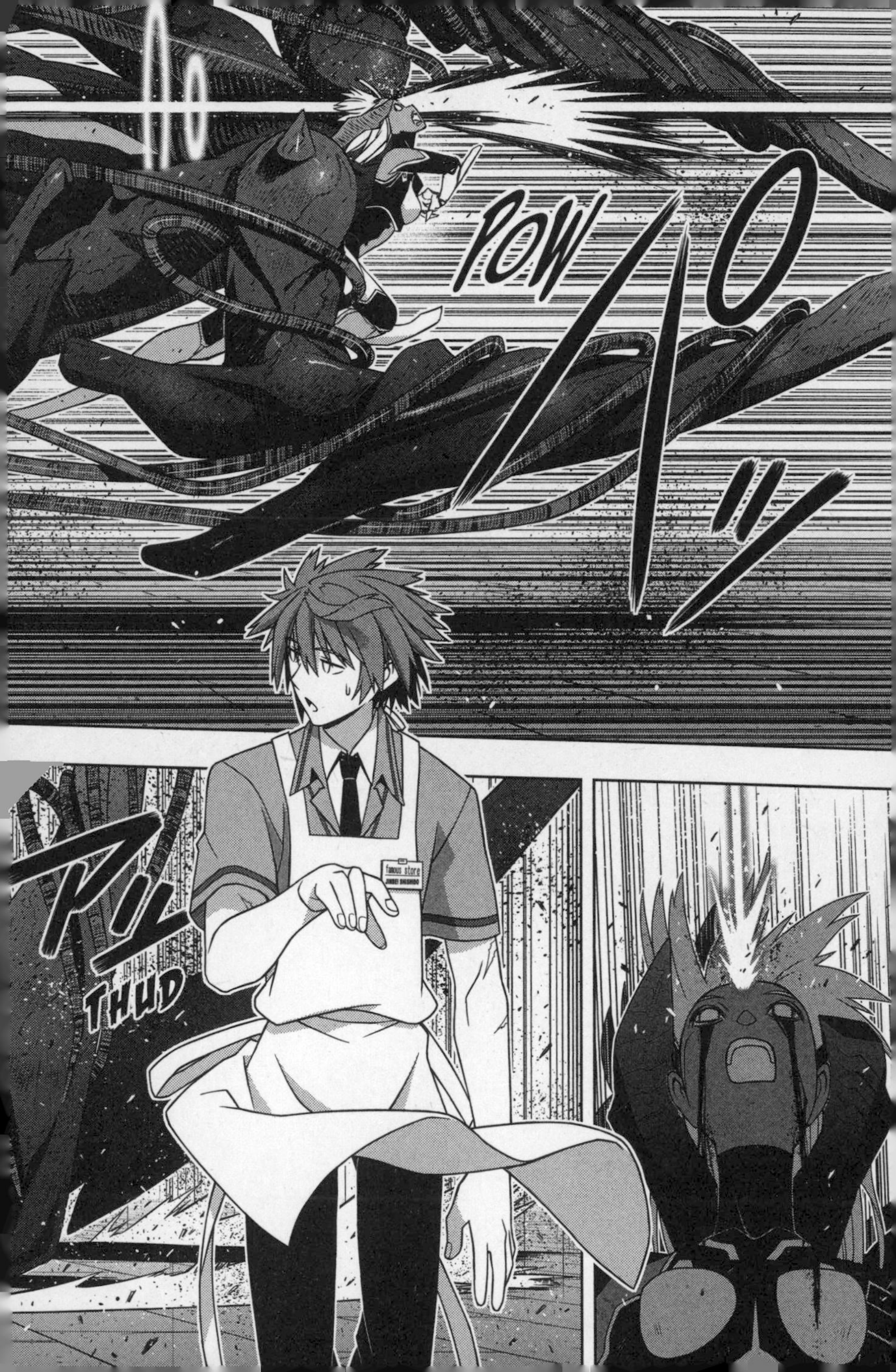
POW
famous store
JINBEI SHISHIDO
THUD

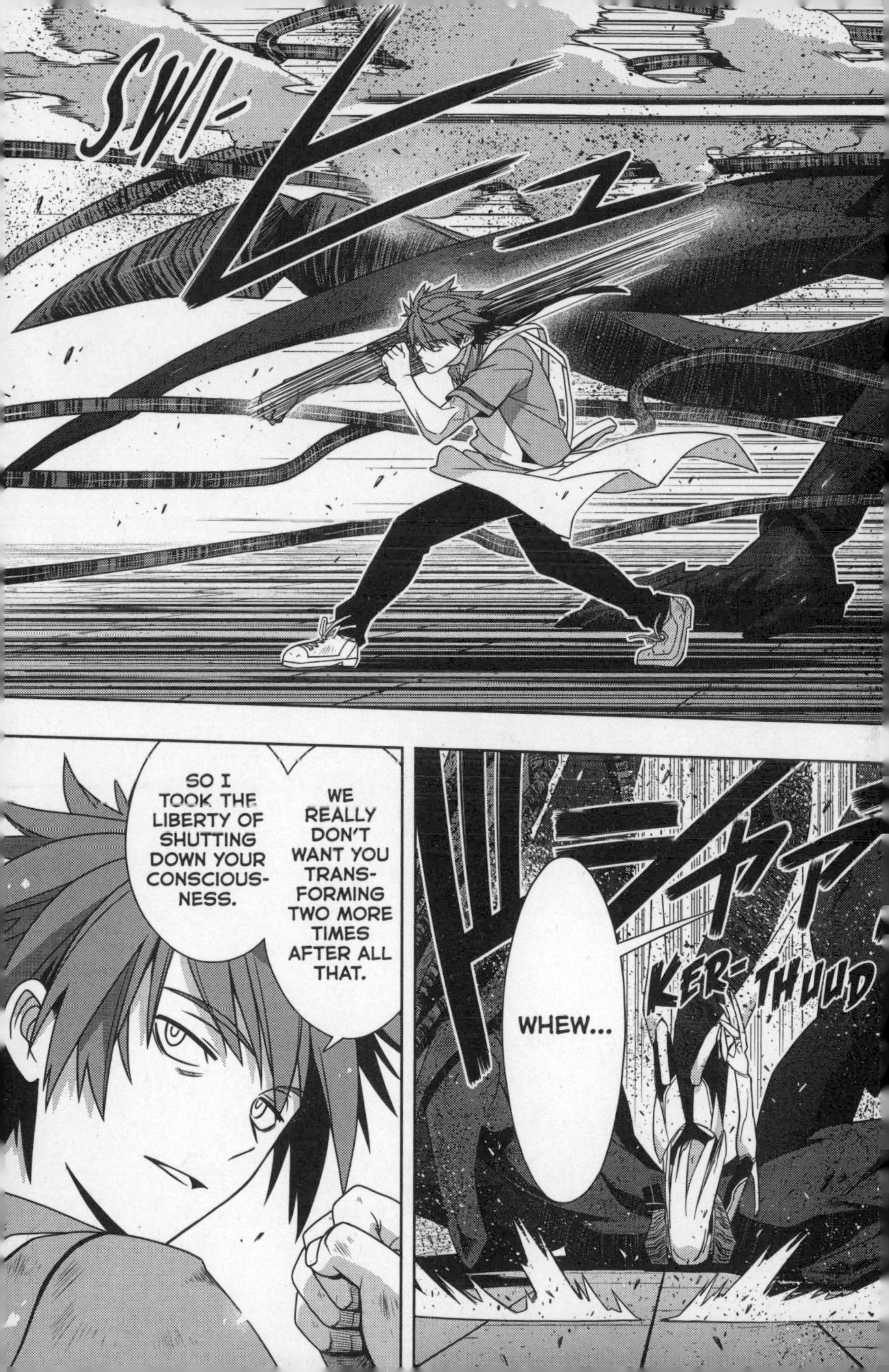
SWI-
KER-THUUD
WHEW...
WE REALLY DON'T WANT YOU TRANS-FORMING TWO MORE TIMES AFTER ALL THAT.
SO I TOOK THE LIBERTY OF SHUTTING DOWN YOUR CONSCIOUS-NESS.

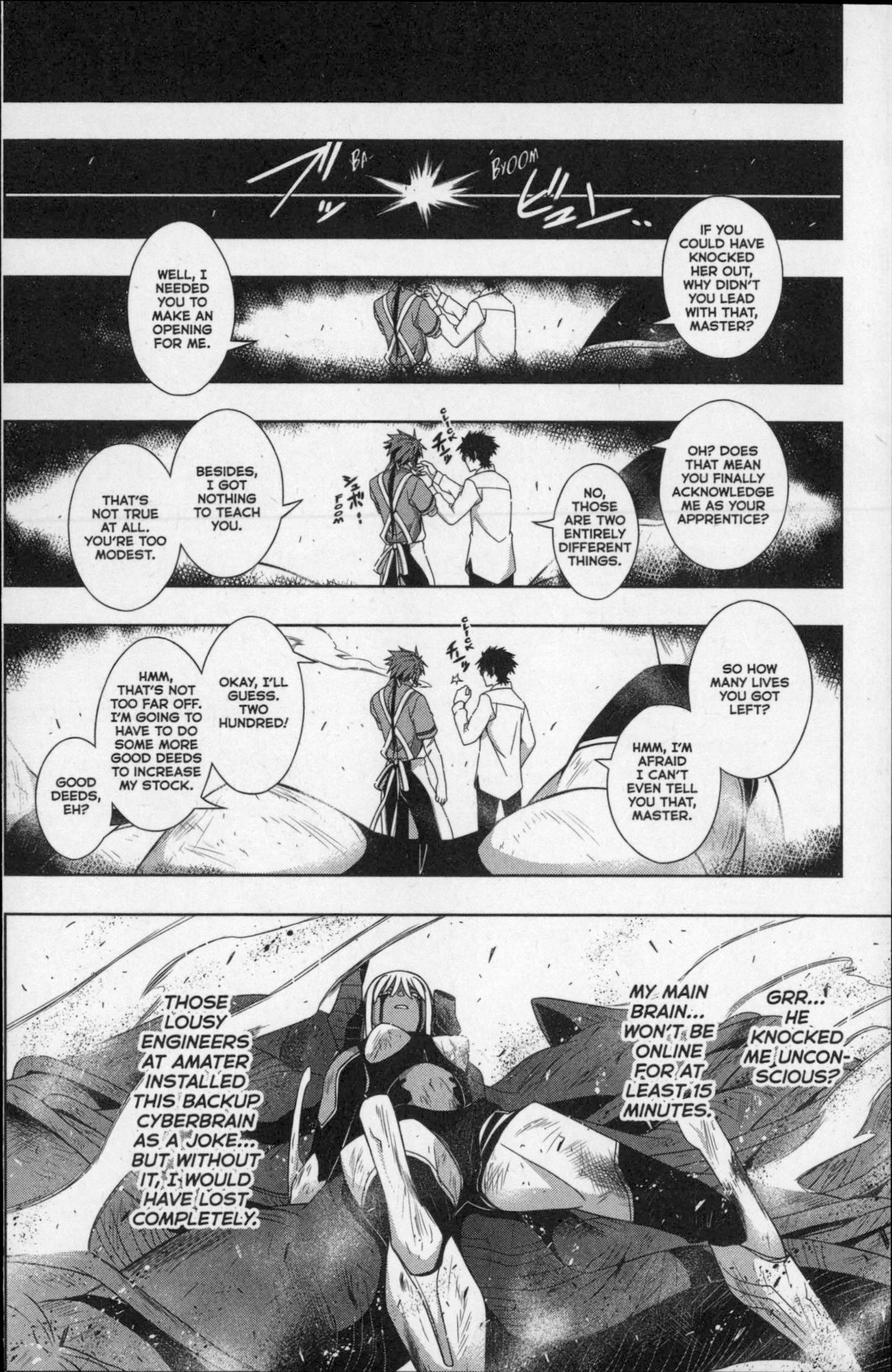
BYOOM
BA-
IF YOU COULD HAVE KNOCKED HER OUT, WHY DIDN'T YOU LEAD WITH THAT, MASTER?
WELL, I NEEDED YOU TO MAKE AN OPENING FOR ME.
OH? DOES THAT MEAN YOU FINALLY ACKNOWLEDGE ME AS YOUR APPRENTICE?
NO, THOSE ARE TWO ENTIRELY DIFFERENT THINGS.
CLICK
FOOM
BESIDES, I GOT NOTHING TO TEACH YOU.
THAT'S NOT TRUE AT ALL. YOU'RE TOO MODEST.
SO HOW MANY LIVES YOU GOT LEFT?
HMM, I'M AFRAID I CAN'T EVEN TELL YOU THAT, MASTER.
CLICK
OKAY, I'LL GUESS. TWO HUNDRED!
HMM, THAT'S NOT TOO FAR OFF. I'M GOING TO HAVE TO DO SOME MORE GOOD DEEDS TO INCREASE MY STOCK.
GOOD DEEDS, EH?
GRR... HE KNOCKED ME UNCONSCIOUS?
MY MAIN BRAIN... WON'T BE ONLINE FOR AT LEAST 15 MINUTES.
THOSE LOUSY ENGINEERS AT AMATER INSTALLED THIS BACKUP CYBERBRAIN AS A JOKE... BUT WITHOUT IT, I WOULD HAVE LOST COMPLETELY.

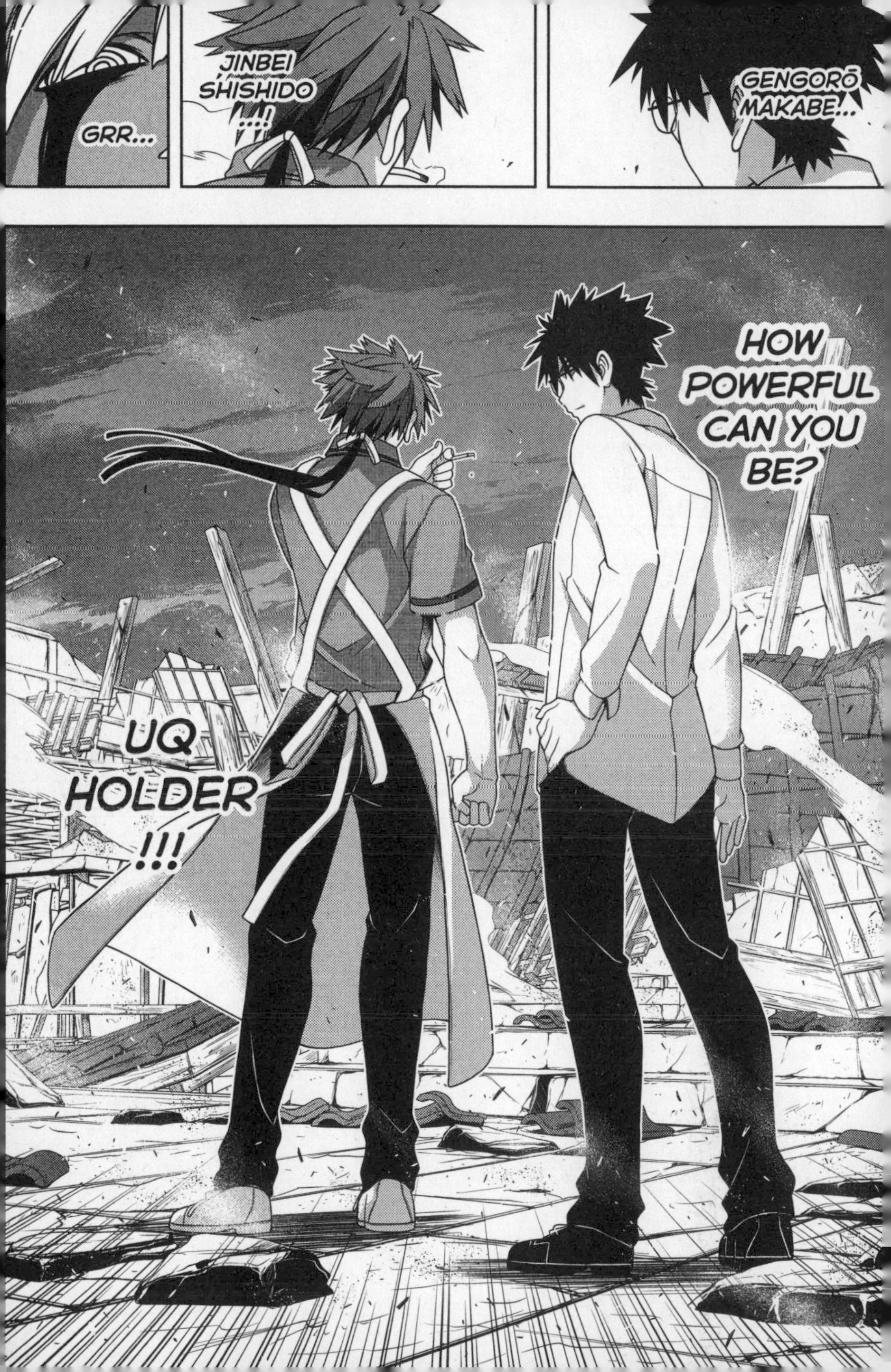
GENGORŌ MAKABE...
JINBEI SHISHIDO
...!!
GRR...
HOW POWERFUL CAN YOU BE?
UQ HOLDER !!!

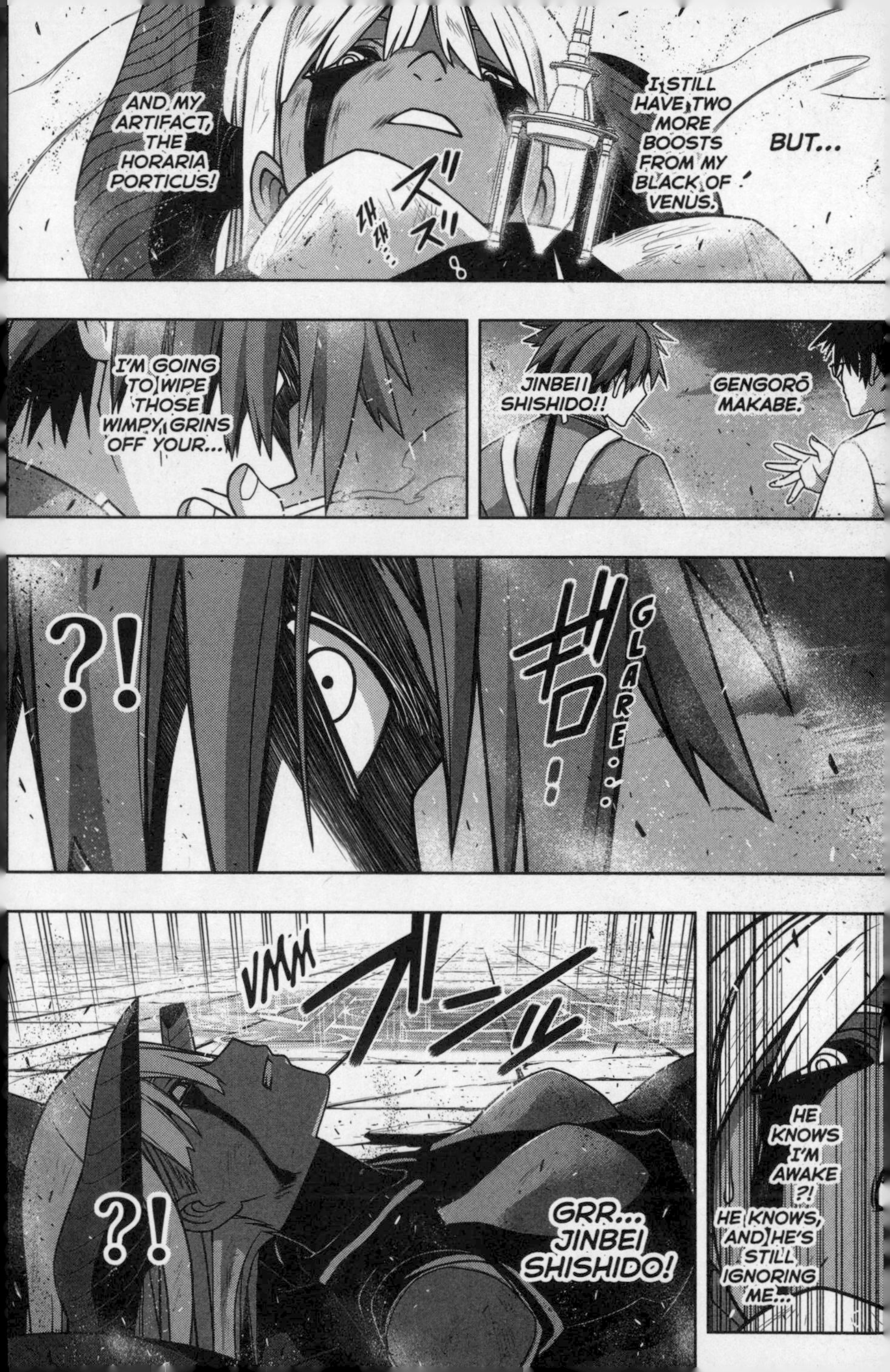
BUT...
I STILL HAVE TWO MORE BOOSTS FROM MY BLACK OF VENUS.
AND MY ARTIFACT, THE HORARIA PORTICUS!
GENGORŌ MAKABE.
JINBEI SHISHIDO!!
I'M GOING TO WIPE THOSE WIMPY GRINS OFF YOUR...
GLARE...
?!
HE KNOWS I'M AWAKE?!
HE KNOWS, AND HE'S STILL IGNORING ME...
VMM
GRR... JINBEI SHISHIDO!
?!

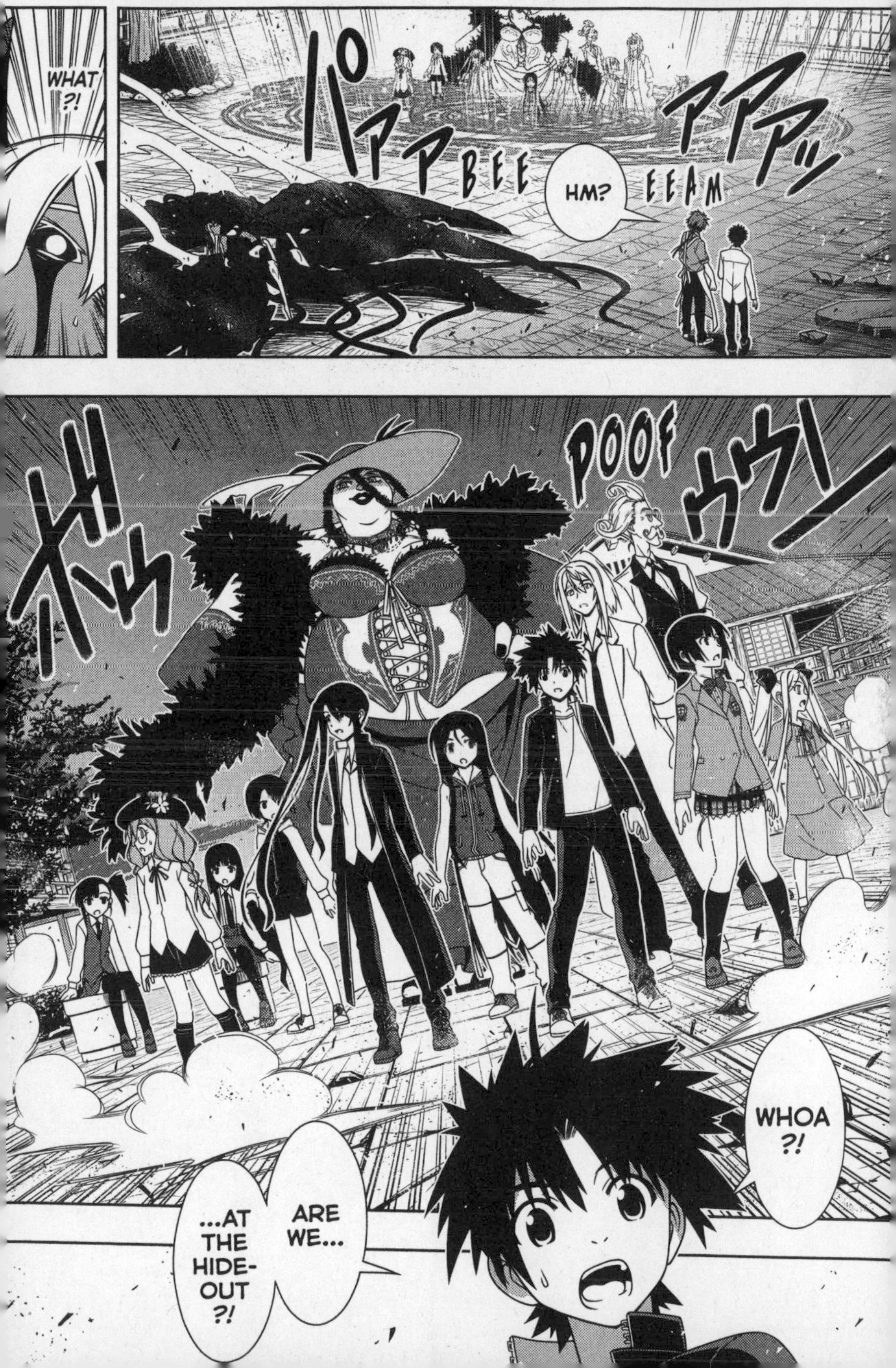
BEEEEAM
HM?
WHAT ?!
POOF
WHOA ?!
ARE WE...
...AT THE HIDE-OUT ?!

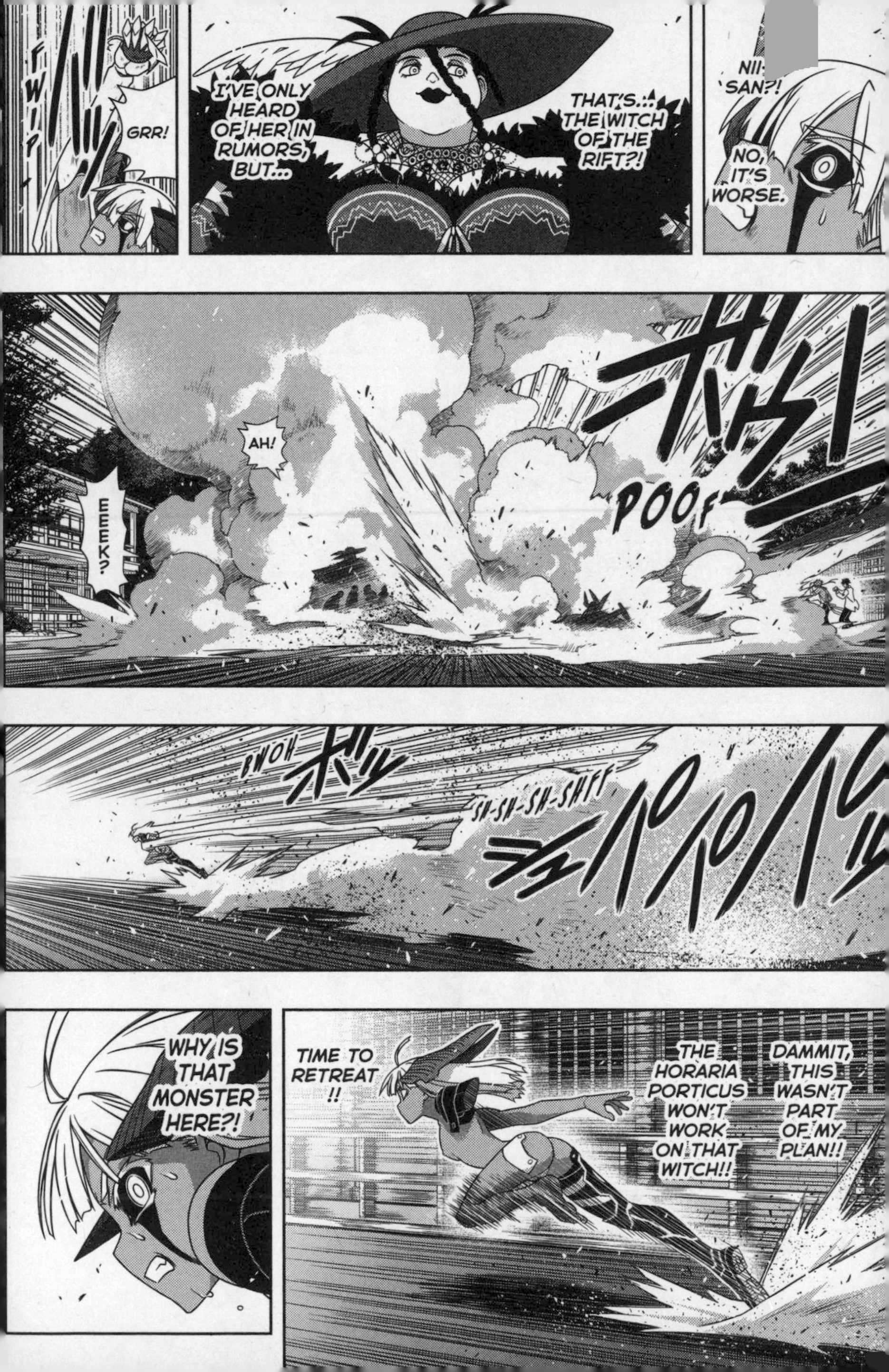
NII-SAN?!
NO, IT'S WORSE.
THAT'S... THE WITCH OF THE RIFT?!
I'VE ONLY HEARD OF HER IN RUMORS, BUT...
FWIP
GRR!
POOF
AH!
EEEK?
BWOH
SH-SH-SH-SHFF
DAMMIT, THIS WASN'T PART OF MY PLAN!!
THE HORARIA PORTICUS WON'T WORK ON THAT WITCH!!
TIME TO RETREAT!!
WHY IS THAT MONSTER HERE?!

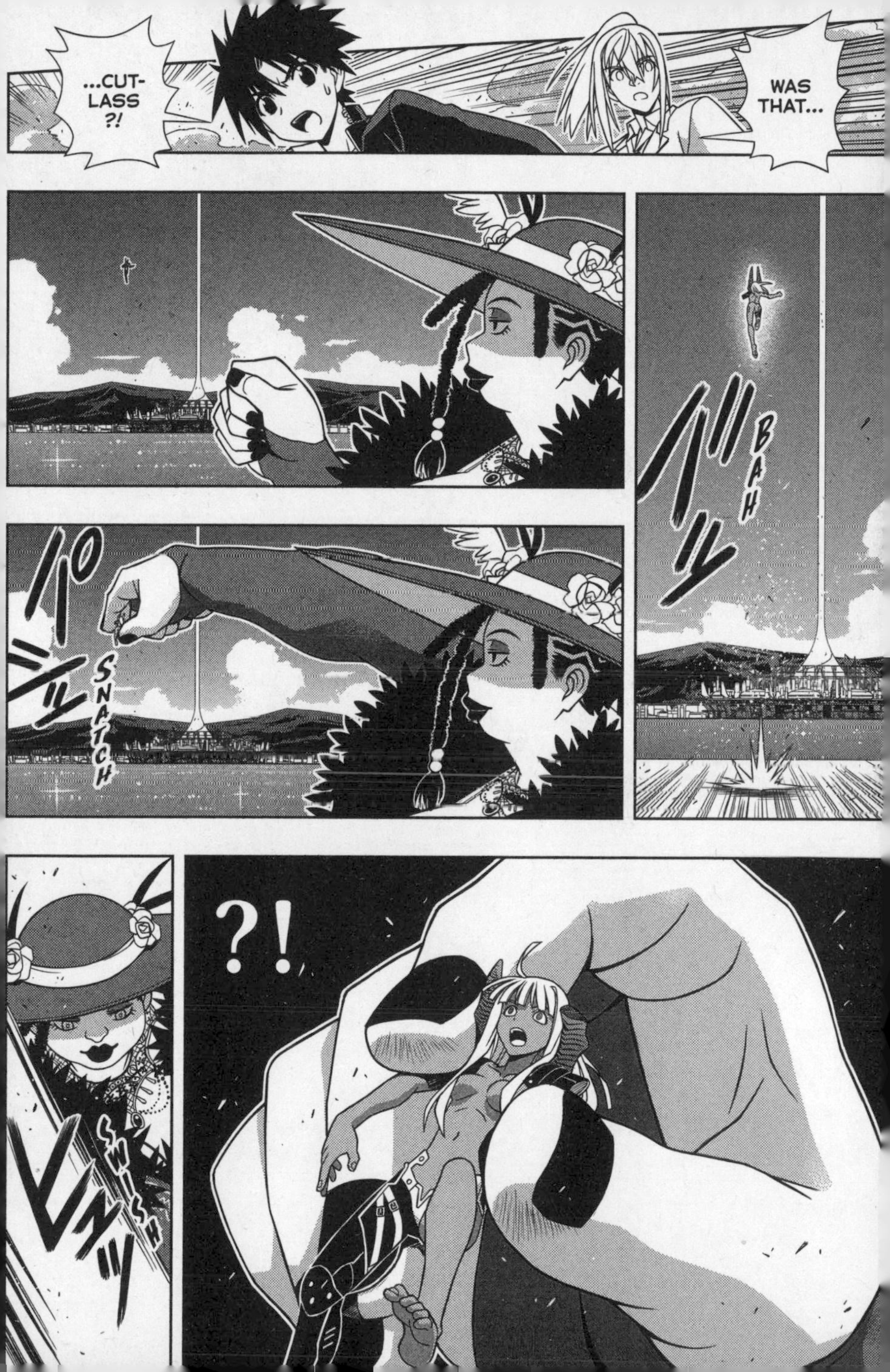
WAS THAT...
...CUT-LASS ?!
BAH
SNATCH
?!
SWISH

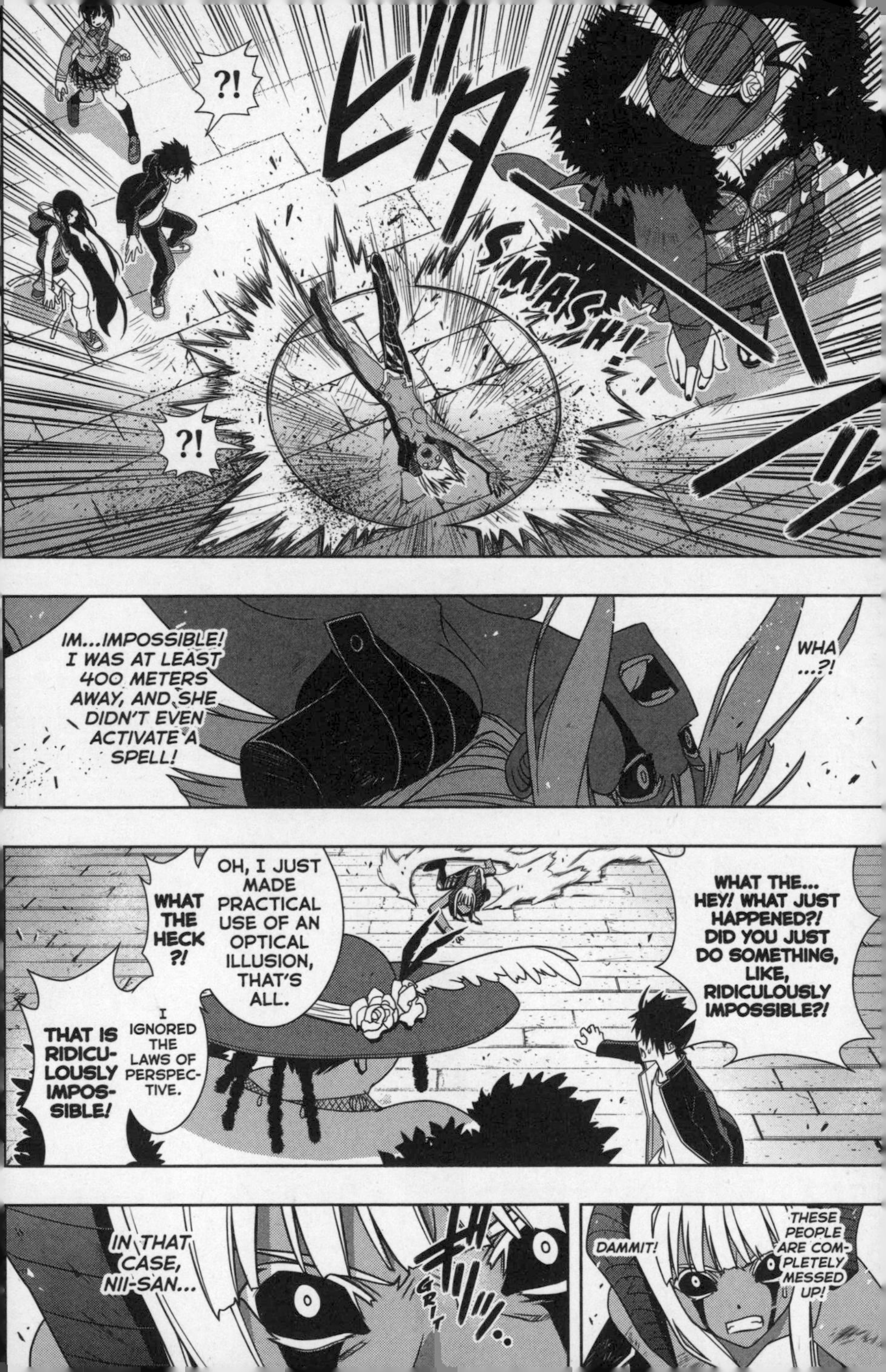
SMASH!!
?!
?!
WHA...?!
IM...IMPOSSIBLE! I WAS AT LEAST 400 METERS AWAY, AND SHE DIDN'T EVEN ACTIVATE A SPELL!
WHAT THE... HEY! WHAT JUST HAPPENED?! DID YOU JUST DO SOMETHING, LIKE, RIDICULOUSLY IMPOSSIBLE?!
OH, I JUST MADE PRACTICAL USE OF AN OPTICAL ILLUSION, THAT'S ALL.
WHAT THE HECK?!
I IGNORED THE LAWS OF PERSPECTIVE.
THAT IS RIDICULOUSLY IMPOSSIBLE!
THESE PEOPLE ARE COMPLETELY MESSED UP!
DAMMIT!
GRIT
IN THAT CASE, NII-SAN...

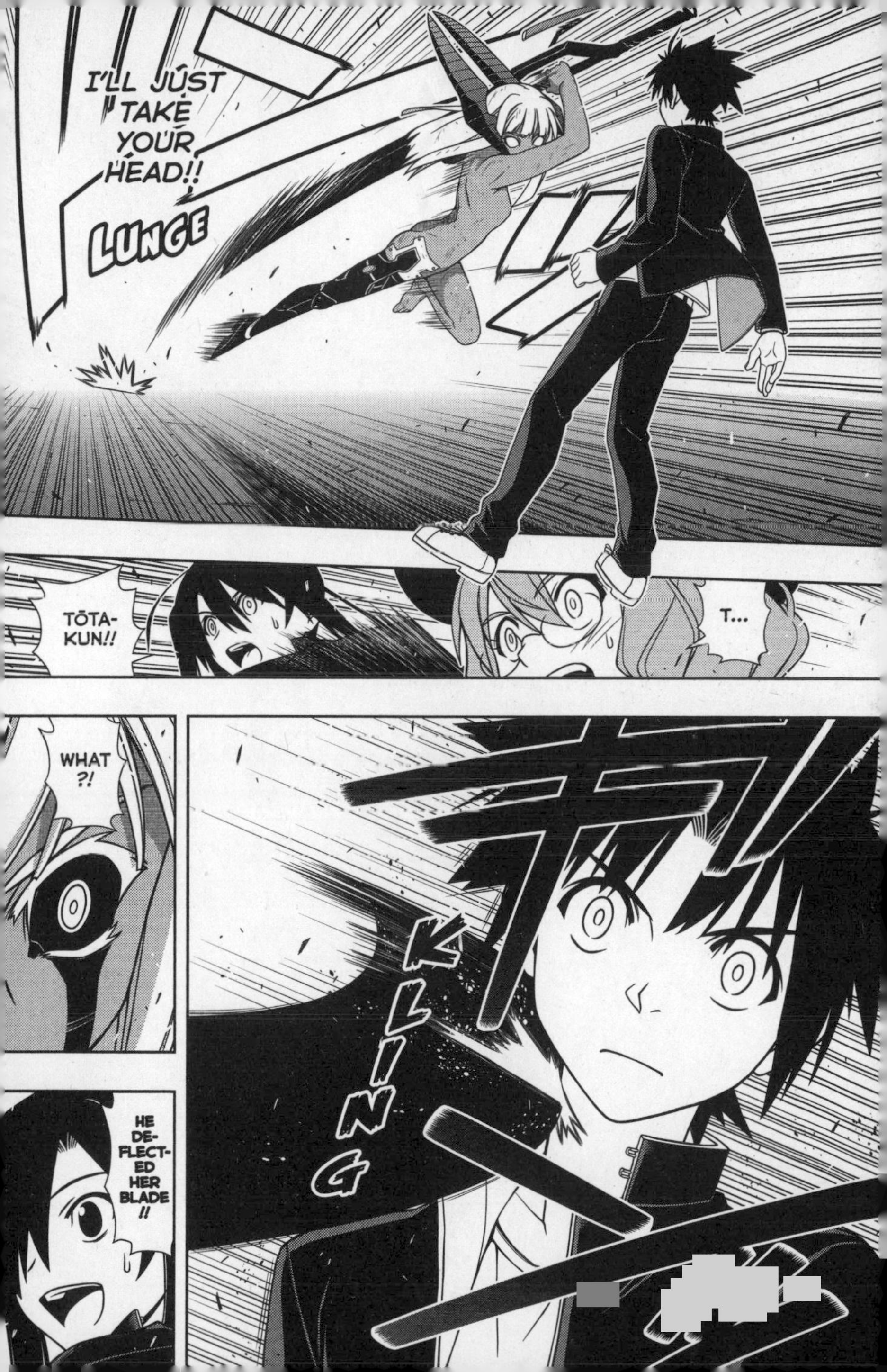
I'LL JUST TAKE YOUR HEAD!!
LUNGE
T...
TŌTA-KUN!!
KLING
WHAT?!
HE DEFLECTED HER BLADE!!

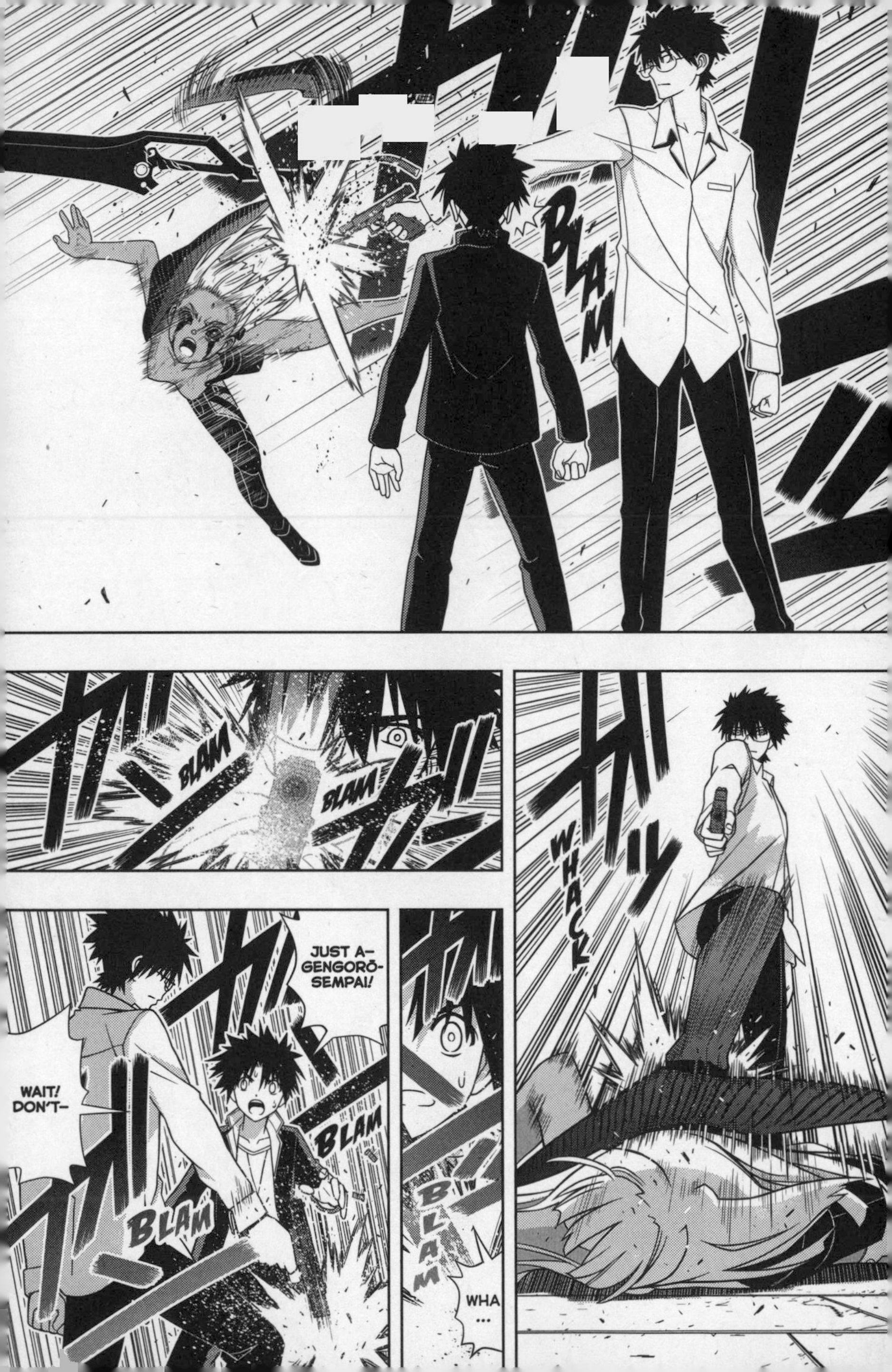
BLAM
WHACK
BLAM
BLAM
BLAM
WHA
...
JUST A-
GENGORŌ-
SEMPAI!
WAIT!
DON'T-
BLAM
BLAM

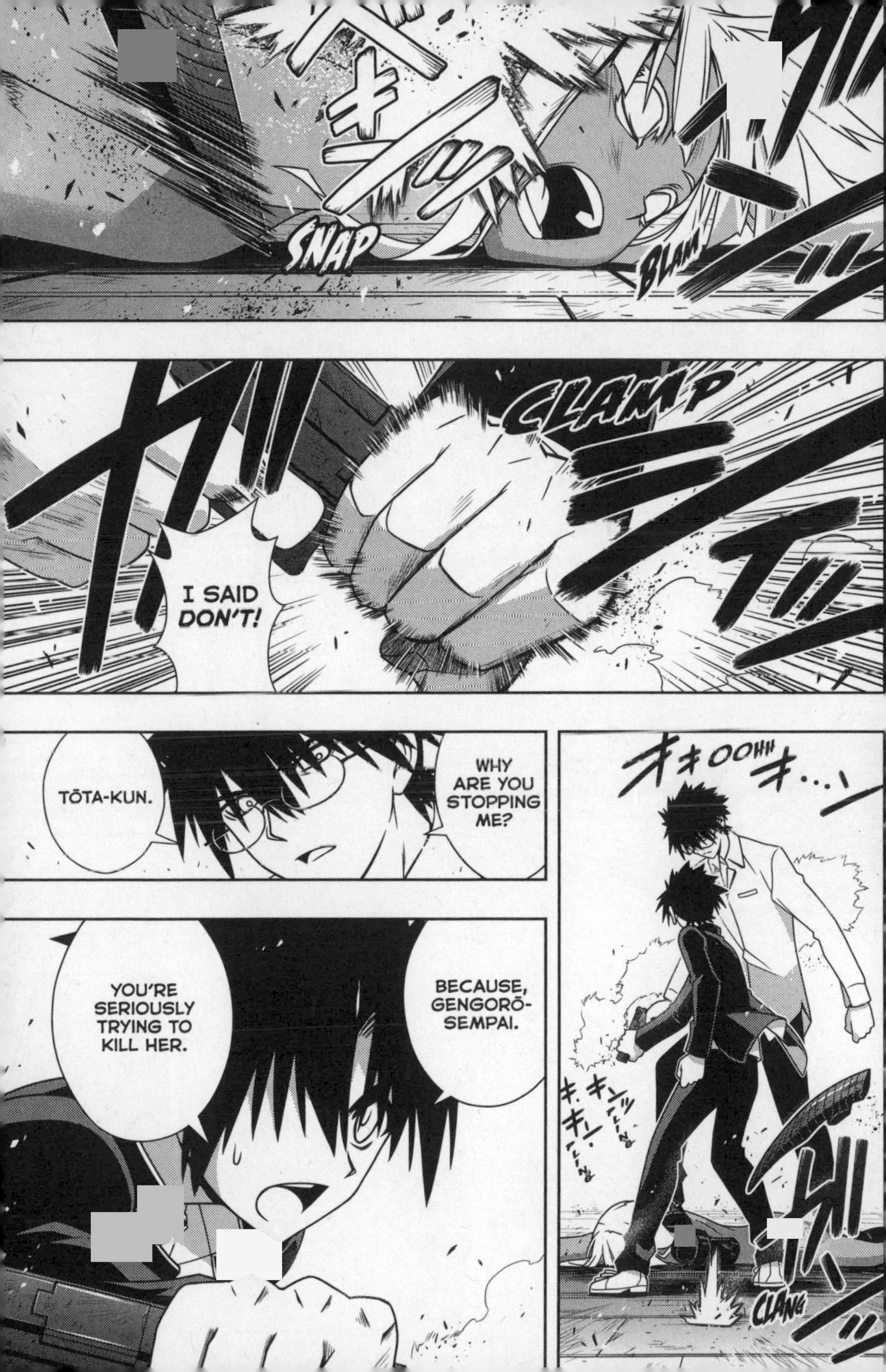
BLAM
SNAP
CLAMP
I SAID DON'T!
OOHH
CLANG
WHY ARE YOU STOPPING ME?
TŌTA-KUN.
BECAUSE, GENGORŌ-SEMPAI.
YOU'RE SERIOUSLY TRYING TO KILL HER.

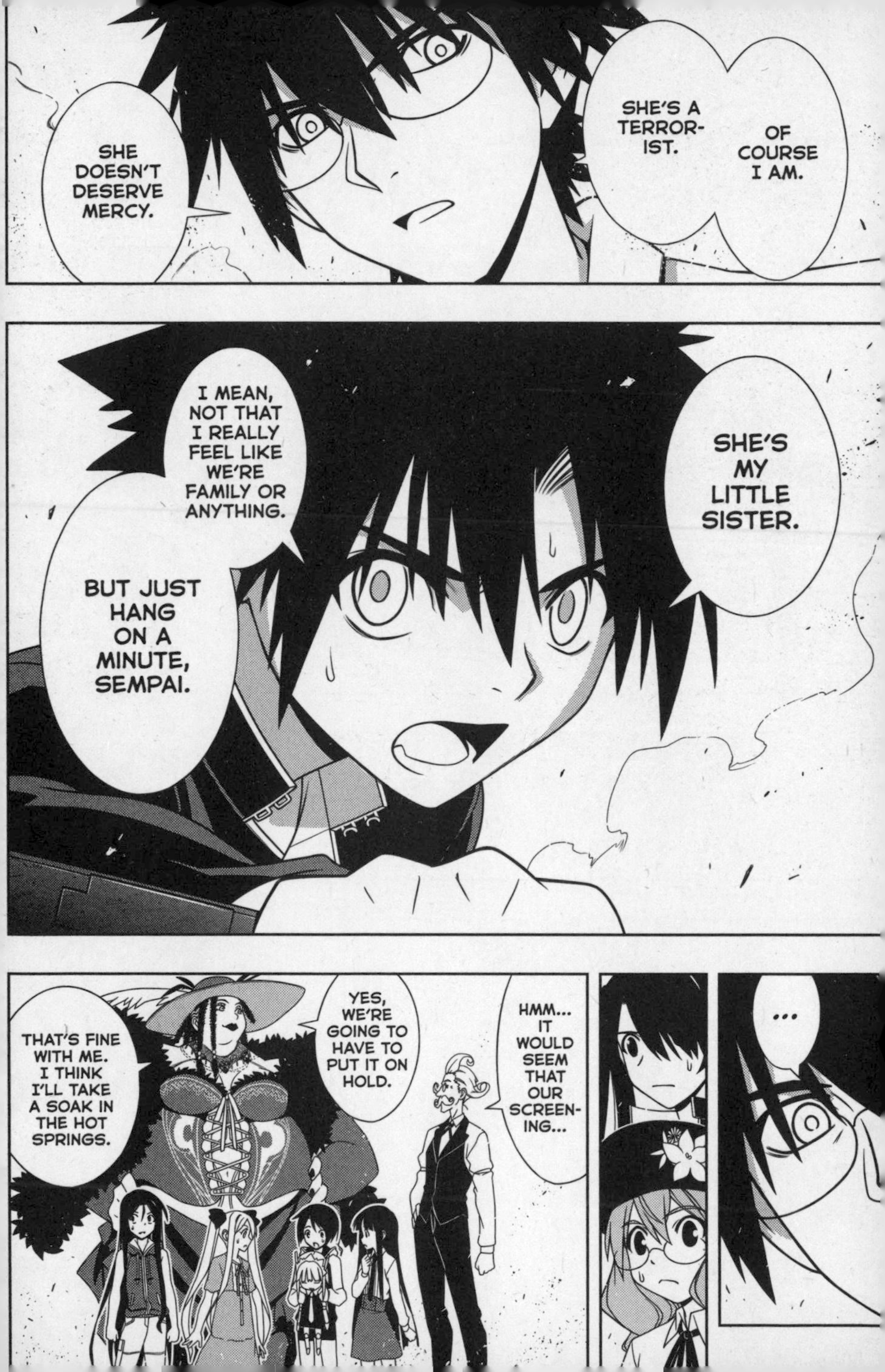
OF COURSE I AM.
SHE'S A TERROR-IST.
SHE DOESN'T DESERVE MERCY.
SHE'S MY LITTLE SISTER.
I MEAN, NOT THAT I REALLY FEEL LIKE WE'RE FAMILY OR ANYTHING.
BUT JUST HANG ON A MINUTE, SEMPAI.
...
HMM... IT WOULD SEEM THAT OUR SCREEN-ING...
YES, WE'RE GOING TO HAVE TO PUT IT ON HOLD.
THAT'S FINE WITH ME. I THINK I'LL TAKE A SOAK IN THE HOT SPRINGS.

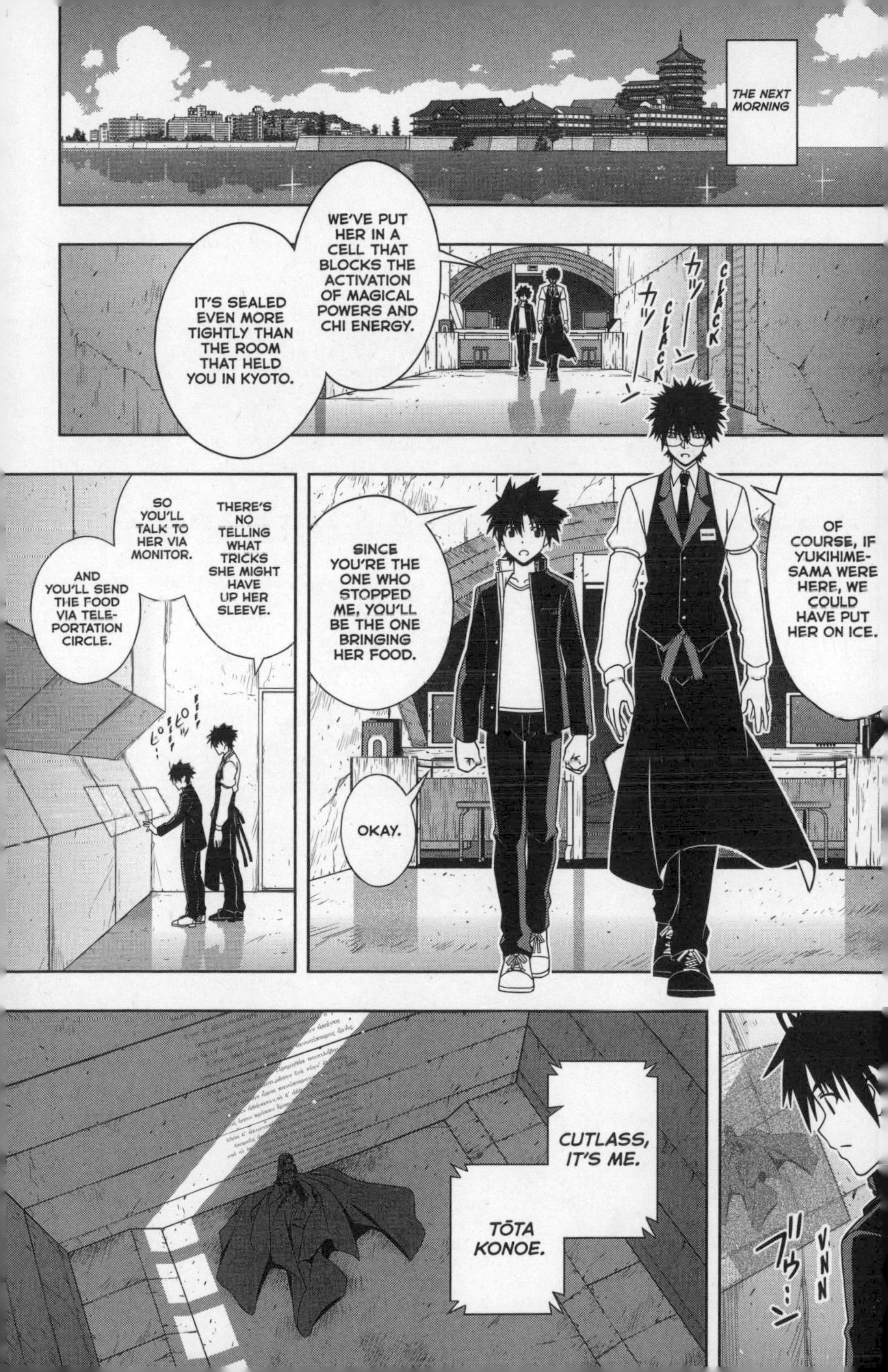
THE NEXT MORNING
WE'VE PUT HER IN A CELL THAT BLOCKS THE ACTIVATION OF MAGICAL POWERS AND CHI ENERGY.
IT'S SEALED EVEN MORE TIGHTLY THAN THE ROOM THAT HELD YOU IN KYOTO.
CLACK
CLACK
OF COURSE, IF YUKIHIME-SAMA WERE HERE, WE COULD HAVE PUT HER ON ICE.
SINCE YOU'RE THE ONE WHO STOPPED ME, YOU'LL BE THE ONE BRINGING HER FOOD.
OKAY.
THERE'S NO TELLING WHAT TRICKS SHE MIGHT HAVE UP HER SLEEVE.
SO YOU'LL TALK TO HER VIA MONITOR.
AND YOU'LL SEND THE FOOD VIA TELE-PORTATION CIRCLE.
VNN
CUTLASS, IT'S ME.
TŌTA KONOE.

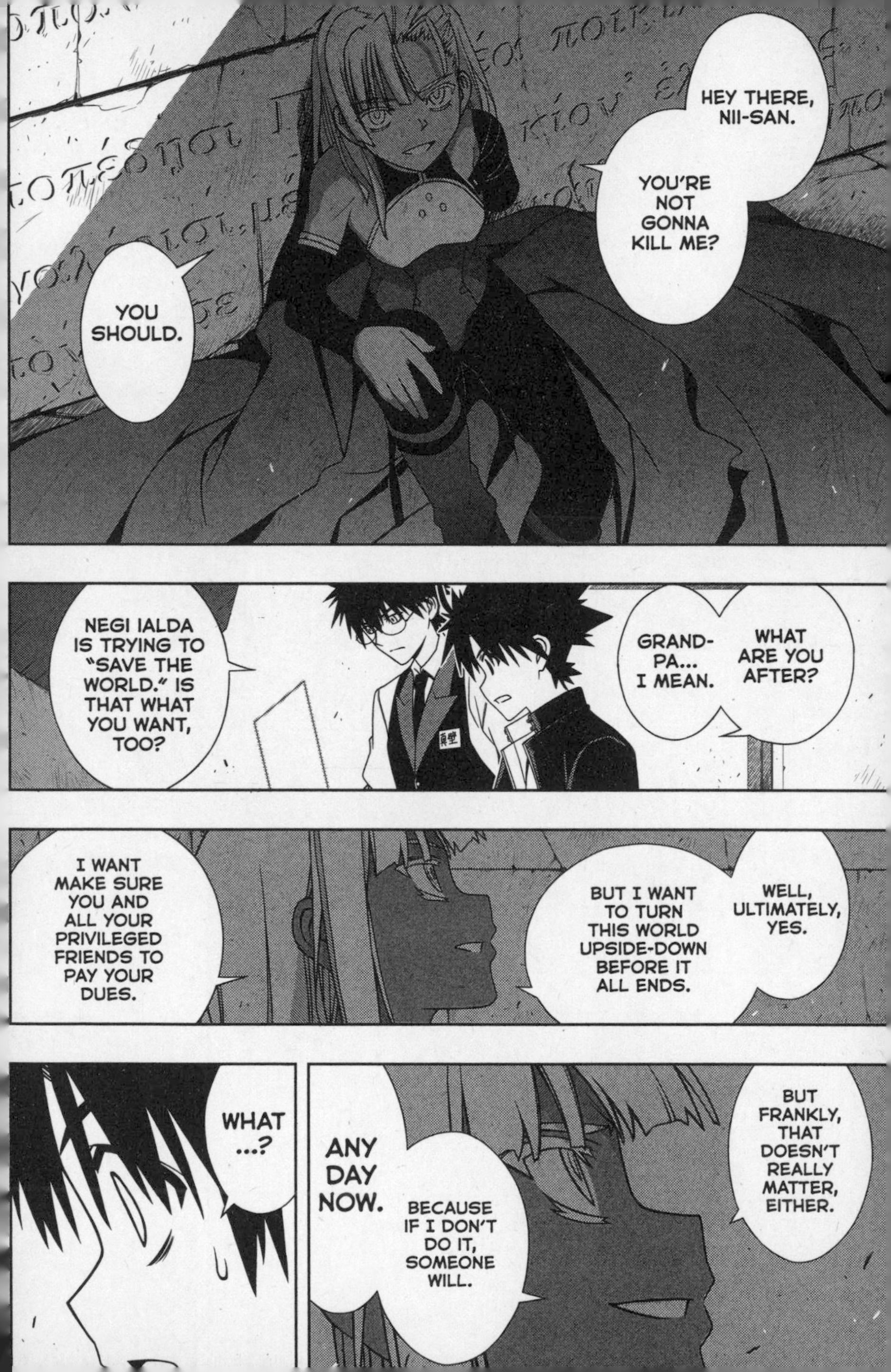
HEY THERE, NII-SAN.
YOU'RE NOT GONNA KILL ME?
YOU SHOULD.
WHAT ARE YOU AFTER?
GRAND-PA... I MEAN.
NEGI IALDA IS TRYING TO "SAVE THE WORLD." IS THAT WHAT YOU WANT, TOO?
WELL, ULTIMATELY, YES.
BUT I WANT TO TURN THIS WORLD UPSIDE-DOWN BEFORE IT ALL ENDS.
I WANT MAKE SURE YOU AND ALL YOUR PRIVILEGED FRIENDS TO PAY YOUR DUES.
BUT FRANKLY, THAT DOESN'T REALLY MATTER, EITHER.
BECAUSE IF I DON'T DO IT, SOMEONE WILL.
ANY DAY NOW.
WHAT ...?

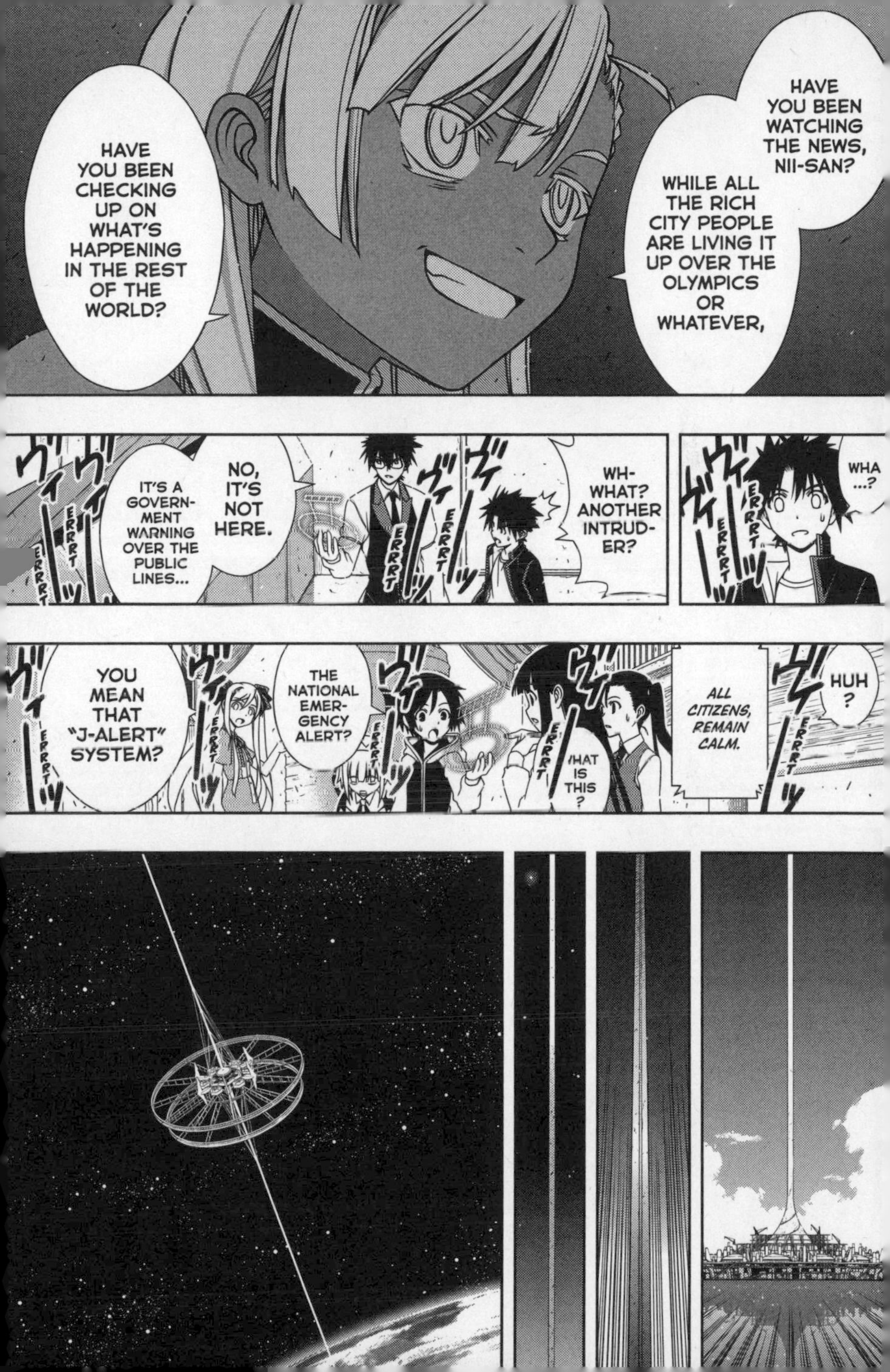
HAVE YOU BEEN WATCHING THE NEWS, NII-SAN?
WHILE ALL THE RICH CITY PEOPLE ARE LIVING IT UP OVER THE OLYMPICS OR WHATEVER,
HAVE YOU BEEN CHECKING UP ON WHAT'S HAPPENING IN THE REST OF THE WORLD?
WHA ...?
ERRRT
ERRRT
WH- WHAT? ANOTHER INTRUD- ER?
ERRRT
ERRRT
NO, IT'S NOT HERE.
IT'S A GOVERN- MENT WARNING OVER THE PUBLIC LINES...
ERRRT
ERRRT
HUH?
ERRRT
ALL CITIZENS, REMAIN CALM.
WHAT IS THIS?
ERRRT
THE NATIONAL EMER- GENCY ALERT?
ERRRT
YOU MEAN THAT "J-ALERT" SYSTEM?
ERRRT
ERRRT

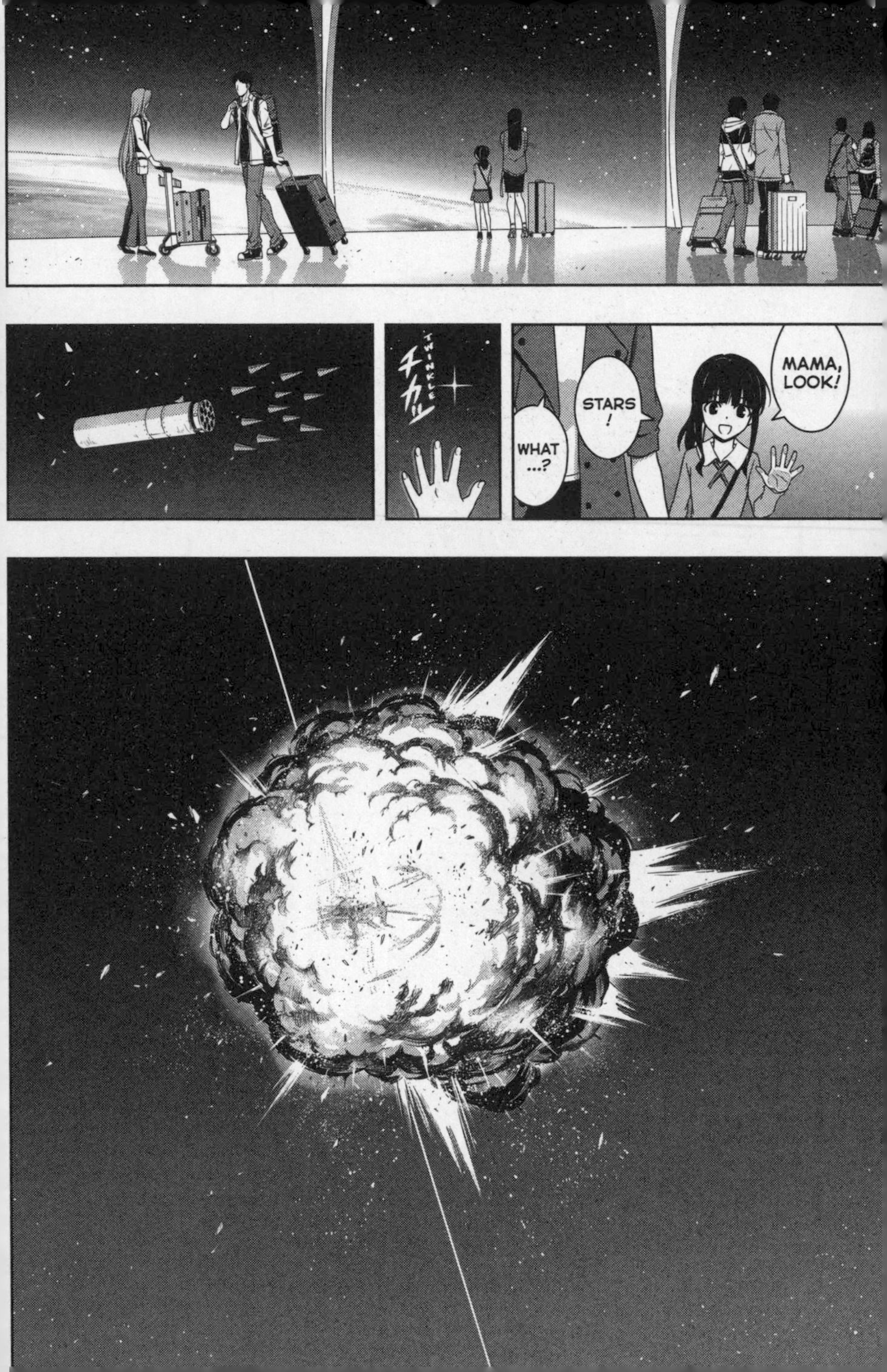
MAMA, LOOK!
STARS!
WHAT ...?
TWINKLE
チカッ

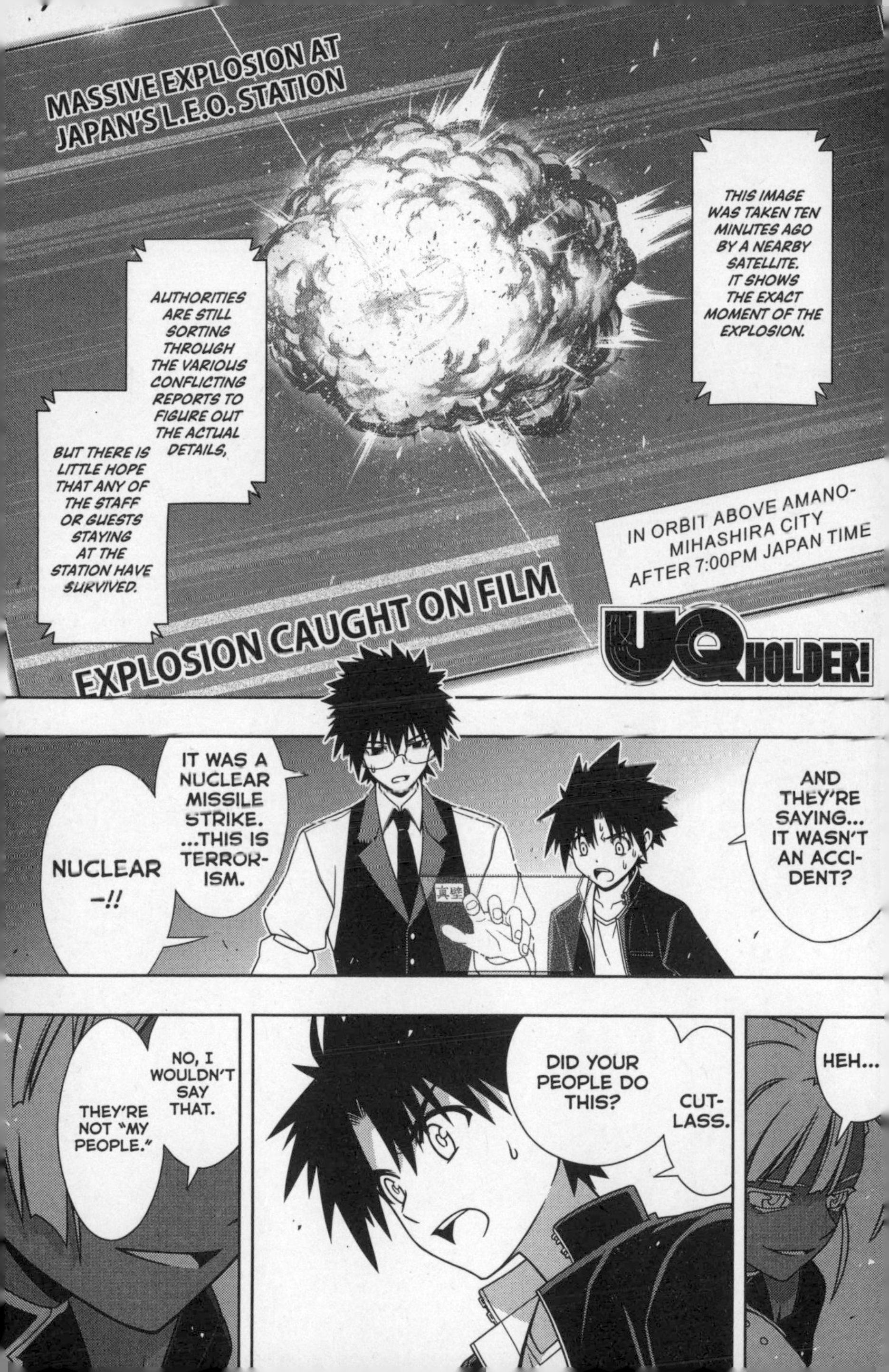
MASSIVE EXPLOSION AT JAPAN'S L.E.O. STATION
THIS IMAGE WAS TAKEN TEN MINUTES AGO BY A NEARBY SATELLITE. IT SHOWS THE EXACT MOMENT OF THE EXPLOSION.
AUTHORITIES ARE STILL SORTING THROUGH THE VARIOUS CONFLICTING REPORTS TO FIGURE OUT THE ACTUAL DETAILS,
BUT THERE IS LITTLE HOPE THAT ANY OF THE STAFF OR GUESTS STAYING AT THE STATION HAVE SURVIVED.
IN ORBIT ABOVE AMANO-MIHASHIRA CITY AFTER 7:00PM JAPAN TIME
EXPLOSION CAUGHT ON FILM
UQ HOLDER!
AND THEY'RE SAYING... IT WASN'T AN ACCI-DENT?
IT WAS A NUCLEAR MISSILE STRIKE. ...THIS IS TERROR-ISM.
NUCLEAR—!!
HEH...
DID YOUR PEOPLE DO THIS?
CUT-LASS.
NO, I WOULDN'T SAY THAT.
THEY'RE NOT "MY PEOPLE."

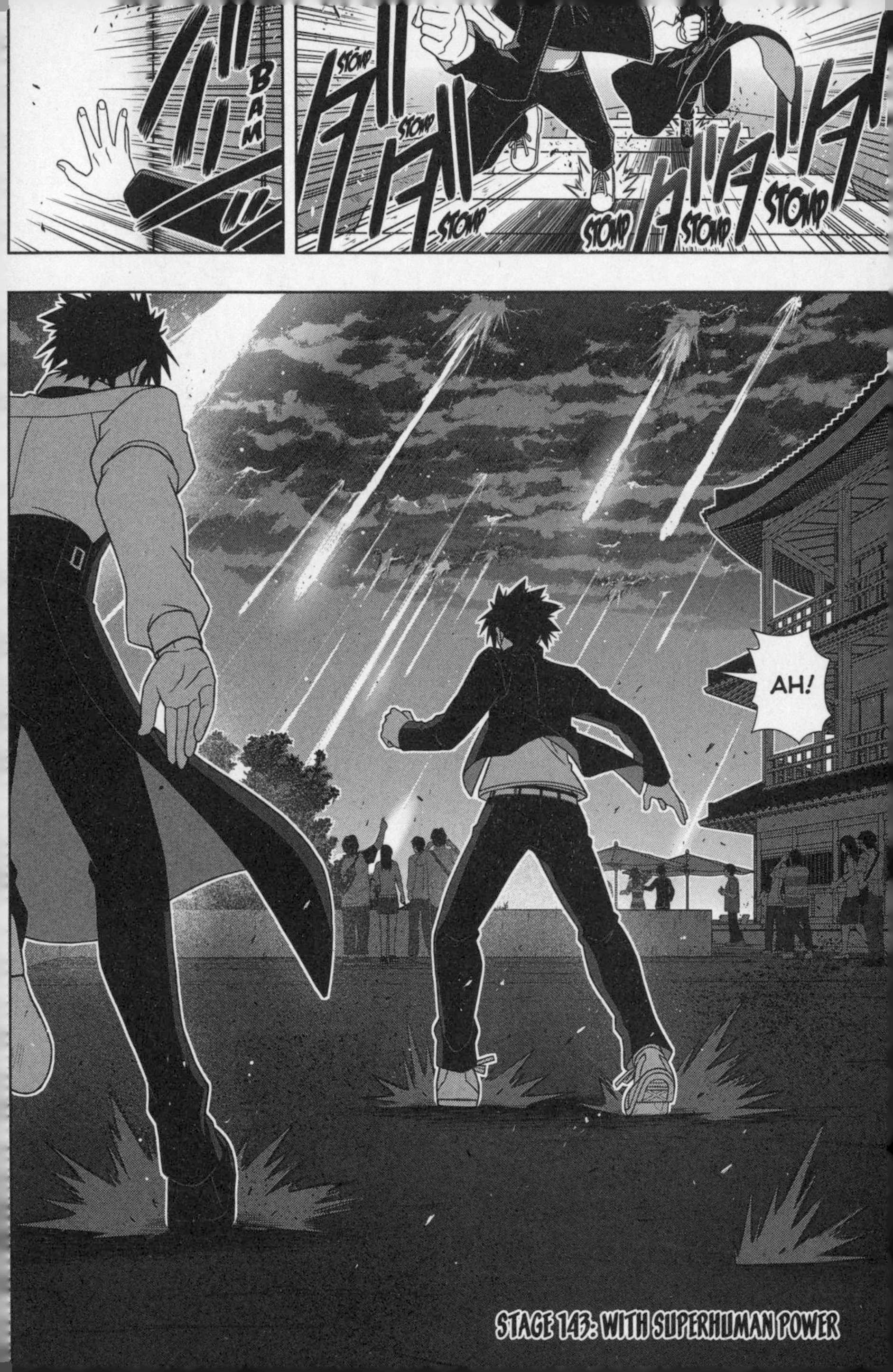

STOMP
STOMP
STOMP
STOMP
STOMP
STOMP
BAM
AH!
STAGE 143: WITH SUPERHUMAN POWER

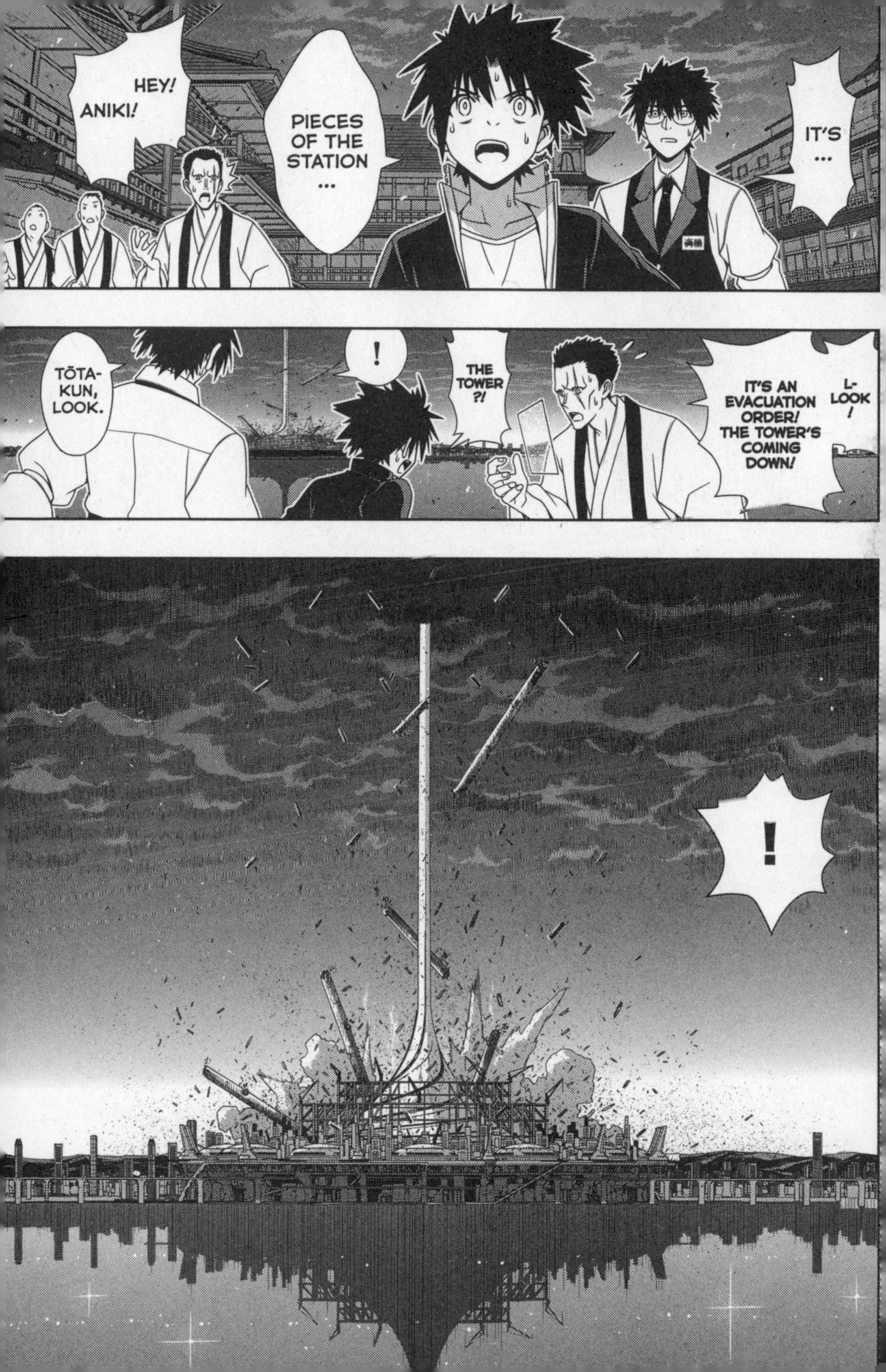
IT'S ...
PIECES OF THE STATION ...
HEY! ANIKI!
L-LOOK!
IT'S AN EVACUATION ORDER! THE TOWER'S COMING DOWN!
THE TOWER?!
!
TŌTA-KUN, LOOK.
!

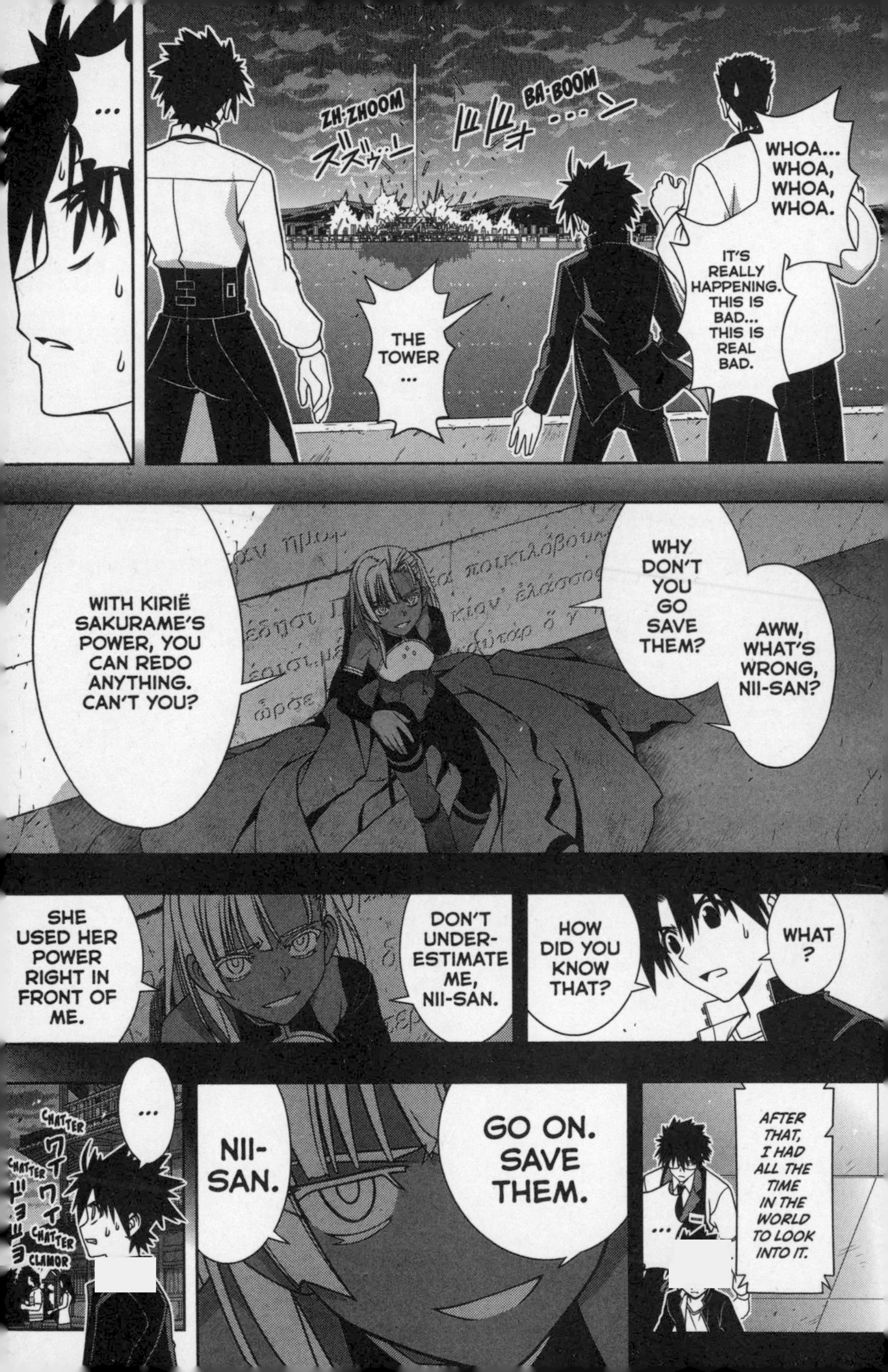
BA-BOOM
WHOA... WHOA, WHOA, WHOA.
IT'S REALLY HAPPENING. THIS IS BAD... THIS IS REAL BAD.
ZH-ZHOOM
THE TOWER ...
...
AWW, WHAT'S WRONG, NII-SAN?
WHY DON'T YOU GO SAVE THEM?
WITH KIRIË SAKURAME'S POWER, YOU CAN REDO ANYTHING. CAN'T YOU?
WHAT?
HOW DID YOU KNOW THAT?
DON'T UNDER-ESTIMATE ME, NII-SAN.
SHE USED HER POWER RIGHT IN FRONT OF ME.
AFTER THAT, I HAD ALL THE TIME IN THE WORLD TO LOOK INTO IT.
...
GO ON. SAVE THEM.
NII-SAN.
...
CHATTER
CHATTER
CHATTER
CLAMOR

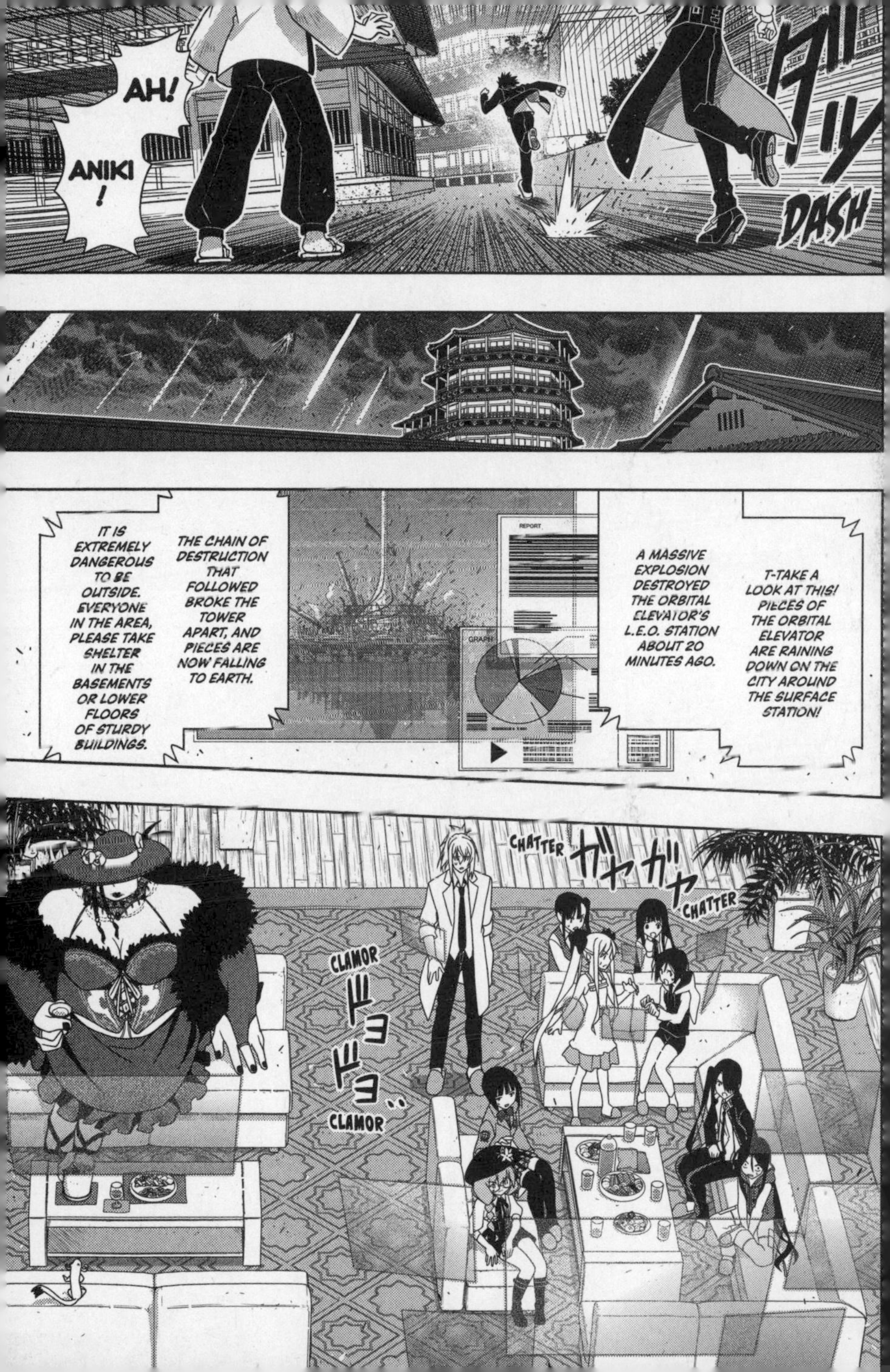

ガッ
DASH
AH!
ANIKI!
T-TAKE A LOOK AT THIS! PIECES OF THE ORBITAL ELEVATOR ARE RAINING DOWN ON THE CITY AROUND THE SURFACE STATION!
A MASSIVE EXPLOSION DESTROYED THE ORBITAL ELEVATOR'S L.E.O. STATION ABOUT 20 MINUTES AGO.
REPORT
GRAPH
THE CHAIN OF DESTRUCTION THAT FOLLOWED BROKE THE TOWER APART, AND PIECES ARE NOW FALLING TO EARTH.
IT IS EXTREMELY DANGEROUS TO BE OUTSIDE. EVERYONE IN THE AREA, PLEASE TAKE SHELTER IN THE BASEMENTS OR LOWER FLOORS OF STURDY BUILDINGS.
CHATTER
ガヤガヤ
CHATTER
CLAMOR
ドョドョ
CLAMOR

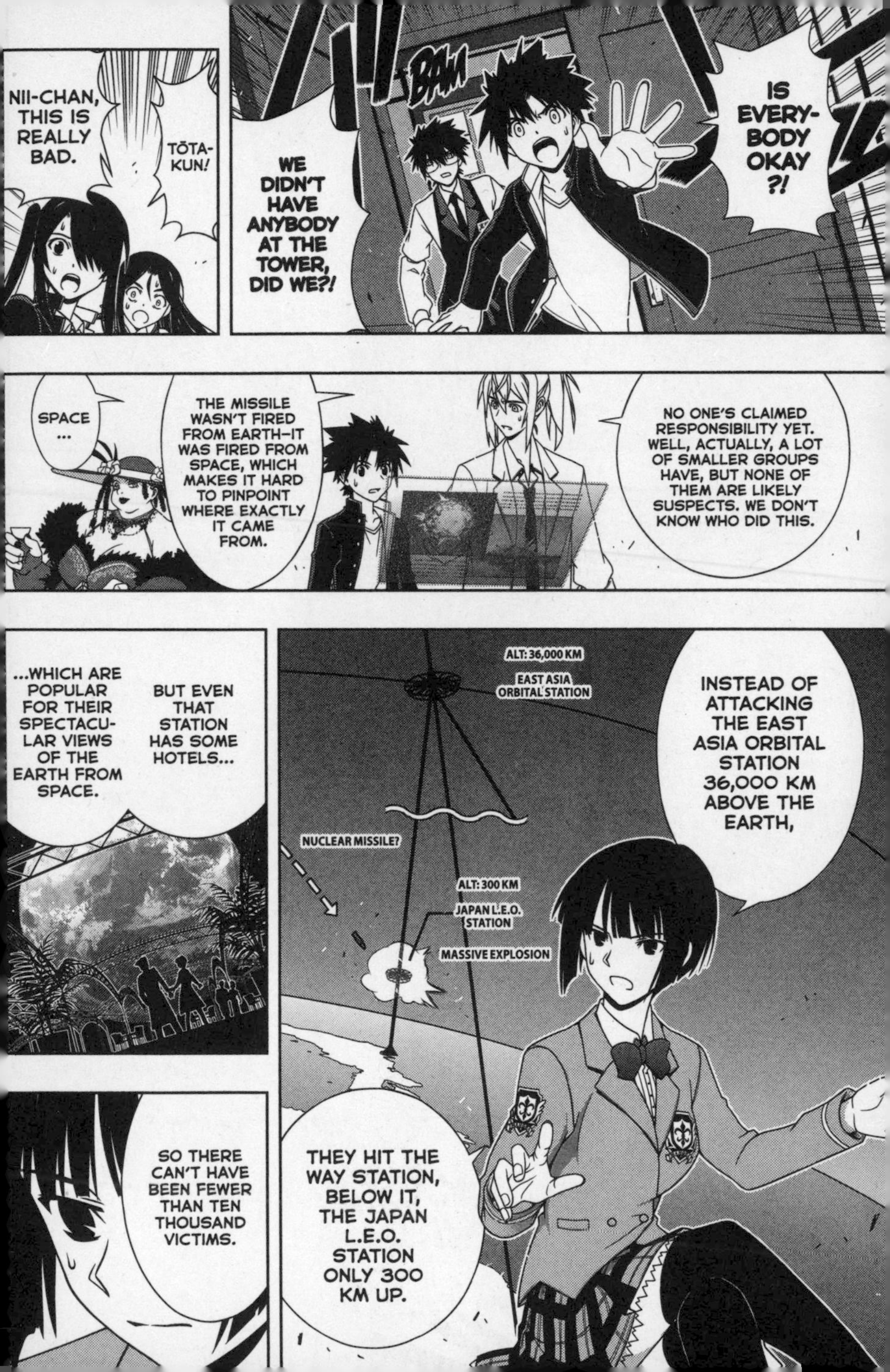
BAM
IS EVERYBODY OKAY ?!
WE DIDN'T HAVE ANYBODY AT THE TOWER, DID WE?!
TŌTA-KUN!
NII-CHAN, THIS IS REALLY BAD.
NO ONE'S CLAIMED RESPONSIBILITY YET. WELL, ACTUALLY, A LOT OF SMALLER GROUPS HAVE, BUT NONE OF THEM ARE LIKELY SUSPECTS. WE DON'T KNOW WHO DID THIS.
THE MISSILE WASN'T FIRED FROM EARTH—IT WAS FIRED FROM SPACE, WHICH MAKES IT HARD TO PINPOINT WHERE EXACTLY IT CAME FROM.
SPACE ...
INSTEAD OF ATTACKING THE EAST ASIA ORBITAL STATION 36,000 KM ABOVE THE EARTH,
ALT: 36,000 KM
EAST ASIA ORBITAL STATION
NUCLEAR MISSILE?
ALT: 300 KM
JAPAN L.E.O. STATION
MASSIVE EXPLOSION
THEY HIT THE WAY STATION, BELOW IT, THE JAPAN L.E.O. STATION ONLY 300 KM UP.
BUT EVEN THAT STATION HAS SOME HOTELS...
...WHICH ARE POPULAR FOR THEIR SPECTACULAR VIEWS OF THE EARTH FROM SPACE.
SO THERE CAN'T HAVE BEEN FEWER THAN TEN THOUSAND VICTIMS.

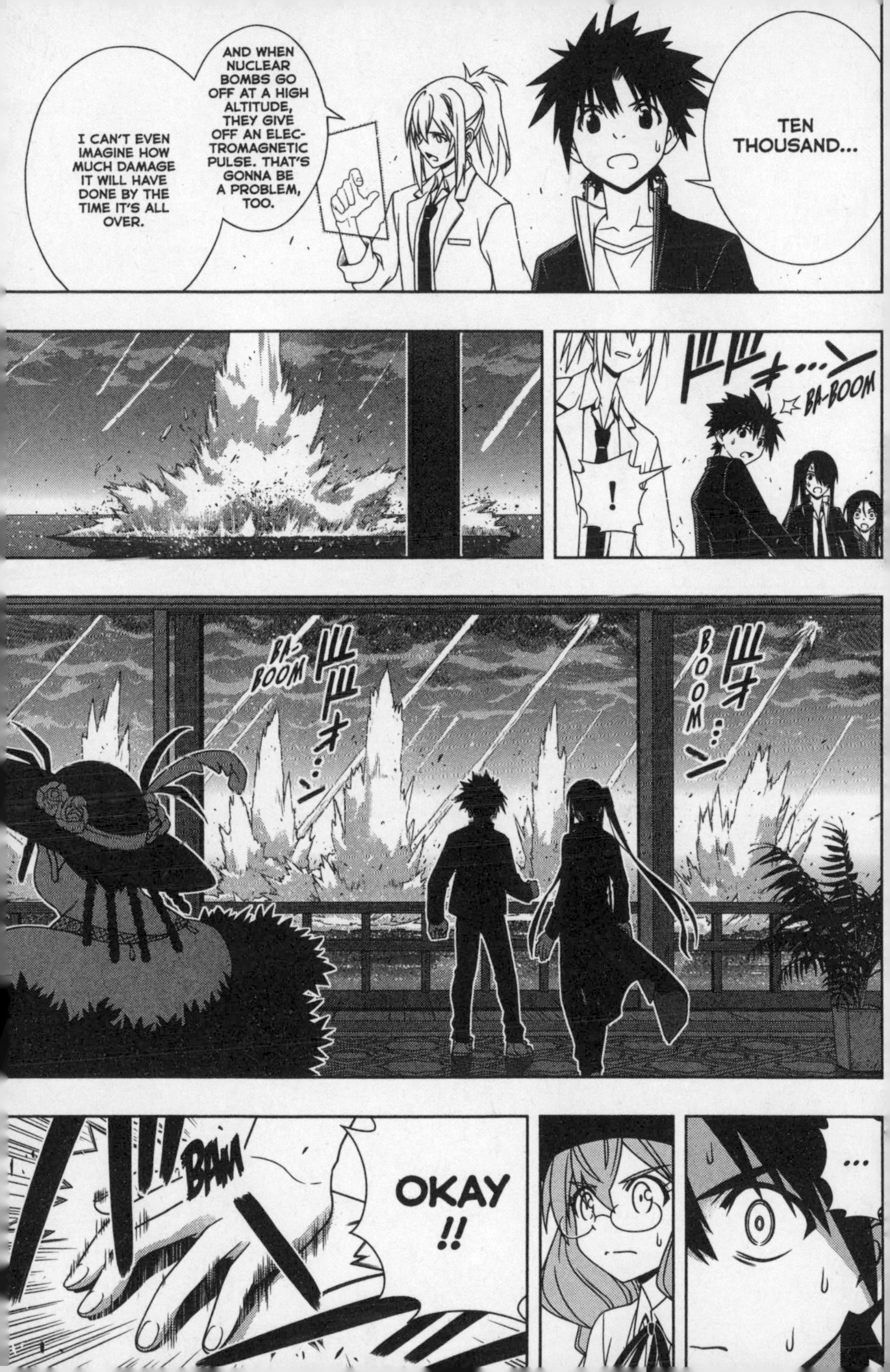
TEN THOUSAND...
AND WHEN NUCLEAR BOMBS GO OFF AT A HIGH ALTITUDE, THEY GIVE OFF AN ELECTROMAGNETIC PULSE. THAT'S GONNA BE A PROBLEM, TOO.
I CAN'T EVEN IMAGINE HOW MUCH DAMAGE IT WILL HAVE DONE BY THE TIME IT'S ALL OVER.
ドドォ…ン
BA-BOOM
!
ドォ…ン
BOOM...
ドドドォ…ン
BA-BOOM
...
BAM
OKAY!!

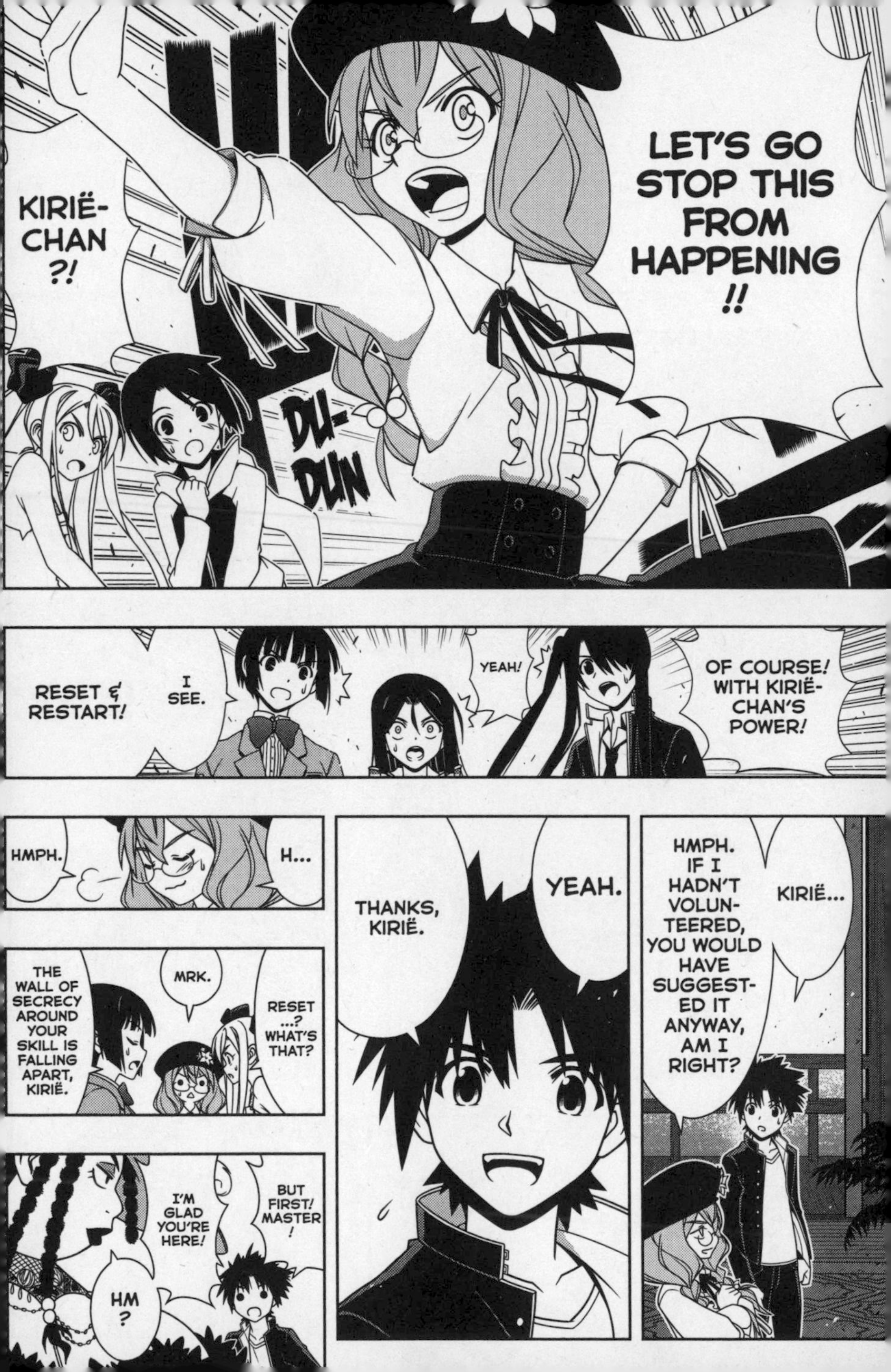
LET'S GO STOP THIS FROM HAPPENING!!
DU-DUN
KIRIË-CHAN?!
OF COURSE! WITH KIRIË-CHAN'S POWER!
YEAH!
I SEE.
RESET & RESTART!
KIRIË...
HMPH. IF I HADN'T VOLUNTEERED, YOU WOULD HAVE SUGGESTED IT ANYWAY, AM I RIGHT?
YEAH.
THANKS, KIRIË.
H...
HMPH.
RESET...? WHAT'S THAT?
MRK.
THE WALL OF SECRECY AROUND YOUR SKILL IS FALLING APART, KIRIË.
BUT FIRST! MASTER!
I'M GLAD YOU'RE HERE!
HM?

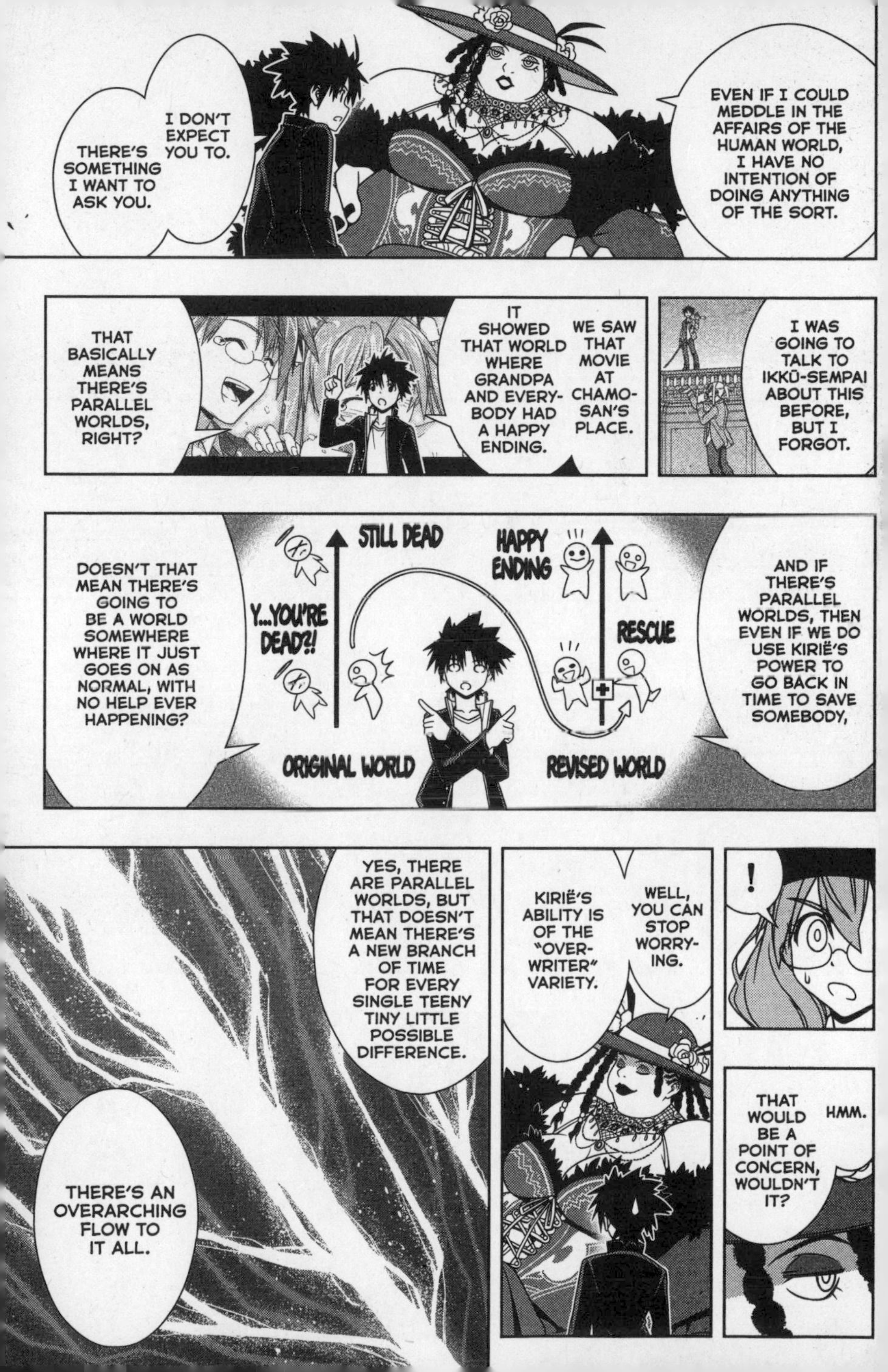
EVEN IF I COULD MEDDLE IN THE AFFAIRS OF THE HUMAN WORLD, I HAVE NO INTENTION OF DOING ANYTHING OF THE SORT.
I DON'T EXPECT YOU TO.
THERE'S SOMETHING I WANT TO ASK YOU.
I WAS GOING TO TALK TO IKKŪ-SEMPAI ABOUT THIS BEFORE, BUT I FORGOT.
WE SAW THAT MOVIE AT CHAMO-SAN'S PLACE.
IT SHOWED THAT WORLD WHERE GRANDPA AND EVERY-BODY HAD A HAPPY ENDING.
THAT BASICALLY MEANS THERE'S PARALLEL WORLDS, RIGHT?
AND IF THERE'S PARALLEL WORLDS, THEN EVEN IF WE DO USE KIRIË'S POWER TO GO BACK IN TIME TO SAVE SOMEBODY,
HAPPY ENDING
RESCUE
REVISED WORLD
STILL DEAD
Y...YOU'RE DEAD?!
ORIGINAL WORLD
DOESN'T THAT MEAN THERE'S GOING TO BE A WORLD SOMEWHERE WHERE IT JUST GOES ON AS NORMAL, WITH NO HELP EVER HAPPENING?
!
HMM.
THAT WOULD BE A POINT OF CONCERN, WOULDN'T IT?
WELL, YOU CAN STOP WORRY-ING.
KIRIË'S ABILITY IS OF THE "OVER-WRITER" VARIETY.
YES, THERE ARE PARALLEL WORLDS, BUT THAT DOESN'T MEAN THERE'S A NEW BRANCH OF TIME FOR EVERY SINGLE TEENY TINY LITTLE POSSIBLE DIFFERENCE.
THERE'S AN OVERARCHING FLOW TO IT ALL.

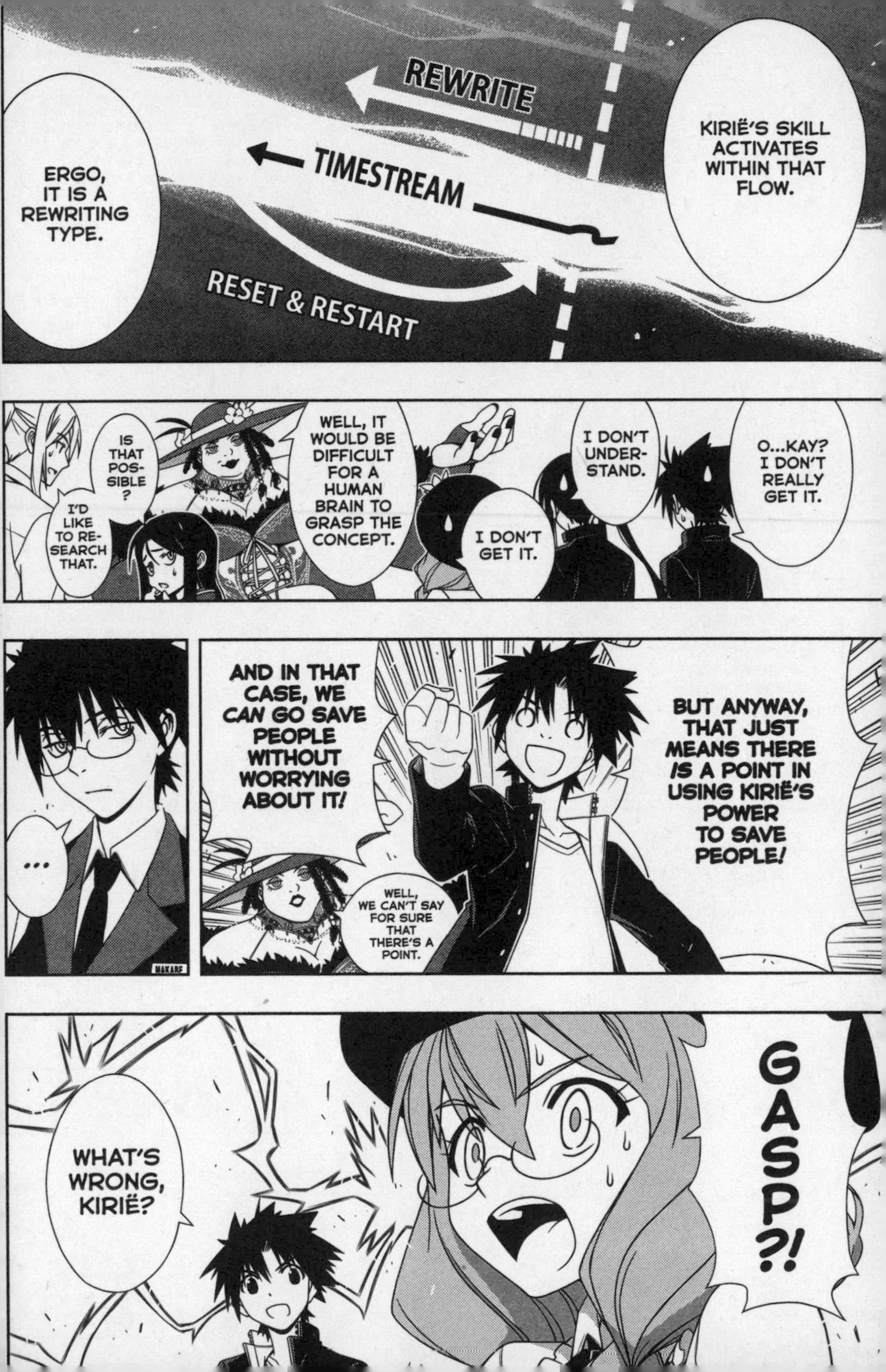
KIRIË'S SKILL ACTIVATES WITHIN THAT FLOW.
REWRITE
TIMESTREAM
RESET & RESTART
ERGO, IT IS A REWRITING TYPE.
O...KAY? I DON'T REALLY GET IT.
I DON'T UNDER-STAND.
I DON'T GET IT.
WELL, IT WOULD BE DIFFICULT FOR A HUMAN BRAIN TO GRASP THE CONCEPT.
IS THAT POS-SIBLE?
I'D LIKE TO RE-SEARCH THAT.
BUT ANYWAY, THAT JUST MEANS THERE IS A POINT IN USING KIRIË'S POWER TO SAVE PEOPLE!
AND IN THAT CASE, WE CAN GO SAVE PEOPLE WITHOUT WORRYING ABOUT IT!
WELL, WE CAN'T SAY FOR SURE THAT THERE'S A POINT.
...
GASP?!
WHAT'S WRONG, KIRIË?

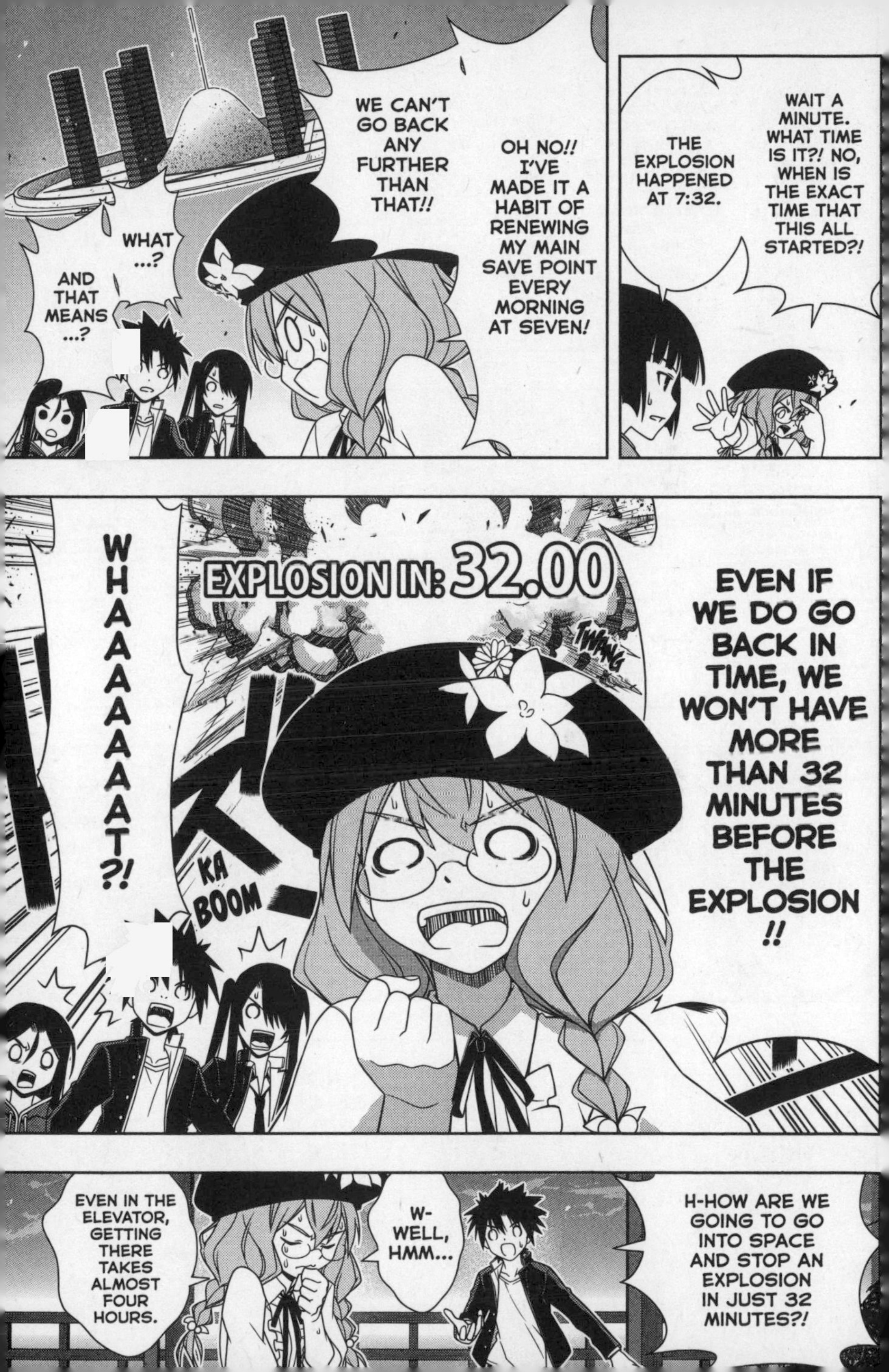
WAIT A MINUTE. WHAT TIME IS IT?! NO, WHEN IS THE EXACT TIME THAT THIS ALL STARTED?!
THE EXPLOSION HAPPENED AT 7:32.
OH NO!! I'VE MADE IT A HABIT OF RENEWING MY MAIN SAVE POINT EVERY MORNING AT SEVEN!
WE CAN'T GO BACK ANY FURTHER THAN THAT!!
WHAT ...?
AND THAT MEANS ...?
EXPLOSION IN: 32.00
EVEN IF WE DO GO BACK IN TIME, WE WON'T HAVE MORE THAN 32 MINUTES BEFORE THE EXPLOSION !!
TWANG
KA BOOM
WHAAAAAAAAAT?!
H-HOW ARE WE GOING TO GO INTO SPACE AND STOP AN EXPLOSION IN JUST 32 MINUTES?!
W- WELL, HMM...
EVEN IN THE ELEVATOR, GETTING THERE TAKES ALMOST FOUR HOURS.

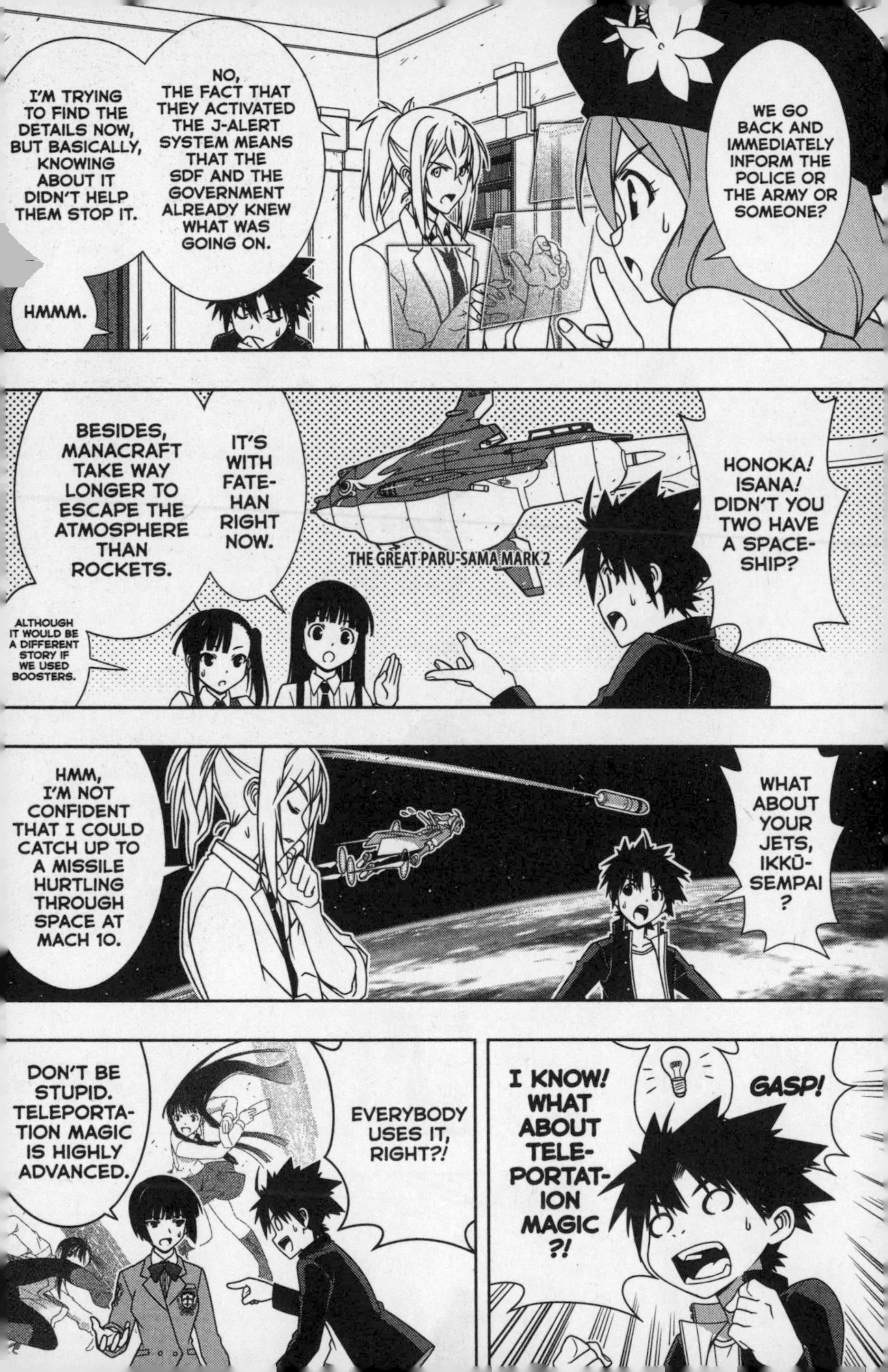
WE GO BACK AND IMMEDIATELY INFORM THE POLICE OR THE ARMY OR SOMEONE?
NO, THE FACT THAT THEY ACTIVATED THE J-ALERT SYSTEM MEANS THAT THE SDF AND THE GOVERNMENT ALREADY KNEW WHAT WAS GOING ON.
I'M TRYING TO FIND THE DETAILS NOW, BUT BASICALLY, KNOWING ABOUT IT DIDN'T HELP THEM STOP IT.
HMMM.
HONOKA! ISANA! DIDN'T YOU TWO HAVE A SPACE-SHIP?
THE GREAT PARU-SAMA MARK 2
IT'S WITH FATE-HAN RIGHT NOW.
BESIDES, MANACRAFT TAKE WAY LONGER TO ESCAPE THE ATMOSPHERE THAN ROCKETS.
ALTHOUGH IT WOULD BE A DIFFERENT STORY IF WE USED BOOSTERS.
WHAT ABOUT YOUR JETS, IKKŪ-SEMPAI?
HMM, I'M NOT CONFIDENT THAT I COULD CATCH UP TO A MISSILE HURTLING THROUGH SPACE AT MACH 10.
GASP!
I KNOW! WHAT ABOUT TELE-PORTAT-ION MAGIC?!
EVERYBODY USES IT, RIGHT?!
DON'T BE STUPID. TELEPORTA-TION MAGIC IS HIGHLY ADVANCED.

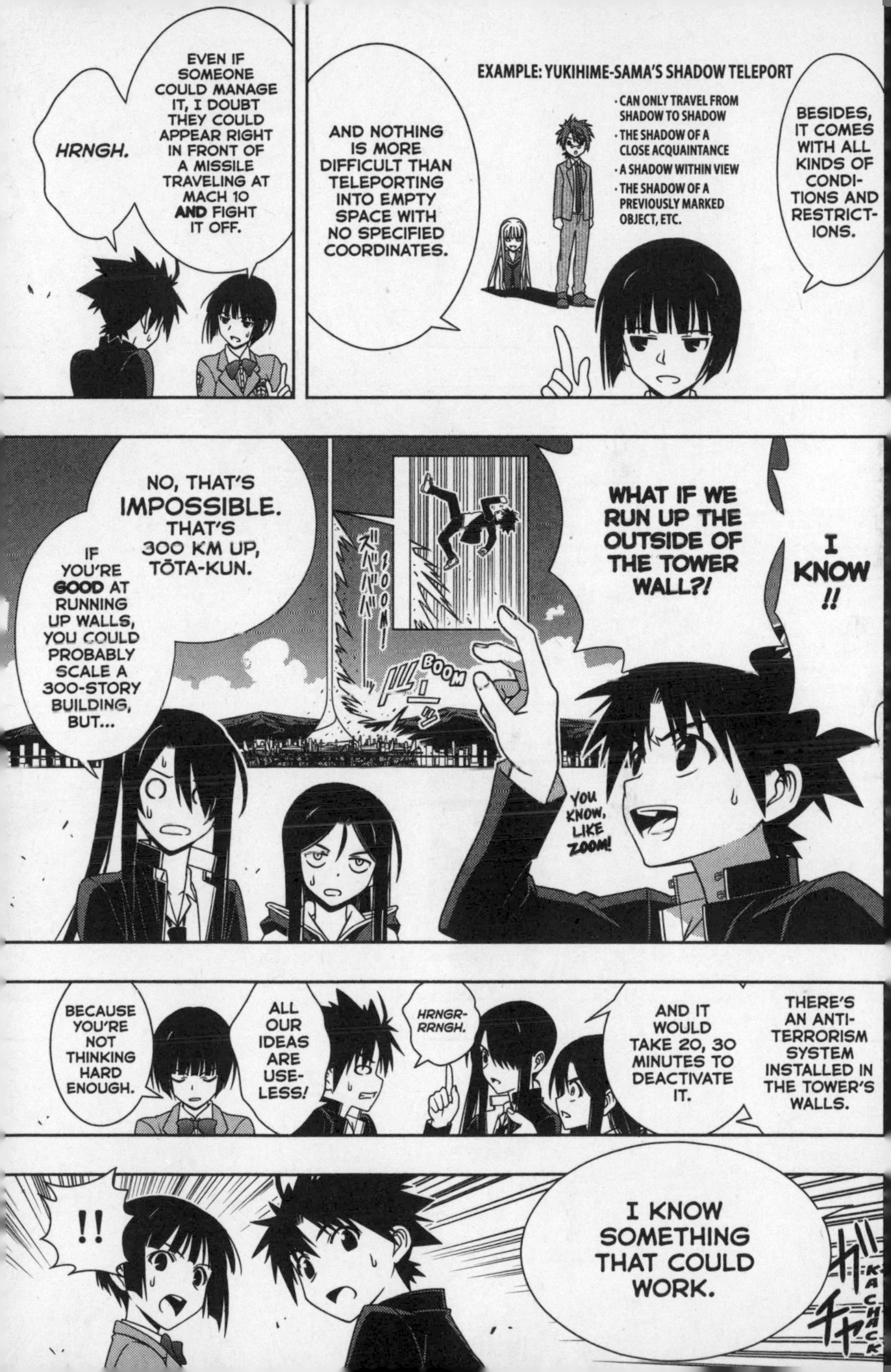
BESIDES, IT COMES WITH ALL KINDS OF CONDITIONS AND RESTRICTIONS.
EXAMPLE: YUKIHIME-SAMA'S SHADOW TELEPORT
· CAN ONLY TRAVEL FROM SHADOW TO SHADOW
· THE SHADOW OF A CLOSE ACQUAINTANCE
· A SHADOW WITHIN VIEW
· THE SHADOW OF A PREVIOUSLY MARKED OBJECT, ETC.
AND NOTHING IS MORE DIFFICULT THAN TELEPORTING INTO EMPTY SPACE WITH NO SPECIFIED COORDINATES.
EVEN IF SOMEONE COULD MANAGE IT, I DOUBT THEY COULD APPEAR RIGHT IN FRONT OF A MISSILE TRAVELING AT MACH 10 AND FIGHT IT OFF.
HRNGH.
I KNOW!!
WHAT IF WE RUN UP THE OUTSIDE OF THE TOWER WALL?!
YOU KNOW, LIKE ZOOM!
1000M!
BOOM
NO, THAT'S IMPOSSIBLE. THAT'S 300 KM UP, TŌTA-KUN.
IF YOU'RE GOOD AT RUNNING UP WALLS, YOU COULD PROBABLY SCALE A 300-STORY BUILDING, BUT...
THERE'S AN ANTI-TERRORISM SYSTEM INSTALLED IN THE TOWER'S WALLS.
AND IT WOULD TAKE 20, 30 MINUTES TO DEACTIVATE IT.
HRNGR-RRNGH.
ALL OUR IDEAS ARE USELESS!
BECAUSE YOU'RE NOT THINKING HARD ENOUGH.
KACHACK
I KNOW SOMETHING THAT COULD WORK.
!!

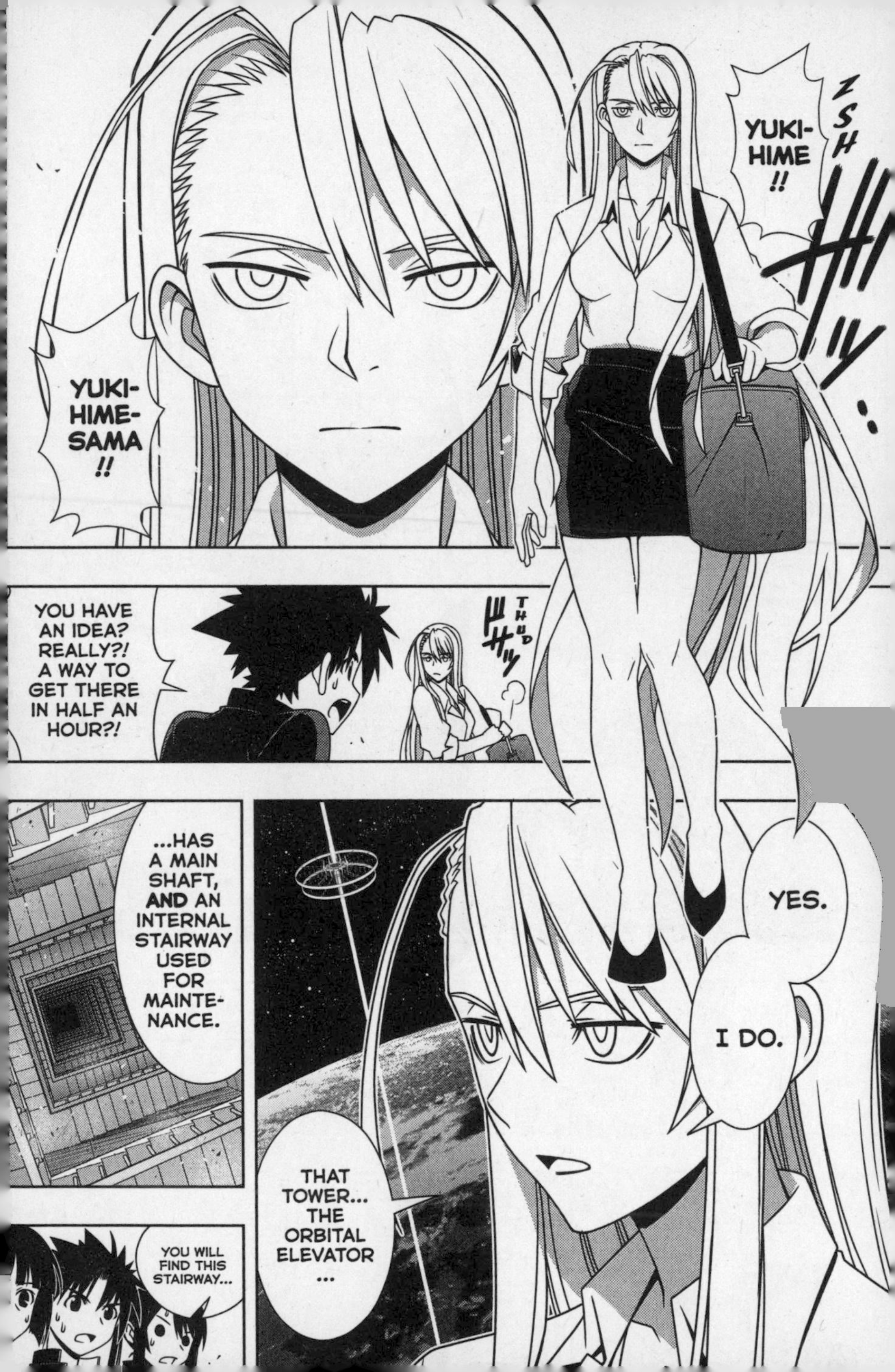
ZSHHHH..
YUKI-HIME!!
YUKI-HIME-SAMA!!
THUD
YOU HAVE AN IDEA? REALLY?! A WAY TO GET THERE IN HALF AN HOUR?!
YES.
I DO.
THAT TOWER... THE ORBITAL ELEVATOR...
...HAS A MAIN SHAFT, AND AN INTERNAL STAIRWAY USED FOR MAINTE-NANCE.
YOU WILL FIND THIS STAIRWAY...

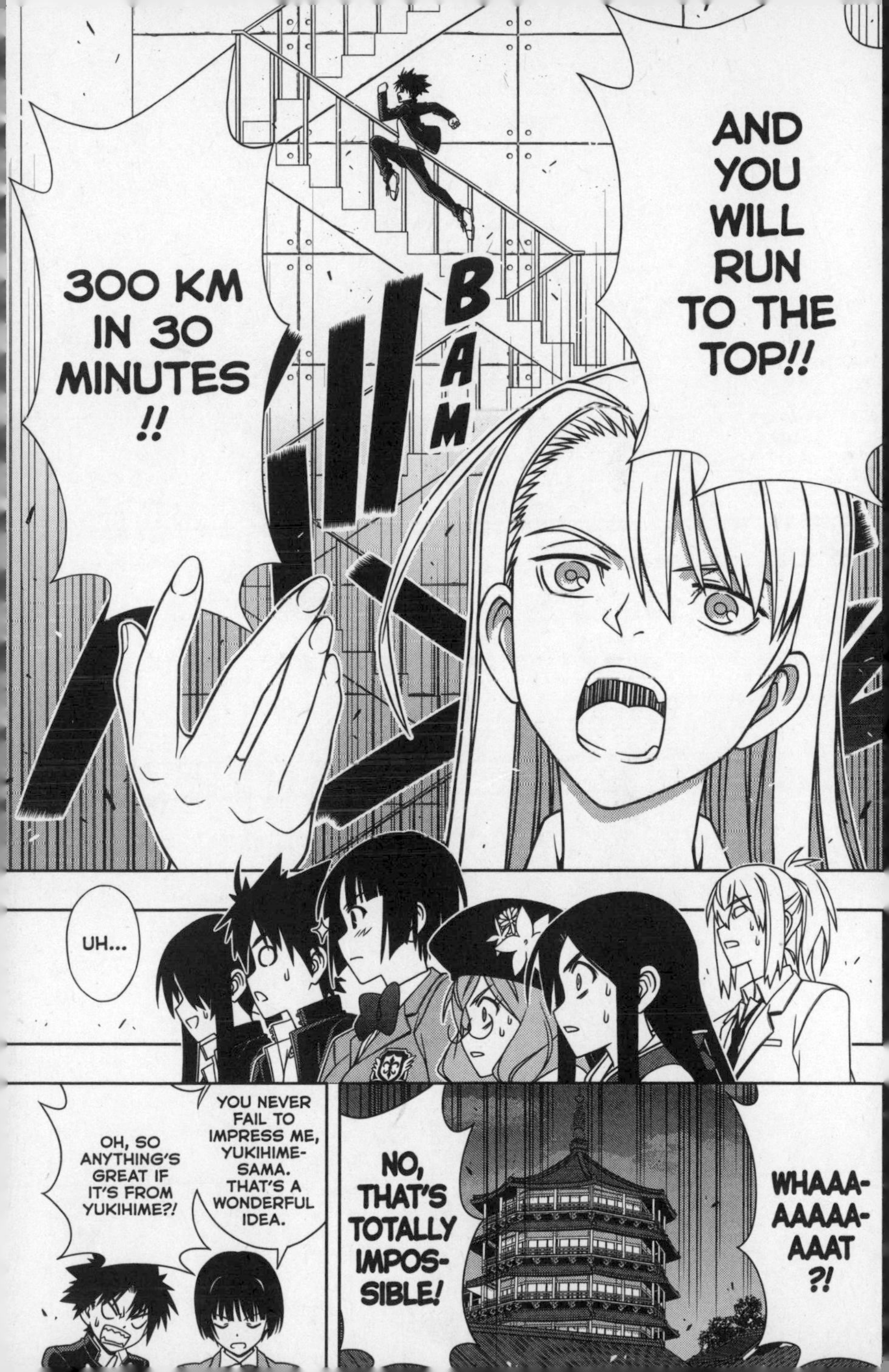
AND YOU WILL RUN TO THE TOP!!
BAM
300 KM IN 30 MINUTES!!
UH...
WHAAA-AAAAA-AAAT?!
NO, THAT'S TOTALLY IMPOS-SIBLE!
YOU NEVER FAIL TO IMPRESS ME, YUKIHIME-SAMA. THAT'S A WONDERFUL IDEA.
OH, SO ANYTHING'S GREAT IF IT'S FROM YUKIHIME?!

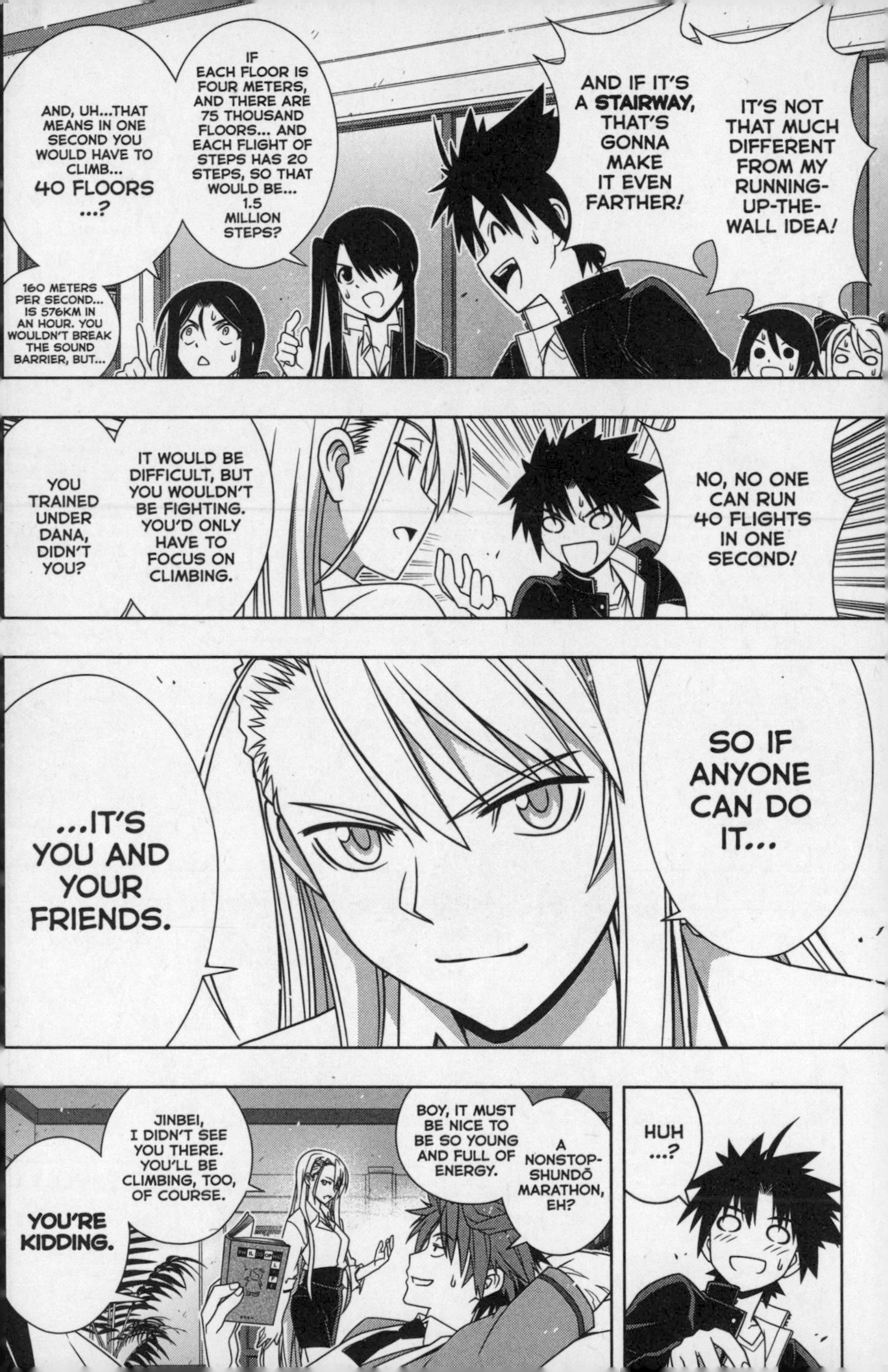

IT'S NOT THAT MUCH DIFFERENT FROM MY RUNNING-UP-THE-WALL IDEA!
AND IF IT'S A STAIRWAY, THAT'S GONNA MAKE IT EVEN FARTHER!
IF EACH FLOOR IS FOUR METERS, AND THERE ARE 75 THOUSAND FLOORS... AND EACH FLIGHT OF STEPS HAS 20 STEPS, SO THAT WOULD BE... 1.5 MILLION STEPS?
AND, UH...THAT MEANS IN ONE SECOND YOU WOULD HAVE TO CLIMB... 40 FLOORS ...?
160 METERS PER SECOND... IS 576KM IN AN HOUR. YOU WOULDN'T BREAK THE SOUND BARRIER, BUT...
NO, NO ONE CAN RUN 40 FLIGHTS IN ONE SECOND!
IT WOULD BE DIFFICULT, BUT YOU WOULDN'T BE FIGHTING. YOU'D ONLY HAVE TO FOCUS ON CLIMBING.
YOU TRAINED UNDER DANA, DIDN'T YOU?
SO IF ANYONE CAN DO IT...
...IT'S YOU AND YOUR FRIENDS.
HUH ...?
A NONSTOP-SHUNDŌ MARATHON, EH?
BOY, IT MUST BE NICE TO BE SO YOUNG AND FULL OF ENERGY.
JINBEI, I DIDN'T SEE YOU THERE. YOU'LL BE CLIMBING, TOO, OF COURSE.
YOU'RE KIDDING.

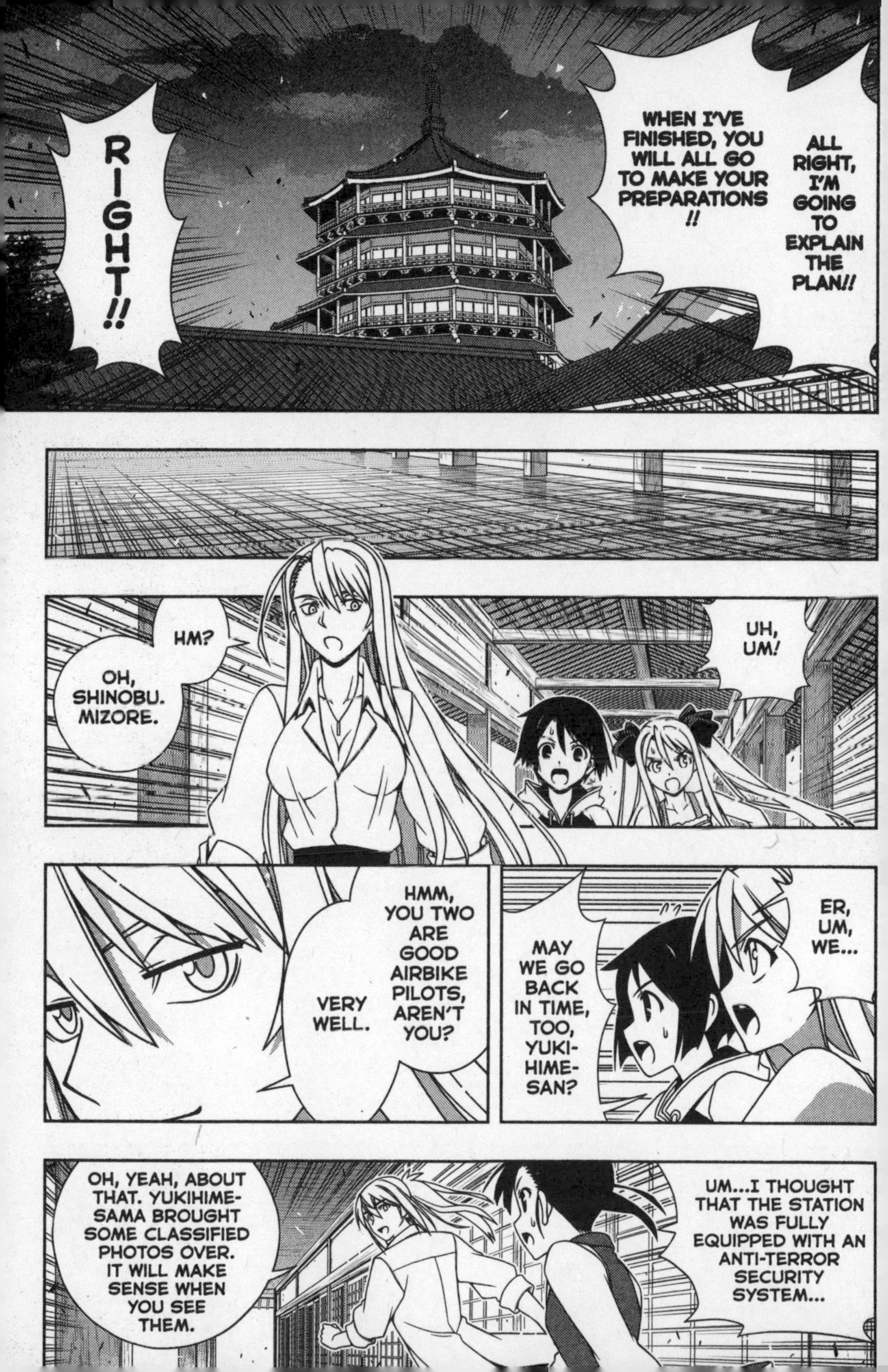
ALL RIGHT, I'M GOING TO EXPLAIN THE PLAN!!
WHEN I'VE FINISHED, YOU WILL ALL GO TO MAKE YOUR PREPARATIONS!!
RIGHT!!
UH, UM!
HM?
OH, SHINOBU. MIZORE.
ER, UM, WE...
MAY WE GO BACK IN TIME, TOO, YUKIHIME-SAN?
HMM, YOU TWO ARE GOOD AIRBIKE PILOTS, AREN'T YOU?
VERY WELL.
UM...I THOUGHT THAT THE STATION WAS FULLY EQUIPPED WITH AN ANTI-TERROR SECURITY SYSTEM...
OH, YEAH, ABOUT THAT. YUKIHIME-SAMA BROUGHT SOME CLASSIFIED PHOTOS OVER. IT WILL MAKE SENSE WHEN YOU SEE THEM.

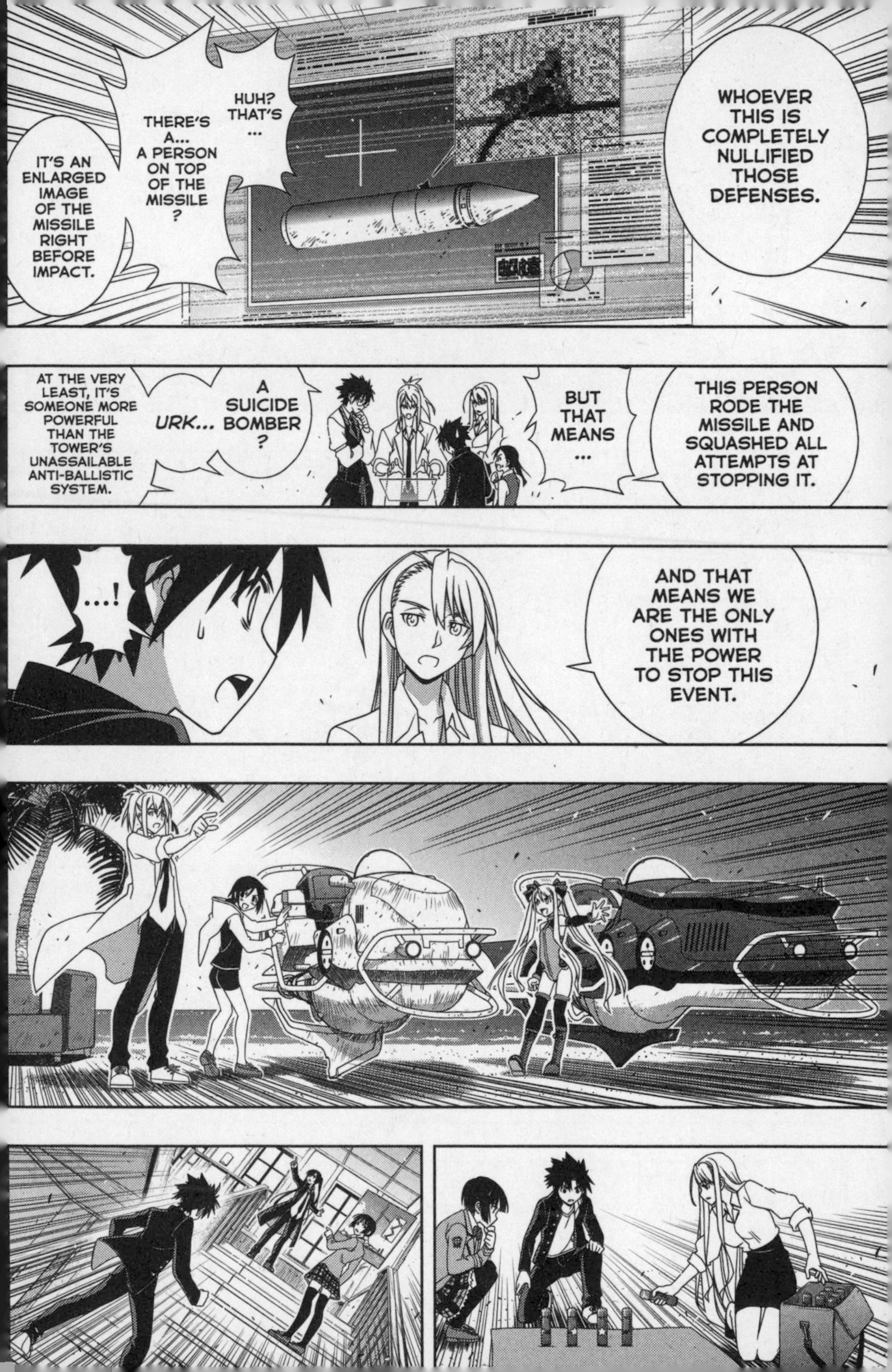
WHOEVER THIS IS COMPLETELY NULLIFIED THOSE DEFENSES.
HUH? THAT'S ...
THERE'S A... A PERSON ON TOP OF THE MISSILE ?
IT'S AN ENLARGED IMAGE OF THE MISSILE RIGHT BEFORE IMPACT.
THIS PERSON RODE THE MISSILE AND SQUASHED ALL ATTEMPTS AT STOPPING IT.
BUT THAT MEANS ...
A SUICIDE BOMBER ?
URK...
AT THE VERY LEAST, IT'S SOMEONE MORE POWERFUL THAN THE TOWER'S UNASSAILABLE ANTI-BALLISTIC SYSTEM.
AND THAT MEANS WE ARE THE ONLY ONES WITH THE POWER TO STOP THIS EVENT.
...!

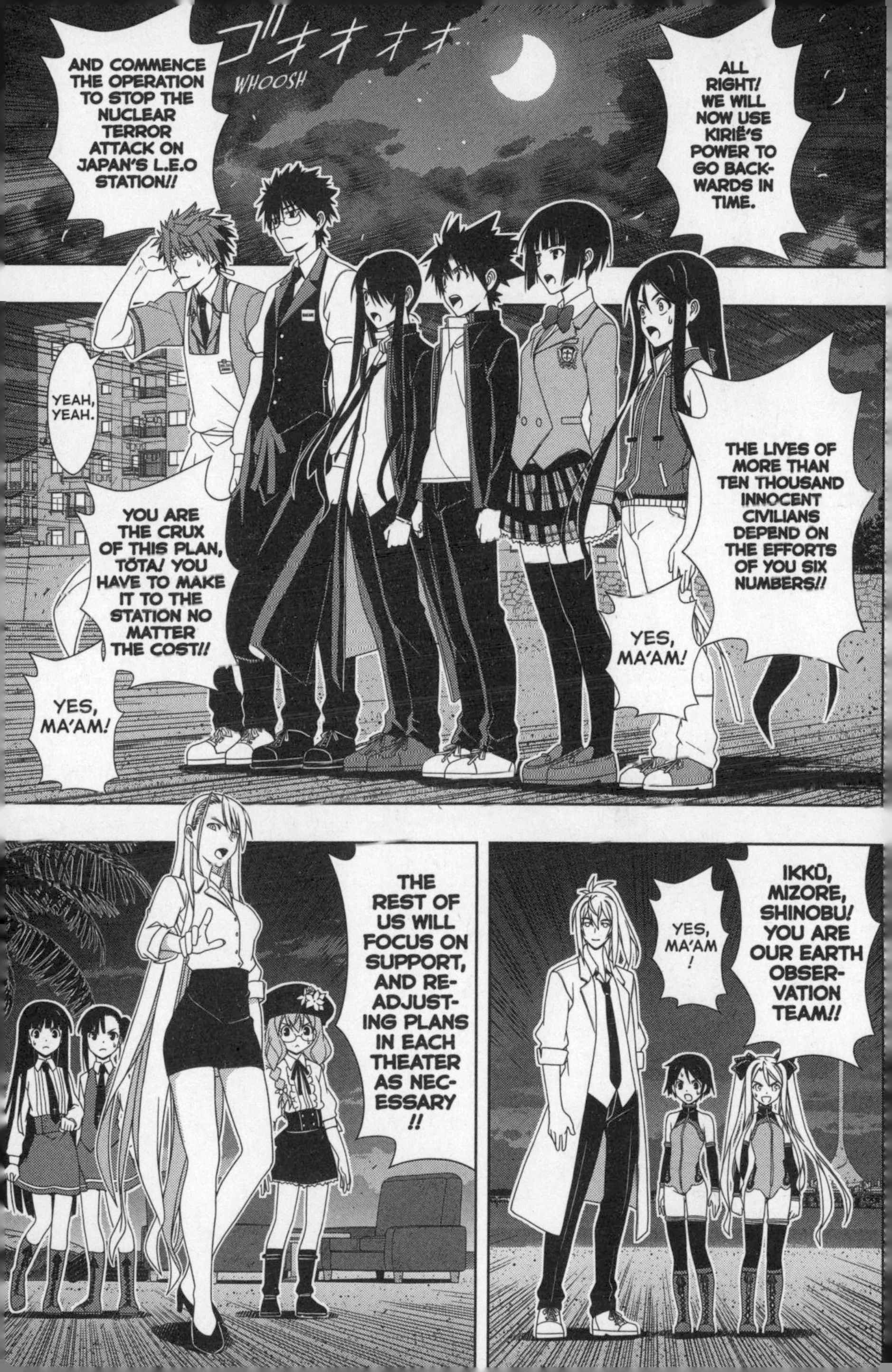
ALL RIGHT! WE WILL NOW USE KIRIĒ'S POWER TO GO BACKWARDS IN TIME.
ゴオオオオ
WHOOSH
AND COMMENCE THE OPERATION TO STOP THE NUCLEAR TERROR ATTACK ON JAPAN'S L.E.O STATION!!
THE LIVES OF MORE THAN TEN THOUSAND INNOCENT CIVILIANS DEPEND ON THE EFFORTS OF YOU SIX NUMBERS!!
YES, MA'AM!
YEAH, YEAH.
YOU ARE THE CRUX OF THIS PLAN, TŌTA! YOU HAVE TO MAKE IT TO THE STATION NO MATTER THE COST!!
YES, MA'AM!
IKKŪ, MIZORE, SHINOBU! YOU ARE OUR EARTH OBSERVATION TEAM!!
YES, MA'AM!
THE REST OF US WILL FOCUS ON SUPPORT, AND RE-ADJUSTING PLANS IN EACH THEATER AS NECESSARY!!

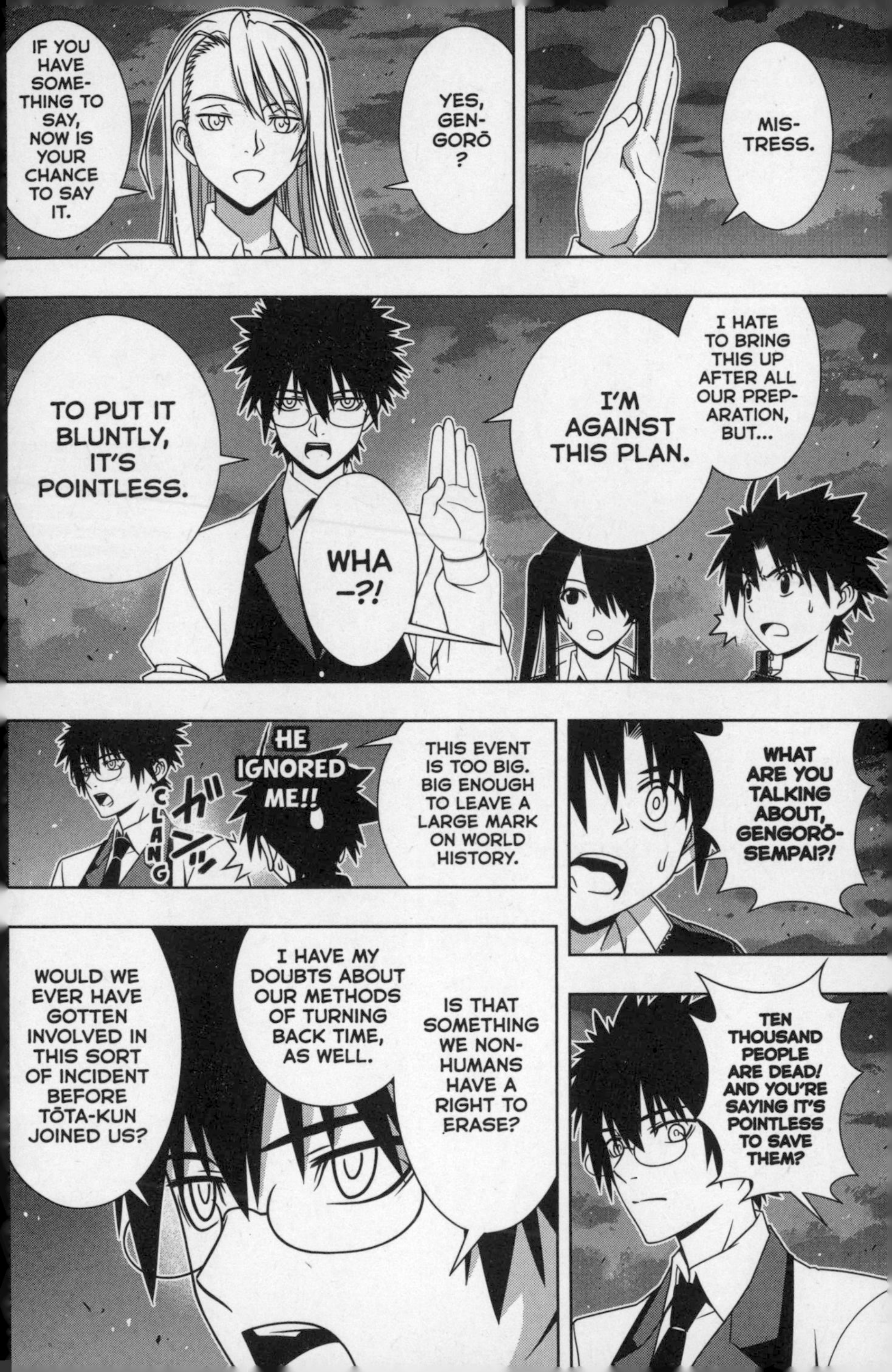
MIS-TRESS.
YES, GEN-GORŌ?
IF YOU HAVE SOME-THING TO SAY, NOW IS YOUR CHANCE TO SAY IT.
I HATE TO BRING THIS UP AFTER ALL OUR PREP-ARATION, BUT...
I'M AGAINST THIS PLAN.
WHA-?!
TO PUT IT BLUNTLY, IT'S POINTLESS.
WHAT ARE YOU TALKING ABOUT, GENGORŌ-SEMPAI?!
THIS EVENT IS TOO BIG. BIG ENOUGH TO LEAVE A LARGE MARK ON WORLD HISTORY.
HE IGNORED ME!!
CLANG
TEN THOUSAND PEOPLE ARE DEAD! AND YOU'RE SAYING IT'S POINTLESS TO SAVE THEM?
IS THAT SOMETHING WE NON-HUMANS HAVE A RIGHT TO ERASE?
I HAVE MY DOUBTS ABOUT OUR METHODS OF TURNING BACK TIME, AS WELL.
WOULD WE EVER HAVE GOTTEN INVOLVED IN THIS SORT OF INCIDENT BEFORE TŌTA-KUN JOINED US?

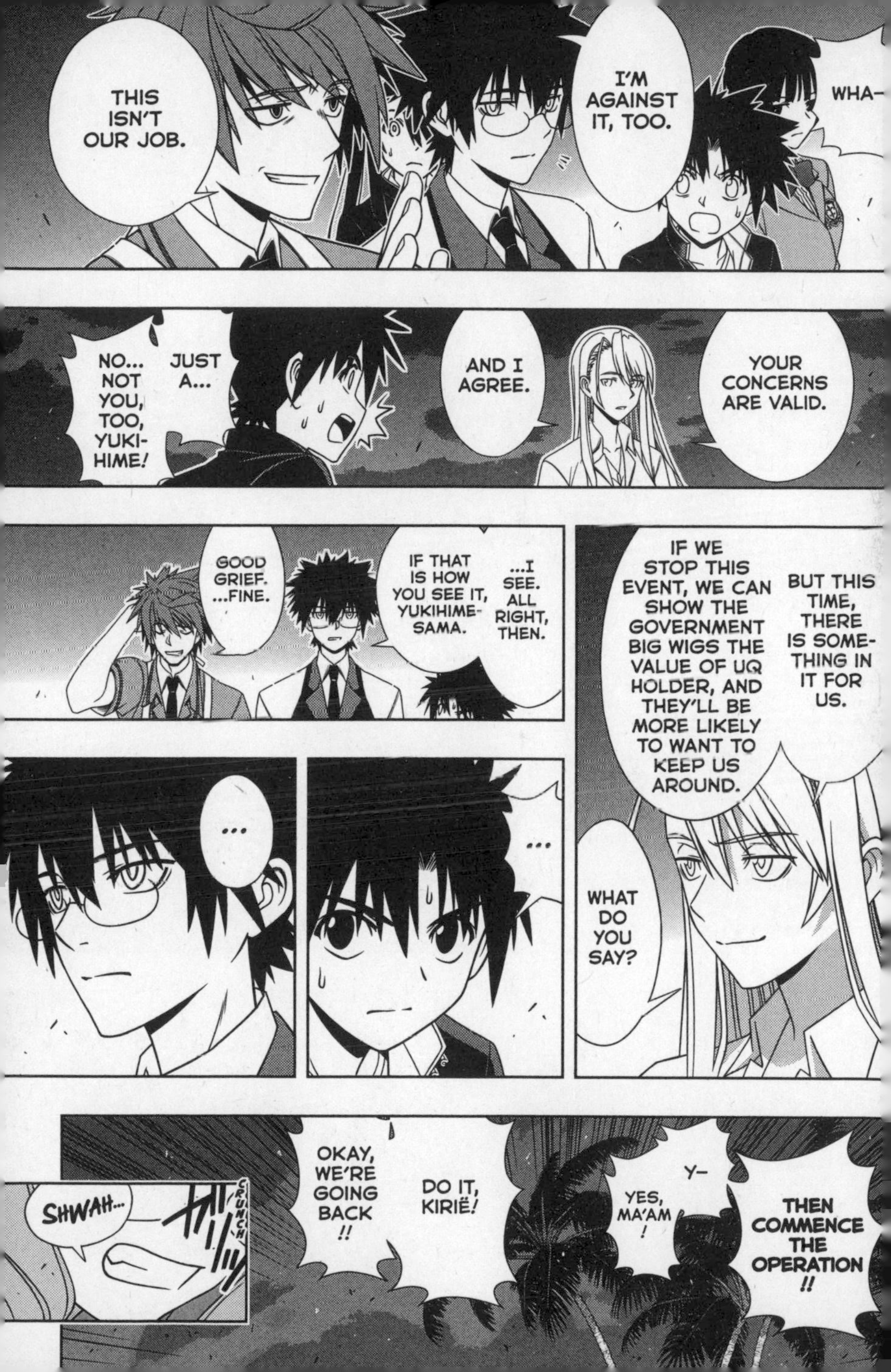
WHA-
I'M AGAINST IT, TOO.
THIS ISN'T OUR JOB.
YOUR CONCERNS ARE VALID.
AND I AGREE.
JUST A...
NO... NOT YOU, TOO, YUKI-HIME!
BUT THIS TIME, THERE IS SOME-THING IN IT FOR US.
IF WE STOP THIS EVENT, WE CAN SHOW THE GOVERNMENT BIG WIGS THE VALUE OF UQ HOLDER, AND THEY'LL BE MORE LIKELY TO WANT TO KEEP US AROUND.
WHAT DO YOU SAY?
...I SEE. ALL RIGHT, THEN.
IF THAT IS HOW YOU SEE IT, YUKIHIME-SAMA.
GOOD GRIEF. ...FINE.
...
...
THEN COMMENCE THE OPERATION!!
Y-
YES, MA'AM!
DO IT, KIRIË!
OKAY, WE'RE GOING BACK!!
CRUNCH
SHWAH...

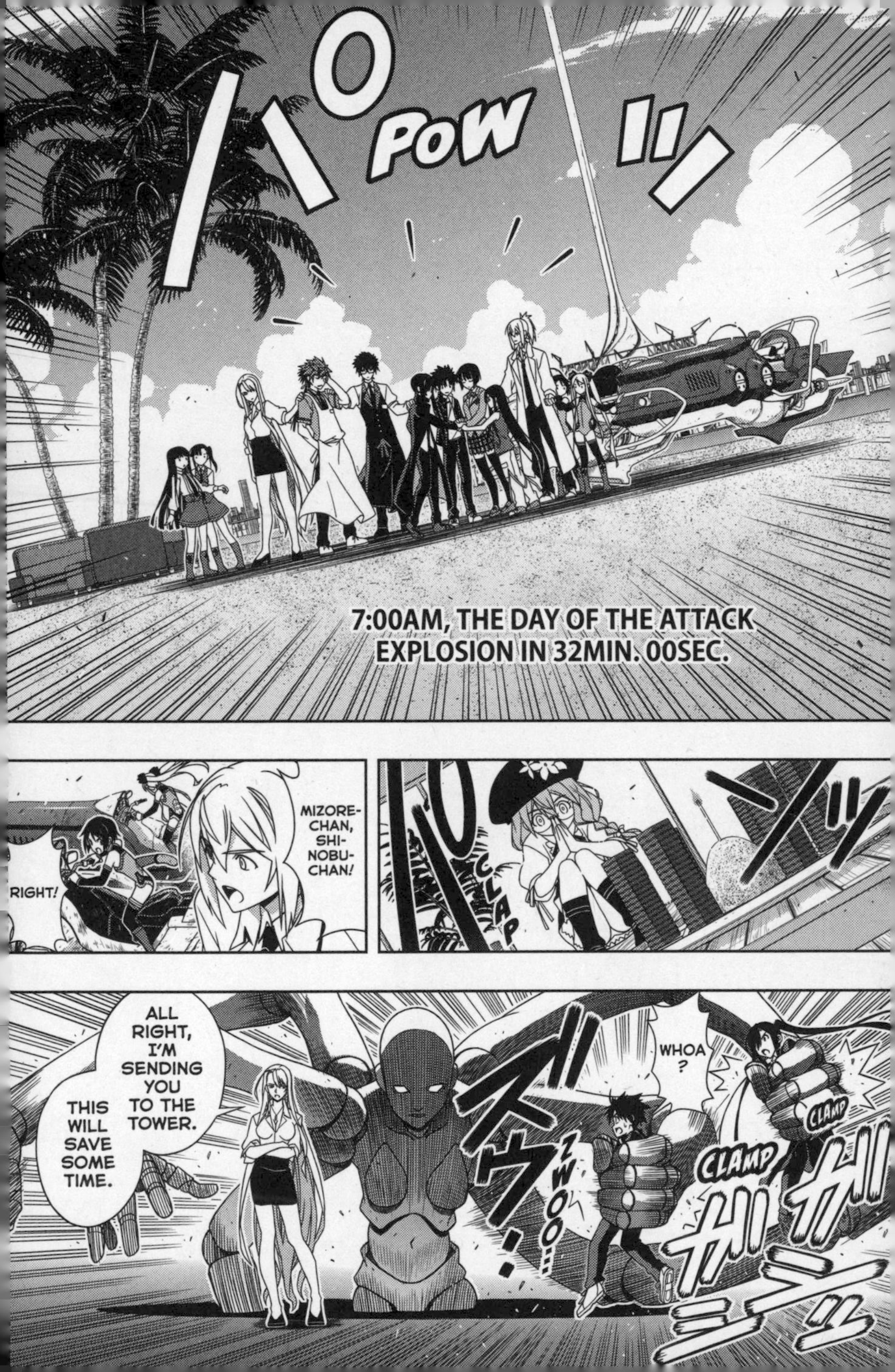
POW
7:00AM, THE DAY OF THE ATTACK
EXPLOSION IN 32MIN. 00SEC.
CLAP
MIZORE-CHAN, SHINOBU-CHAN!
RIGHT!
CLAMP
CLAMP
WHOA?
ZWOO...
ALL RIGHT, I'M SENDING YOU TO THE TOWER.
THIS WILL SAVE SOME TIME.

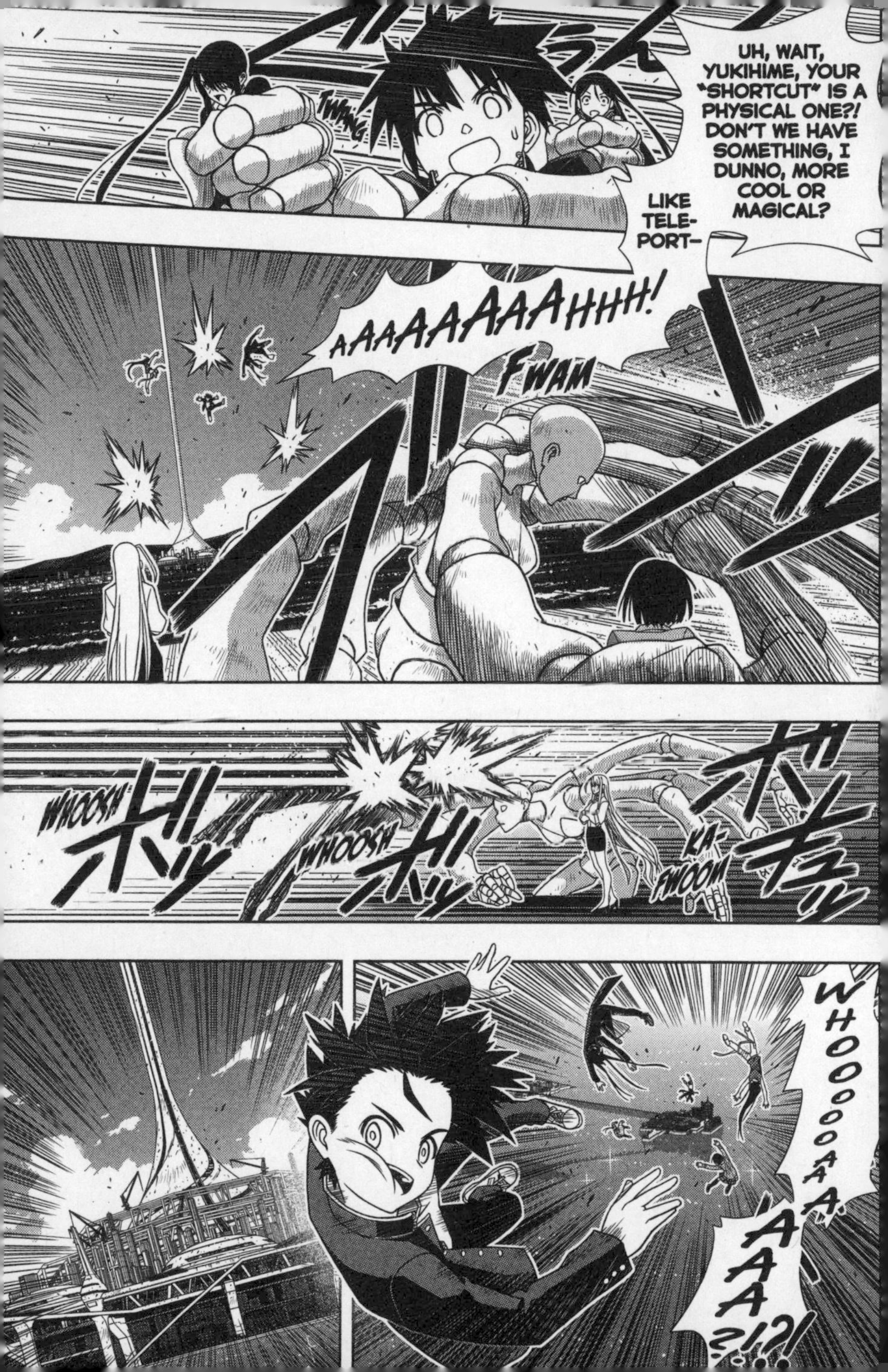
UH, WAIT, YUKIHIME, YOUR "SHORTCUT" IS A PHYSICAL ONE?! DON'T WE HAVE SOMETHING, I DUNNO, MORE COOL OR MAGICAL?
LIKE TELE-PORT–
TWANG
AAAAAAAAAHHHH!
FWAM
KA-FWOOM
WHOOSH
WHOOSH
WHOOOOOOOAAAAAAAA?!?!

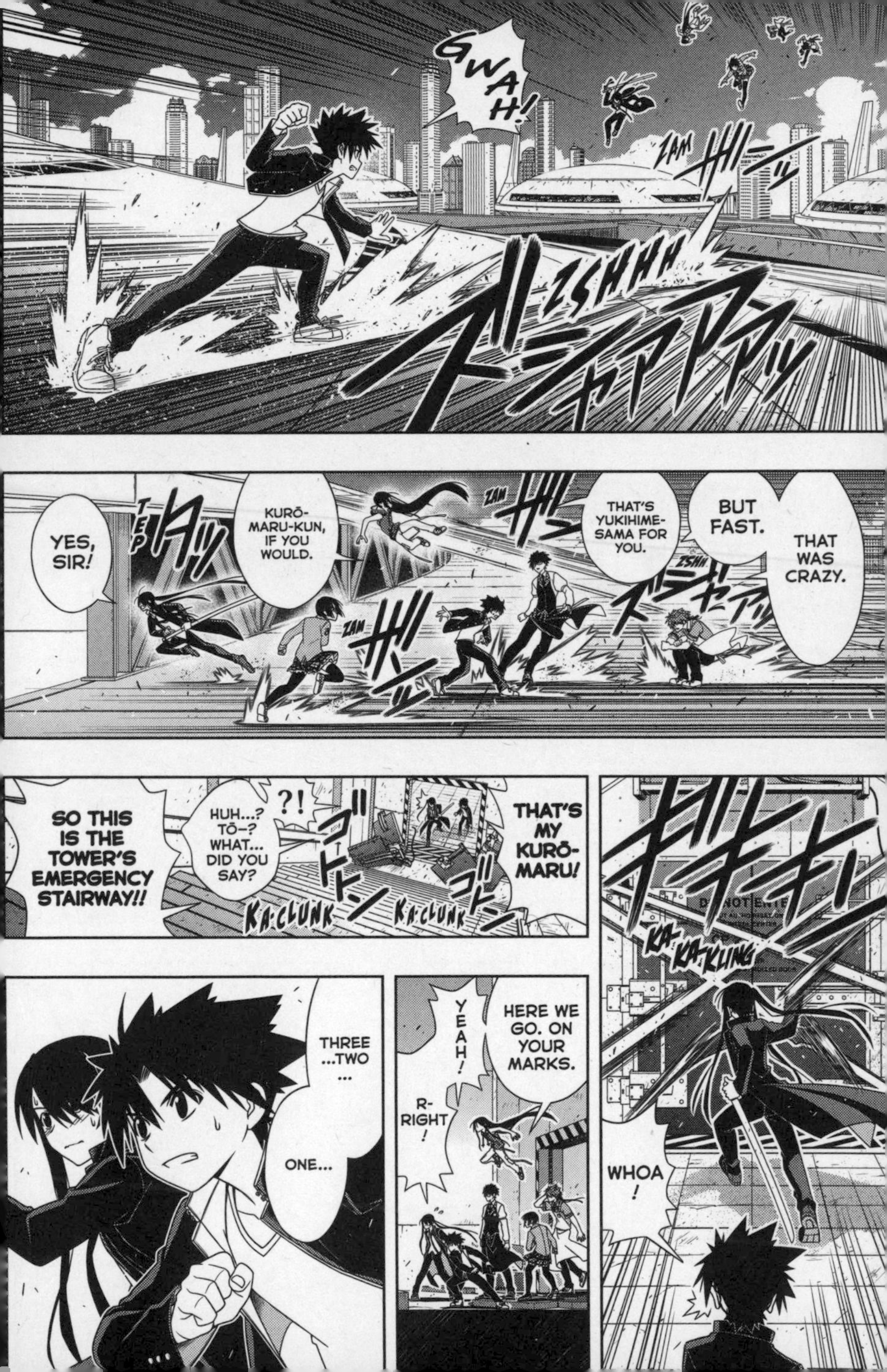
GWAH!
ZAM
ZSHHH
THAT WAS CRAZY.
BUT FAST.
THAT'S YUKIHIME-SAMA FOR YOU.
ZSHH
ZAM
KURŌ-MARU-KUN, IF YOU WOULD.
TEP
YES, SIR!
ZAM
KA-KA-KLING
DO NOT ENTER
WHOA!
THAT'S MY KURŌ-MARU!
?!
HUH...? TŌ–? WHAT... DID YOU SAY?
KA-CLUNK
KA-CLUNK
SO THIS IS THE TOWER'S EMERGENCY STAIRWAY!!
HERE WE GO. ON YOUR MARKS.
YEAH!
R-RIGHT!
THREE ...TWO ...
ONE...

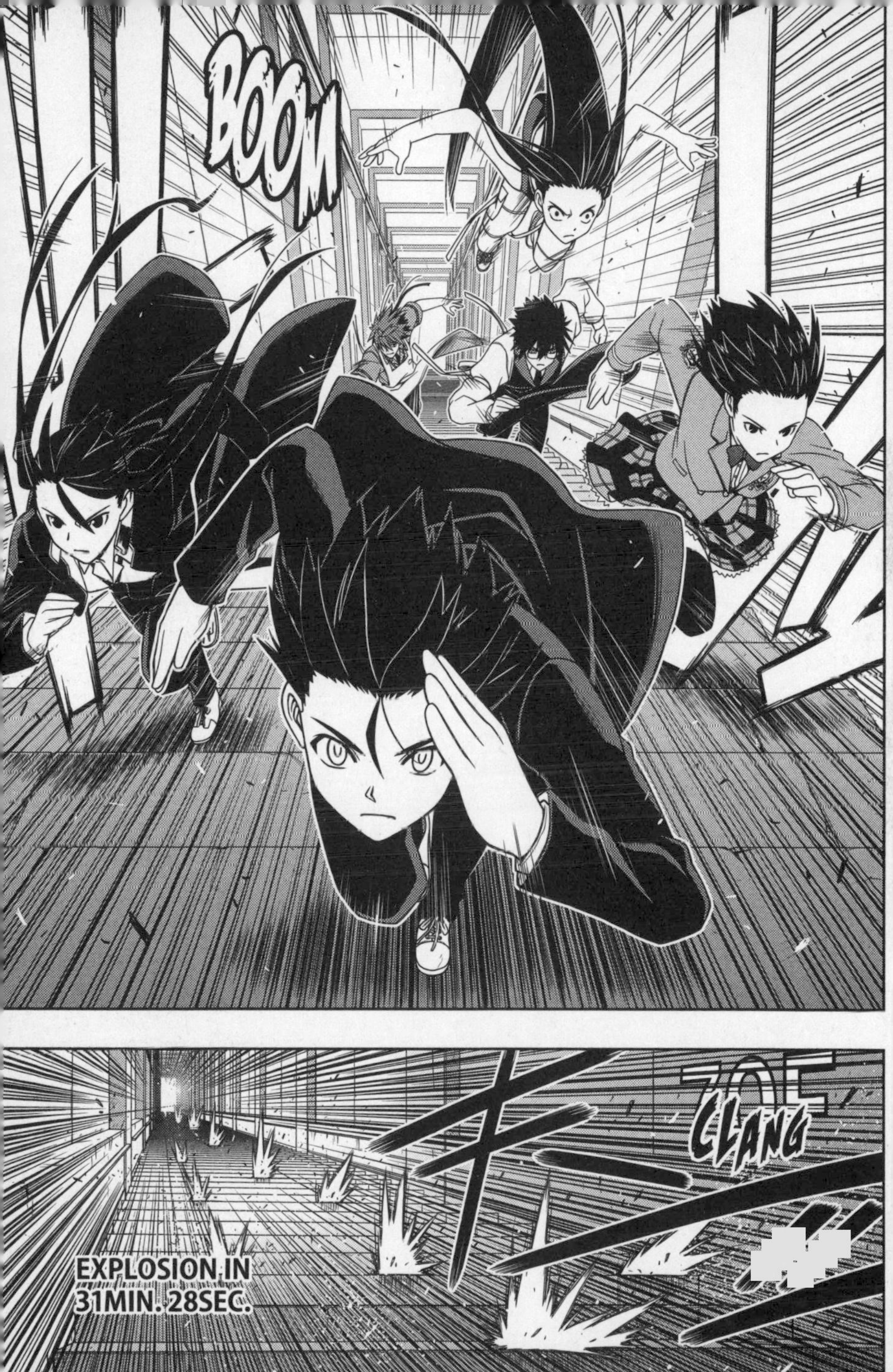
BOOM
CLANG
EXPLOSION IN
31MIN. 28SEC.

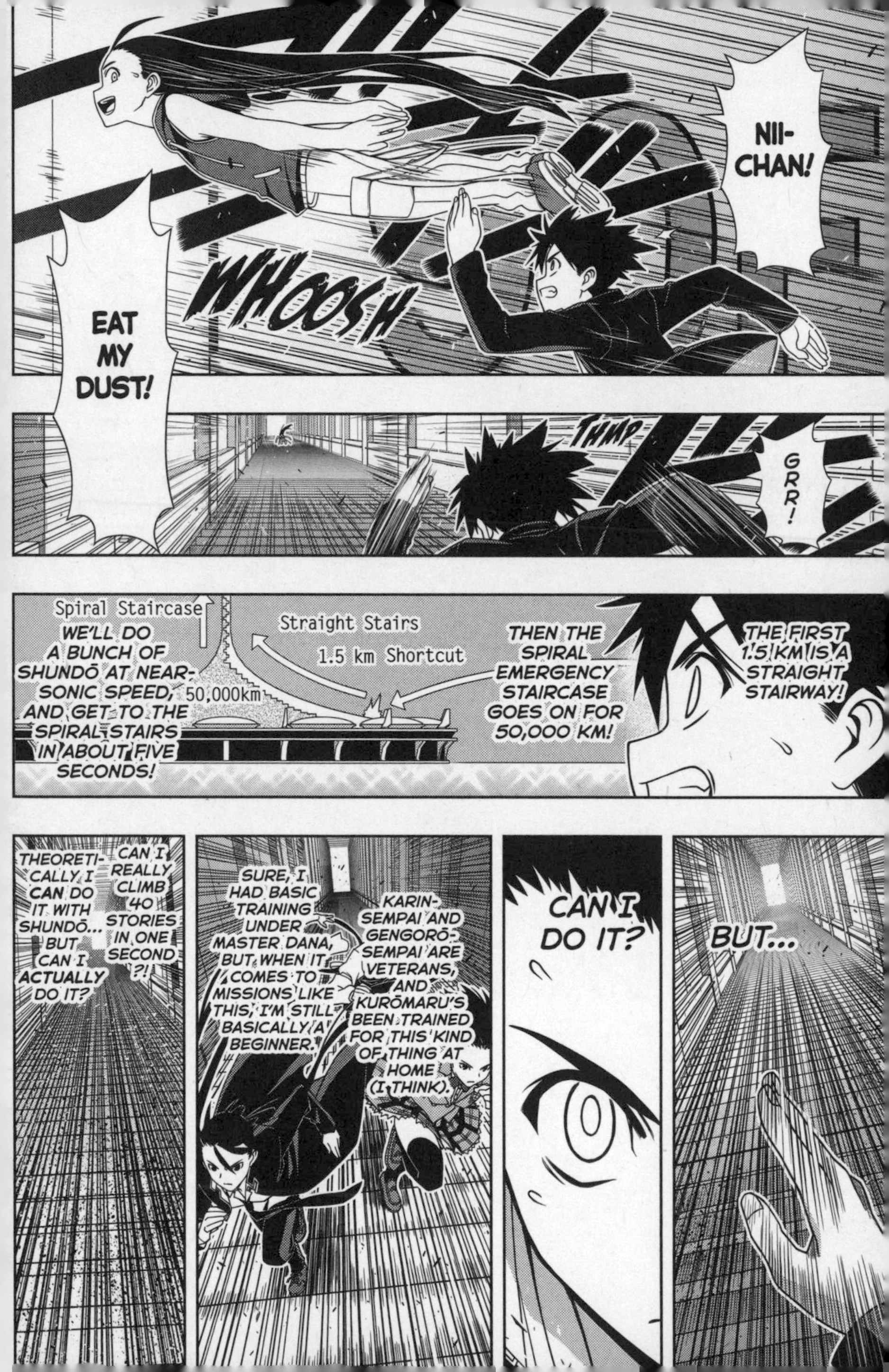
NII-CHAN!
WHOOSH
EAT MY DUST!
GRR!
THMP
THE FIRST 1.5 KM IS A STRAIGHT STAIRWAY!
THEN THE SPIRAL EMERGENCY STAIRCASE GOES ON FOR 50,000 KM!
Straight Stairs
1.5 km Shortcut
Spiral Staircase
50,000km
WE'LL DO A BUNCH OF SHUNDŌ AT NEAR-SONIC SPEED, AND GET TO THE SPIRAL STAIRS IN ABOUT FIVE SECONDS!
BUT...
CAN I DO IT?
KARIN-SEMPAI AND GENGORŌ-SEMPAI ARE VETERANS, AND KURŌMARU'S BEEN TRAINED FOR THIS KIND OF THING AT HOME (I THINK).
SURE, I HAD BASIC TRAINING UNDER MASTER DANA, BUT WHEN IT COMES TO MISSIONS LIKE THIS, I'M STILL BASICALLY A BEGINNER.
CAN I REALLY CLIMB 40 STORIES IN ONE SECOND?!
THEORETICALLY I CAN DO IT WITH SHUNDŌ... BUT CAN I ACTUALLY DO IT?

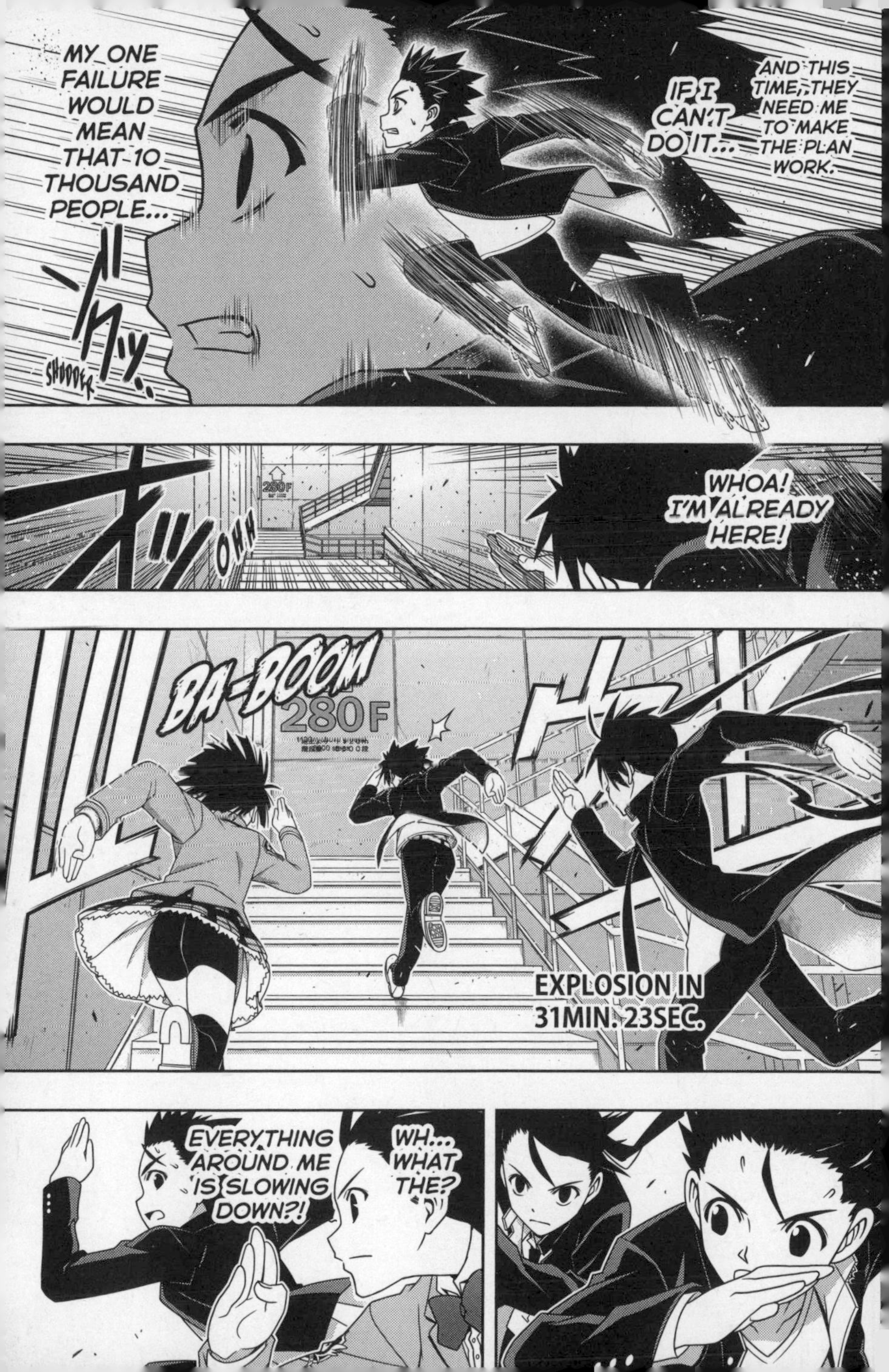

AND THIS TIME, THEY NEED ME TO MAKE THE PLAN WORK.
IF I CAN'T DO IT...
MY ONE FAILURE WOULD MEAN THAT 10 THOUSAND PEOPLE...
SHUDDER
280F
WHOA! I'M ALREADY HERE!
BA-BOOM
280F
EXPLOSION IN 31MIN. 23SEC.
WH... WHAT THE?
EVERYTHING AROUND ME IS SLOWING DOWN?!

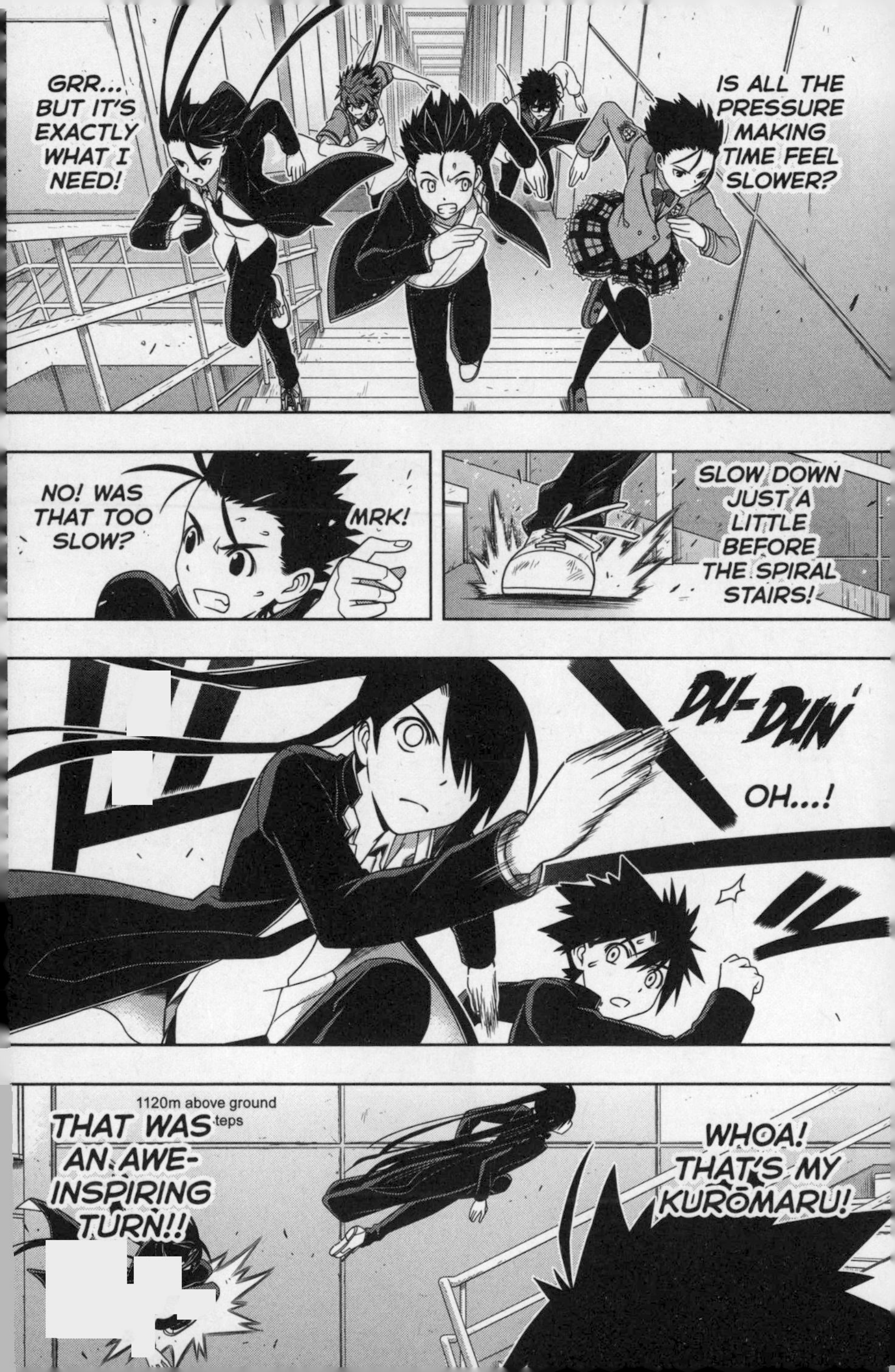
IS ALL THE PRESSURE MAKING TIME FEEL SLOWER?
GRR... BUT IT'S EXACTLY WHAT I NEED!
SLOW DOWN JUST A LITTLE BEFORE THE SPIRAL STAIRS!
MRK!
NO! WAS THAT TOO SLOW?
DU-DUN
OH...!
WHOA! THAT'S MY KUROMARU!
1120m above ground
THAT WAS AN AWE-INSPIRING TURN!!

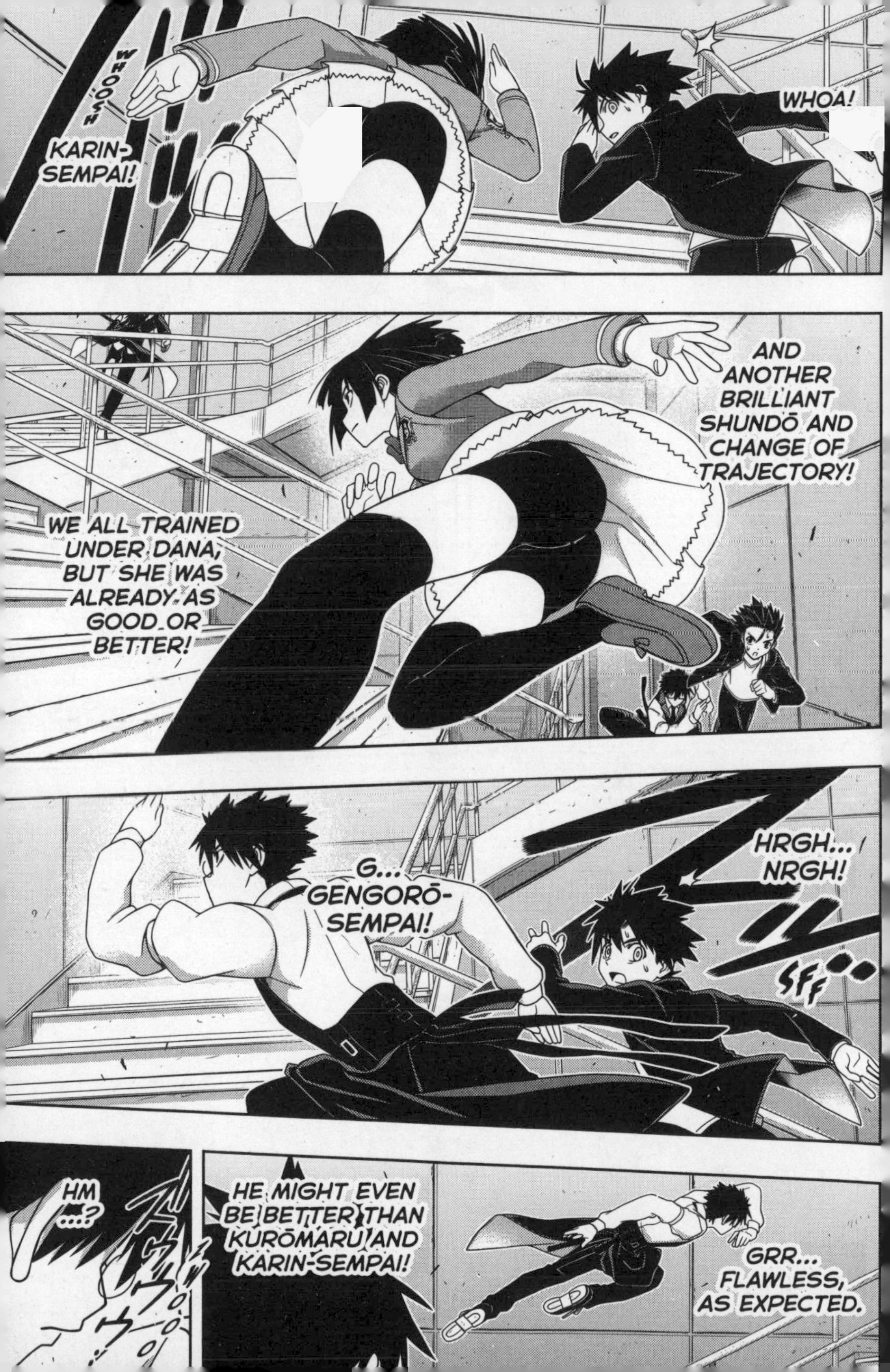
WHOA!
WHOOSH
KARIN-SEMPAI!
AND ANOTHER BRILLIANT SHUNDŌ AND CHANGE OF TRAJECTORY!
WE ALL TRAINED UNDER DANA, BUT SHE WAS ALREADY AS GOOD OR BETTER!
HRGH... NRGH!
SFF
G... GENGORŌ-SEMPAI!
GRR... FLAWLESS, AS EXPECTED.
HE MIGHT EVEN BE BETTER THAN KURŌMARU AND KARIN-SEMPAI!
HM ...?

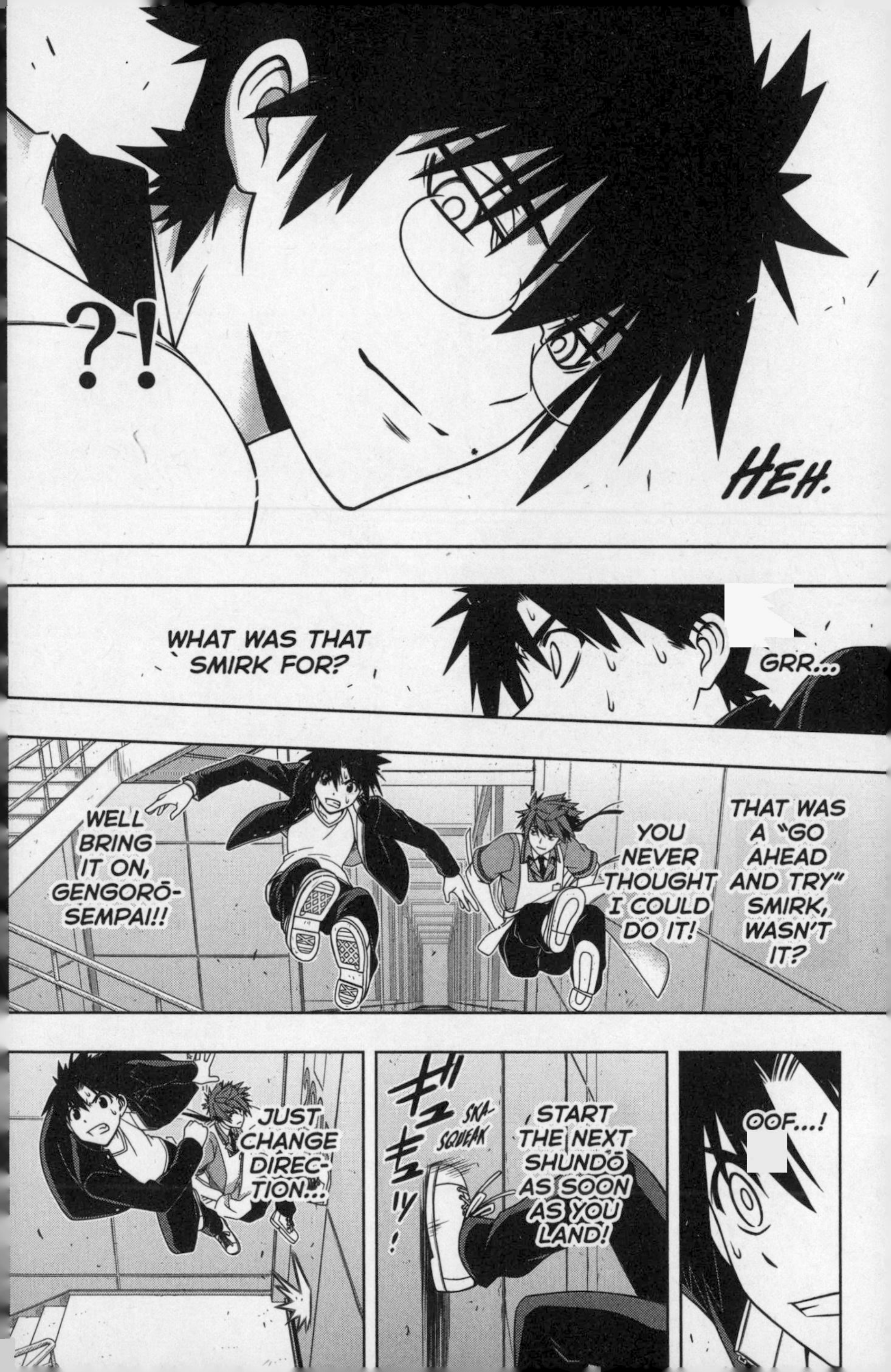
HEH.
?!
GRR...
WHAT WAS THAT SMIRK FOR?
THAT WAS A "GO AHEAD AND TRY" SMIRK, WASN'T IT?
YOU NEVER THOUGHT I COULD DO IT!
WELL BRING IT ON, GENGORŌ-SEMPAI!!
OOF...!
START THE NEXT SHUNDŌ AS SOON AS YOU LAND!
SKA-SQUEAK
JUST CHANGE DIRECTION...

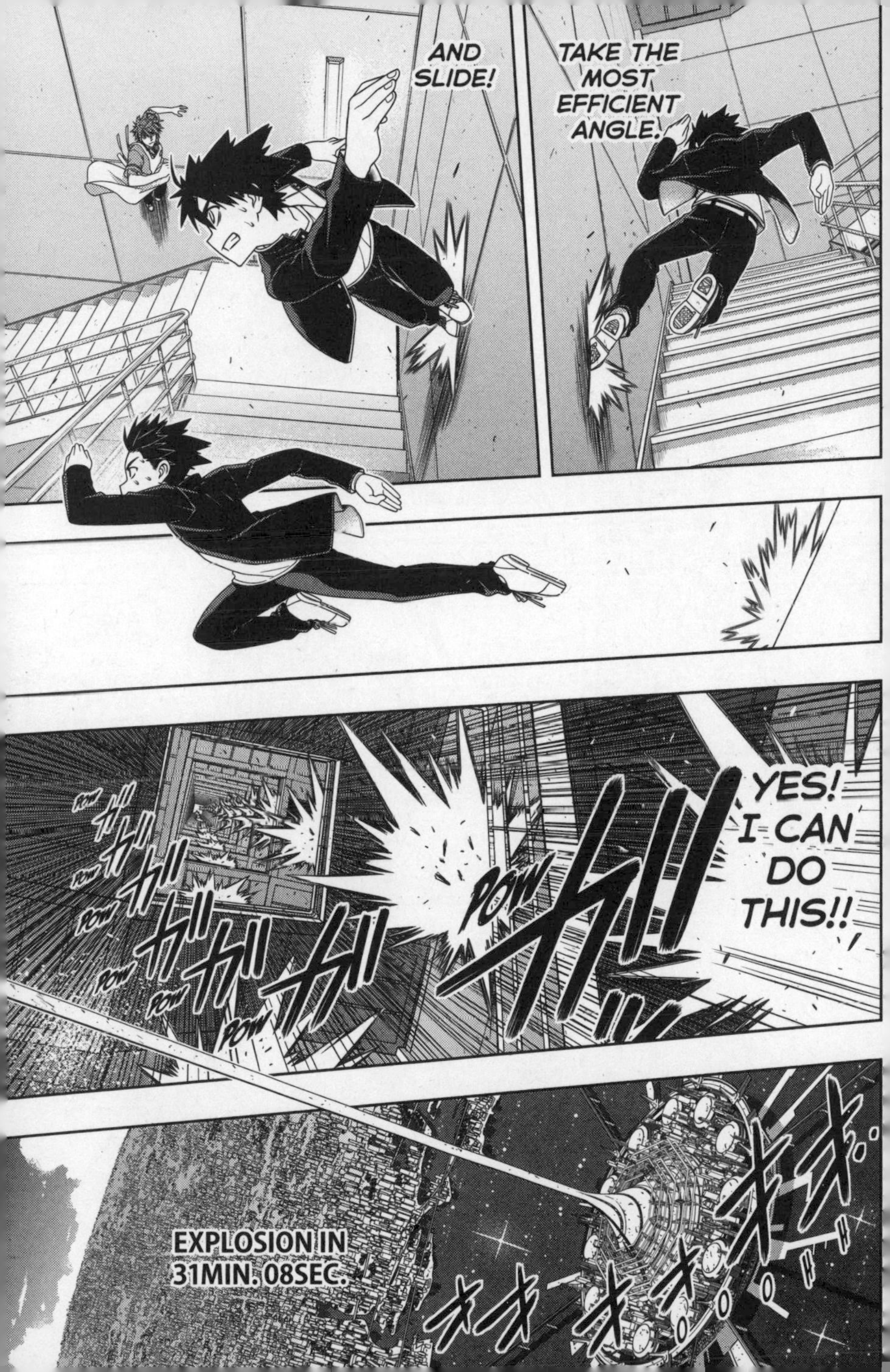
TAKE THE MOST EFFICIENT ANGLE.
AND SLIDE!
YES! I CAN DO THIS!!
POW
POW
POW
POW
POW
POW
POW
EXPLOSION IN 31MIN. 08SEC.

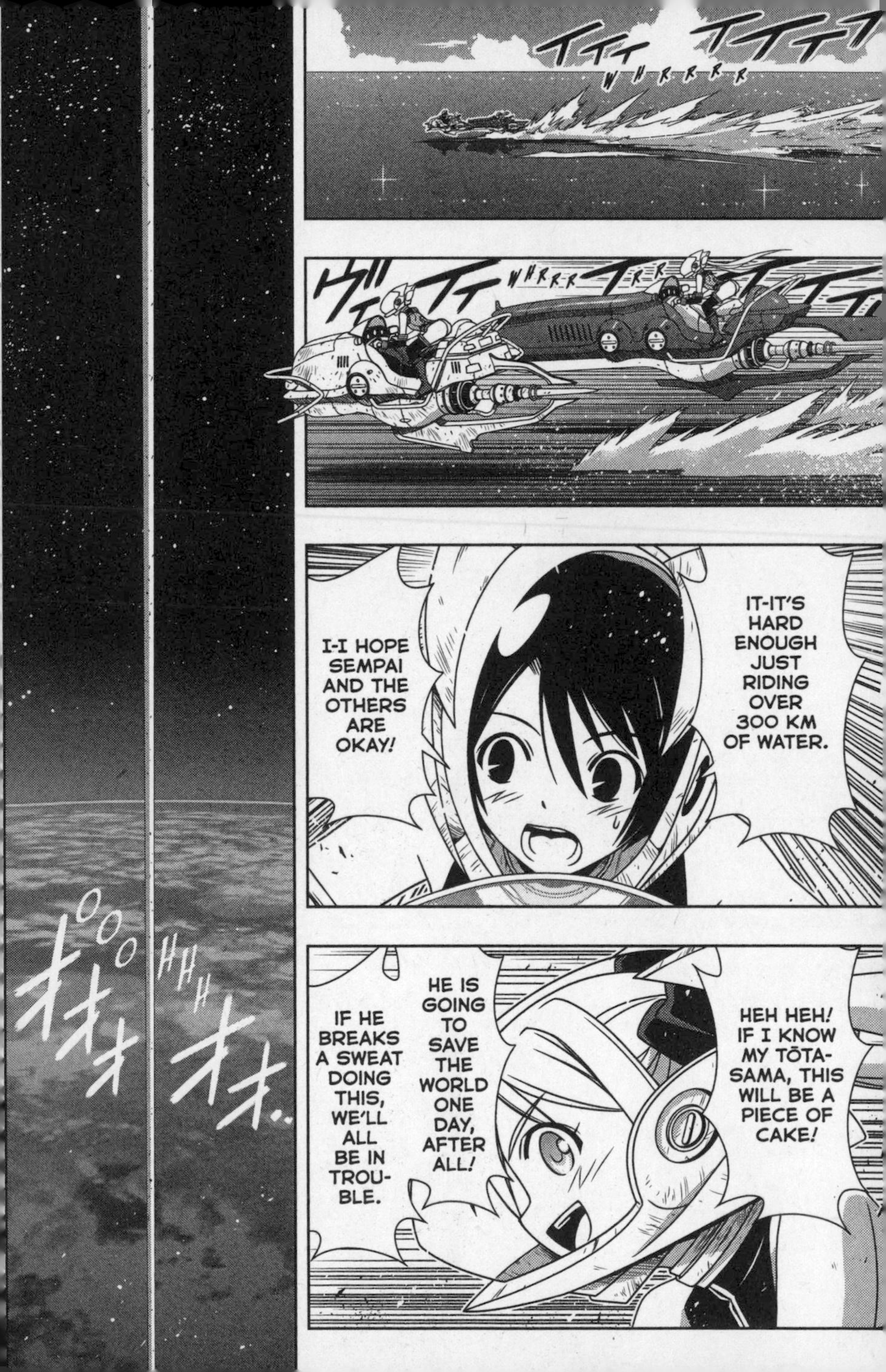
WHRRRRR
WHRR-R-R
R-R-R
IT-IT'S HARD ENOUGH JUST RIDING OVER 300 KM OF WATER.
I-I HOPE SEMPAI AND THE OTHERS ARE OKAY!
HEH HEH! IF I KNOW MY TŌTA-SAMA, THIS WILL BE A PIECE OF CAKE!
HE IS GOING TO SAVE THE WORLD ONE DAY, AFTER ALL!
IF HE BREAKS A SWEAT DOING THIS, WE'LL ALL BE IN TROU-BLE.
OOO
HHHH

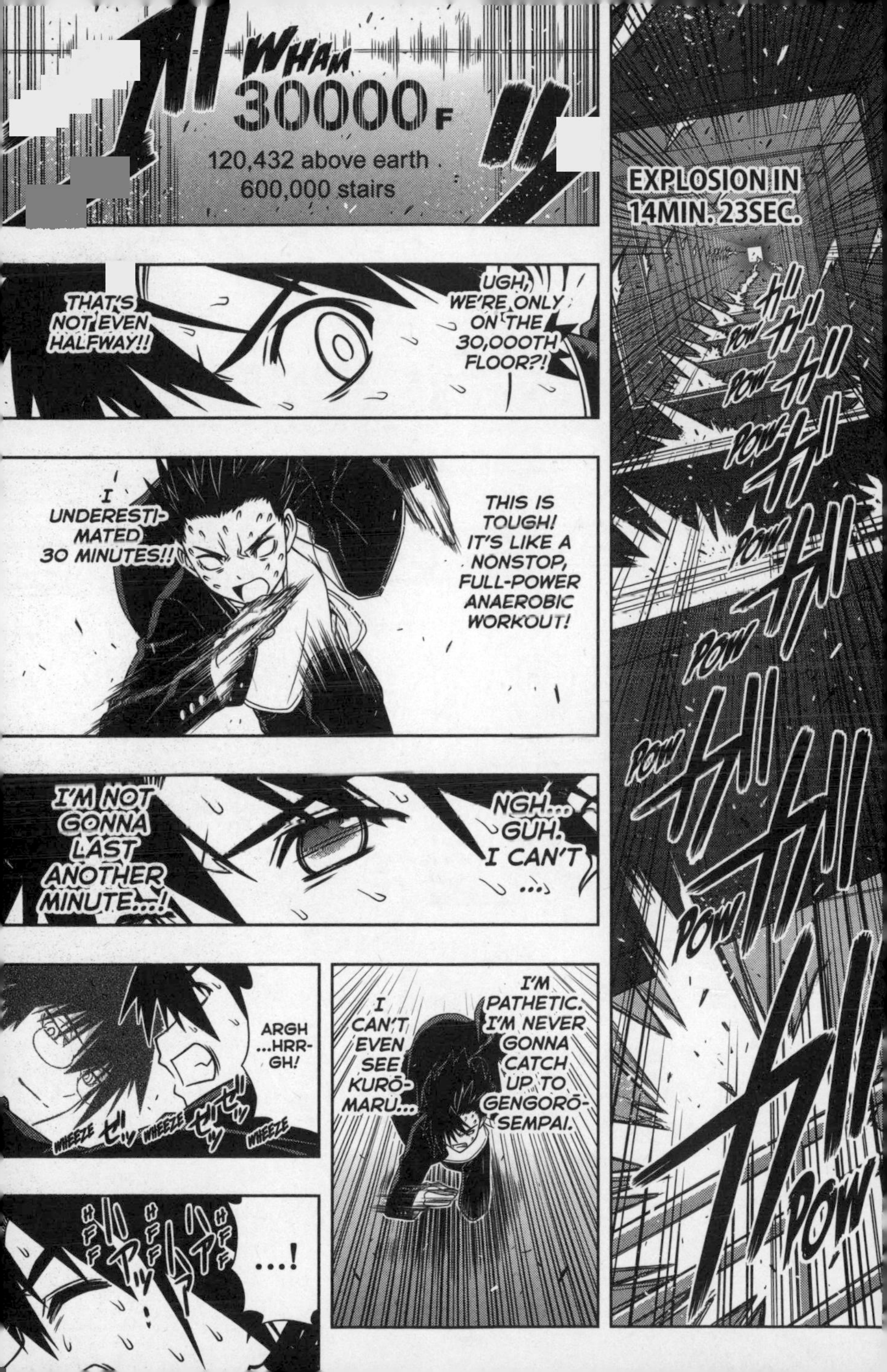
EXPLOSION IN 14MIN. 23SEC.
POW POW POW POW POW POW POW POW POW
WHAM
30000F
120,432 above earth
600,000 stairs
UGH, WE'RE ONLY ON THE 30,000TH FLOOR?!
THAT'S NOT EVEN HALFWAY!!
THIS IS TOUGH! IT'S LIKE A NONSTOP, FULL-POWER ANAEROBIC WORKOUT!
I UNDERESTIMATED 30 MINUTES!!
NGH... GUH. I CAN'T ...
I'M NOT GONNA LAST ANOTHER MINUTE...!
I'M PATHETIC. I'M NEVER GONNA CATCH UP TO GENGORŌ-SEMPAI.
I CAN'T EVEN SEE KURŌMARU...
ARGH ...HRR-GH!
WHEEZE WHEEZE WHEEZE
...!
HFF HFF HFF

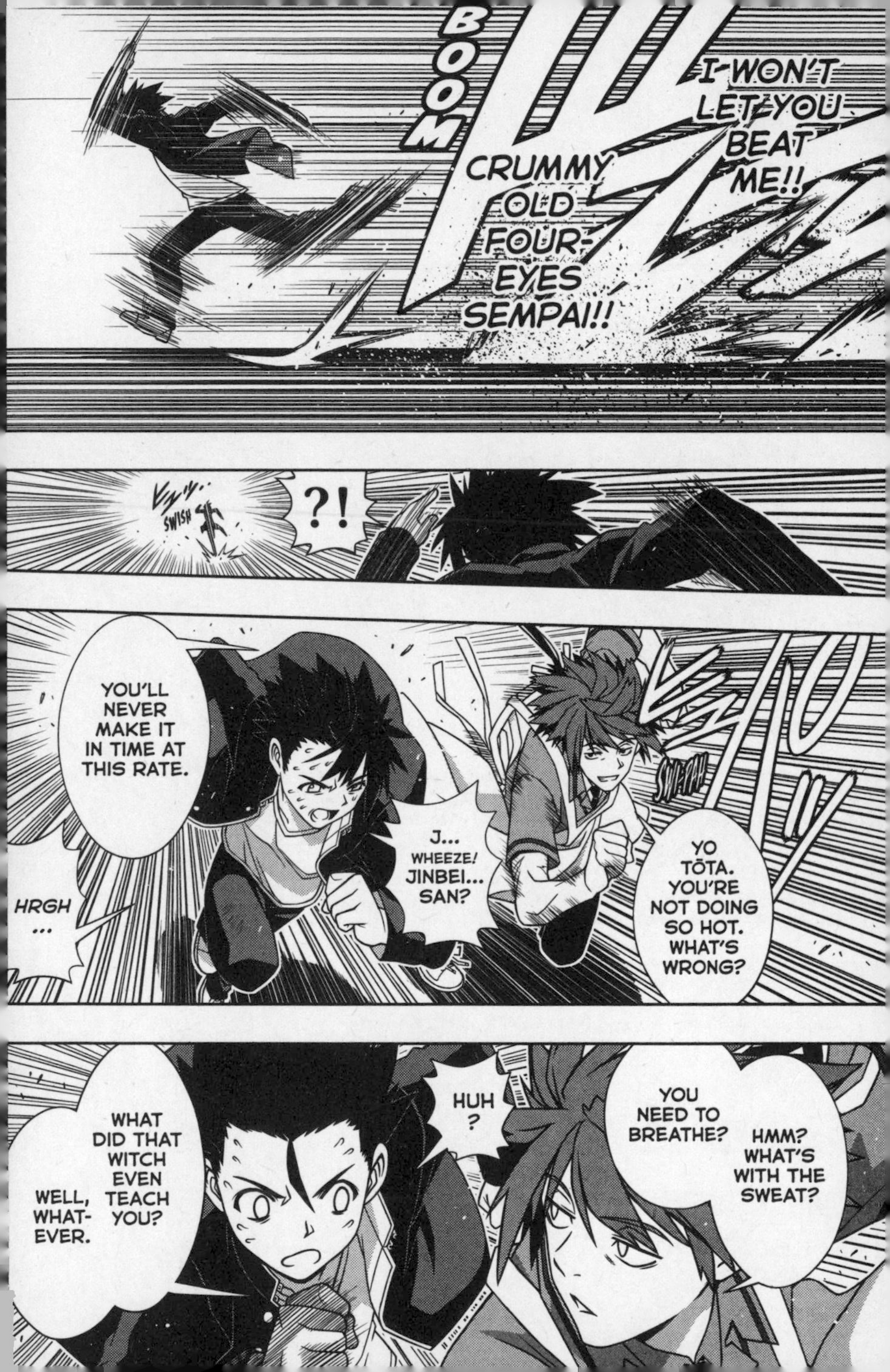
I WON'T LET YOU BEAT ME!!
CRUMMY OLD FOUR-EYES SEMPAI!!
BOOM
?!
SWISH
YO TŌTA. YOU'RE NOT DOING SO HOT. WHAT'S WRONG?
J... WHEEZE! JINBEI... SAN?
YOU'LL NEVER MAKE IT IN TIME AT THIS RATE.
HRGH ...
HMM? WHAT'S WITH THE SWEAT?
YOU NEED TO BREATHE?
HUH?
WHAT DID THAT WITCH EVEN TEACH YOU?
WELL, WHAT-EVER.

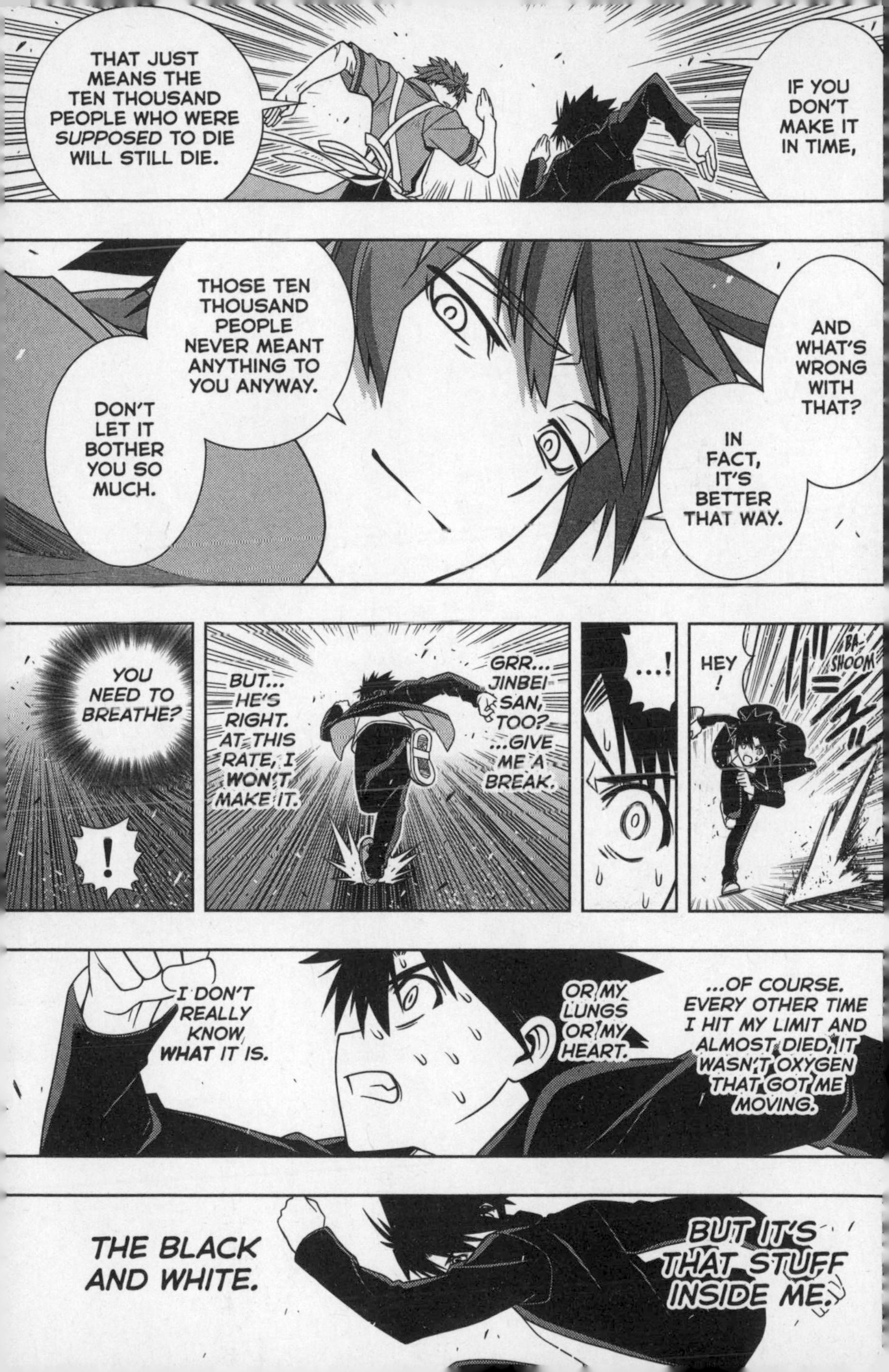
IF YOU DON'T MAKE IT IN TIME,
THAT JUST MEANS THE TEN THOUSAND PEOPLE WHO WERE *SUPPOSED* TO DIE WILL STILL DIE.
AND WHAT'S WRONG WITH THAT?
IN FACT, IT'S BETTER THAT WAY.
THOSE TEN THOUSAND PEOPLE NEVER MEANT ANYTHING TO YOU ANYWAY.
DON'T LET IT BOTHER YOU SO MUCH.
HEY!
BA-SHOOM
...!
GRR... JINBEI-SAN, TOO? ...GIVE ME A BREAK.
BUT... HE'S RIGHT. AT THIS RATE, I WON'T MAKE IT.
YOU NEED TO BREATHE?
!
...OF COURSE. EVERY OTHER TIME I HIT MY LIMIT AND ALMOST DIED, IT WASN'T OXYGEN THAT GOT ME MOVING.
OR MY LUNGS OR MY HEART.
I DON'T REALLY KNOW WHAT IT IS.
BUT IT'S THAT STUFF INSIDE ME.
THE BLACK AND WHITE.

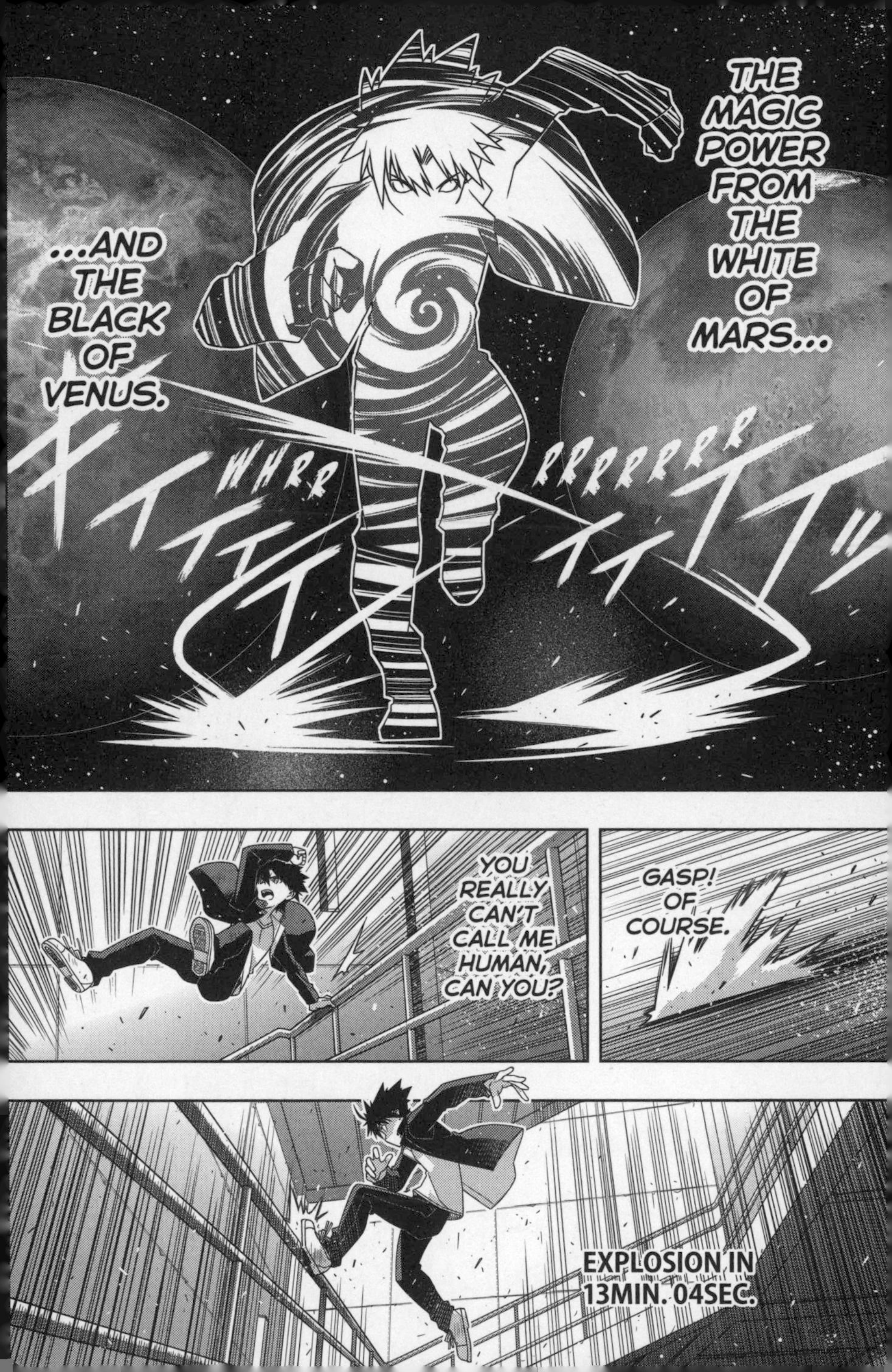
THE MAGIC POWER FROM THE WHITE OF MARS...
...AND THE BLACK OF VENUS.
WHRR RRRRRRR
GASP! OF COURSE.
YOU REALLY CAN'T CALL ME HUMAN, CAN YOU?
EXPLOSION IN 13MIN. 04SEC.

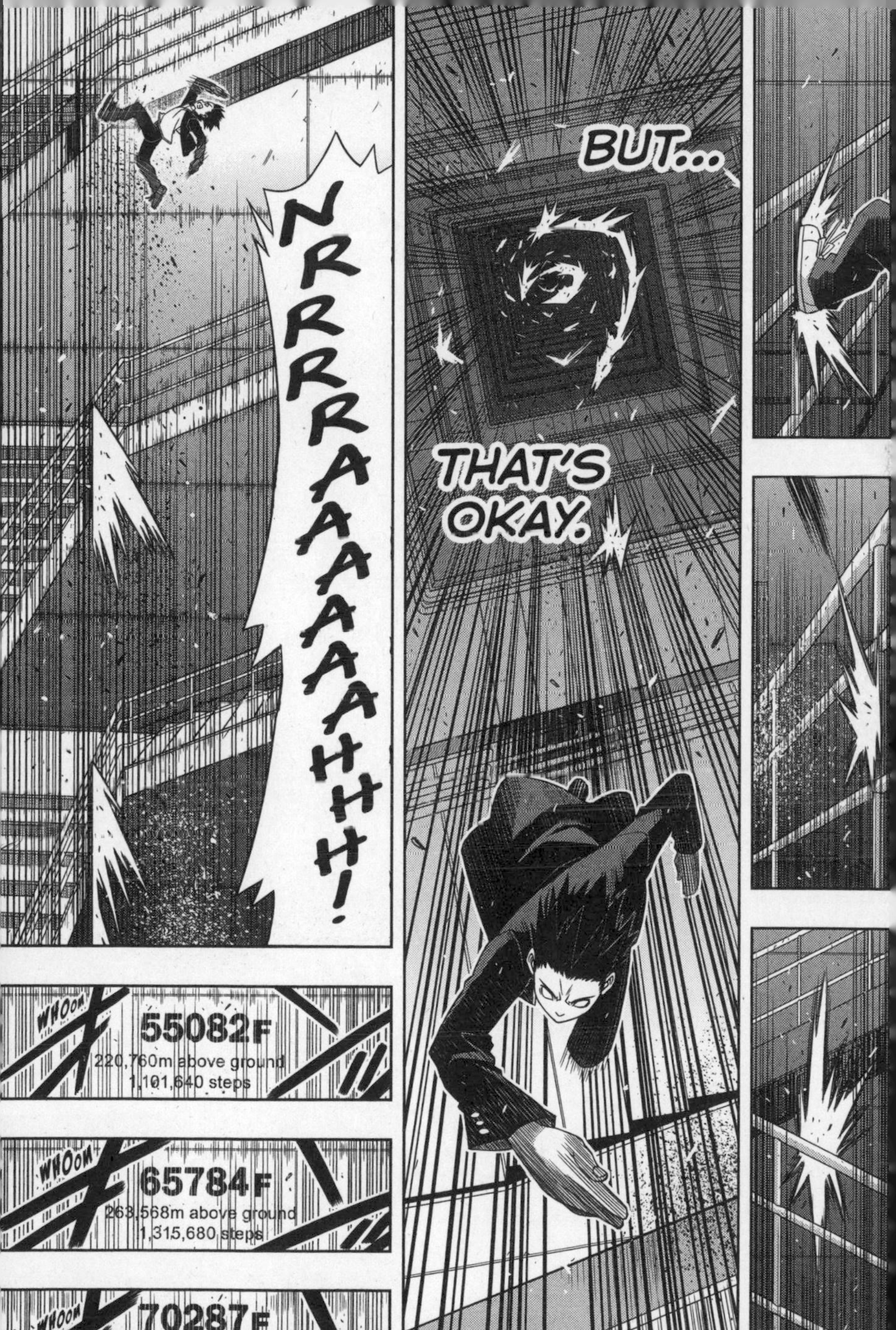
BUT...
THAT'S OKAY.
NRRRAAAAAAHHH!
WHOOM
55082F
220,760m above ground
1,101,640 steps
WHOOM
65784F
263,568m above ground
1,315,680 steps
WHOOM
70287F
281,580m above ground
1,405,740 steps

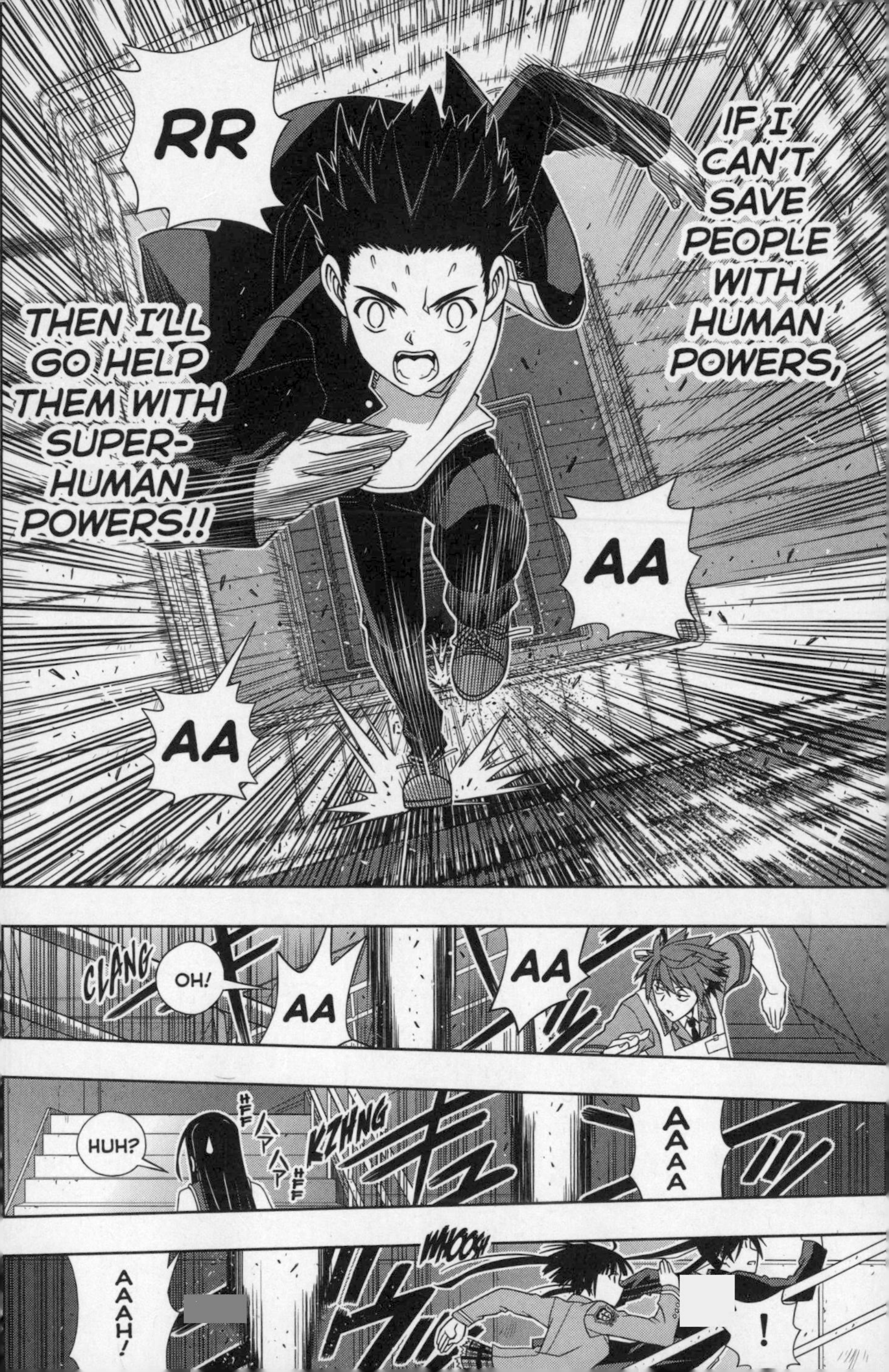
IF I CAN'T SAVE PEOPLE WITH HUMAN POWERS,
RR
THEN I'LL GO HELP THEM WITH SUPER-HUMAN POWERS!!
AA
AA
AA
AA
OH!
CLANG
AAAA
KZHNG
HFF HFF
HUH?
WHOOSH
!
AAAH!

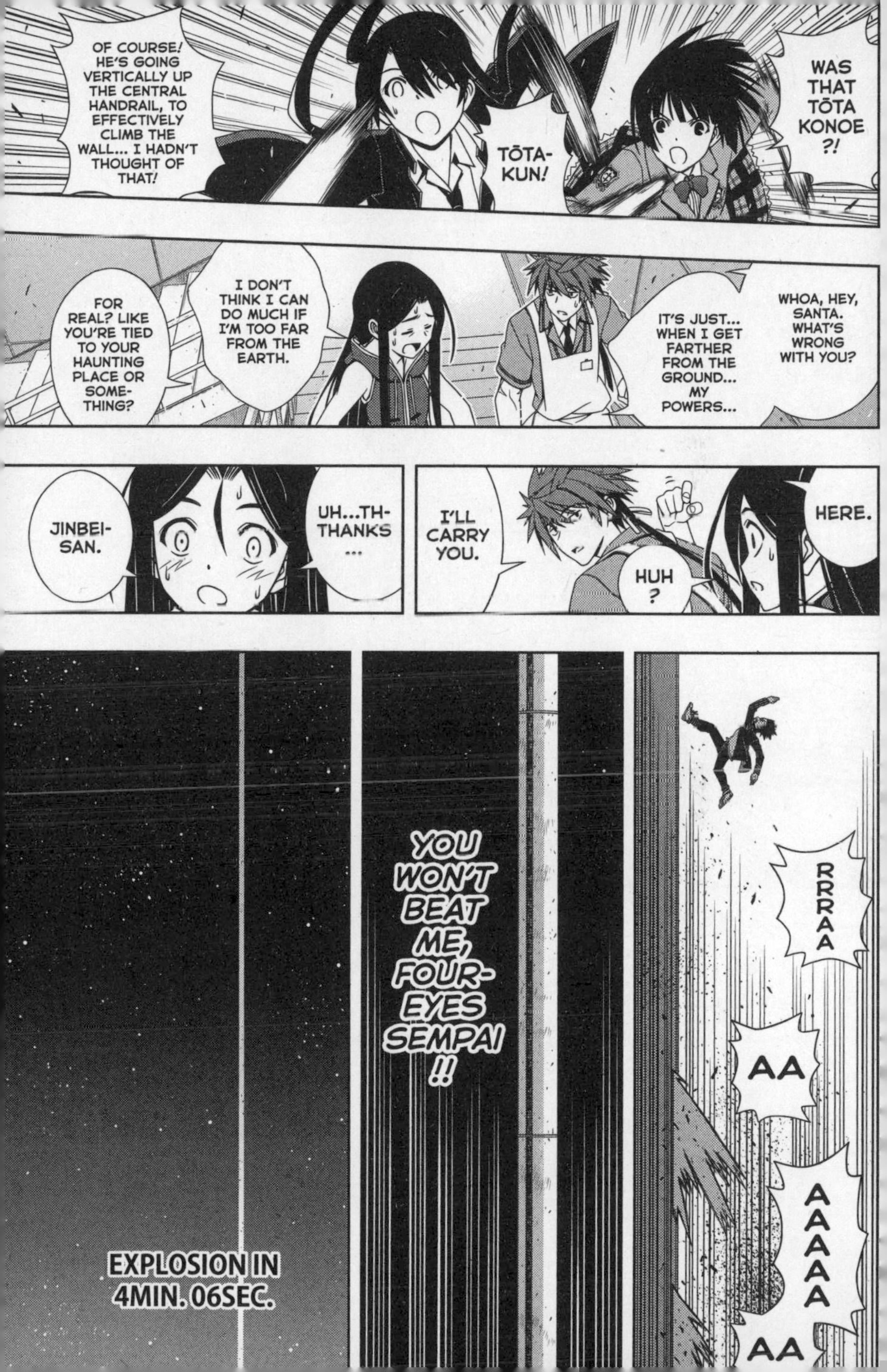
WAS THAT TŌTA KONOE?!
TŌTA-KUN!
OF COURSE! HE'S GOING VERTICALLY UP THE CENTRAL HANDRAIL, TO EFFECTIVELY CLIMB THE WALL... I HADN'T THOUGHT OF THAT!
WHOA, HEY, SANTA. WHAT'S WRONG WITH YOU?
IT'S JUST... WHEN I GET FARTHER FROM THE GROUND... MY POWERS...
I DON'T THINK I CAN DO MUCH IF I'M TOO FAR FROM THE EARTH.
FOR REAL? LIKE YOU'RE TIED TO YOUR HAUNTING PLACE OR SOME-THING?
HERE.
HUH?
I'LL CARRY YOU.
UH...TH-THANKS...
JINBEI-SAN.
RRRAA
AA
AAAAA
AA
YOU WON'T BEAT ME, FOUR-EYES SEMPAI!!
EXPLOSION IN 4MIN. 06SEC.

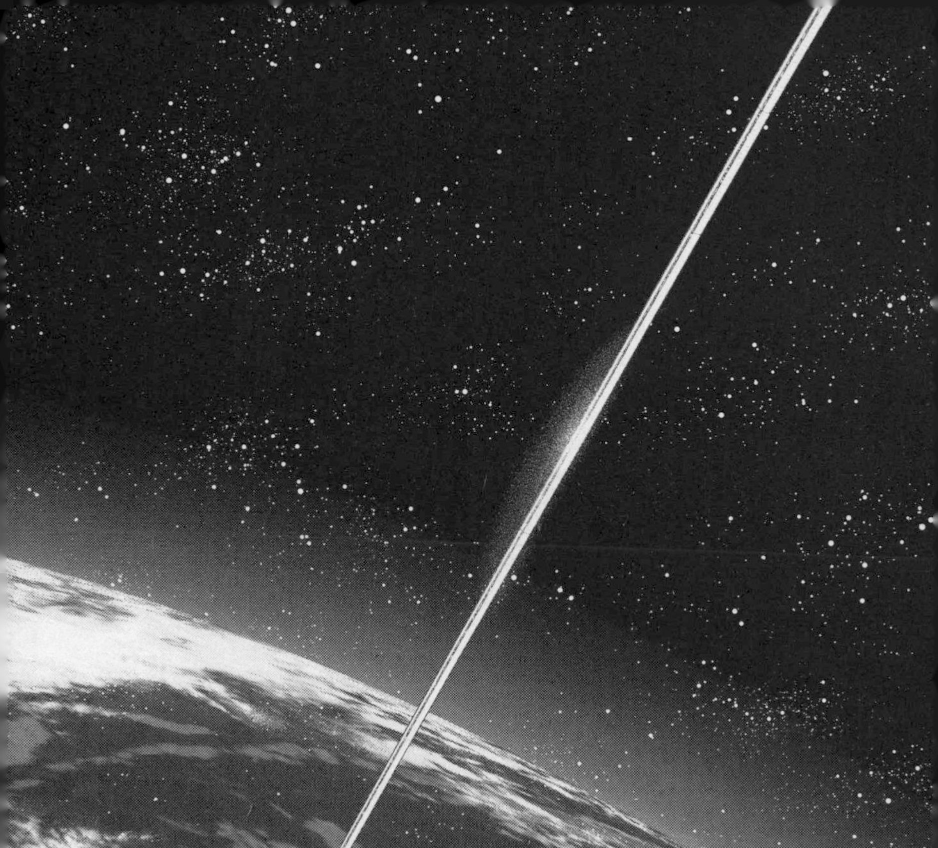
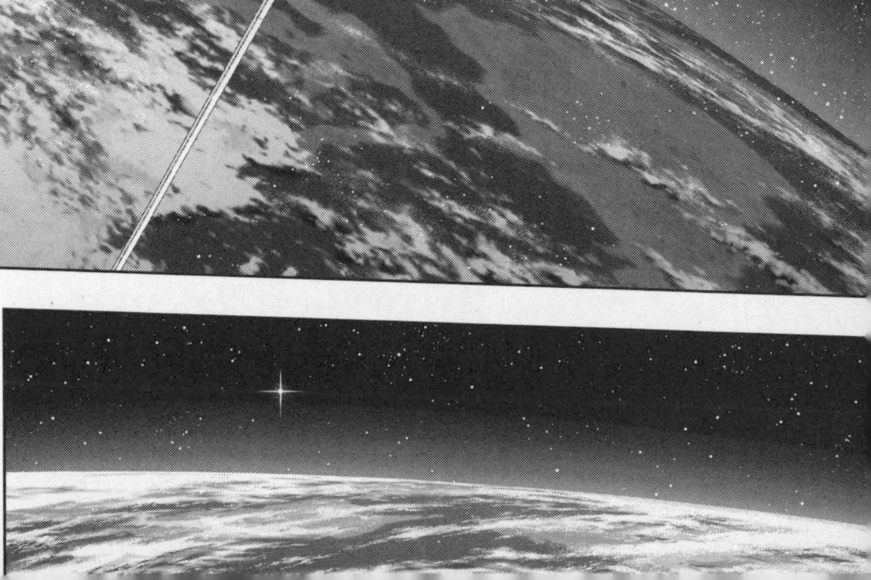

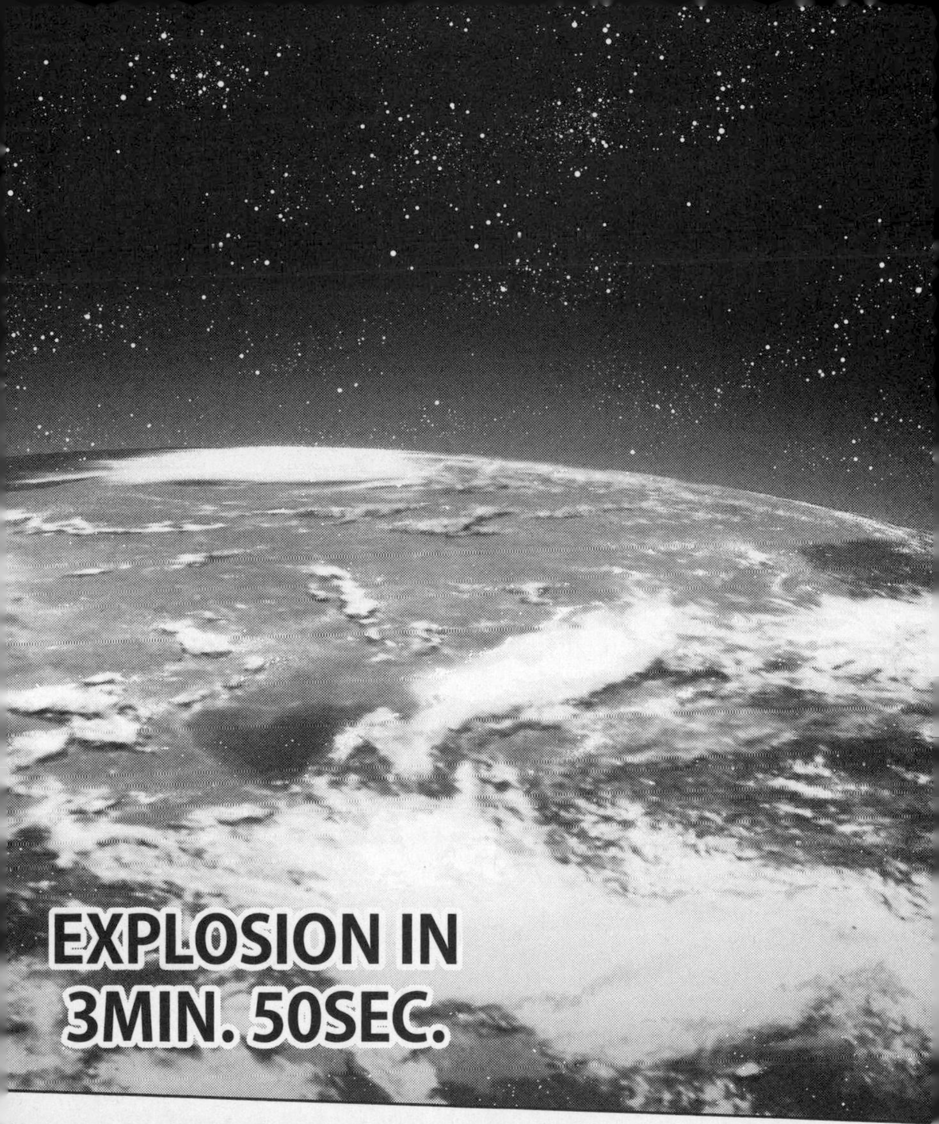
EXPLOSION IN
3MIN. 50SEC.
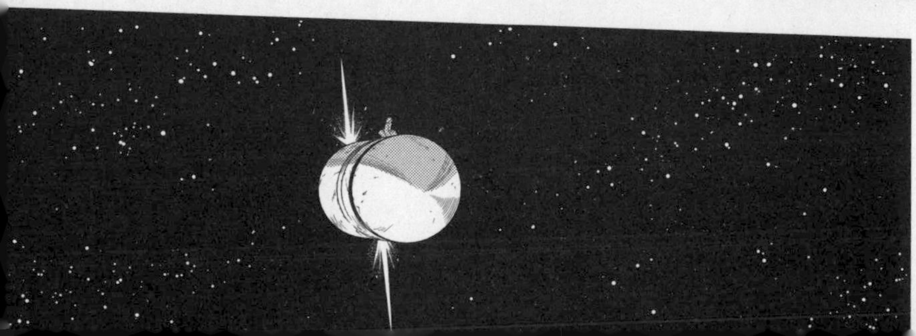

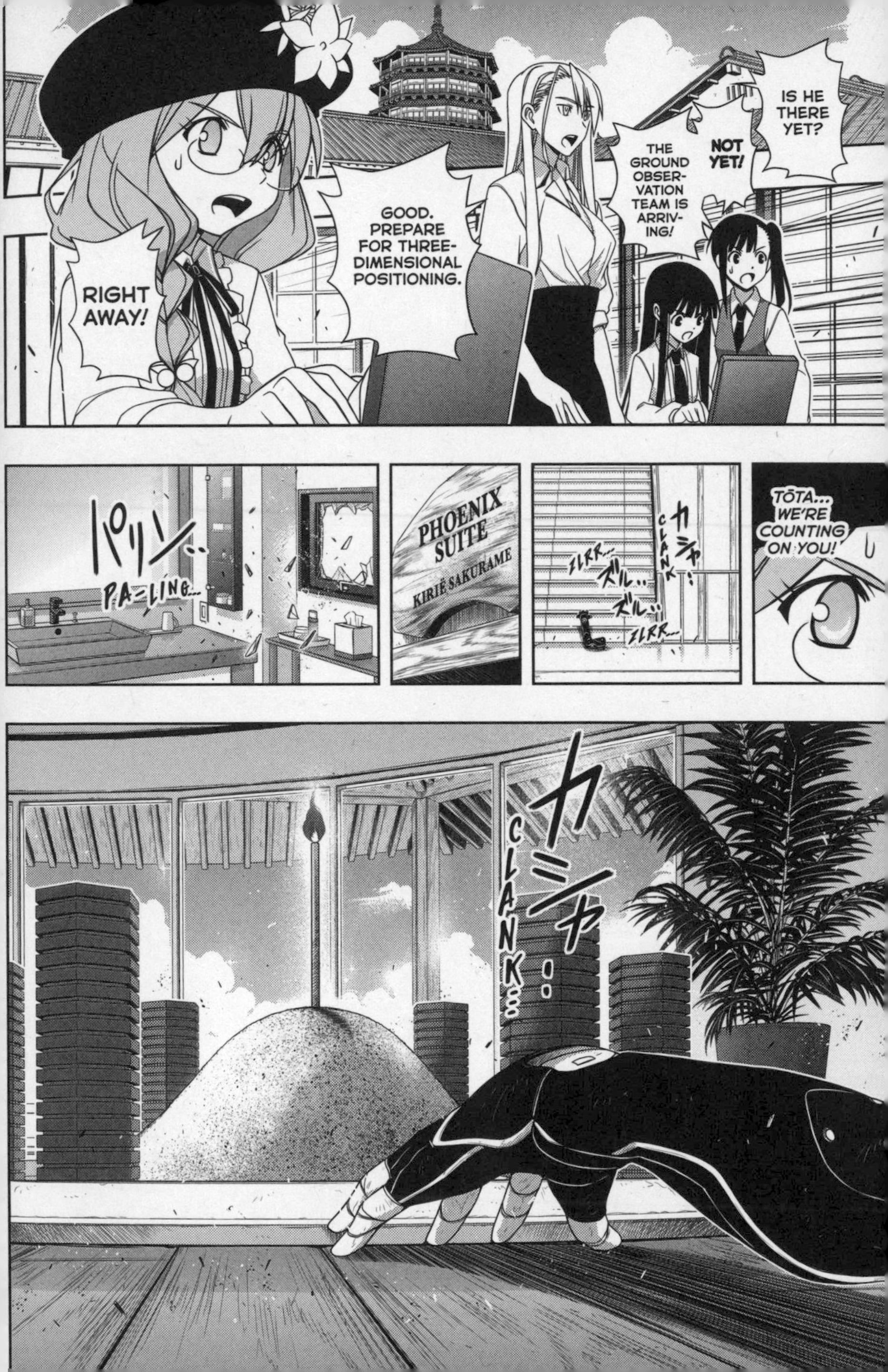
IS HE THERE YET?
NOT YET!
THE GROUND OBSERVATION TEAM IS ARRIVING!
GOOD. PREPARE FOR THREE-DIMENSIONAL POSITIONING.
RIGHT AWAY!
TŌTA... WE'RE COUNTING ON YOU!
カシャ!
CLANK!
ズル.. ズル..
ZLRR... ZLRR...
PHOENIX SUITE
KIRIÉ SAKURAME
パリン..
PA-LING...
カシャ..
CLANK...

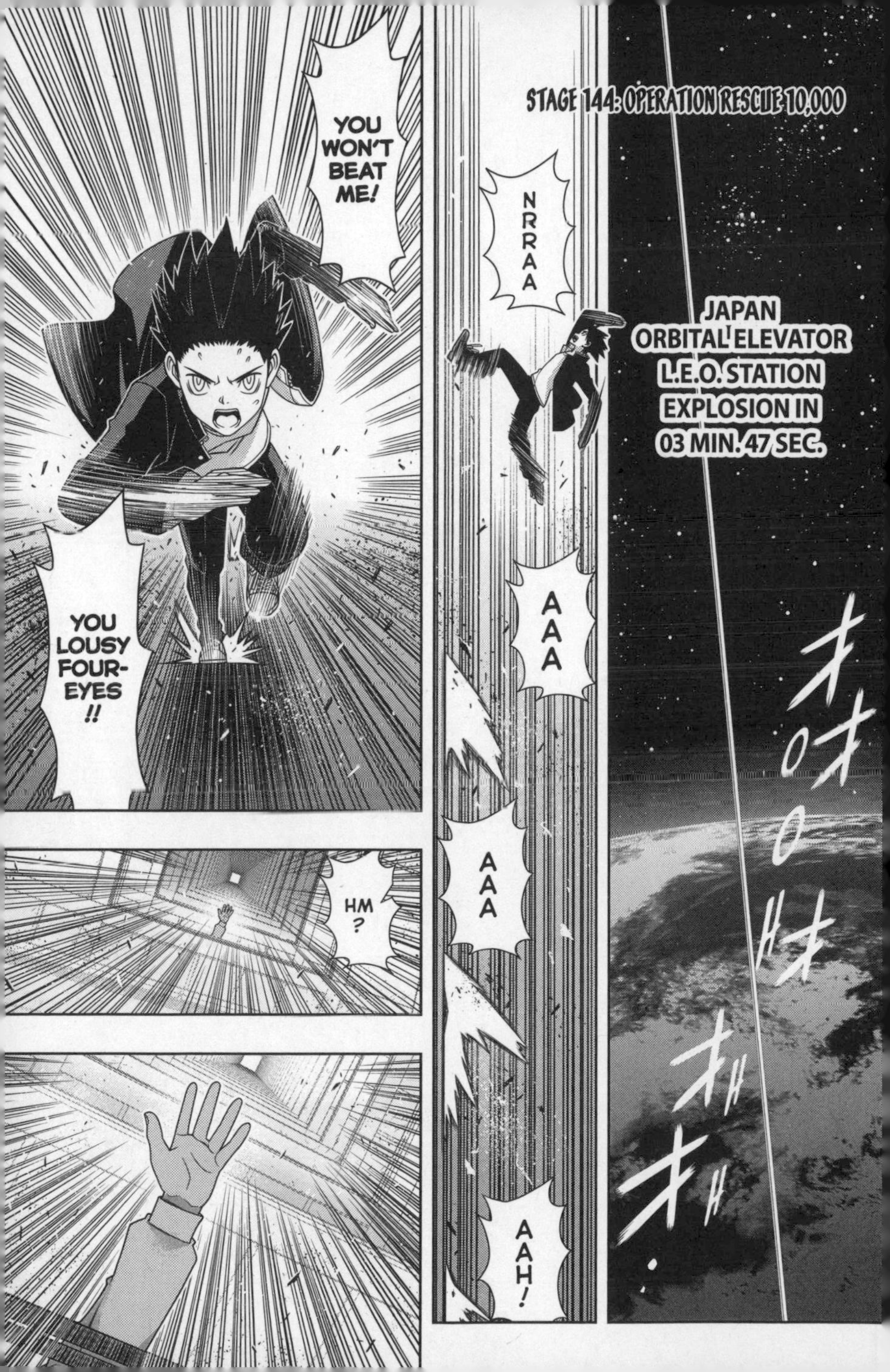
STAGE 144: OPERATION RESCUE 10,000
JAPAN ORBITAL ELEVATOR L.E.O. STATION EXPLOSION IN 03 MIN. 47 SEC.
NRRAA
AAA
AAA
AAH!
YOU WON'T BEAT ME!
YOU LOUSY FOUR-EYES!!
HM?

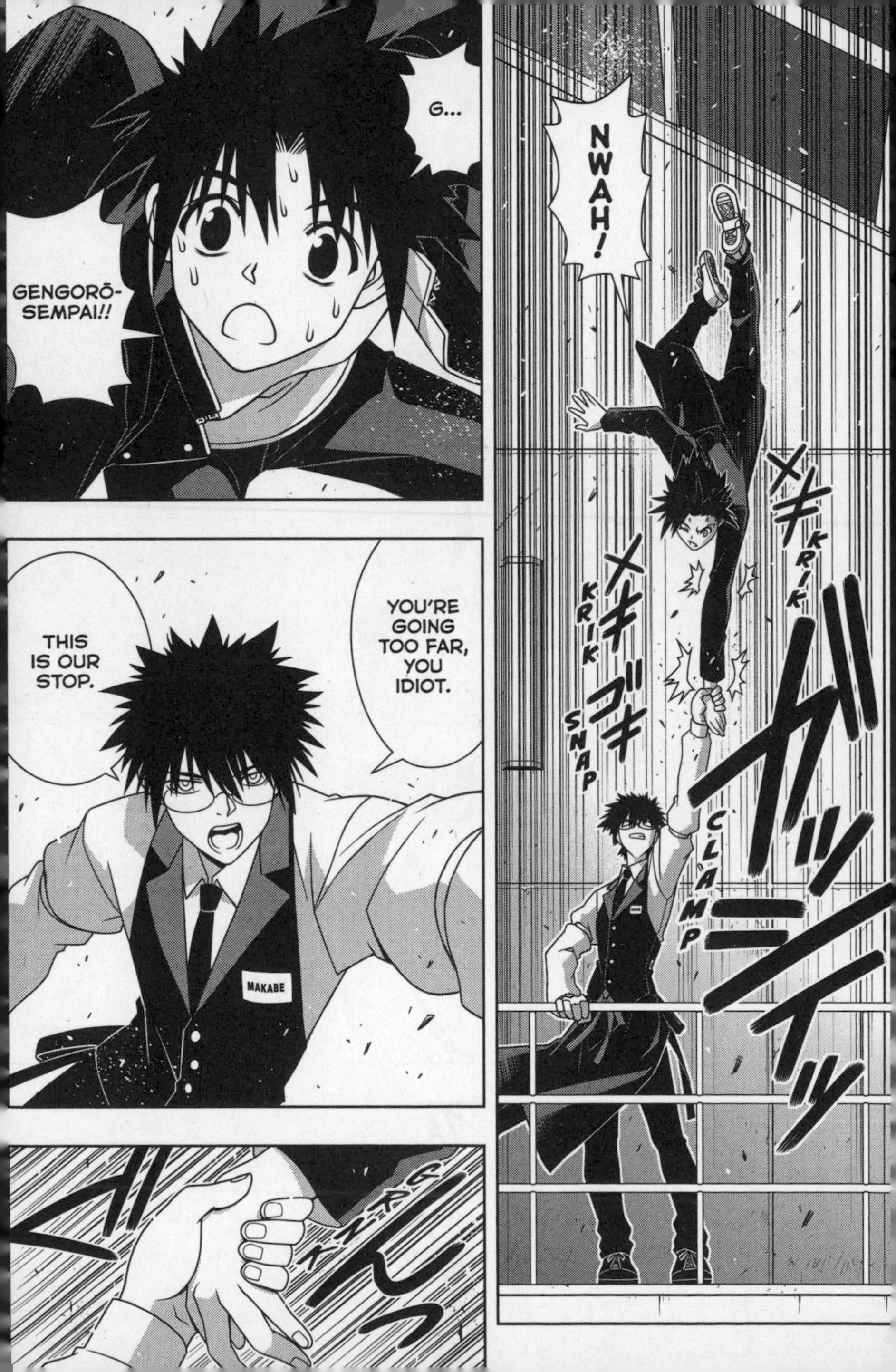
NWAH!
KRIK
KRIK
SNAP
CLAMP
G...
GENGORŌ-SEMPAI!!
YOU'RE GOING TOO FAR, YOU IDIOT.
THIS IS OUR STOP.
MAKABE
GRZK

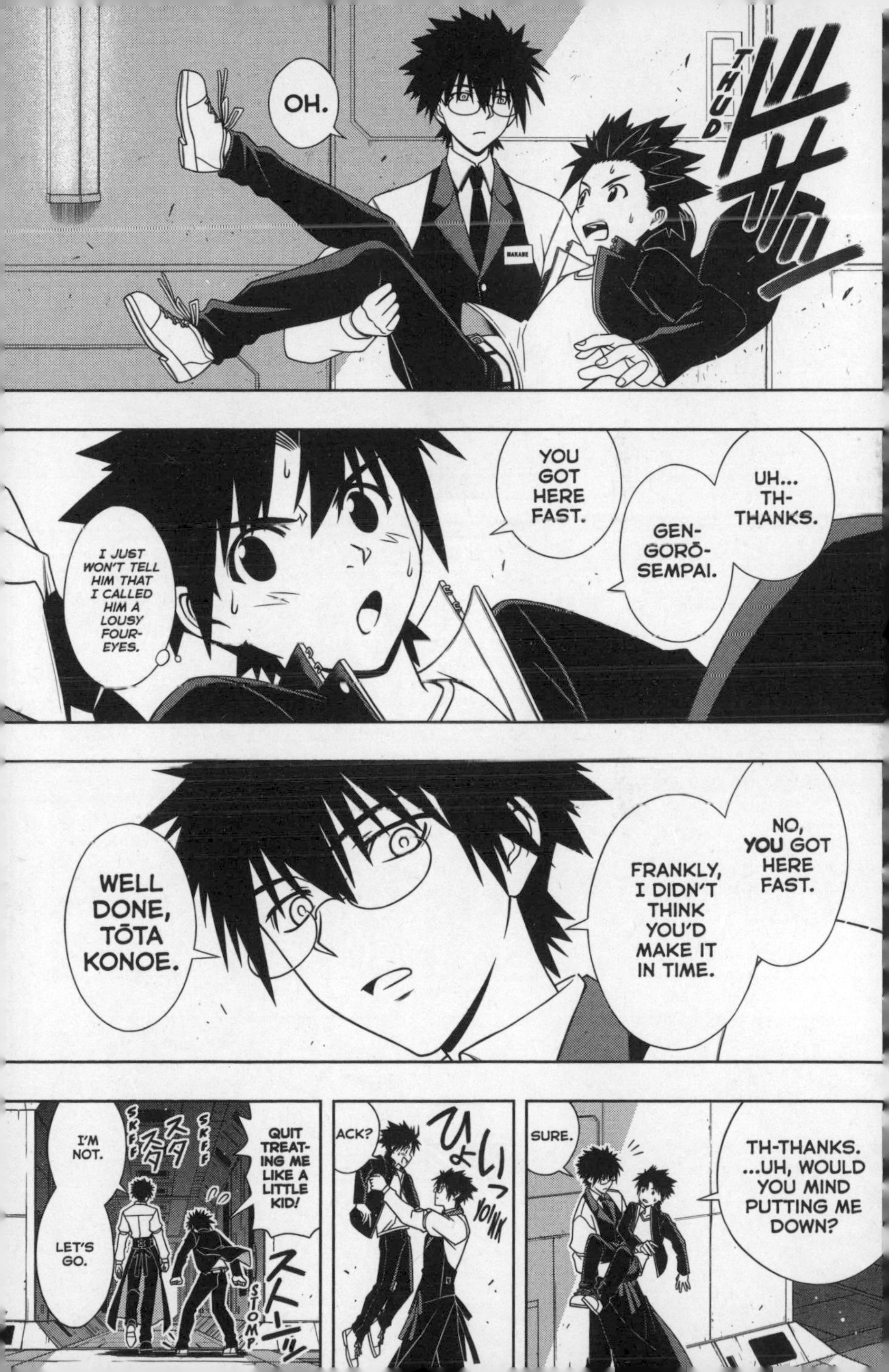
THUD
OH.
UH... TH-THANKS.
GEN-GORŌ-SEMPAI.
YOU GOT HERE FAST.
I JUST WON'T TELL HIM THAT I CALLED HIM A LOUSY FOUR-EYES.
NO, YOU GOT HERE FAST.
FRANKLY, I DIDN'T THINK YOU'D MAKE IT IN TIME.
WELL DONE, TŌTA KONOE.
TH-THANKS. ...UH, WOULD YOU MIND PUTTING ME DOWN?
SURE.
YOINK
ACK?
QUIT TREATING ME LIKE A LITTLE KID!
STOMP
SKFF SKFF
I'M NOT.
LET'S GO.

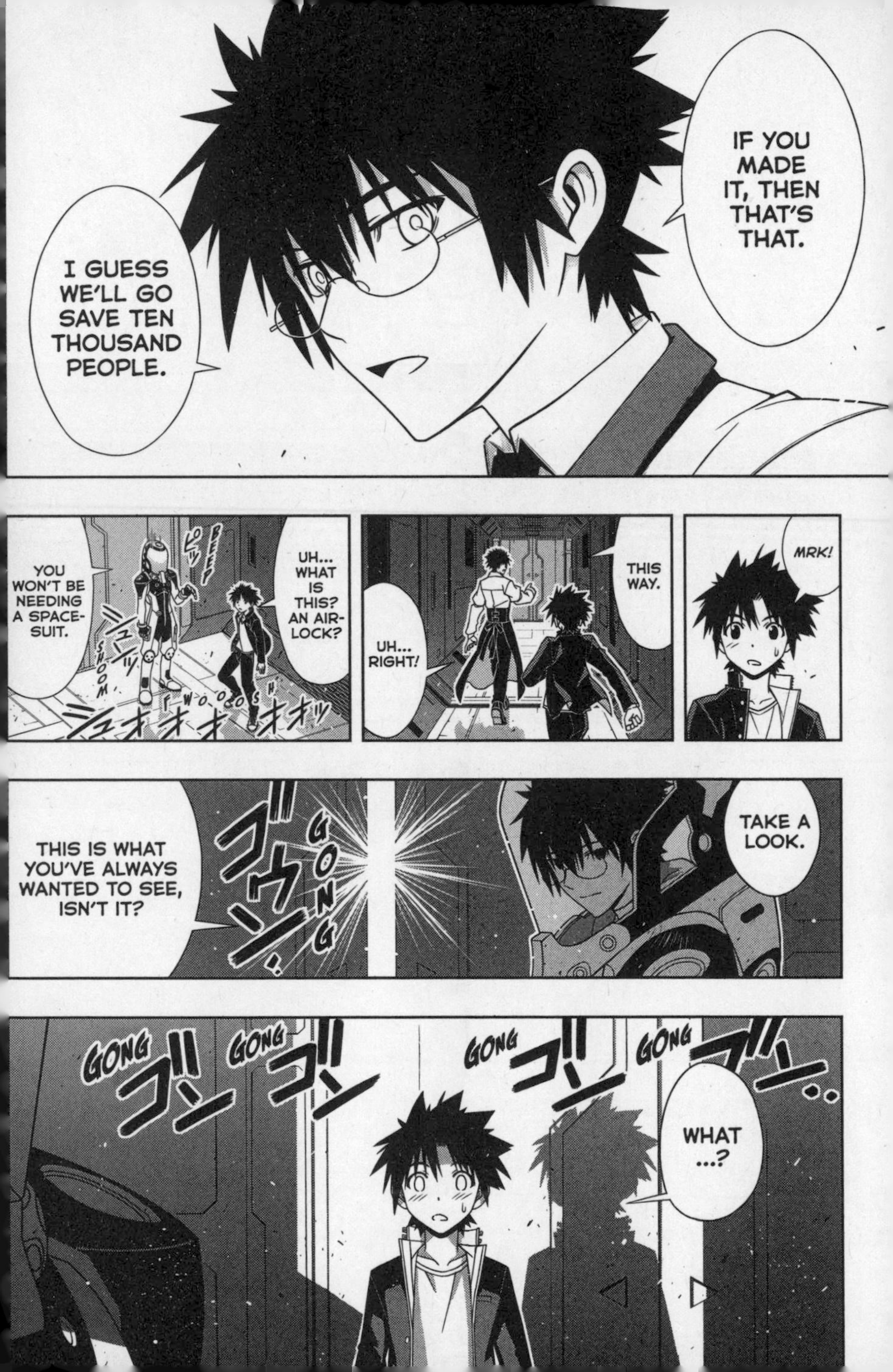
IF YOU MADE IT, THEN THAT'S THAT.
I GUESS WE'LL GO SAVE TEN THOUSAND PEOPLE.
MRK!
THIS WAY.
UH... RIGHT!
UH... WHAT IS THIS? AN AIR-LOCK?
BEEP
YOU WON'T BE NEEDING A SPACE-SUIT.
SHOOM
WOOOSH
TAKE A LOOK.
GONG
THIS IS WHAT YOU'VE ALWAYS WANTED TO SEE, ISN'T IT?
GONG
GONG
GONG
GONG
WHAT ...?

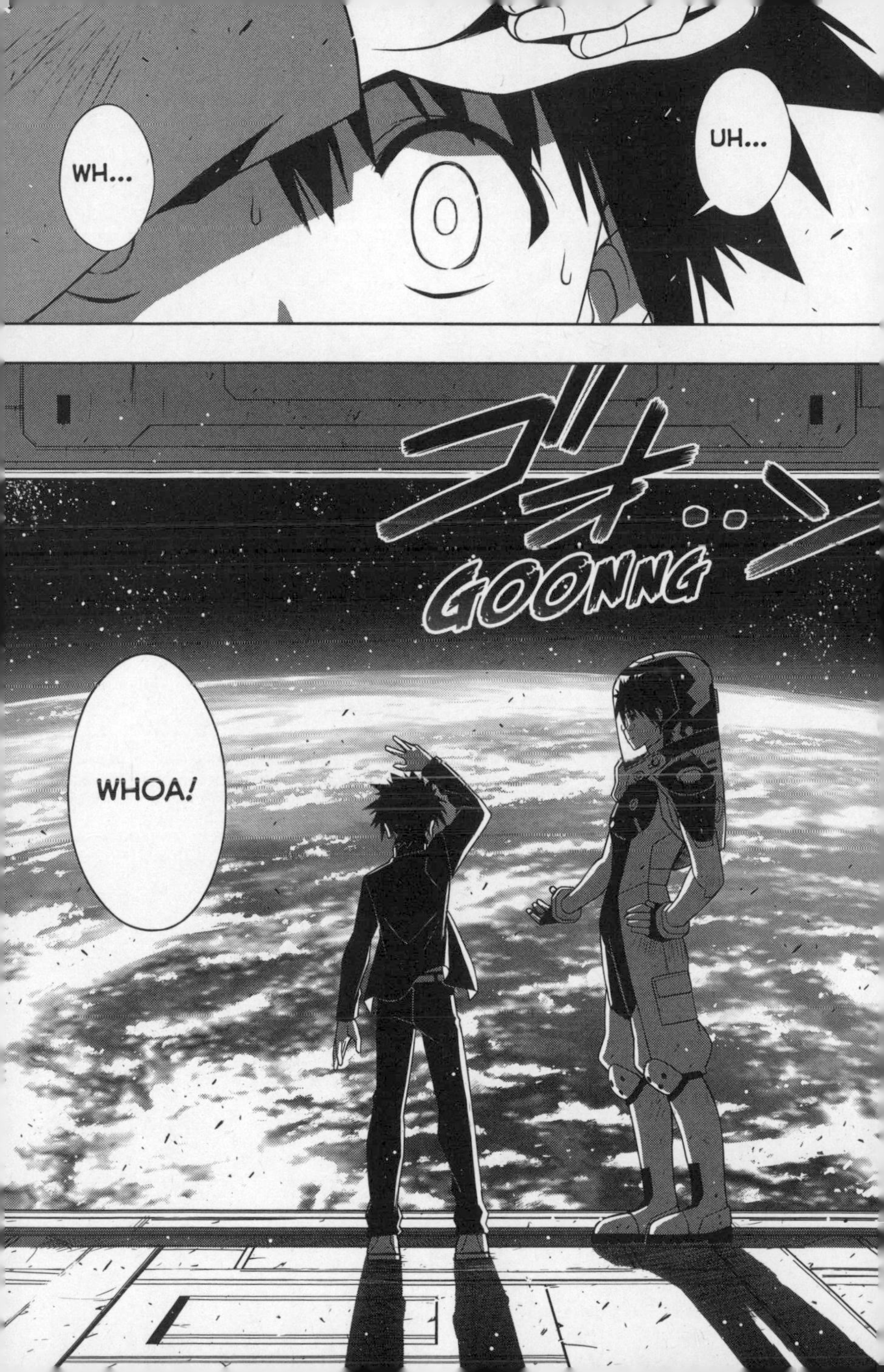
UH...
WH...
ゴォ‥ン
GOONNG
WHOA!

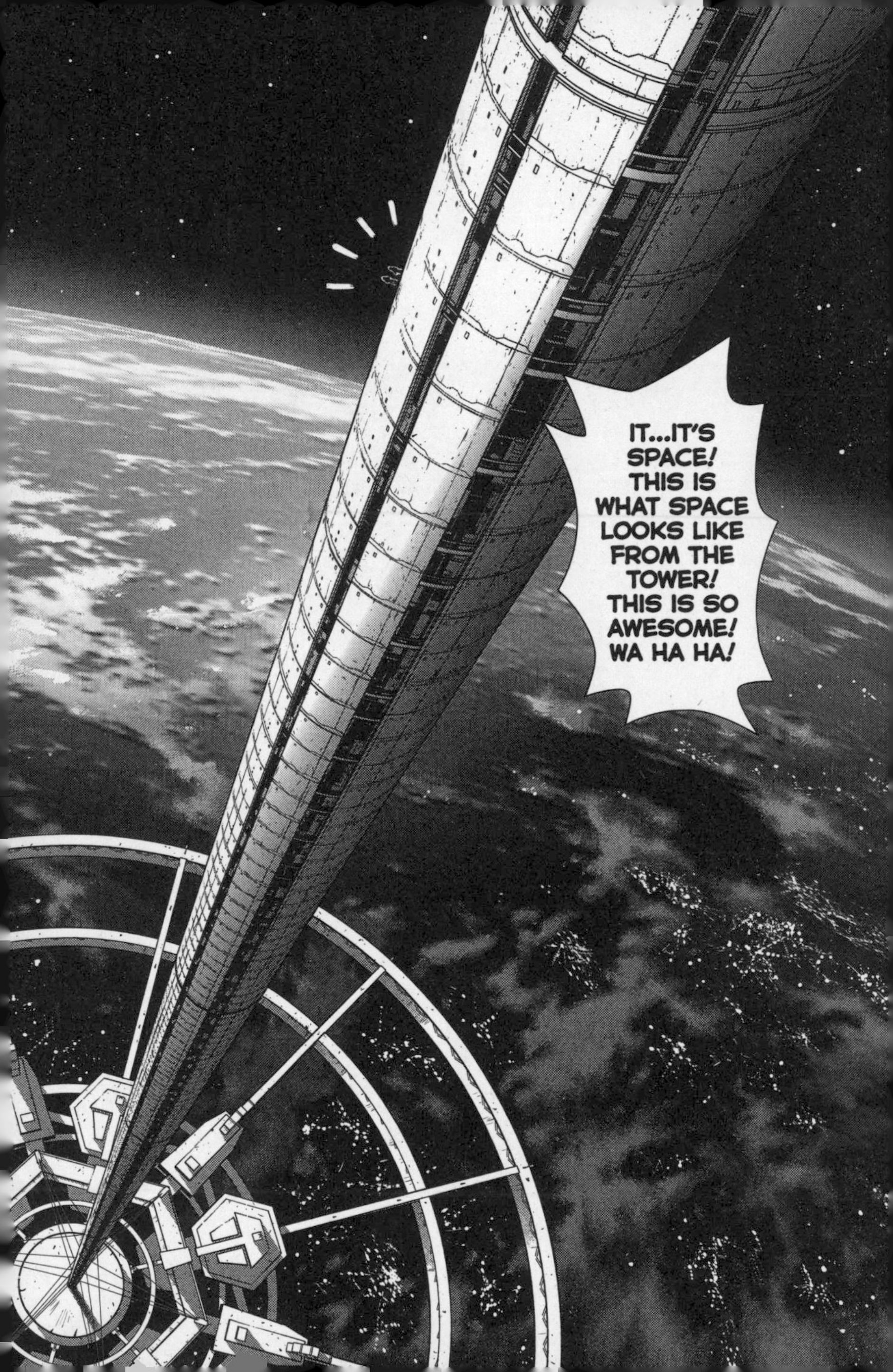
IT...IT'S SPACE! THIS IS WHAT SPACE LOOKS LIKE FROM THE TOWER! THIS IS SO AWESOME! WA HA HA!

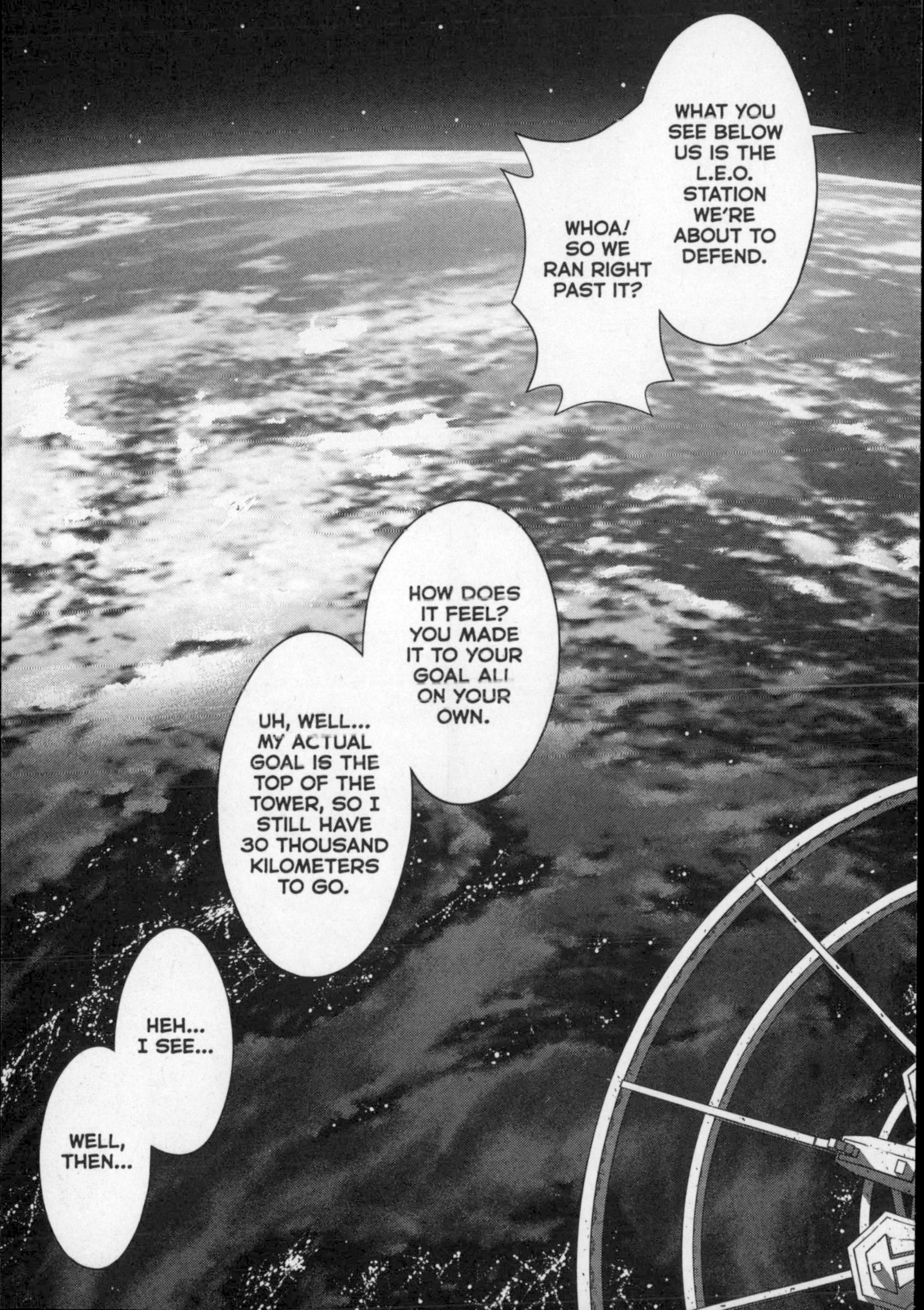
WHAT YOU SEE BELOW US IS THE L.E.O. STATION WE'RE ABOUT TO DEFEND.
WHOA! SO WE RAN RIGHT PAST IT?
HOW DOES IT FEEL? YOU MADE IT TO YOUR GOAL ALL ON YOUR OWN.
UH, WELL... MY ACTUAL GOAL IS THE TOP OF THE TOWER, SO I STILL HAVE 30 THOUSAND KILOMETERS TO GO.
HEH... I SEE...
WELL, THEN...

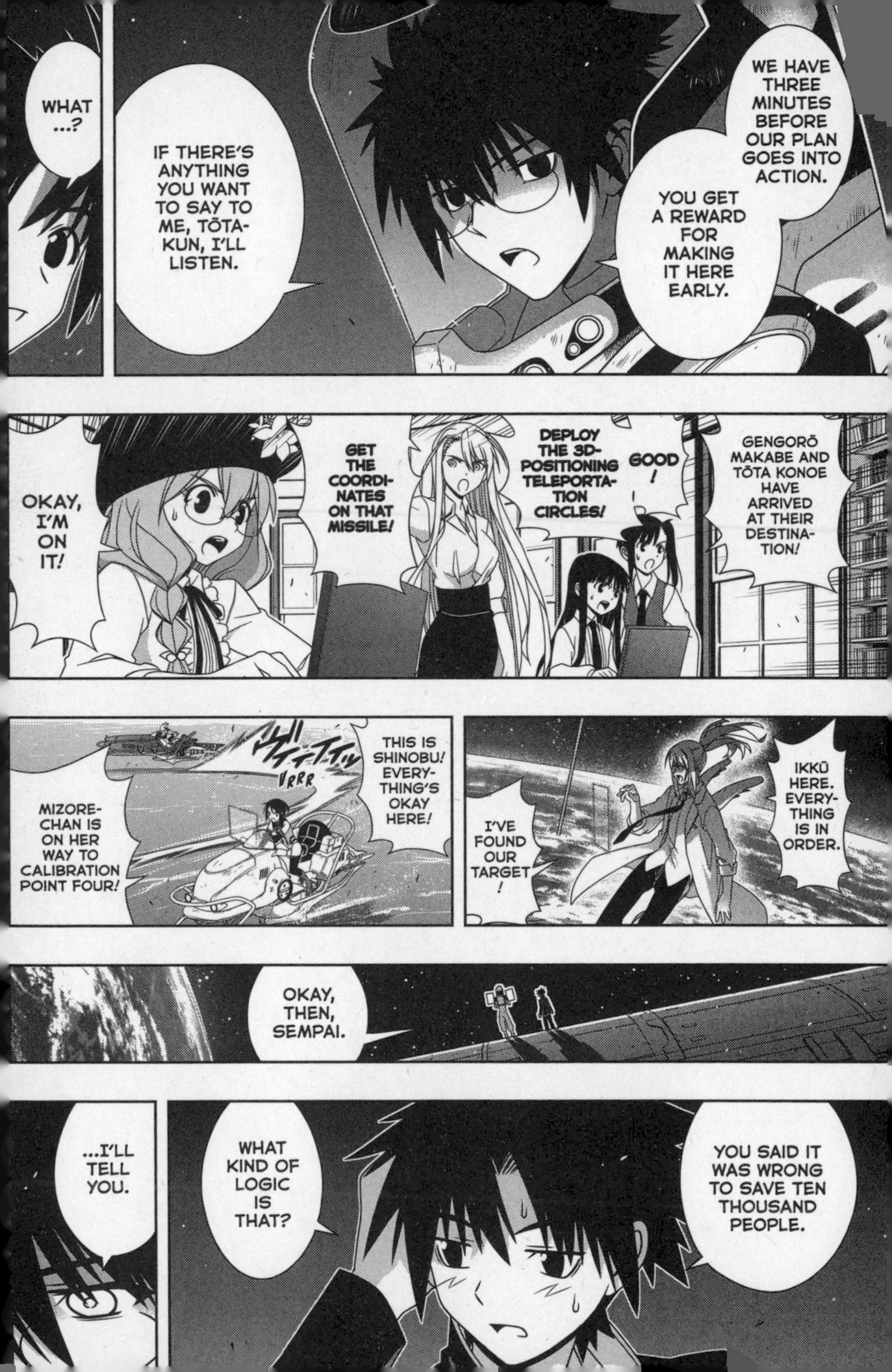
WE HAVE THREE MINUTES BEFORE OUR PLAN GOES INTO ACTION.
YOU GET A REWARD FOR MAKING IT HERE EARLY.
IF THERE'S ANYTHING YOU WANT TO SAY TO ME, TŌTA-KUN, I'LL LISTEN.
WHAT ...?
GENGORŌ MAKABE AND TŌTA KONOE HAVE ARRIVED AT THEIR DESTINATION!
GOOD!
DEPLOY THE 3D-POSITIONING TELEPORTATION CIRCLES!
GET THE COORDINATES ON THAT MISSILE!
OKAY, I'M ON IT!
IKKŪ HERE. EVERYTHING IS IN ORDER.
I'VE FOUND OUR TARGET!
THIS IS SHINOBU! EVERYTHING'S OKAY HERE!
VRRR
MIZORE-CHAN IS ON HER WAY TO CALIBRATION POINT FOUR!
OKAY, THEN, SEMPAI.
YOU SAID IT WAS WRONG TO SAVE TEN THOUSAND PEOPLE.
WHAT KIND OF LOGIC IS THAT?
...I'LL TELL YOU.

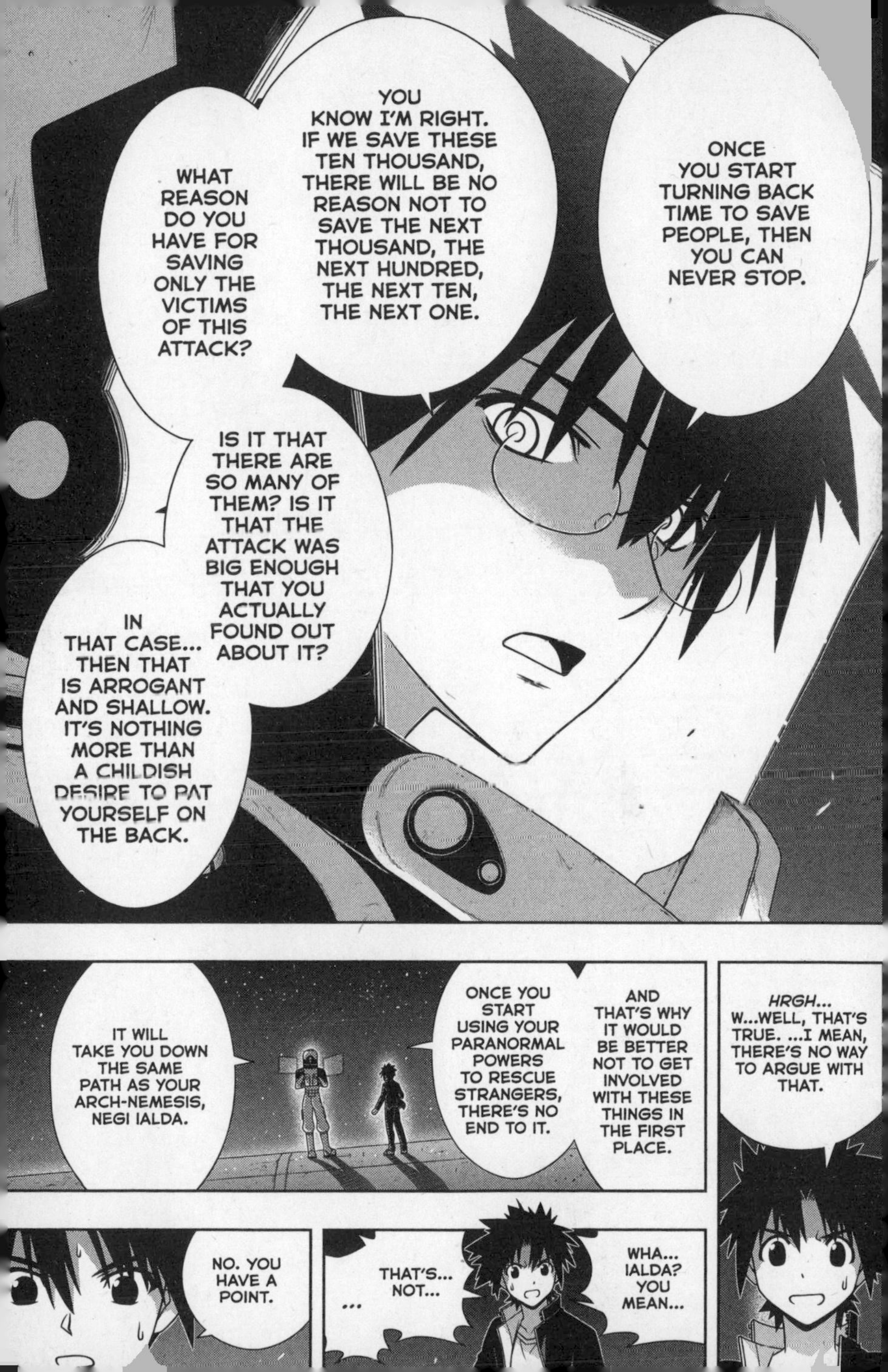
ONCE YOU START TURNING BACK TIME TO SAVE PEOPLE, THEN YOU CAN NEVER STOP.
YOU KNOW I'M RIGHT. IF WE SAVE THESE TEN THOUSAND, THERE WILL BE NO REASON NOT TO SAVE THE NEXT THOUSAND, THE NEXT HUNDRED, THE NEXT TEN, THE NEXT ONE.
WHAT REASON DO YOU HAVE FOR SAVING ONLY THE VICTIMS OF THIS ATTACK?
IS IT THAT THERE ARE SO MANY OF THEM? IS IT THAT THE ATTACK WAS BIG ENOUGH THAT YOU ACTUALLY FOUND OUT ABOUT IT?
IN THAT CASE... THEN THAT IS ARROGANT AND SHALLOW. IT'S NOTHING MORE THAN A CHILDISH DESIRE TO PAT YOURSELF ON THE BACK.
HRGH... W...WELL, THAT'S TRUE. ...I MEAN, THERE'S NO WAY TO ARGUE WITH THAT.
ONCE YOU START USING YOUR PARANORMAL POWERS TO RESCUE STRANGERS, THERE'S NO END TO IT.
AND THAT'S WHY IT WOULD BE BETTER NOT TO GET INVOLVED WITH THESE THINGS IN THE FIRST PLACE.
IT WILL TAKE YOU DOWN THE SAME PATH AS YOUR ARCH-NEMESIS, NEGI IALDA.
WHA... IALDA? YOU MEAN...
THAT'S... NOT...
...
NO. YOU HAVE A POINT.

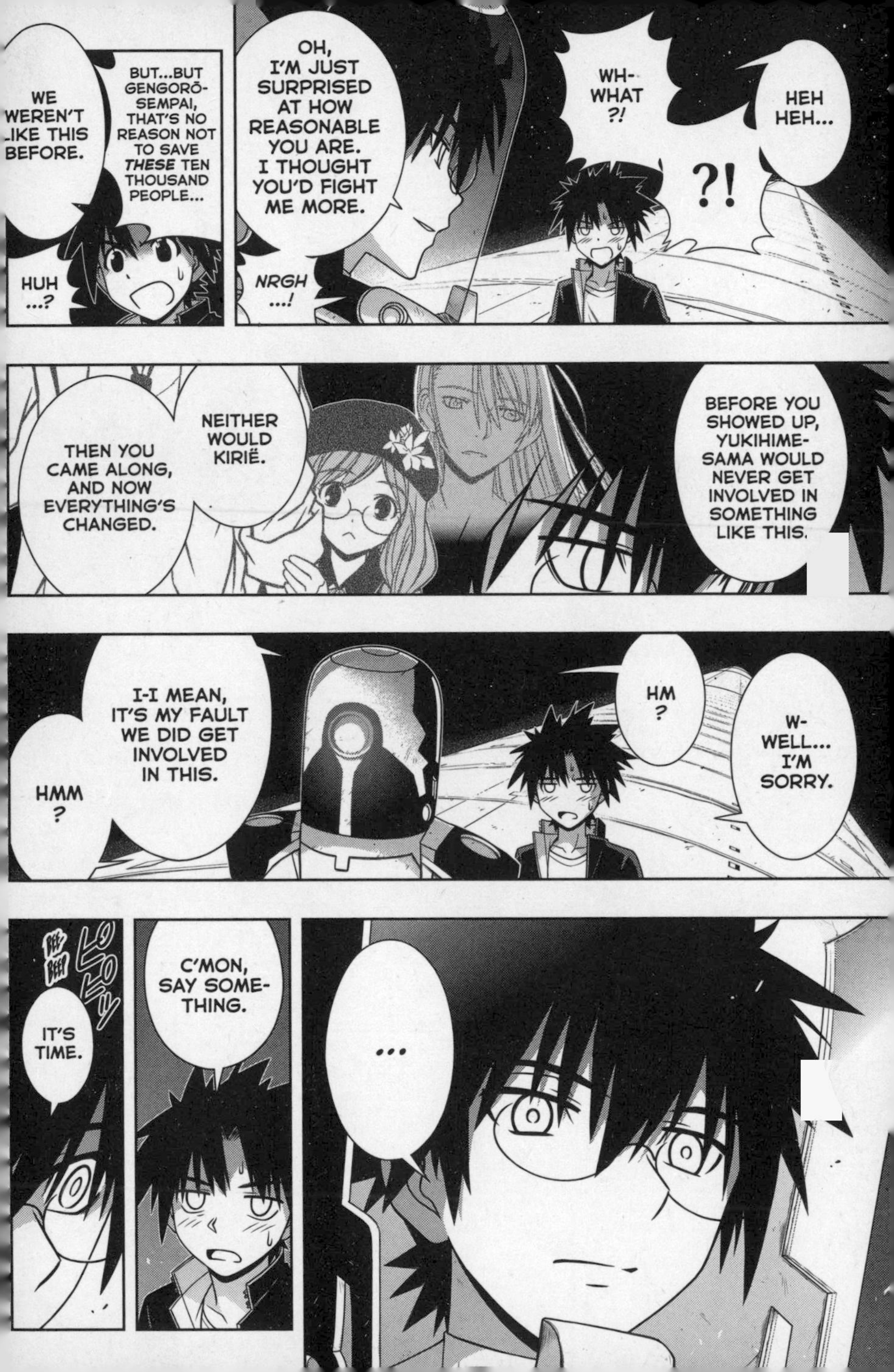
HEH HEH...
?!
WH-WHAT ?!
OH, I'M JUST SURPRISED AT HOW REASONABLE YOU ARE. I THOUGHT YOU'D FIGHT ME MORE.
NRGH ...!
BUT...BUT GENGORŌ-SEMPAI, THAT'S NO REASON NOT TO SAVE *THESE* TEN THOUSAND PEOPLE...
WE WEREN'T LIKE THIS BEFORE.
HUH ...?
BEFORE YOU SHOWED UP, YUKIHIME-SAMA WOULD NEVER GET INVOLVED IN SOMETHING LIKE THIS.
NEITHER WOULD KIRIË.
THEN YOU CAME ALONG, AND NOW EVERYTHING'S CHANGED.
W-WELL... I'M SORRY.
HM ?
I-I MEAN, IT'S MY FAULT WE DID GET INVOLVED IN THIS.
HMM ?
...
C'MON, SAY SOME-THING.
BEE-BEEP
IT'S TIME.

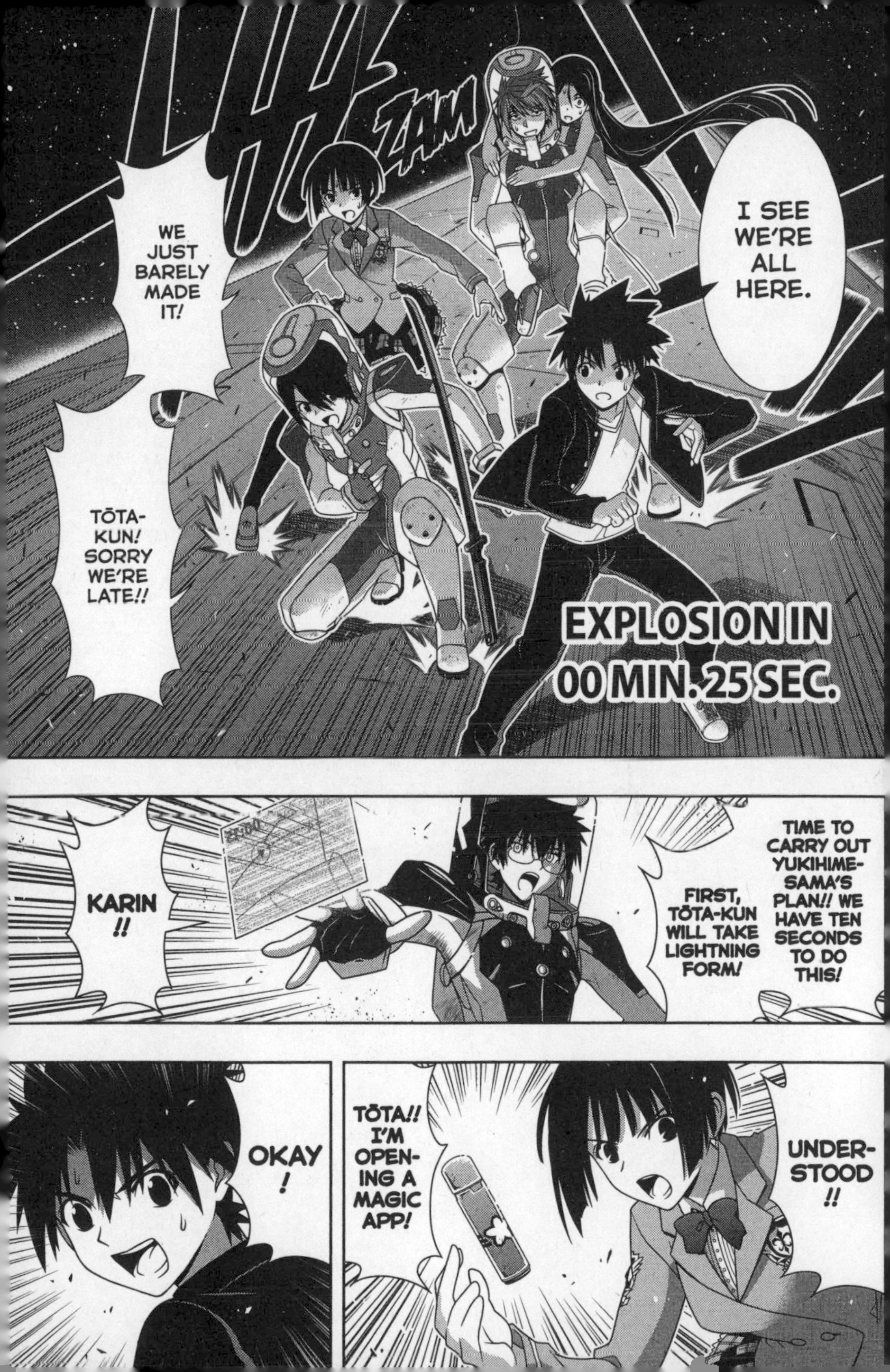
ZAM
I SEE WE'RE ALL HERE.
WE JUST BARELY MADE IT!
TŌTA-KUN! SORRY WE'RE LATE!!
EXPLOSION IN 00 MIN. 25 SEC.
TIME TO CARRY OUT YUKIHIME-SAMA'S PLAN!! WE HAVE TEN SECONDS TO DO THIS!
FIRST, TŌTA-KUN WILL TAKE LIGHTNING FORM!
KARIN !!
UNDER-STOOD !!
TŌTA!! I'M OPEN-ING A MAGIC APP!
OKAY !

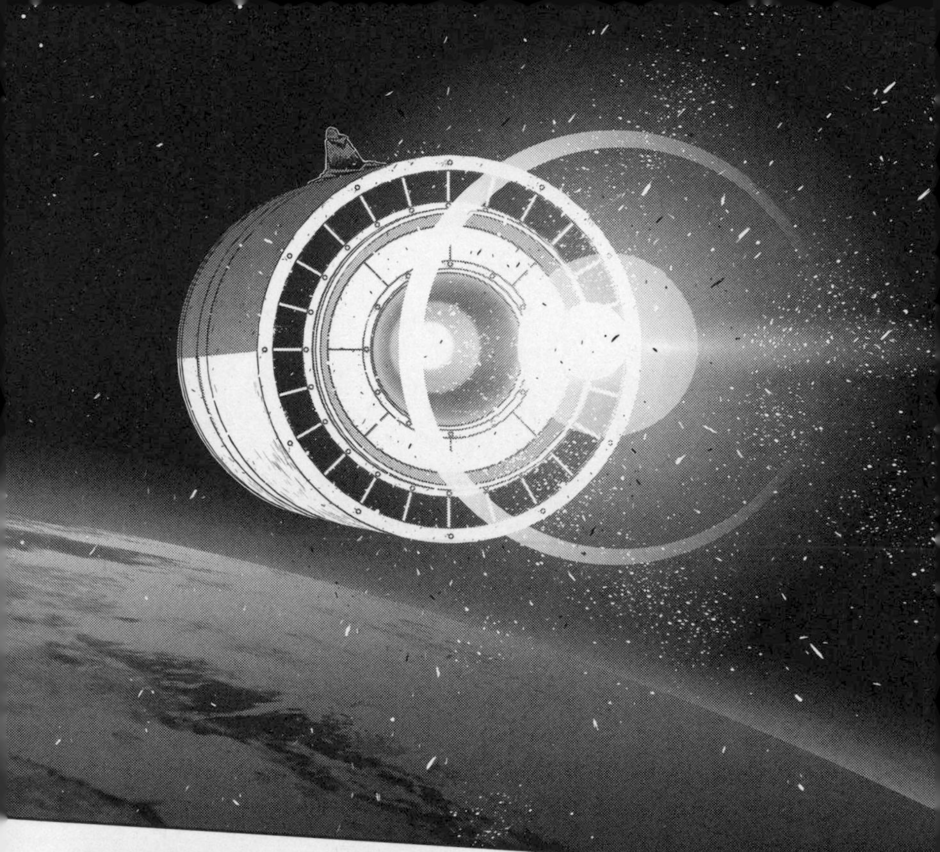
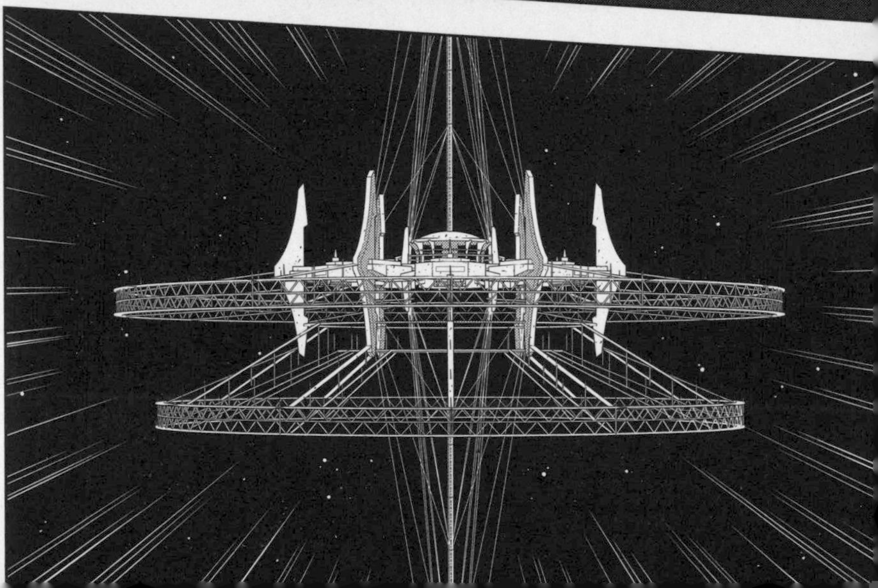

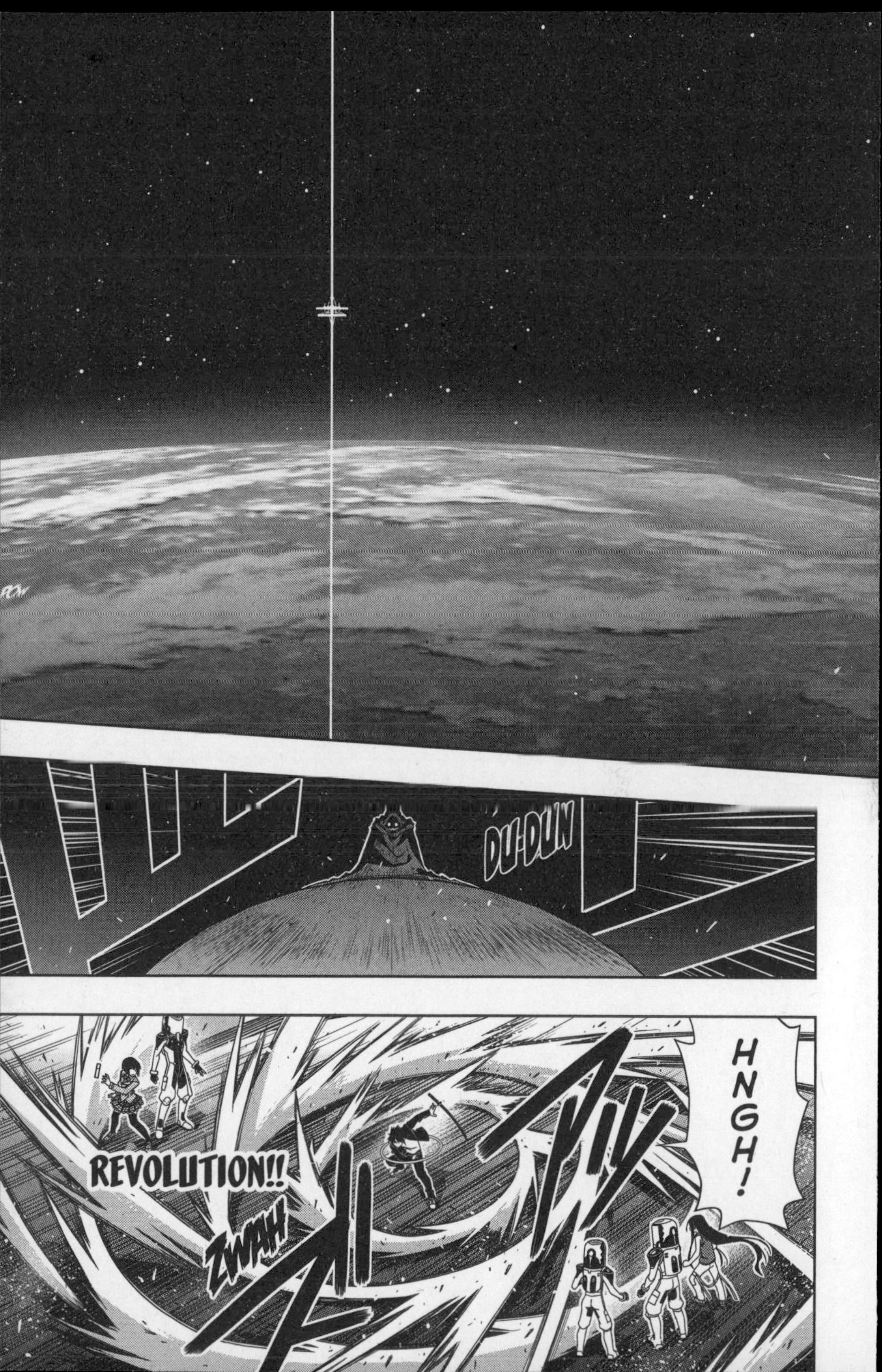
DU-DUN
HNGH!
REVOLUTION!!
ZWAH

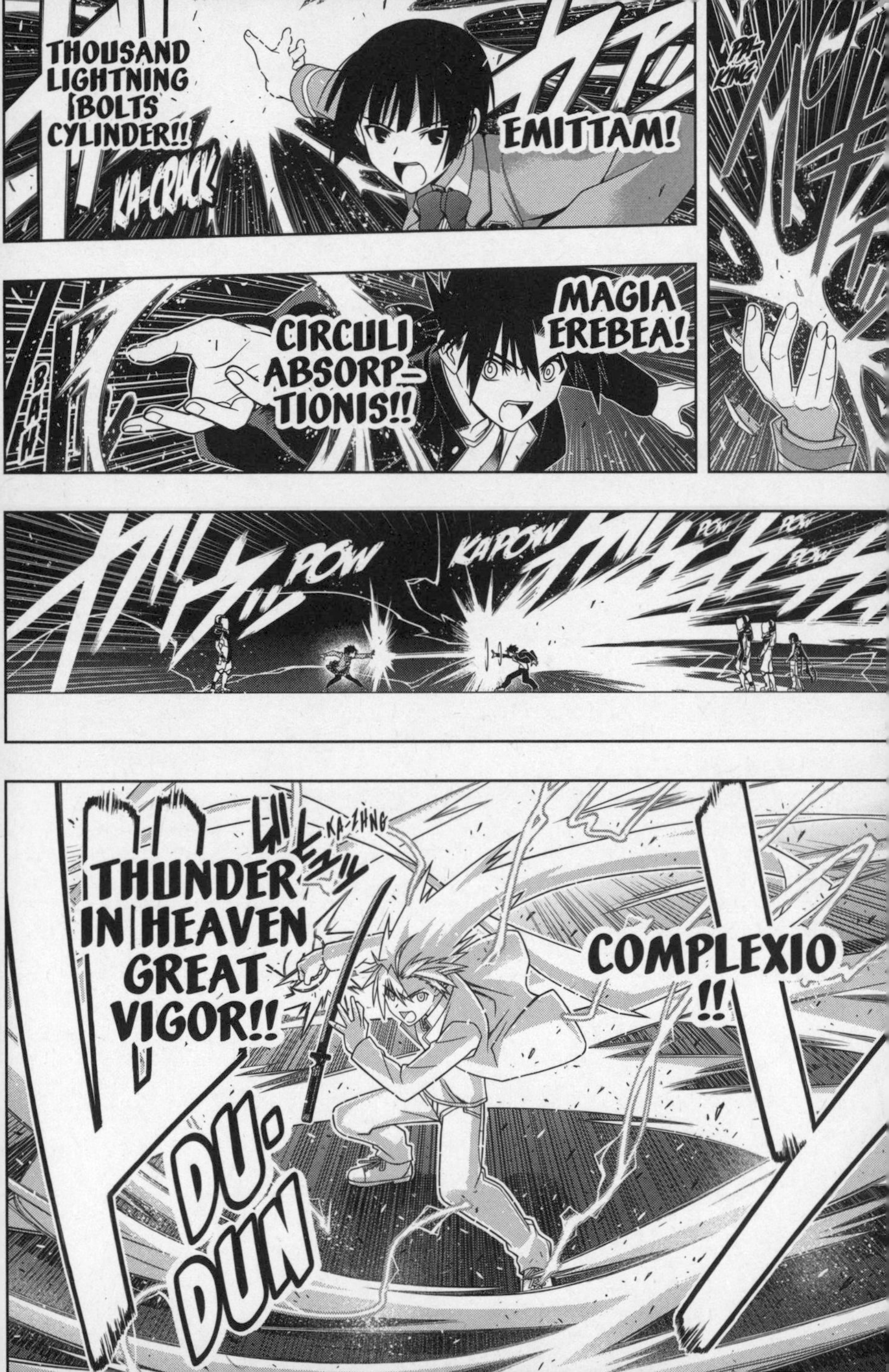
PA-KING
EMITTAM!
THOUSAND LIGHTNING BOLTS CYLINDER!!
KA-CRACK
MAGIA EREBEA!
CIRCULI ABSORPTIONIS!!
BAH
POW
POW
POW
KA-POW
POW
COMPLEXIO!!
KA-ZHNG
THUNDER IN HEAVEN GREAT VIGOR!!
DU-DUN

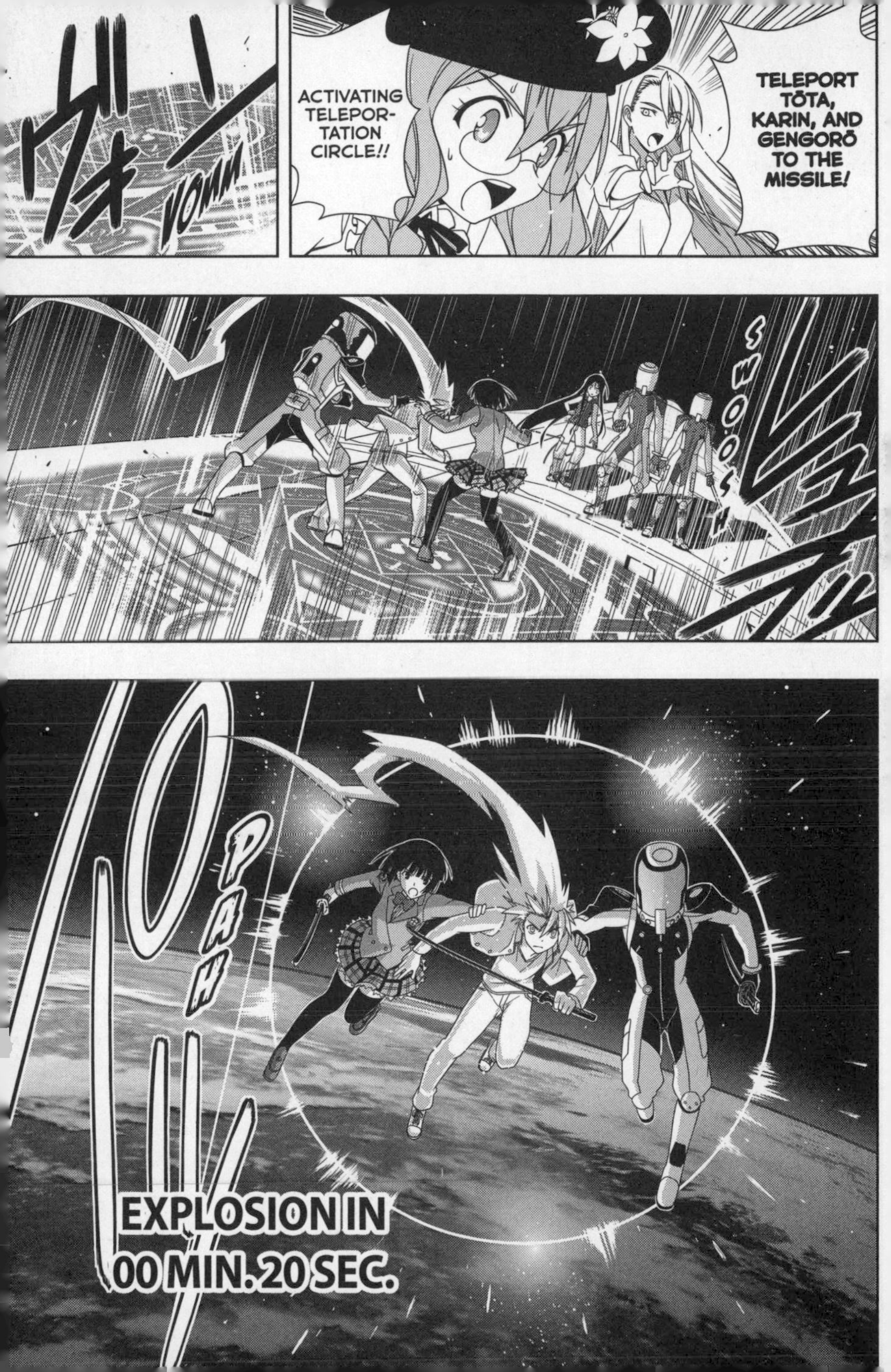
TELEPORT TŌTA, KARIN, AND GENGORŌ TO THE MISSILE!
ACTIVATING TELEPOR-TATION CIRCLE!!
VOMM
SWOOSH
PAAH
EXPLOSION IN 00 MIN. 20 SEC.

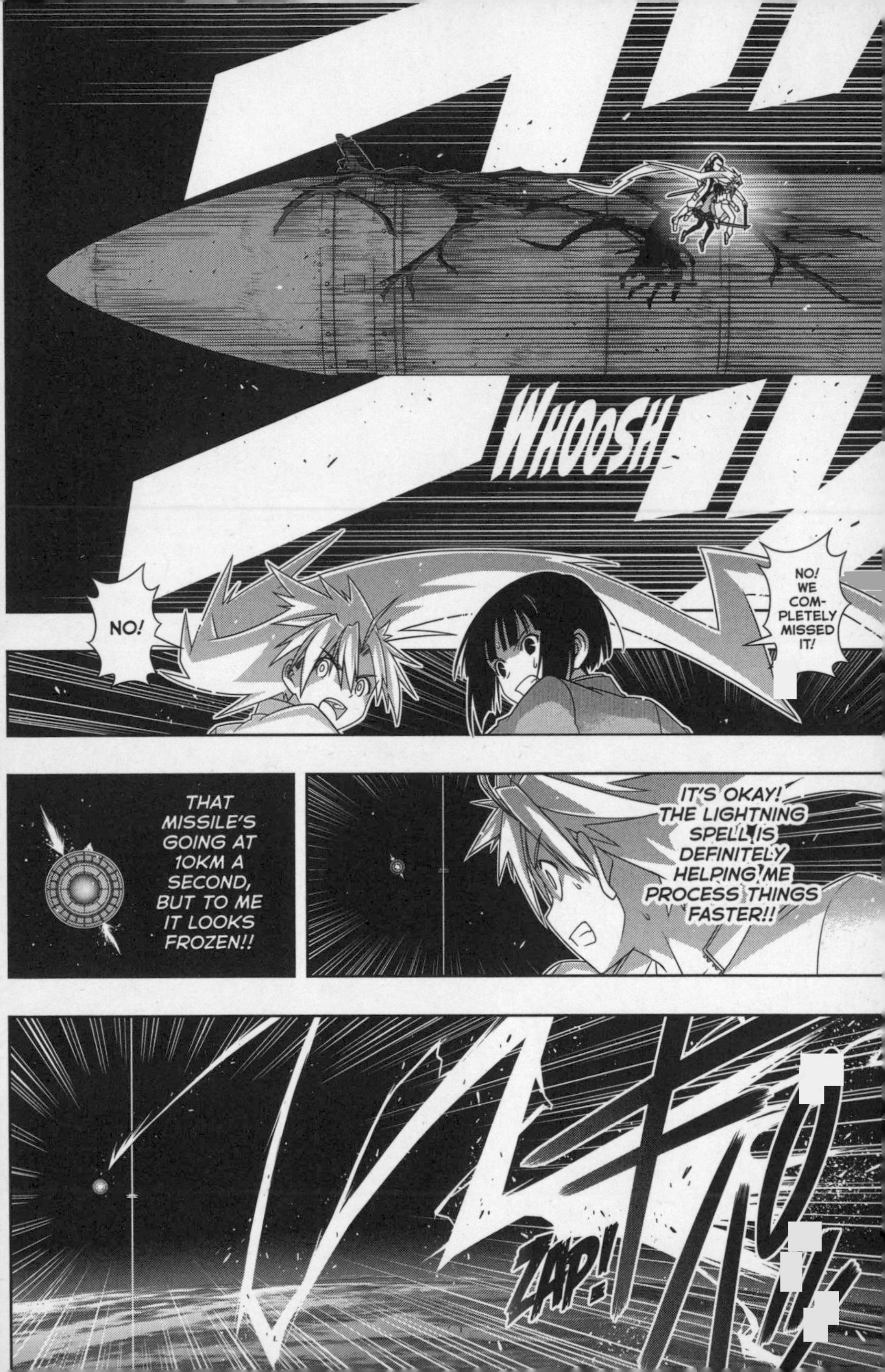
WHOOSH
NO! WE COM-PLETELY MISSED IT!
NO!
IT'S OKAY! THE LIGHTNING SPELL IS DEFINITELY HELPING ME PROCESS THINGS FASTER!!
THAT MISSILE'S GOING AT 10KM A SECOND, BUT TO ME IT LOOKS FROZEN!!
ZAP!!

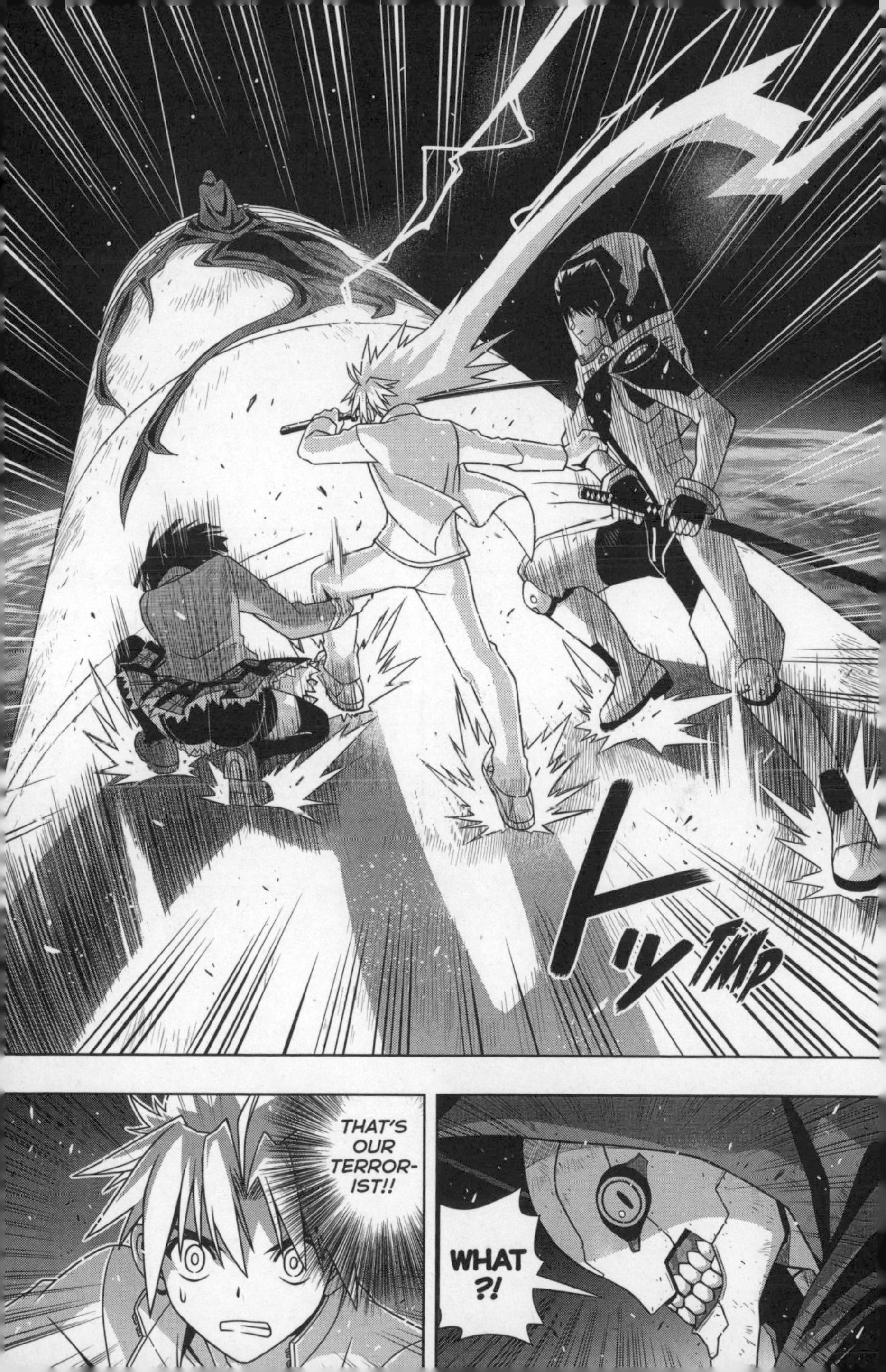
TMP
WHAT ?!
THAT'S OUR TERROR-IST!!

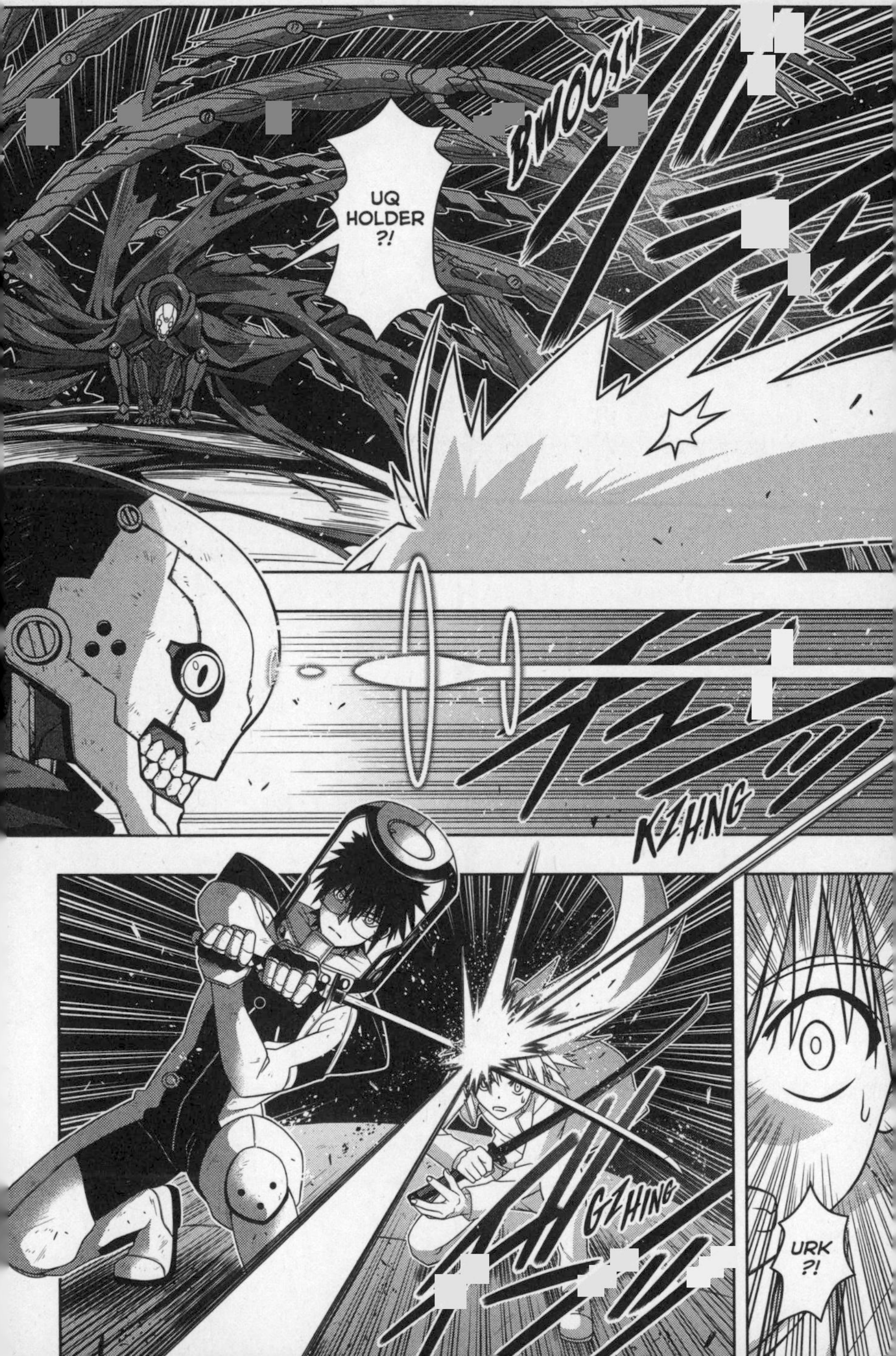
BWOOSH
UQ HOLDER ?!
KZHING
URK ?!
GZHING

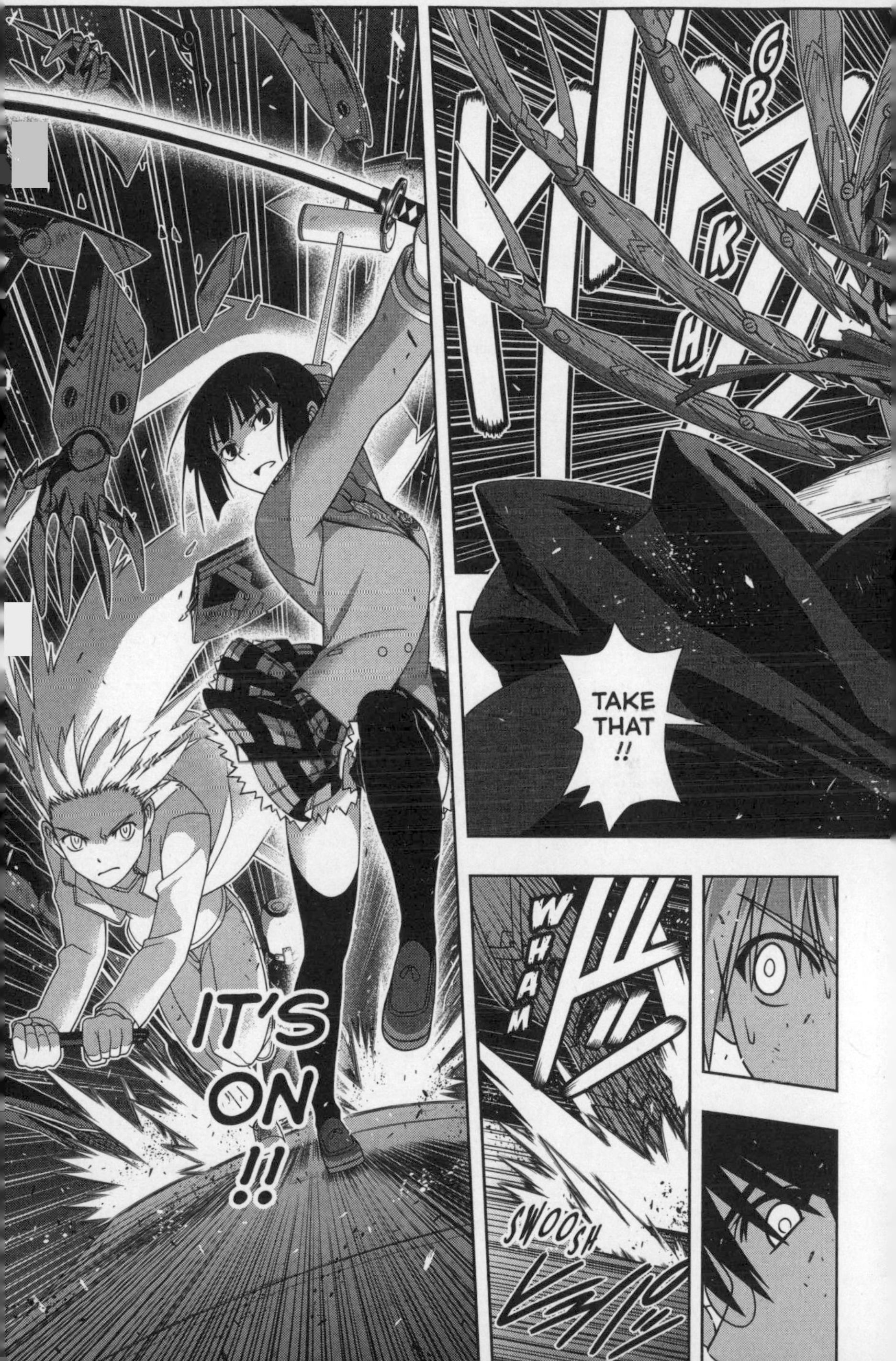

GRKKH
TAKE THAT!!
WHAM
SWOOSH
IT'S ON!!

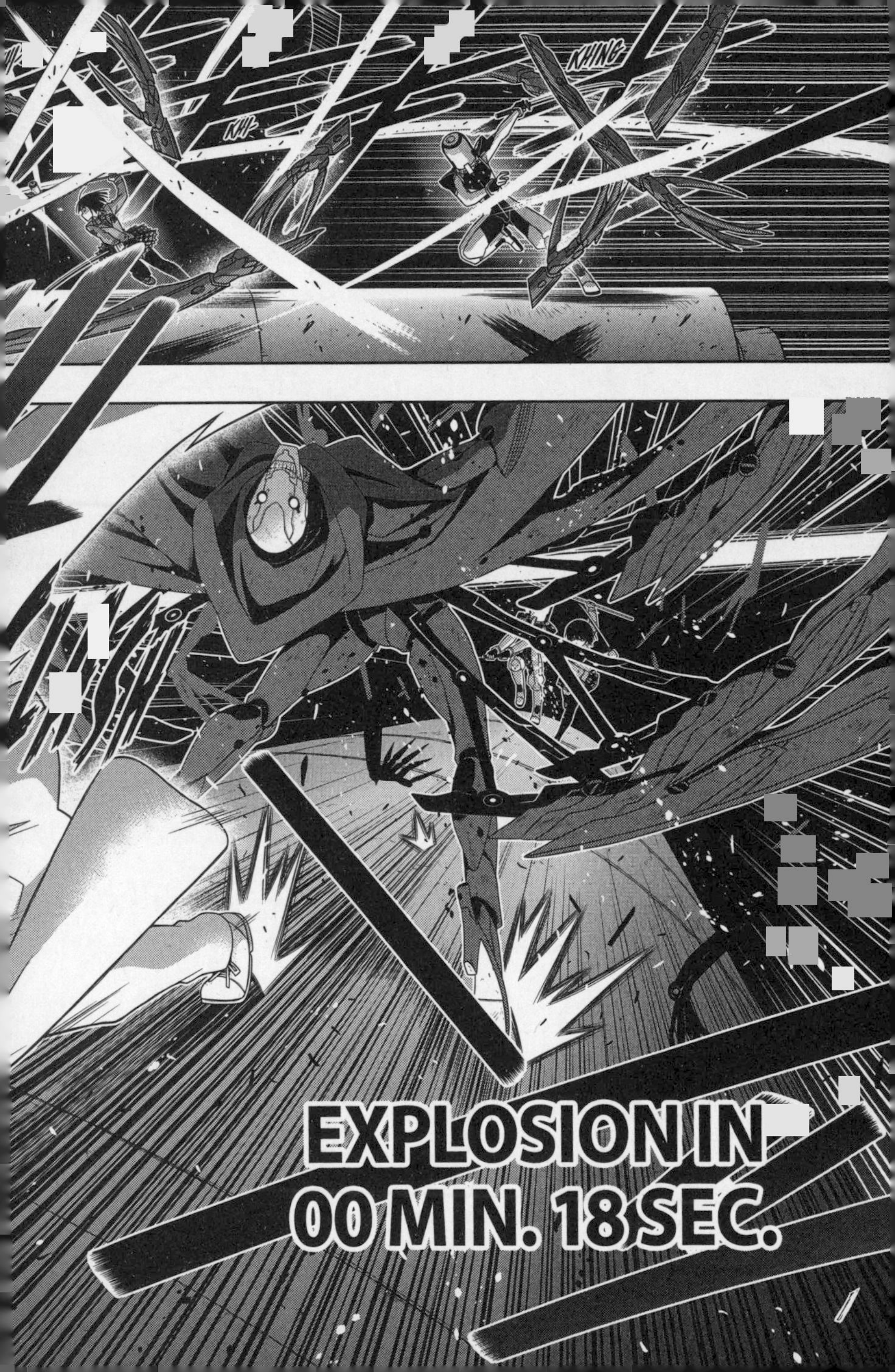
KHING
KHI
EXPLOSION IN
00 MIN. 18 SEC.

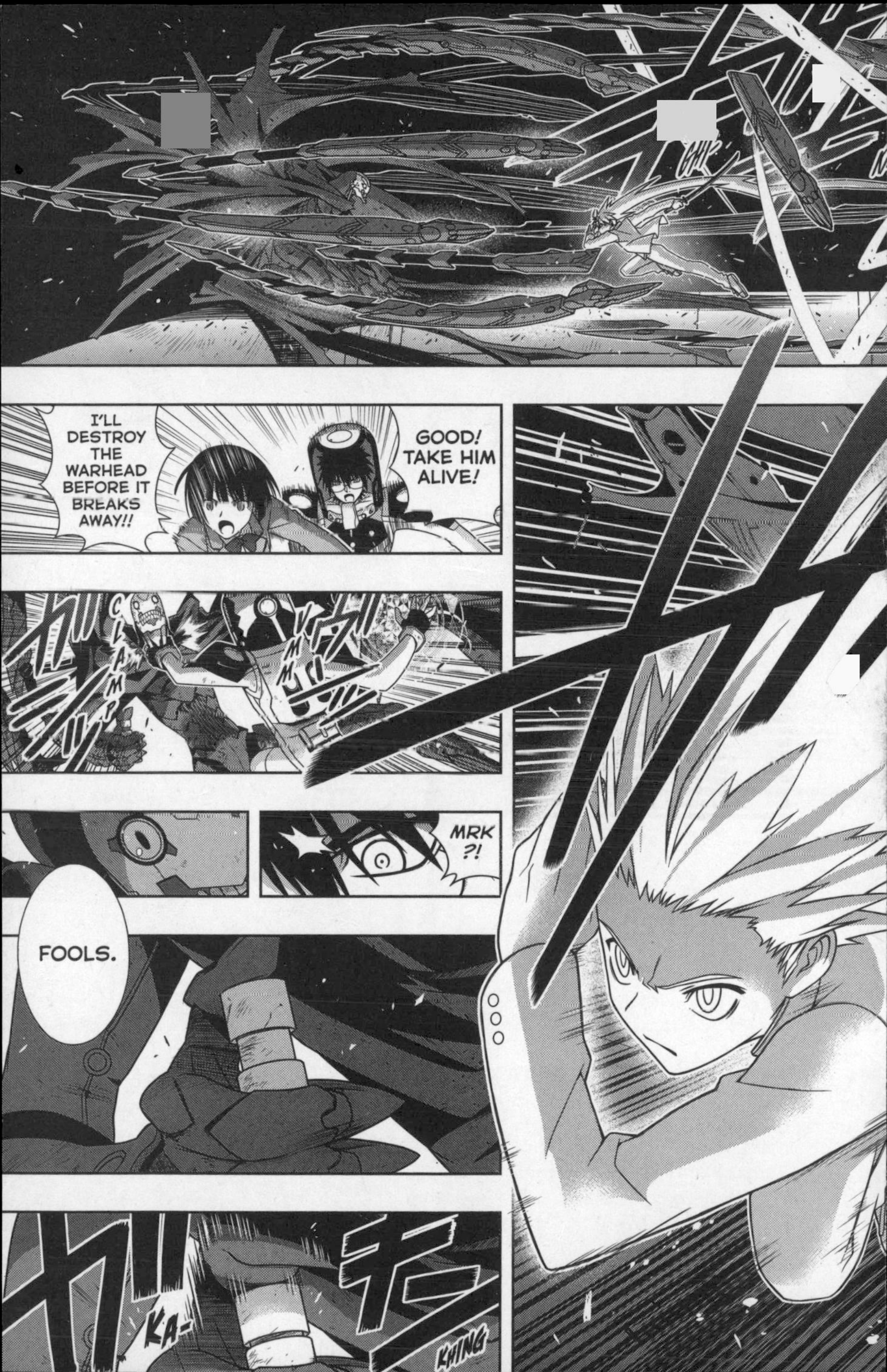
GOOD! TAKE HIM ALIVE!
I'LL DESTROY THE WARHEAD BEFORE IT BREAKS AWAY!!
VMMM
CLAMP
MRK ?!
FOOLS.
KA-
KHING

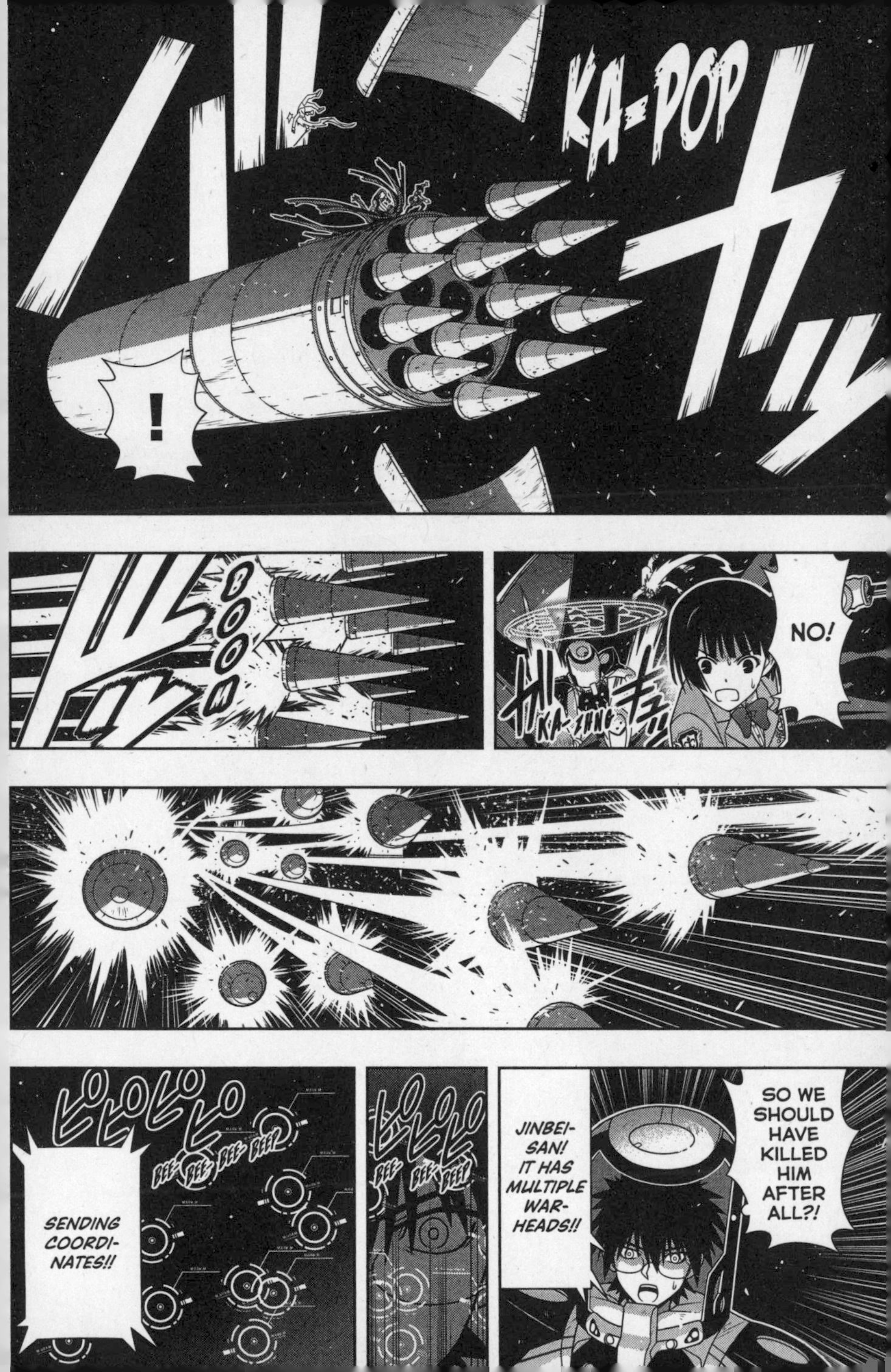
KA-POP
!
NO!
KA-CHING
BOOOM
SO WE SHOULD HAVE KILLED HIM AFTER ALL?!
JINBEI-SAN! IT HAS MULTIPLE WAR-HEADS!!
BEE-BEE-BEEP
BEE-BEE-BEE-BEEP
SENDING COORDI-NATES!!

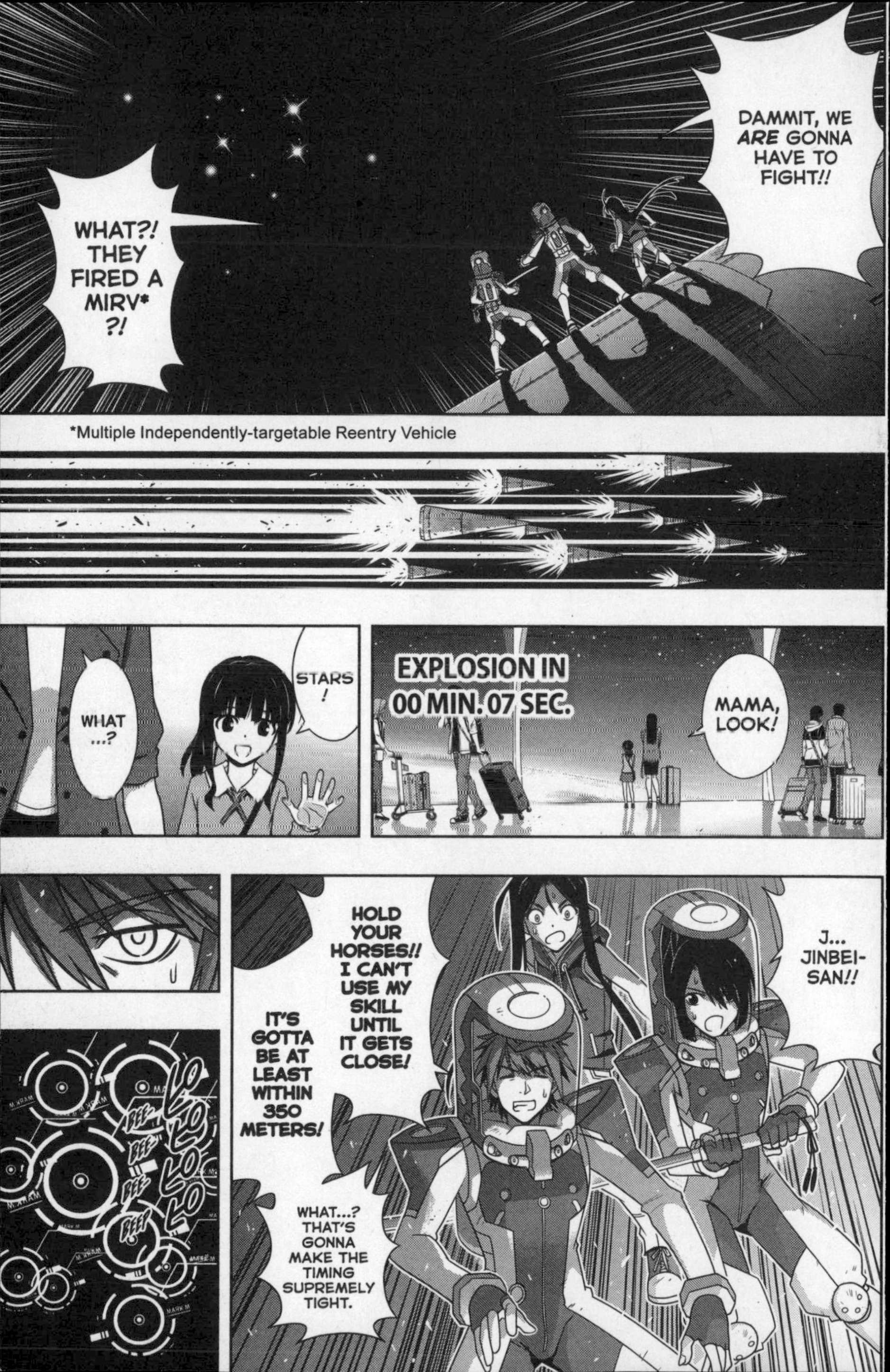
DAMMIT, WE *ARE* GONNA HAVE TO FIGHT!!
WHAT?! THEY FIRED A MIRV*?!
MAMA, LOOK!
EXPLOSION IN 00 MIN. 07 SEC.
STARS!
WHAT...?
J... JINBEI-SAN!!
HOLD YOUR HORSES!! I CAN'T USE MY SKILL UNTIL IT GETS CLOSE!
IT'S GOTTA BE AT LEAST WITHIN 350 METERS!
WHAT...? THAT'S GONNA MAKE THE TIMING SUPREMELY TIGHT.
BEE- BEE- BEE- BEEP

*Multiple Independently-targetable Reentry Vehicle

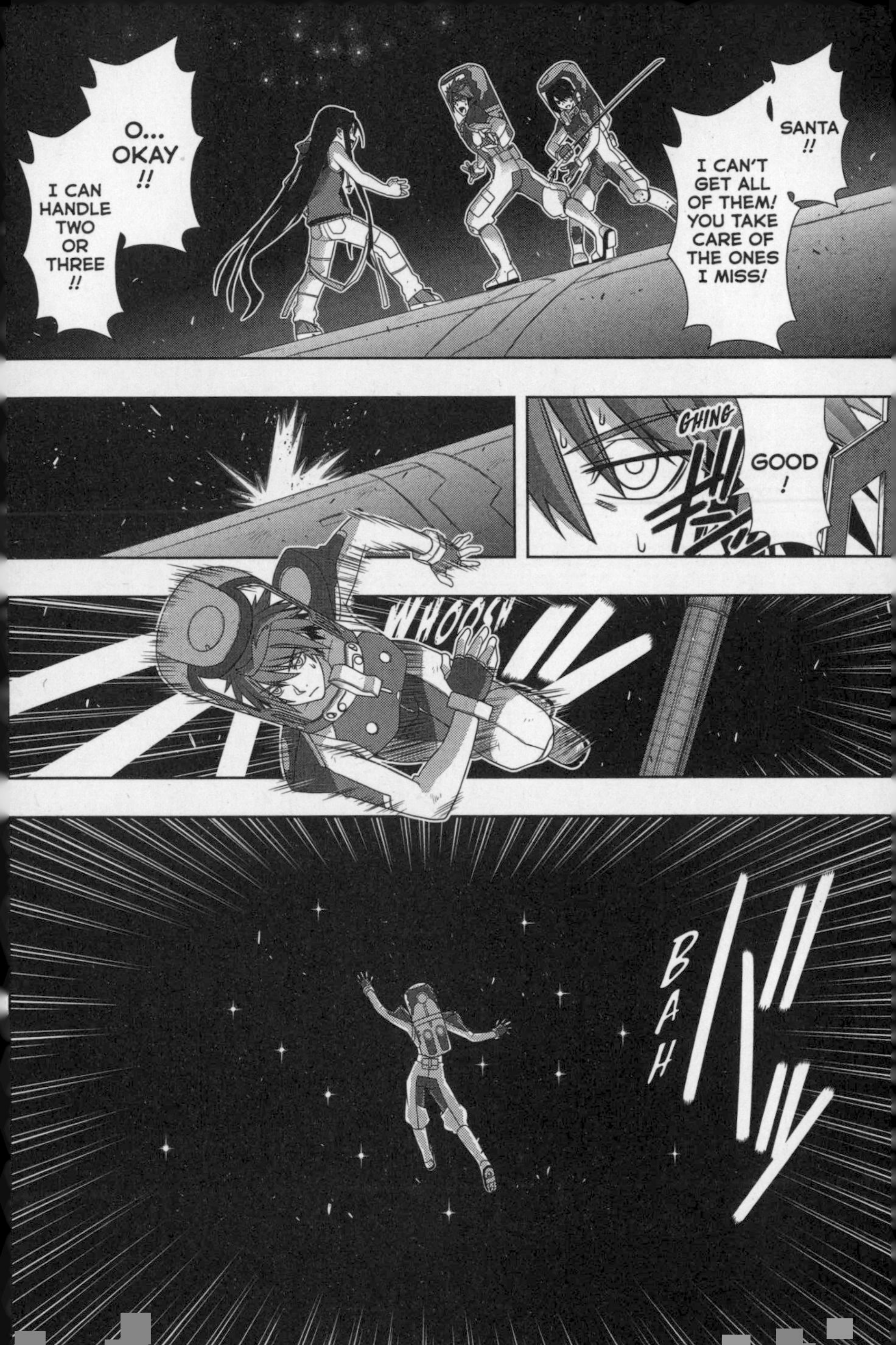
SANTA!!
I CAN'T GET ALL OF THEM! YOU TAKE CARE OF THE ONES I MISS!
O... OKAY!!
I CAN HANDLE TWO OR THREE!!
GHING
GOOD!
WHOOSH
BAH

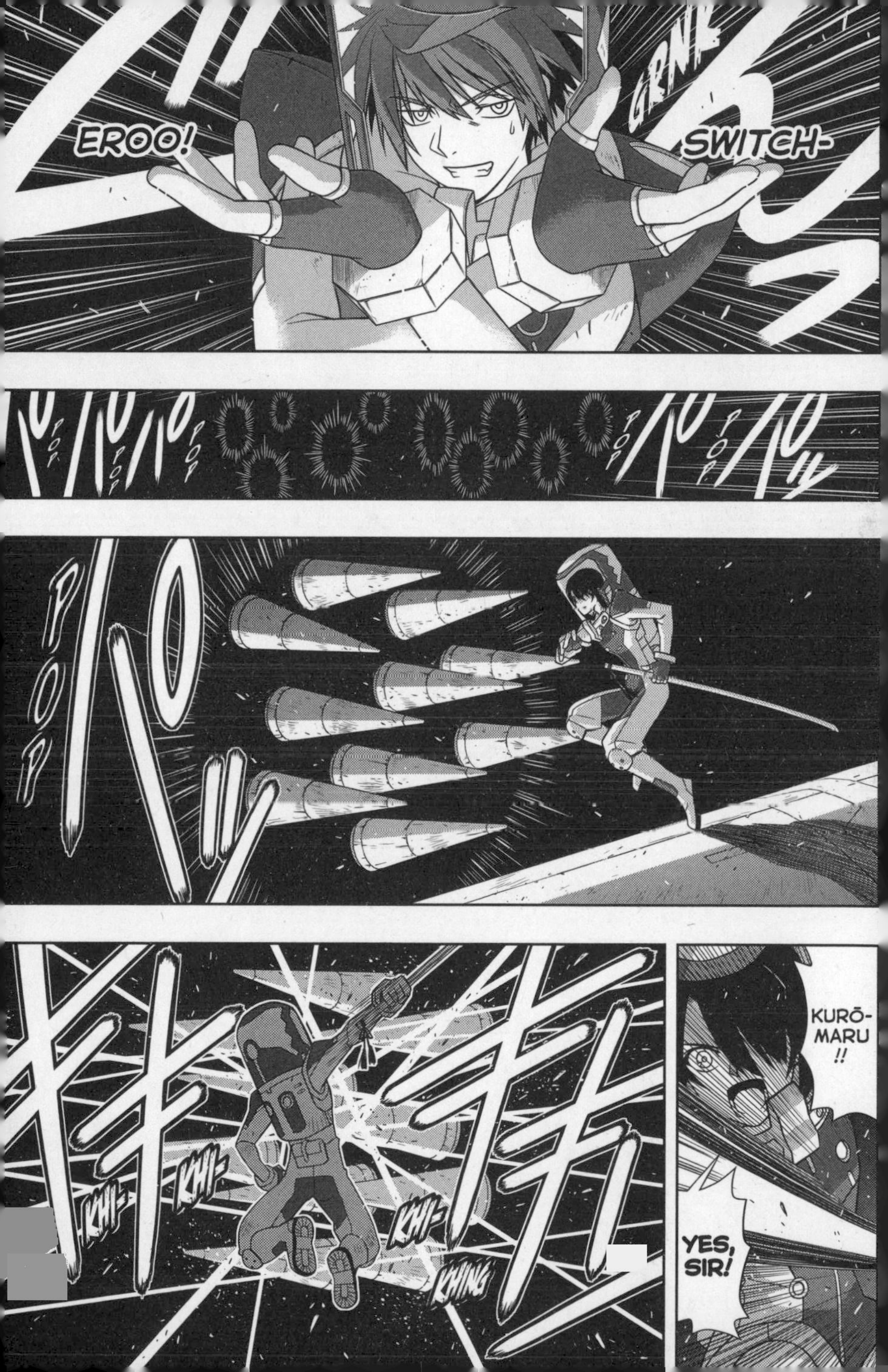
GRNK
SWITCH-
EROO!
POP
POP
POP
POP
POP
POP
KURŌ-MARU!!
YES, SIR!
KHI-
KHI-
KHI-
KHING

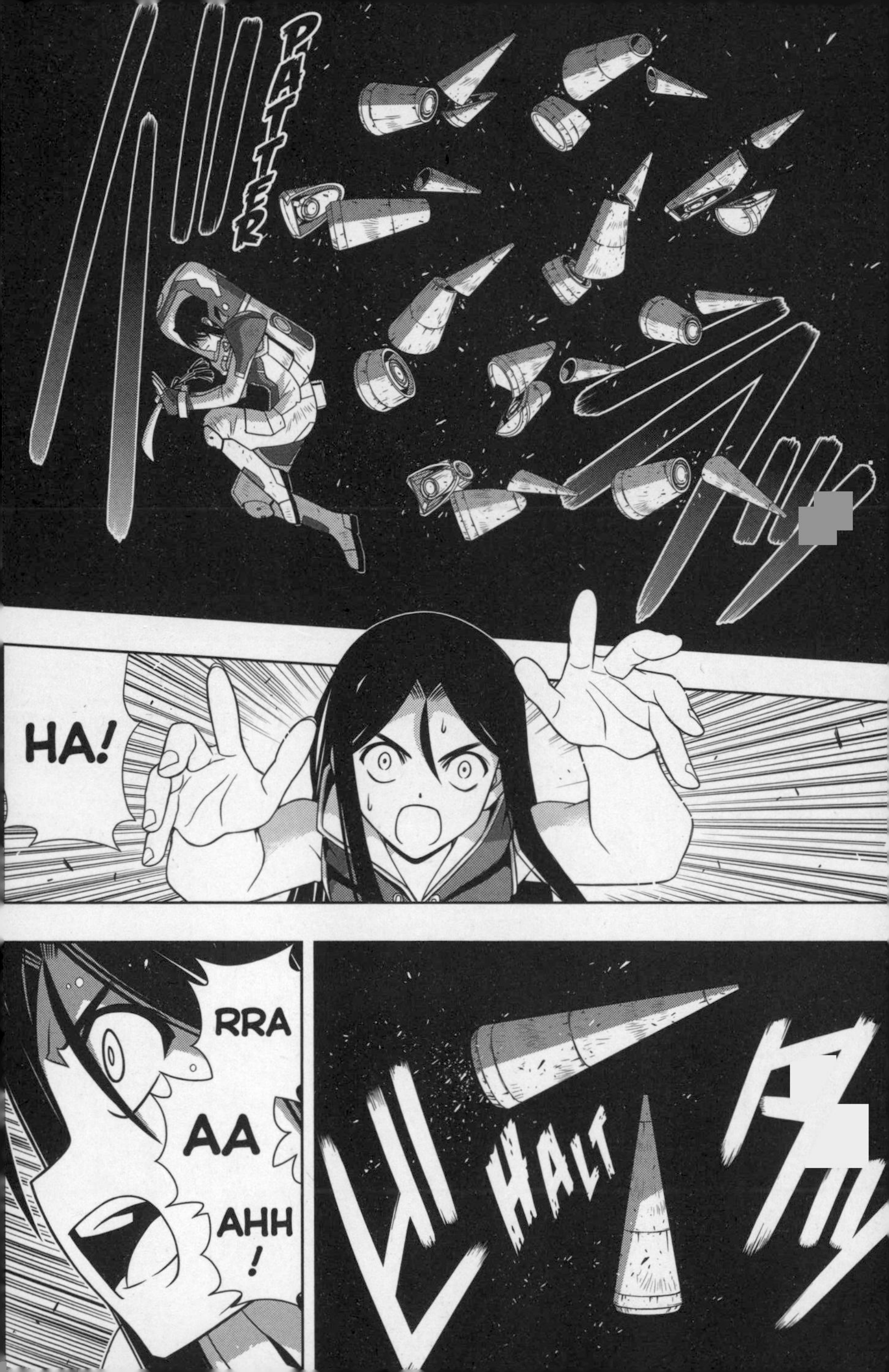
PATTER
HA!
HALT
RRA
AA
AHH!

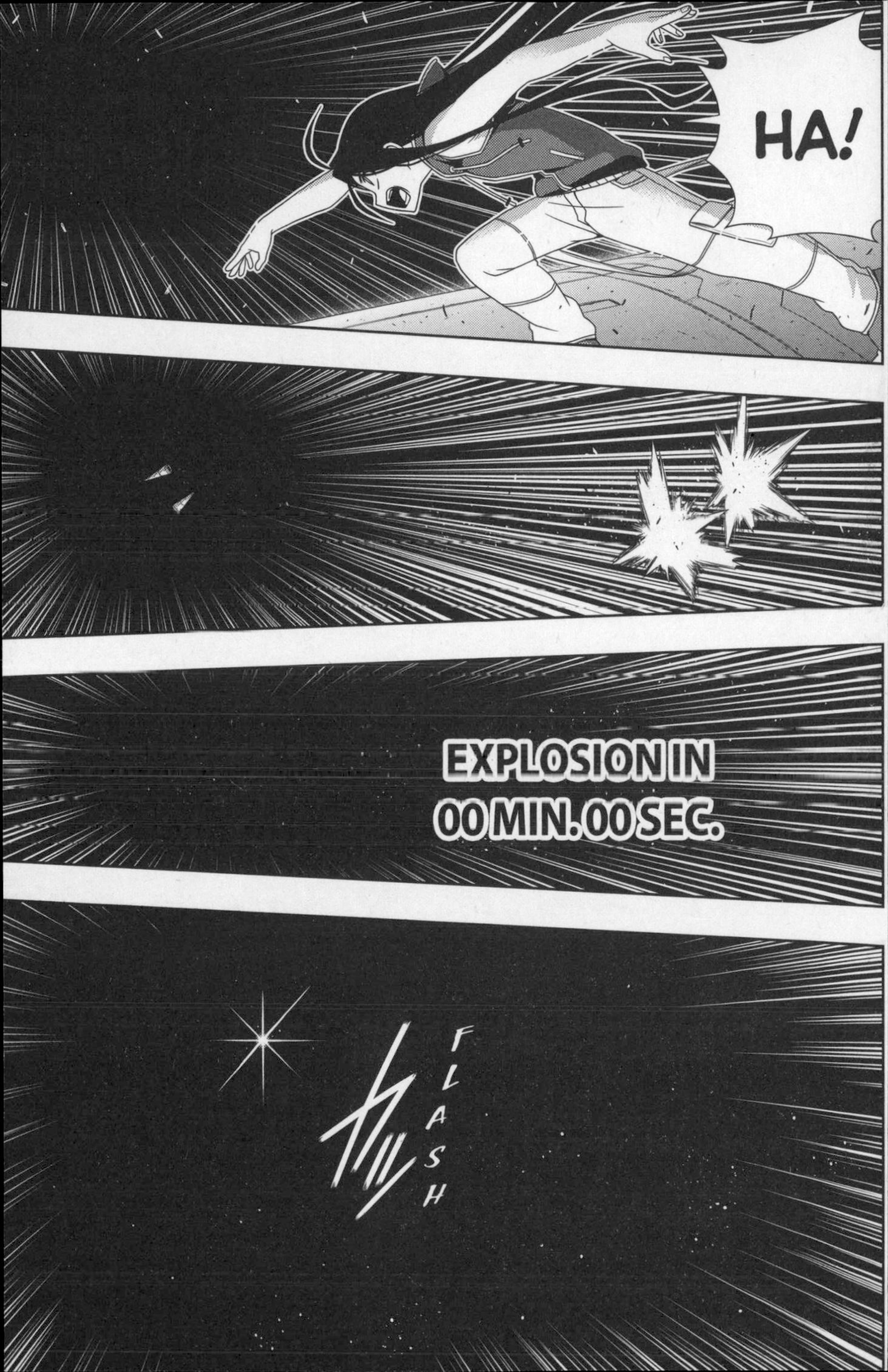
HA!
EXPLOSION IN
00 MIN. 00 SEC.
FLASH

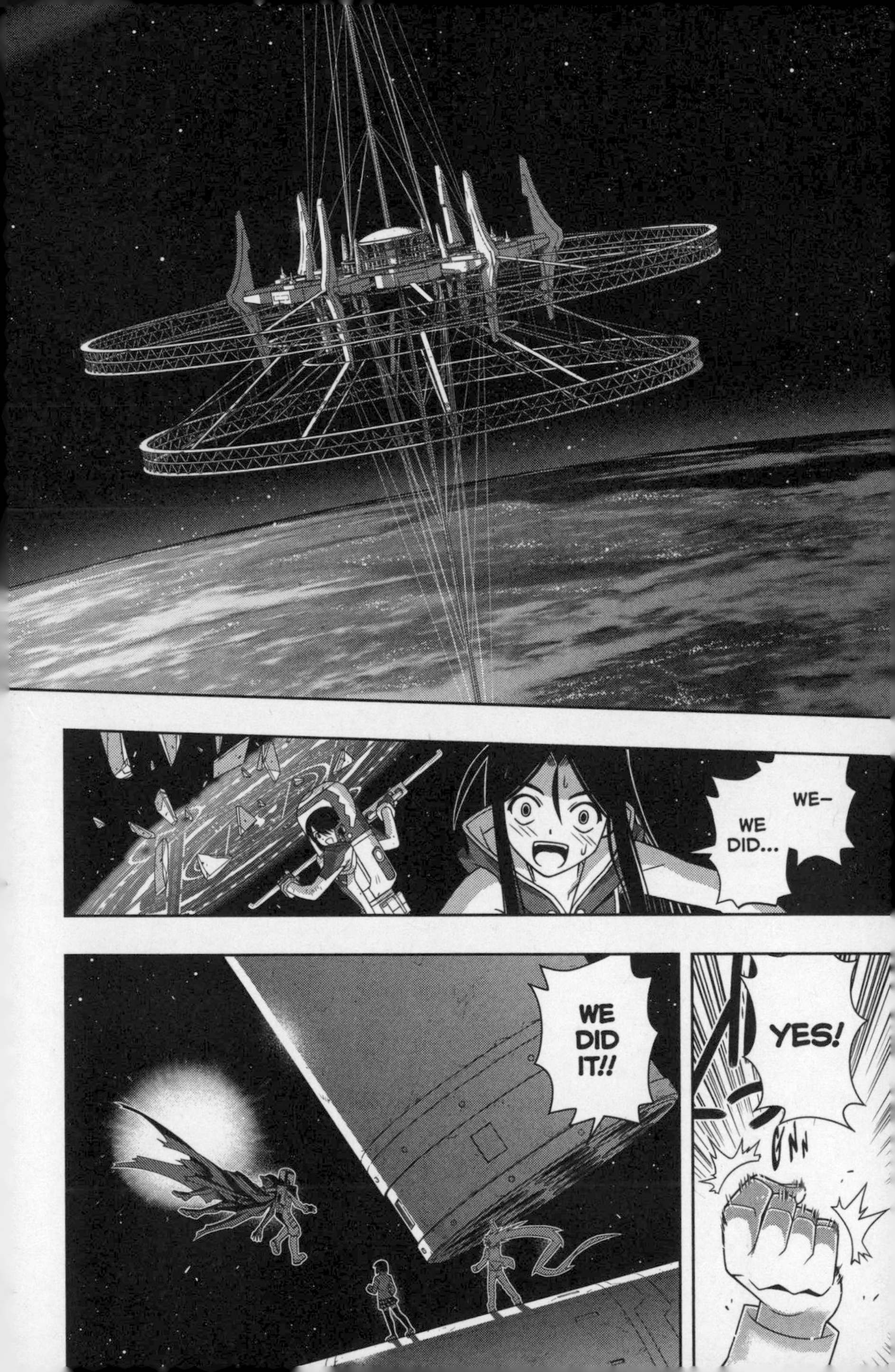
WE-
WE DID...
YES!
GNN
WE DID IT!!

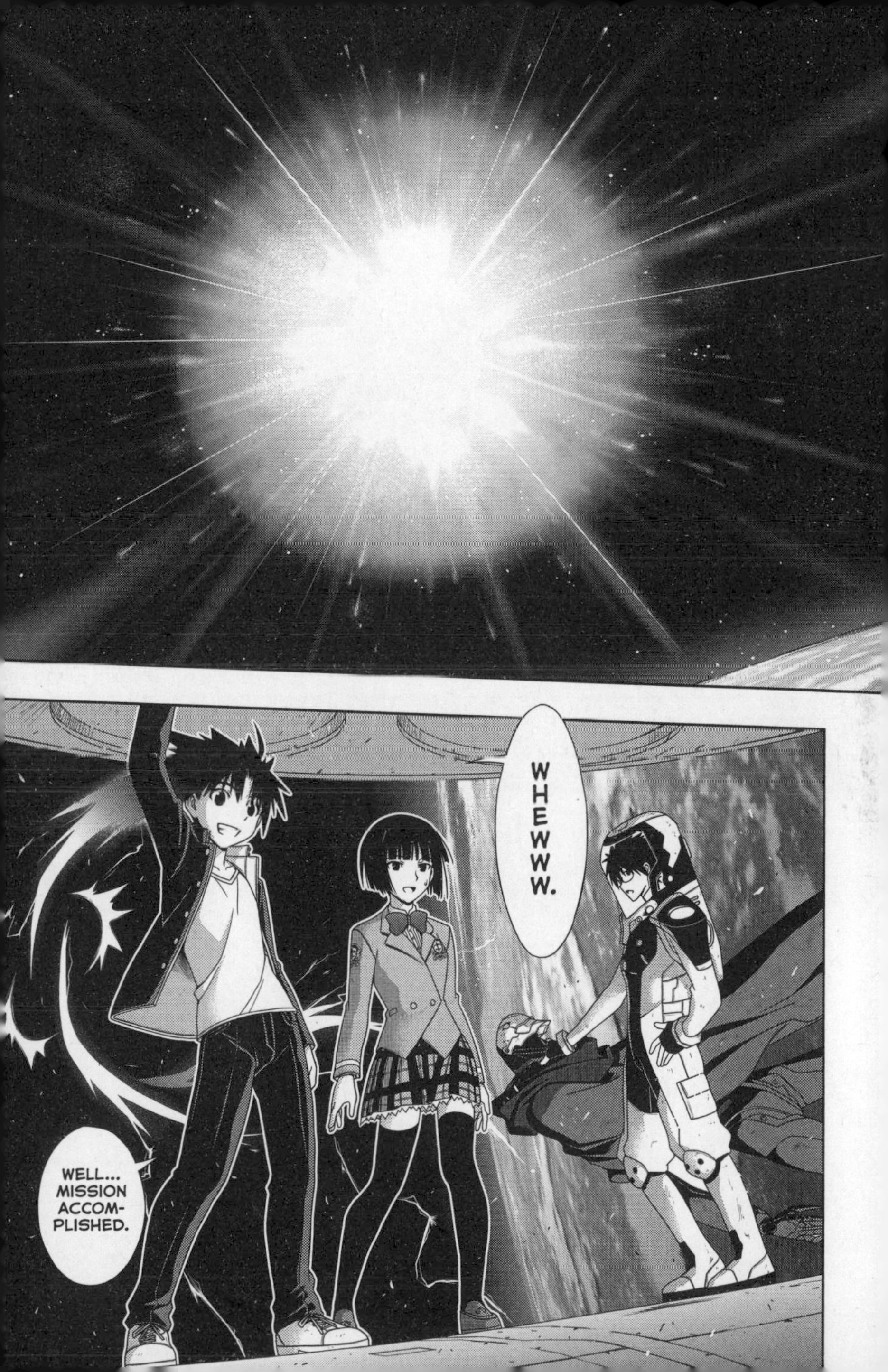
WHEWWW.
WELL... MISSION ACCOMPLISHED.

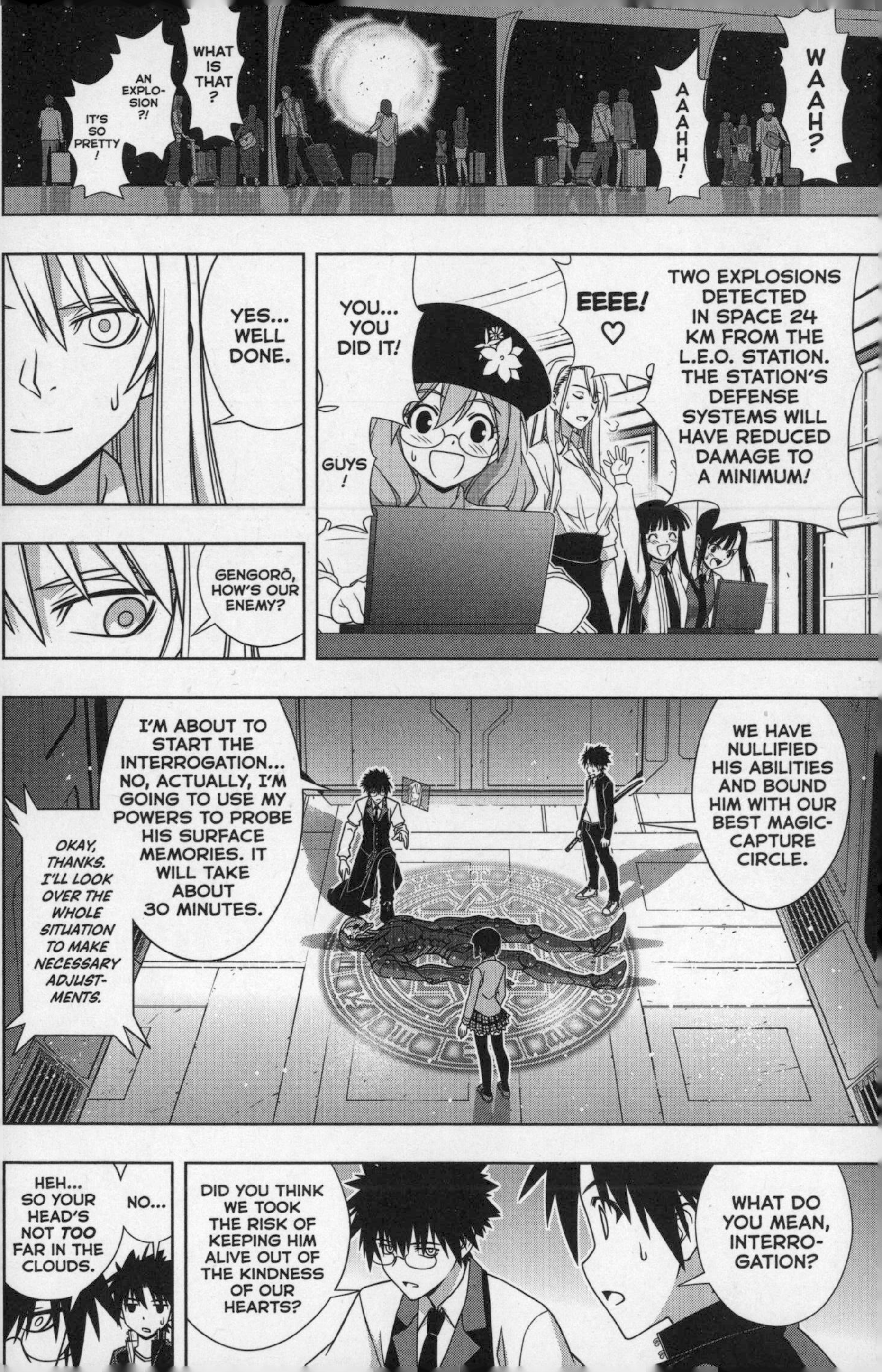
WAAH?
AAAHH!
WHAT IS THAT?
AN EXPLOSION?!
IT'S SO PRETTY!
TWO EXPLOSIONS DETECTED IN SPACE 24 KM FROM THE L.E.O. STATION. THE STATION'S DEFENSE SYSTEMS WILL HAVE REDUCED DAMAGE TO A MINIMUM!
EEEE! ♡
YOU... YOU DID IT!
GUYS!
YES... WELL DONE.
GENGORŌ, HOW'S OUR ENEMY?
WE HAVE NULLIFIED HIS ABILITIES AND BOUND HIM WITH OUR BEST MAGIC-CAPTURE CIRCLE.
I'M ABOUT TO START THE INTERROGATION... NO, ACTUALLY, I'M GOING TO USE MY POWERS TO PROBE HIS SURFACE MEMORIES. IT WILL TAKE ABOUT 30 MINUTES.
OKAY, THANKS. I'LL LOOK OVER THE WHOLE SITUATION TO MAKE NECESSARY ADJUSTMENTS.
WHAT DO YOU MEAN, INTERROGATION?
DID YOU THINK WE TOOK THE RISK OF KEEPING HIM ALIVE OUT OF THE KINDNESS OF OUR HEARTS?
NO...
HEH... SO YOUR HEAD'S NOT TOO FAR IN THE CLOUDS.

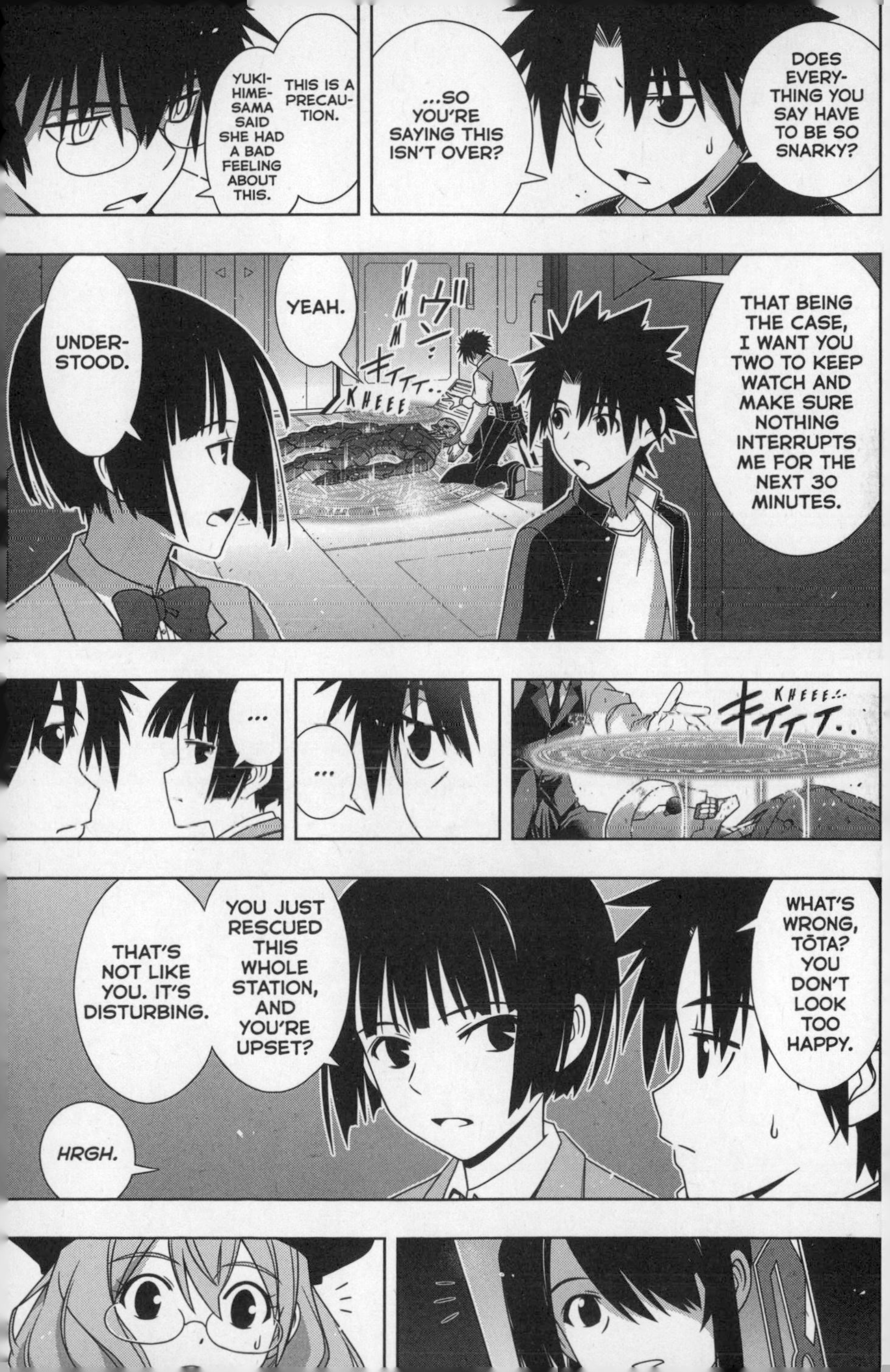
DOES EVERYTHING YOU SAY HAVE TO BE SO SNARKY?
...SO YOU'RE SAYING THIS ISN'T OVER?
THIS IS A PRECAUTION.
YUKI-HIME-SAMA SAID SHE HAD A BAD FEELING ABOUT THIS.
THAT BEING THE CASE, I WANT YOU TWO TO KEEP WATCH AND MAKE SURE NOTHING INTERRUPTS ME FOR THE NEXT 30 MINUTES.
VMMM
KHEEE
YEAH.
UNDERSTOOD.
KHEEE...
...
...
WHAT'S WRONG, TŌTA? YOU DON'T LOOK TOO HAPPY.
YOU JUST RESCUED THIS WHOLE STATION, AND YOU'RE UPSET?
THAT'S NOT LIKE YOU. IT'S DISTURBING.
HRGH.

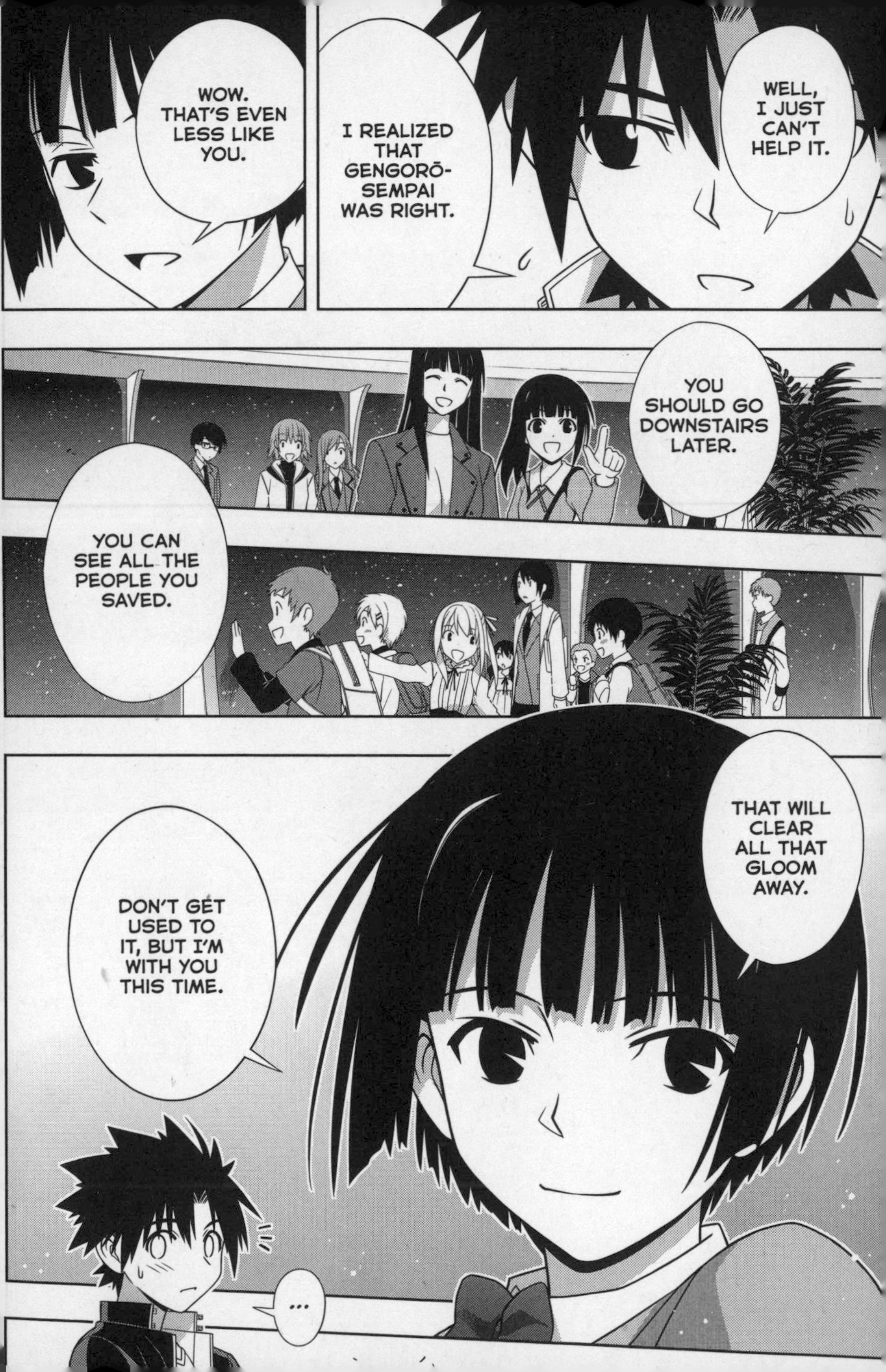
WELL, I JUST CAN'T HELP IT.
I REALIZED THAT GENGORŌ-SEMPAI WAS RIGHT.
WOW. THAT'S EVEN LESS LIKE YOU.
YOU SHOULD GO DOWNSTAIRS LATER.
YOU CAN SEE ALL THE PEOPLE YOU SAVED.
THAT WILL CLEAR ALL THAT GLOOM AWAY.
DON'T GET USED TO IT, BUT I'M WITH YOU THIS TIME.
...

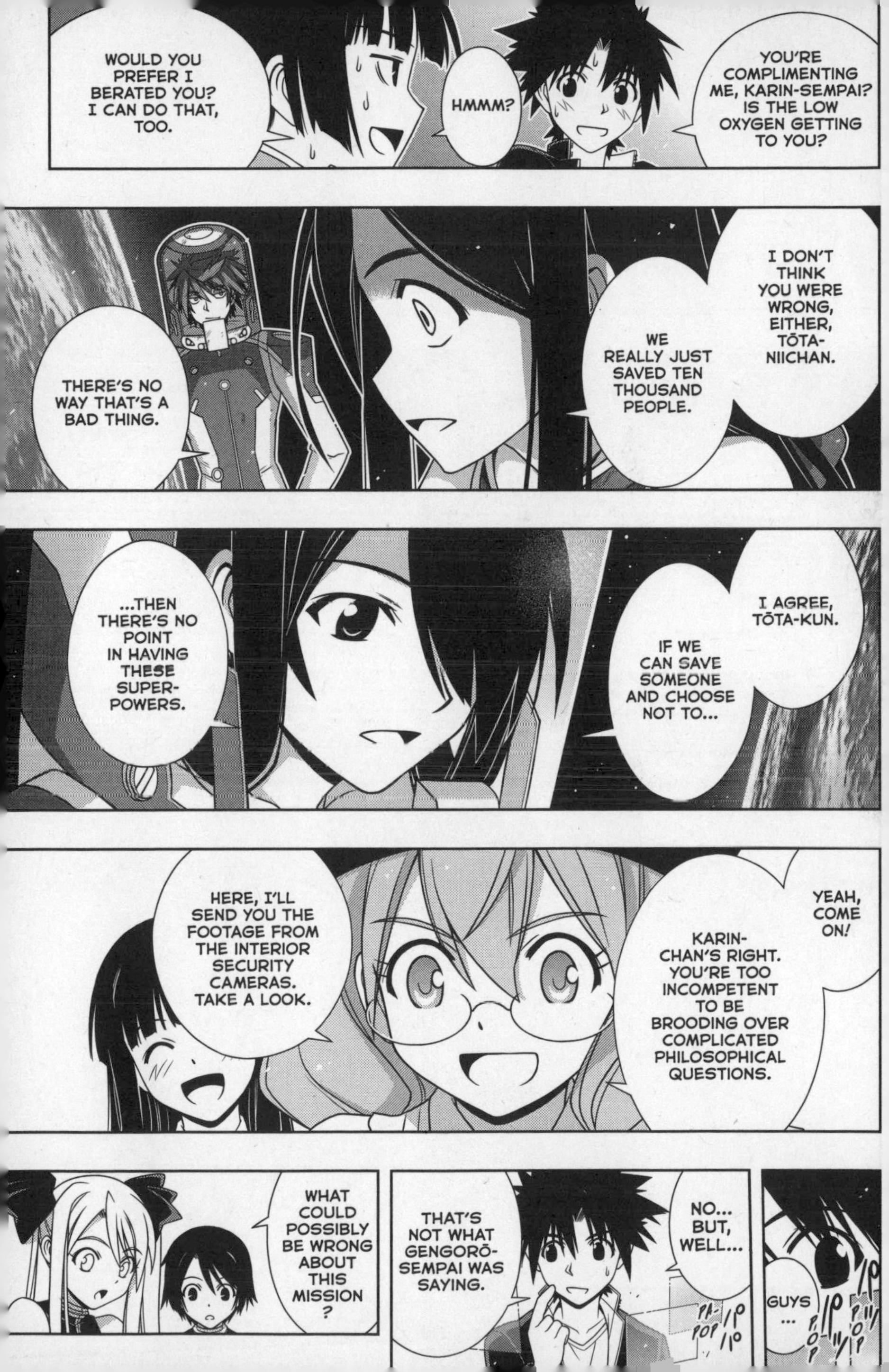
YOU'RE COMPLIMENTING ME, KARIN-SEMPAI? IS THE LOW OXYGEN GETTING TO YOU?
HMMM?
WOULD YOU PREFER I BERATED YOU? I CAN DO THAT, TOO.
I DON'T THINK YOU WERE WRONG, EITHER, TŌTA-NIICHAN.
WE REALLY JUST SAVED TEN THOUSAND PEOPLE.
THERE'S NO WAY THAT'S A BAD THING.
I AGREE, TŌTA-KUN.
IF WE CAN SAVE SOMEONE AND CHOOSE NOT TO...
...THEN THERE'S NO POINT IN HAVING THESE SUPER-POWERS.
YEAH, COME ON!
KARIN-CHAN'S RIGHT. YOU'RE TOO INCOMPETENT TO BE BROODING OVER COMPLICATED PHILOSOPHICAL QUESTIONS.
HERE, I'LL SEND YOU THE FOOTAGE FROM THE INTERIOR SECURITY CAMERAS. TAKE A LOOK.
GUYS ...
NO... BUT, WELL...
THAT'S NOT WHAT GENGORŌ-SEMPAI WAS SAYING.
PA-POP
WHAT COULD POSSIBLY BE WRONG ABOUT THIS MISSION?

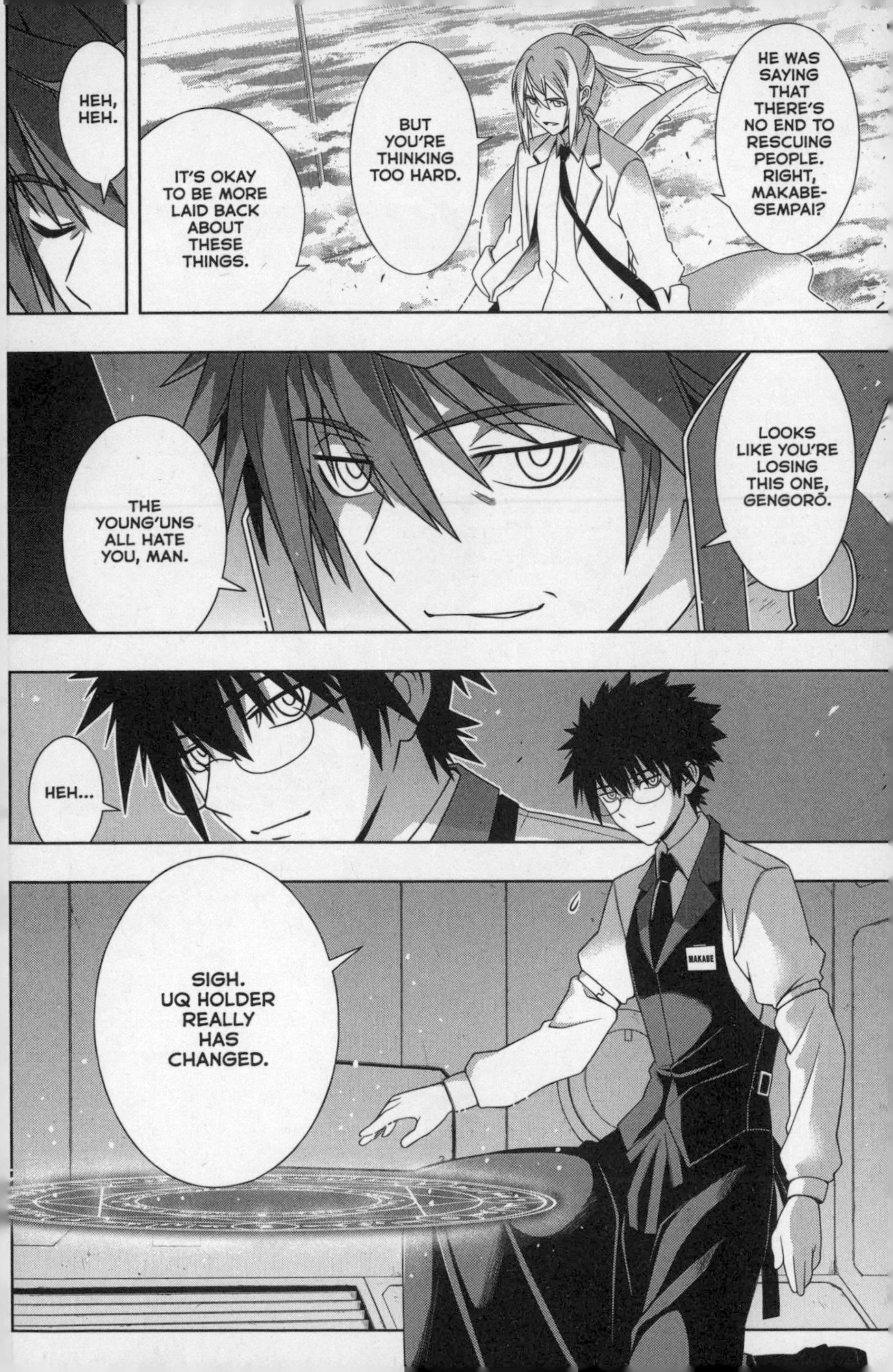
HE WAS SAYING THAT THERE'S NO END TO RESCUING PEOPLE. RIGHT, MAKABE-SEMPAI?
BUT YOU'RE THINKING TOO HARD.
IT'S OKAY TO BE MORE LAID BACK ABOUT THESE THINGS.
HEH, HEH.
LOOKS LIKE YOU'RE LOSING THIS ONE, GENGORŌ.
THE YOUNG'UNS ALL HATE YOU, MAN.
HEH...
MAKABE
SIGH. UQ HOLDER REALLY HAS CHANGED.

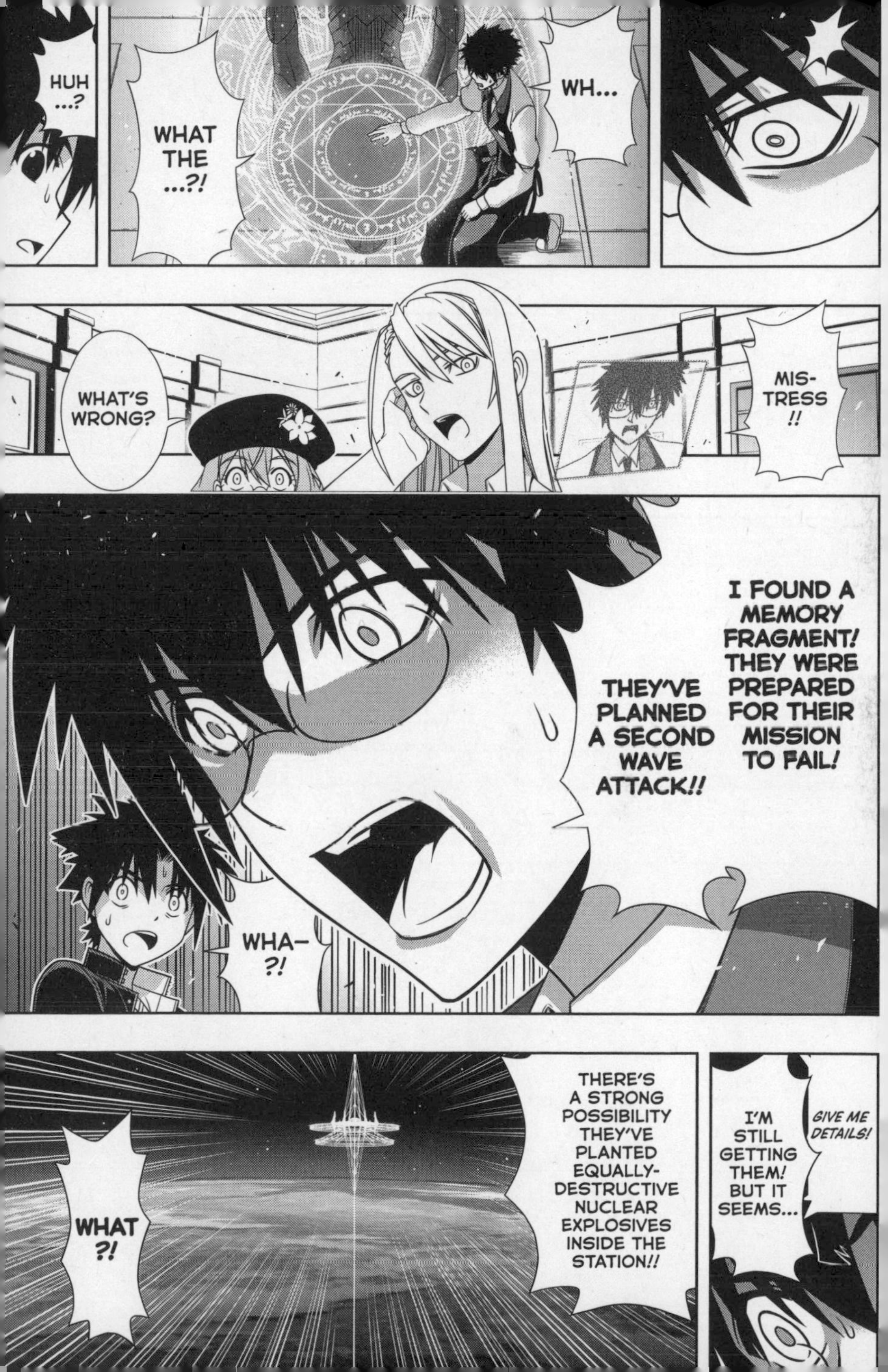
WH...
WHAT THE ...?!
HUH ...?
MIS-TRESS !!
WHAT'S WRONG?
I FOUND A MEMORY FRAGMENT! THEY WERE PREPARED FOR THEIR MISSION TO FAIL!
THEY'VE PLANNED A SECOND WAVE ATTACK!!
WHA– ?!
GIVE ME DETAILS!
I'M STILL GETTING THEM! BUT IT SEEMS...
THERE'S A STRONG POSSIBILITY THEY'VE PLANTED EQUALLY-DESTRUCTIVE NUCLEAR EXPLOSIVES INSIDE THE STATION!!
WHAT ?!

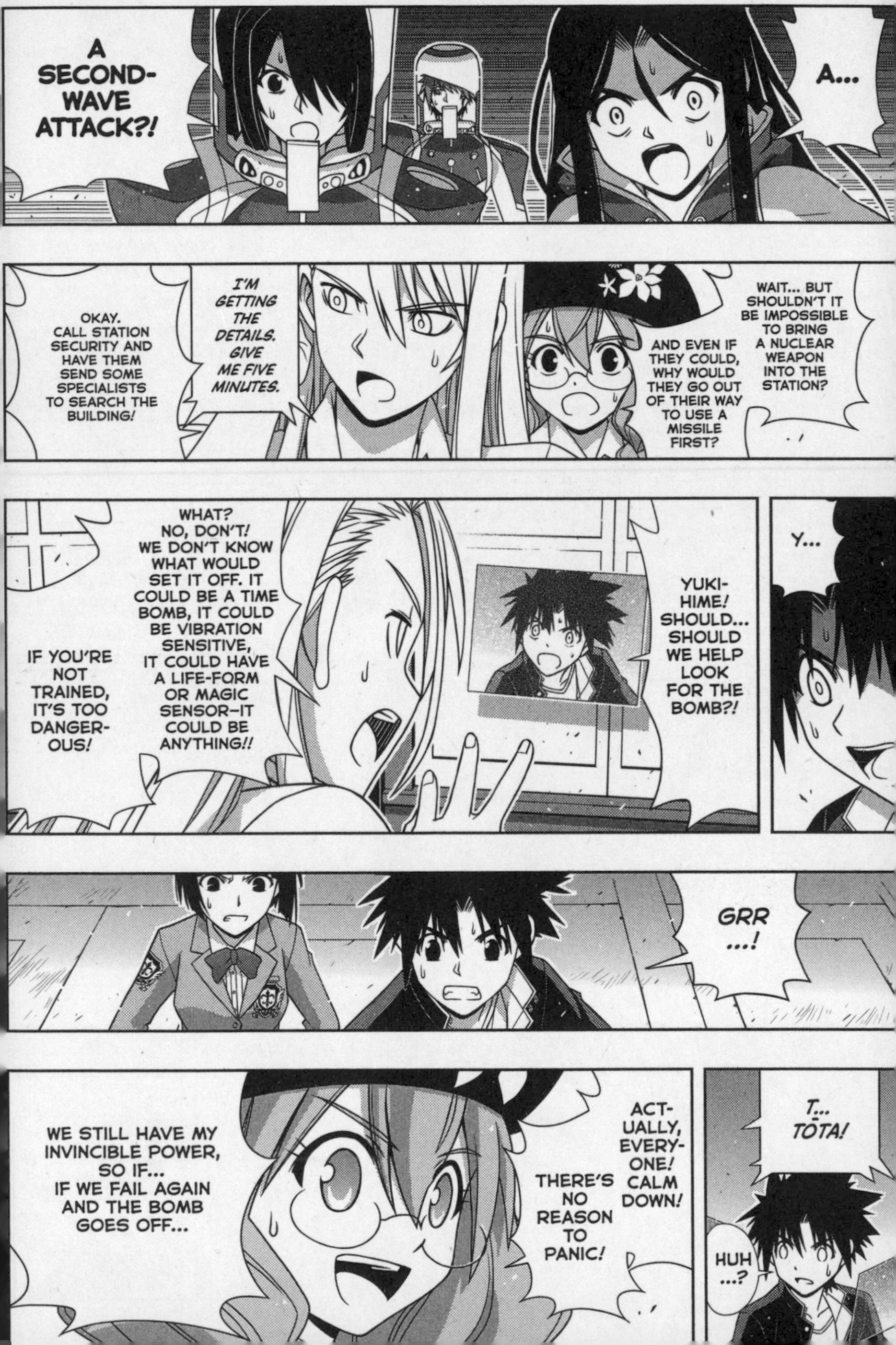
A...
A SECOND-WAVE ATTACK?!
WAIT... BUT SHOULDN'T IT BE IMPOSSIBLE TO BRING A NUCLEAR WEAPON INTO THE STATION?
AND EVEN IF THEY COULD, WHY WOULD THEY GO OUT OF THEIR WAY TO USE A MISSILE FIRST?
I'M GETTING THE DETAILS. GIVE ME FIVE MINUTES.
OKAY. CALL STATION SECURITY AND HAVE THEM SEND SOME SPECIALISTS TO SEARCH THE BUILDING!
Y...
YUKI-HIME! SHOULD... SHOULD WE HELP LOOK FOR THE BOMB?!
WHAT? NO, DON'T! WE DON'T KNOW WHAT WOULD SET IT OFF. IT COULD BE A TIME BOMB, IT COULD BE VIBRATION SENSITIVE, IT COULD HAVE A LIFE-FORM OR MAGIC SENSOR—IT COULD BE ANYTHING!!
IF YOU'RE NOT TRAINED, IT'S TOO DANGEROUS!
GRR...!
T... TŌTA!
HUH...?
ACTUALLY, EVERYONE! CALM DOWN!
THERE'S NO REASON TO PANIC!
WE STILL HAVE MY INVINCIBLE POWER, SO IF... IF WE FAIL AGAIN AND THE BOMB GOES OFF...

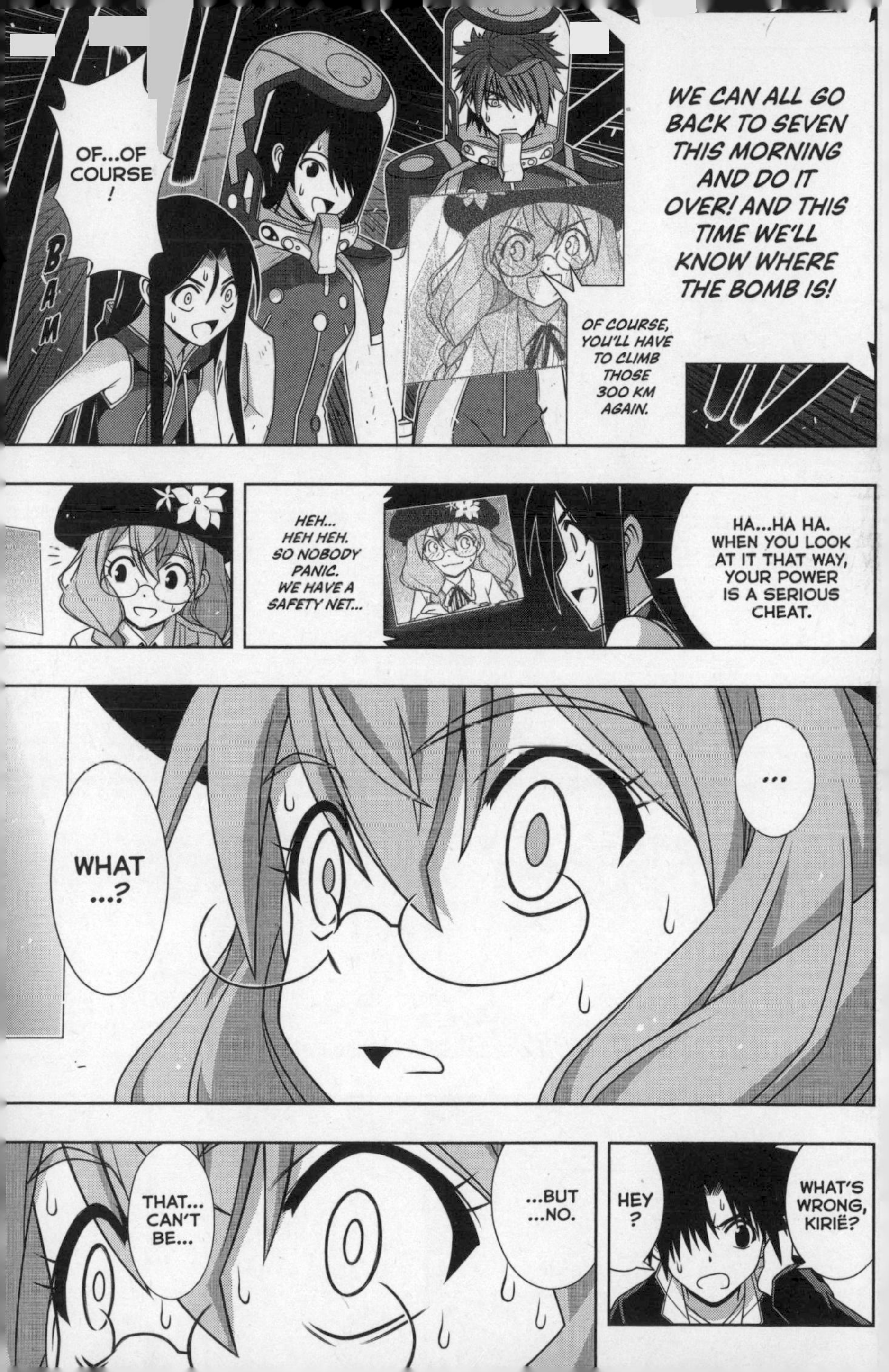
WE CAN ALL GO BACK TO SEVEN THIS MORNING AND DO IT OVER! AND THIS TIME WE'LL KNOW WHERE THE BOMB IS!
OF COURSE, YOU'LL HAVE TO CLIMB THOSE 300 KM AGAIN.
OF...OF COURSE!
BAM
HA...HA HA. WHEN YOU LOOK AT IT THAT WAY, YOUR POWER IS A SERIOUS CHEAT.
HEH... HEH HEH. SO NOBODY PANIC. WE HAVE A SAFETY NET...
...
WHAT ...?
WHAT'S WRONG, KIRIË?
HEY ?
...BUT ...NO.
THAT... CAN'T BE...

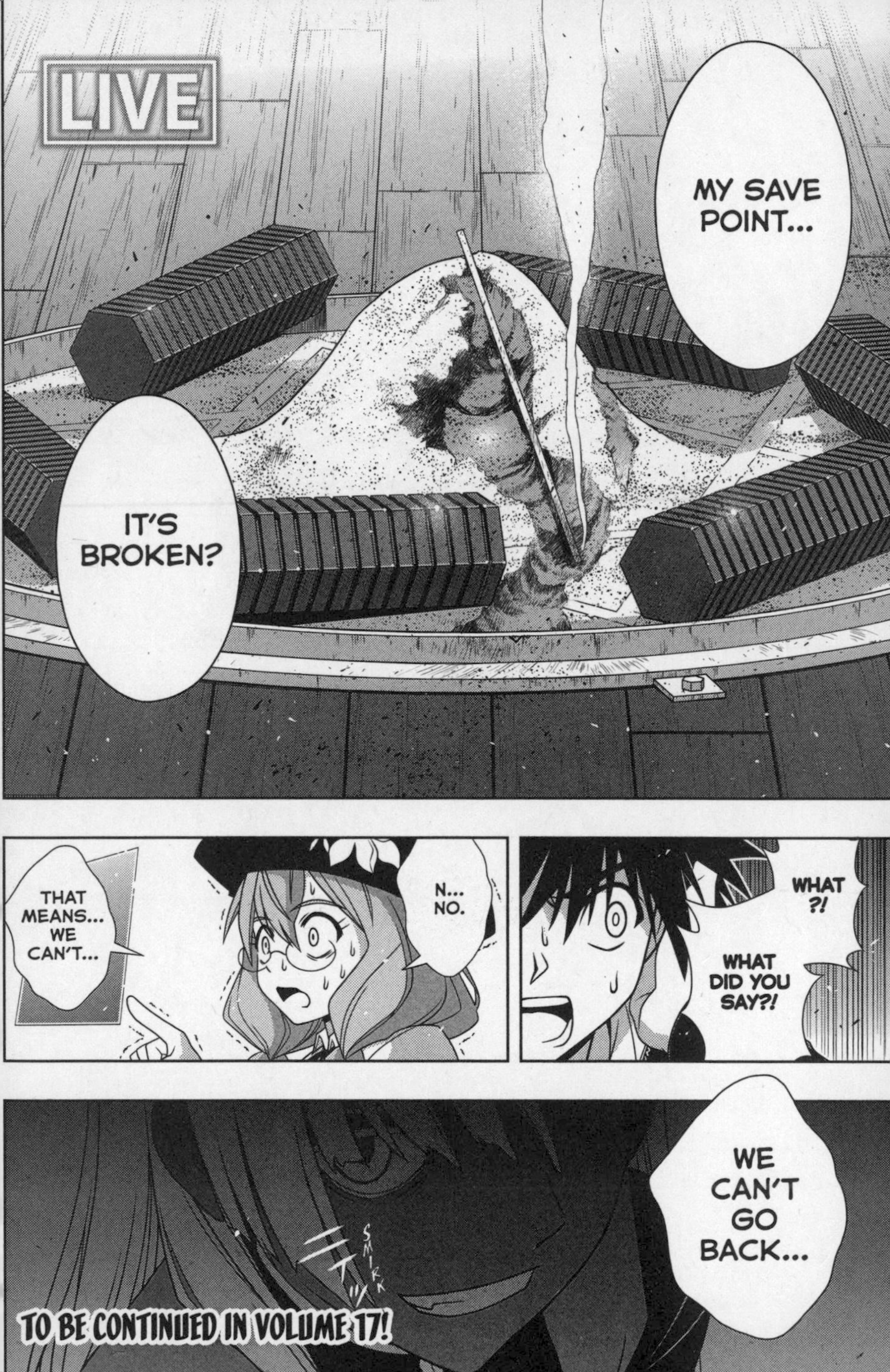
MY SAVE POINT...
LIVE
IT'S BROKEN?
WHAT?!
WHAT DID YOU SAY?!
N... NO.
THAT MEANS... WE CAN'T...
WE CAN'T GO BACK...
SMIRK
TO BE CONTINUED IN VOLUME 17!

UQ HOLDER!

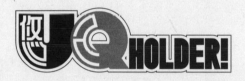

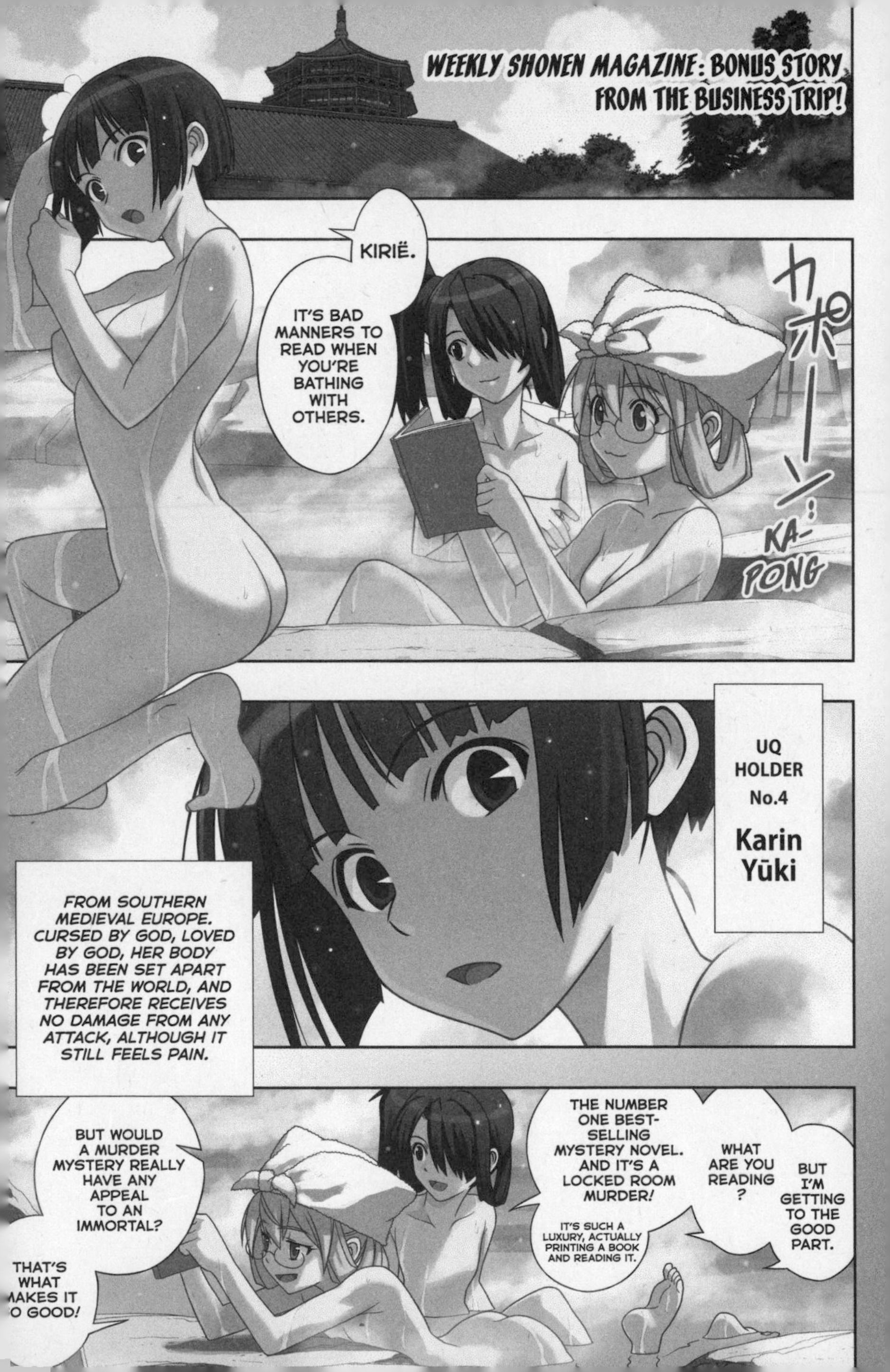
WEEKLY SHONEN MAGAZINE: BONUS STORY FROM THE BUSINESS TRIP!
KA-PONG
KIRIË.
IT'S BAD MANNERS TO READ WHEN YOU'RE BATHING WITH OTHERS.
UQ HOLDER No.4 Karin Yūki
FROM SOUTHERN MEDIEVAL EUROPE. CURSED BY GOD, LOVED BY GOD, HER BODY HAS BEEN SET APART FROM THE WORLD, AND THEREFORE RECEIVES NO DAMAGE FROM ANY ATTACK, ALTHOUGH IT STILL FEELS PAIN.
BUT I'M GETTING TO THE GOOD PART.
WHAT ARE YOU READING?
THE NUMBER ONE BEST-SELLING MYSTERY NOVEL. AND IT'S A LOCKED ROOM MURDER!
IT'S SUCH A LUXURY, ACTUALLY PRINTING A BOOK AND READING IT.
BUT WOULD A MURDER MYSTERY REALLY HAVE ANY APPEAL TO AN IMMORTAL?
THAT'S WHAT MAKES IT O GOOD!

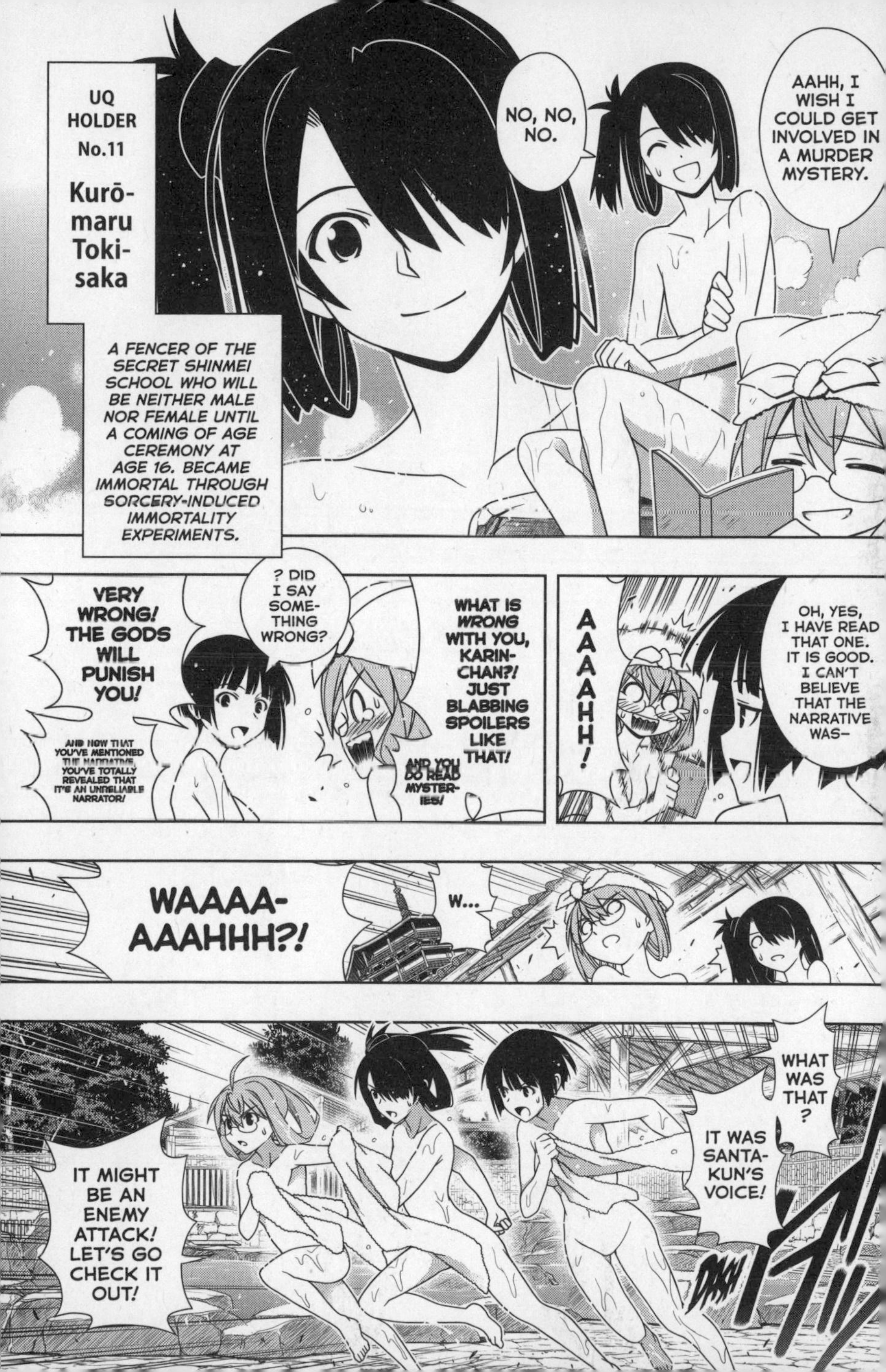
AAHH, I WISH I COULD GET INVOLVED IN A MURDER MYSTERY.
NO, NO, NO.
UQ HOLDER No.11 Kurō-maru Toki-saka
A FENCER OF THE SECRET SHINMEI SCHOOL WHO WILL BE NEITHER MALE NOR FEMALE UNTIL A COMING OF AGE CEREMONY AT AGE 16. BECAME IMMORTAL THROUGH SORCERY-INDUCED IMMORTALITY EXPERIMENTS.
OH, YES, I HAVE READ THAT ONE. IT IS GOOD. I CAN'T BELIEVE THAT THE NARRATIVE WAS—
AAAAAH!
WHAT IS WRONG WITH YOU, KARIN-CHAN?! JUST BLABBING SPOILERS LIKE THAT!
AND YOU DO READ MYSTER-IES!
? DID I SAY SOME-THING WRONG?
VERY WRONG! THE GODS WILL PUNISH YOU!
AND NOW THAT YOU'VE MENTIONED THE NARRATIVE, YOU'VE TOTALLY REVEALED THAT IT'S AN UNRELIABLE NARRATOR!
W...
WAAAA-AAAHHH?!
WHAT WAS THAT?
IT WAS SANTA-KUN'S VOICE!
DASH
IT MIGHT BE AN ENEMY ATTACK! LET'S GO CHECK IT OUT!

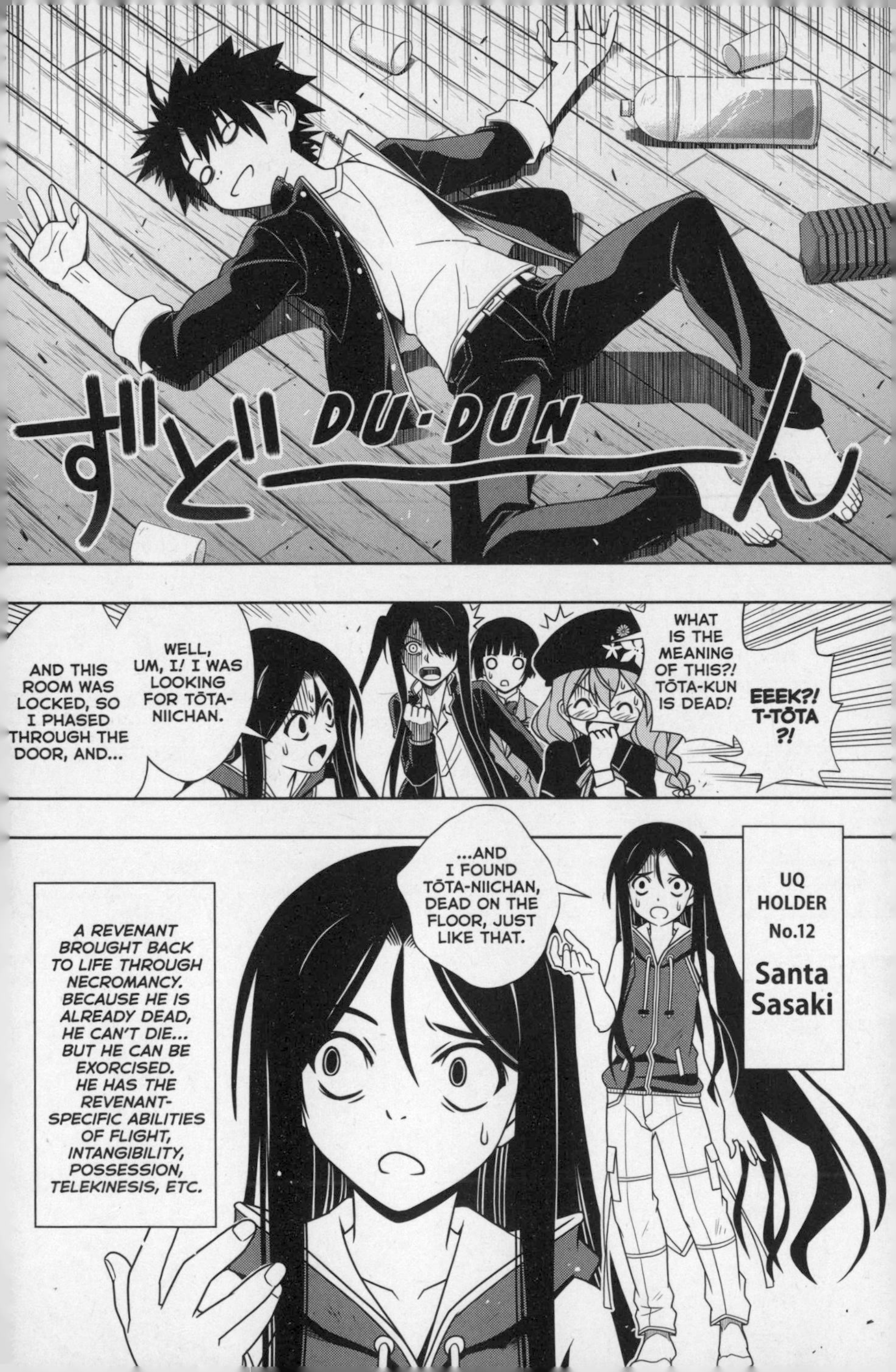
ずどーん
DU-DUN
EEEK?! T-TŌTA?!
WHAT IS THE MEANING OF THIS?! TŌTA-KUN IS DEAD!
WELL, UM, I! I WAS LOOKING FOR TŌTA-NIICHAN.
AND THIS ROOM WAS LOCKED, SO I PHASED THROUGH THE DOOR, AND...
UQ HOLDER No.12 Santa Sasaki
...AND I FOUND TŌTA-NIICHAN, DEAD ON THE FLOOR, JUST LIKE THAT.
A REVENANT BROUGHT BACK TO LIFE THROUGH NECROMANCY. BECAUSE HE IS ALREADY DEAD, HE CAN'T DIE... BUT HE CAN BE EXORCISED. HE HAS THE REVENANT-SPECIFIC ABILITIES OF FLIGHT, INTANGIBILITY, POSSESSION, TELEKINESIS, ETC.

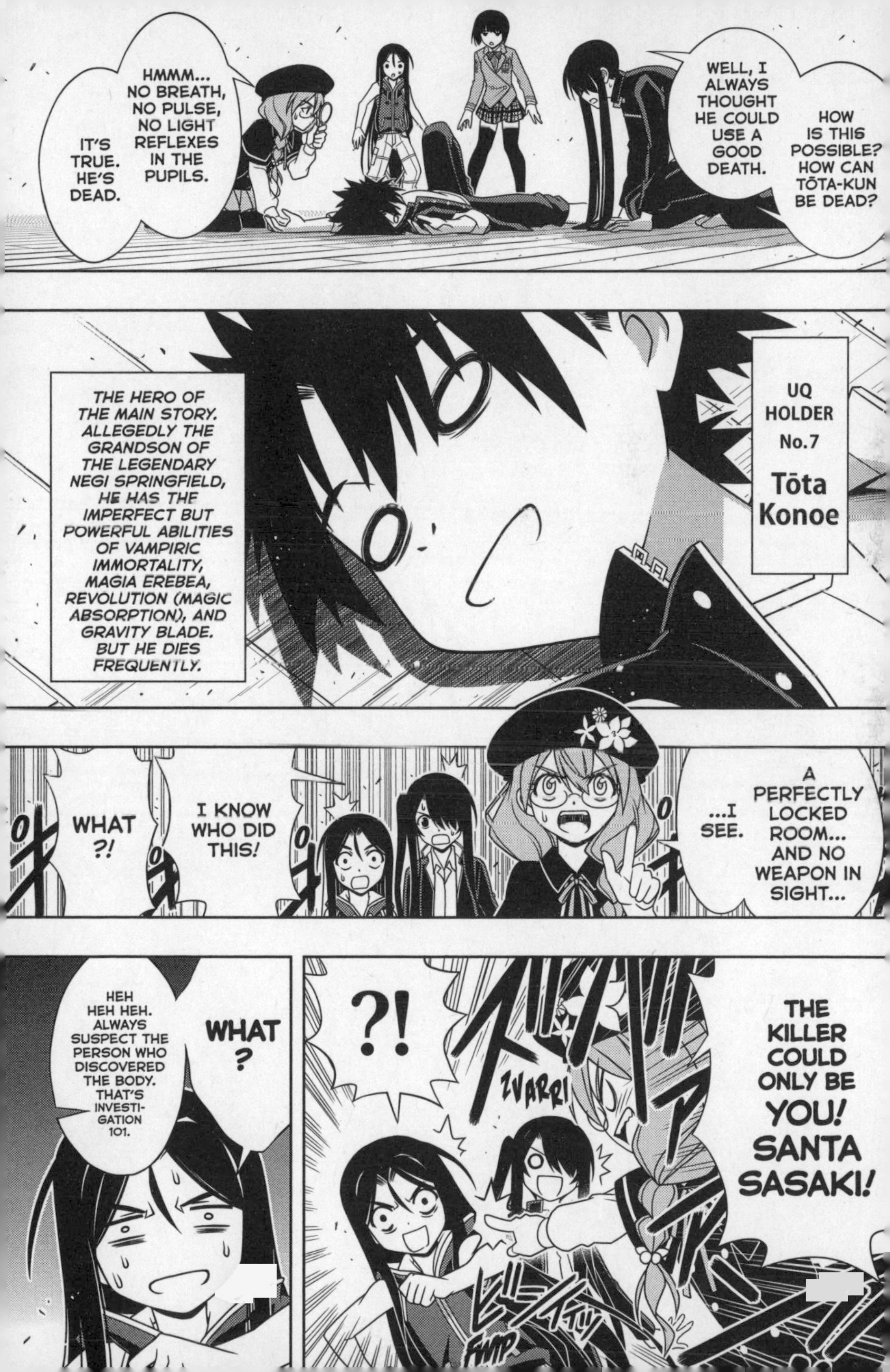
HOW IS THIS POSSIBLE? HOW CAN TŌTA-KUN BE DEAD?
WELL, I ALWAYS THOUGHT HE COULD USE A GOOD DEATH.
HMMM... NO BREATH, NO PULSE, NO LIGHT REFLEXES IN THE PUPILS.
IT'S TRUE. HE'S DEAD.
UQ HOLDER No.7 Tōta Konoe
THE HERO OF THE MAIN STORY. ALLEGEDLY THE GRANDSON OF THE LEGENDARY NEGI SPRINGFIELD, HE HAS THE IMPERFECT BUT POWERFUL ABILITIES OF VAMPIRIC IMMORTALITY, MAGIA EREBEA, REVOLUTION (MAGIC ABSORPTION), AND GRAVITY BLADE. BUT HE DIES FREQUENTLY.
A PERFECTLY LOCKED ROOM... AND NO WEAPON IN SIGHT...
...I SEE.
I KNOW WHO DID THIS!
WHAT?!
THE KILLER COULD ONLY BE YOU! SANTA SASAKI!
ZVARRI
?!
FWIP
WHAT?
HEH HEH HEH. ALWAYS SUSPECT THE PERSON WHO DISCOVERED THE BODY. THAT'S INVESTIGATION 101.

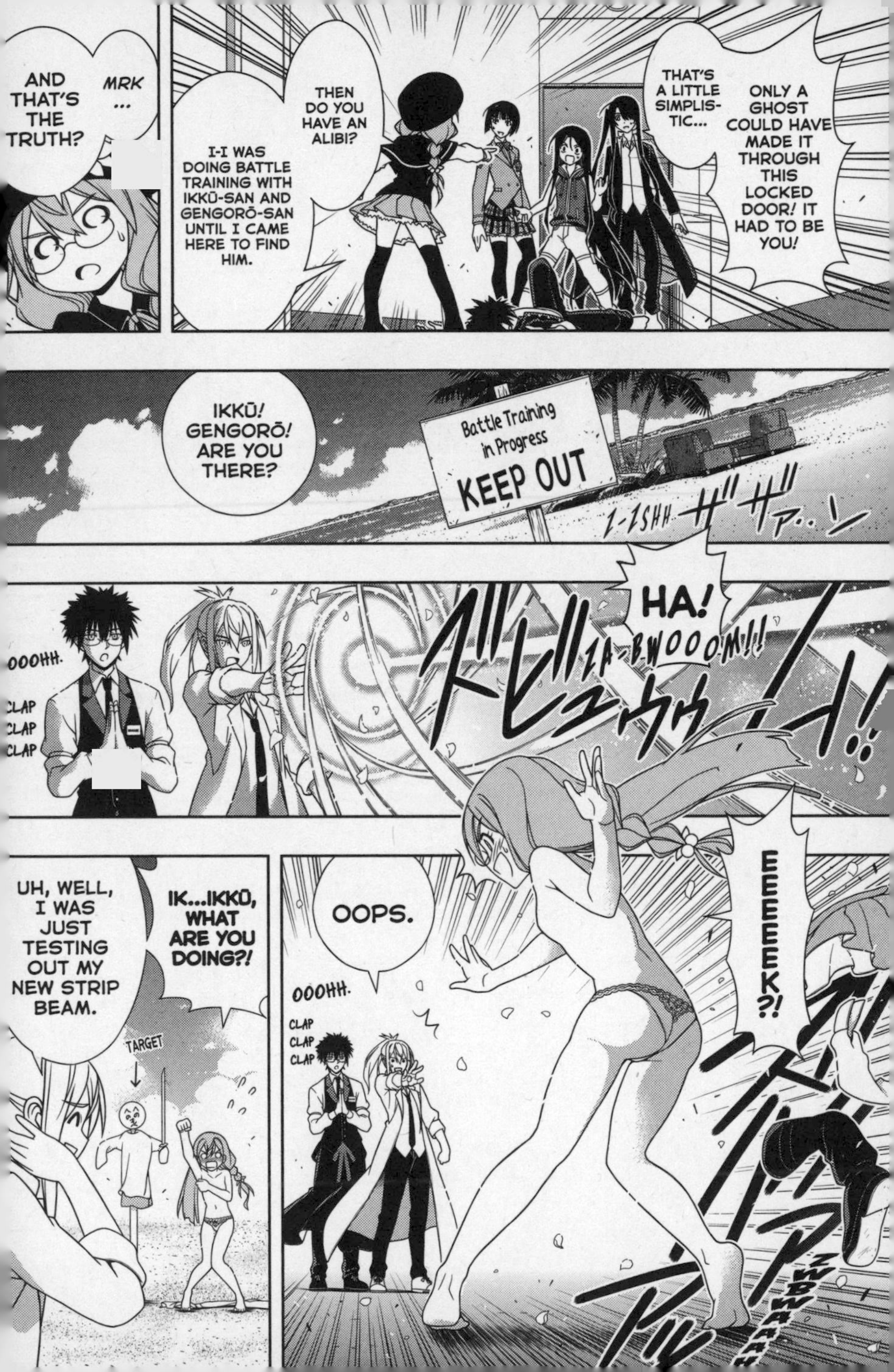
ONLY A GHOST COULD HAVE MADE IT THROUGH THIS LOCKED DOOR! IT HAD TO BE YOU!
THAT'S A LITTLE SIMPLISTIC...
THEN DO YOU HAVE AN ALIBI?
I-I WAS DOING BATTLE TRAINING WITH IKKŪ-SAN AND GENGORŌ-SAN UNTIL I CAME HERE TO FIND HIM.
MRK ...
AND THAT'S THE TRUTH?
IKKŪ! GENGORŌ! ARE YOU THERE?
Battle Training in Progress KEEP OUT
Z-ZSHH
HA!
ZA-BWOOOM!!!
OOOHH.
CLAP CLAP CLAP
EEEEEEK?!
OOPS.
OOOHH.
CLAP CLAP CLAP
IK...IKKŪ, WHAT ARE YOU DOING?!
UH, WELL, I WAS JUST TESTING OUT MY NEW STRIP BEAM.
TARGET

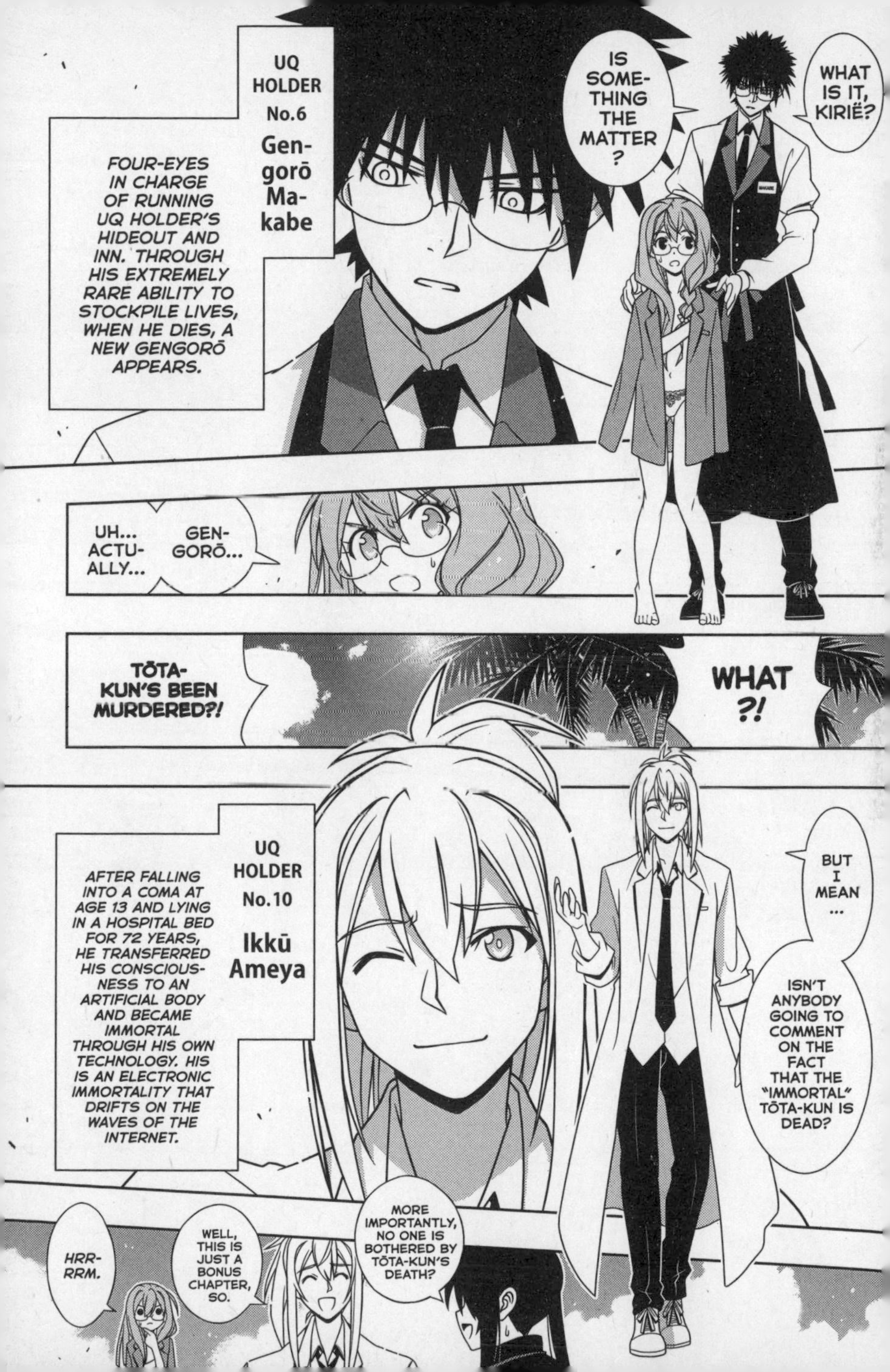

WHAT IS IT, KIRIË?
IS SOMETHING THE MATTER?
UQ HOLDER No.6 Gengorō Makabe
FOUR-EYES IN CHARGE OF RUNNING UQ HOLDER'S HIDEOUT AND INN. THROUGH HIS EXTREMELY RARE ABILITY TO STOCKPILE LIVES, WHEN HE DIES, A NEW GENGORŌ APPEARS.
GENGORŌ...
UH... ACTUALLY...
WHAT?!
TŌTA-KUN'S BEEN MURDERED?!
BUT I MEAN...
ISN'T ANYBODY GOING TO COMMENT ON THE FACT THAT THE "IMMORTAL" TŌTA-KUN IS DEAD?
UQ HOLDER No.10 Ikkū Ameya
AFTER FALLING INTO A COMA AT AGE 13 AND LYING IN A HOSPITAL BED FOR 72 YEARS, HE TRANSFERRED HIS CONSCIOUSNESS TO AN ARTIFICIAL BODY AND BECAME IMMORTAL THROUGH HIS OWN TECHNOLOGY. HIS IS AN ELECTRONIC IMMORTALITY THAT DRIFTS ON THE WAVES OF THE INTERNET.
MORE IMPORTANTLY, NO ONE IS BOTHERED BY TŌTA-KUN'S DEATH?
WELL, THIS IS JUST A BONUS CHAPTER, SO.
HRR-RRM.

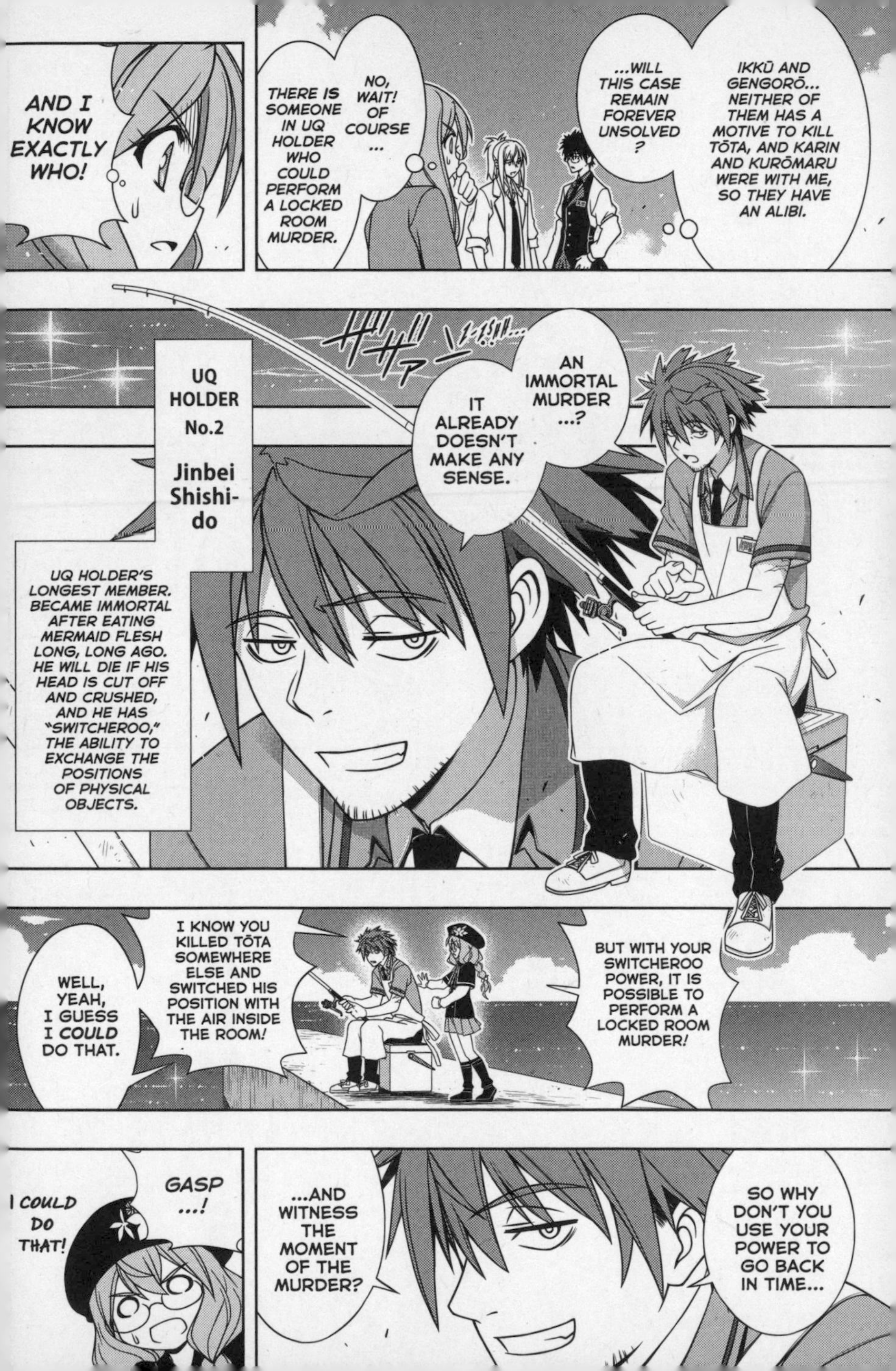
IKKŪ AND GENGORŌ... NEITHER OF THEM HAS A MOTIVE TO KILL TŌTA, AND KARIN AND KURŌMARU WERE WITH ME, SO THEY HAVE AN ALIBI.
...WILL THIS CASE REMAIN FOREVER UNSOLVED?
NO, WAIT! OF COURSE...
THERE IS SOMEONE IN UQ HOLDER WHO COULD PERFORM A LOCKED ROOM MURDER.
AND I KNOW EXACTLY WHO!
AN IMMORTAL MURDER...?
IT ALREADY DOESN'T MAKE ANY SENSE.
UQ HOLDER No.2 Jinbei Shishi-do
UQ HOLDER'S LONGEST MEMBER. BECAME IMMORTAL AFTER EATING MERMAID FLESH LONG, LONG AGO. HE WILL DIE IF HIS HEAD IS CUT OFF AND CRUSHED, AND HE HAS "SWITCHEROO," THE ABILITY TO EXCHANGE THE POSITIONS OF PHYSICAL OBJECTS.
BUT WITH YOUR SWITCHEROO POWER, IT IS POSSIBLE TO PERFORM A LOCKED ROOM MURDER!
I KNOW YOU KILLED TŌTA SOMEWHERE ELSE AND SWITCHED HIS POSITION WITH THE AIR INSIDE THE ROOM!
WELL, YEAH, I GUESS I COULD DO THAT.
SO WHY DON'T YOU USE YOUR POWER TO GO BACK IN TIME...
...AND WITNESS THE MOMENT OF THE MURDER?
GASP...!
I COULD DO THAT!

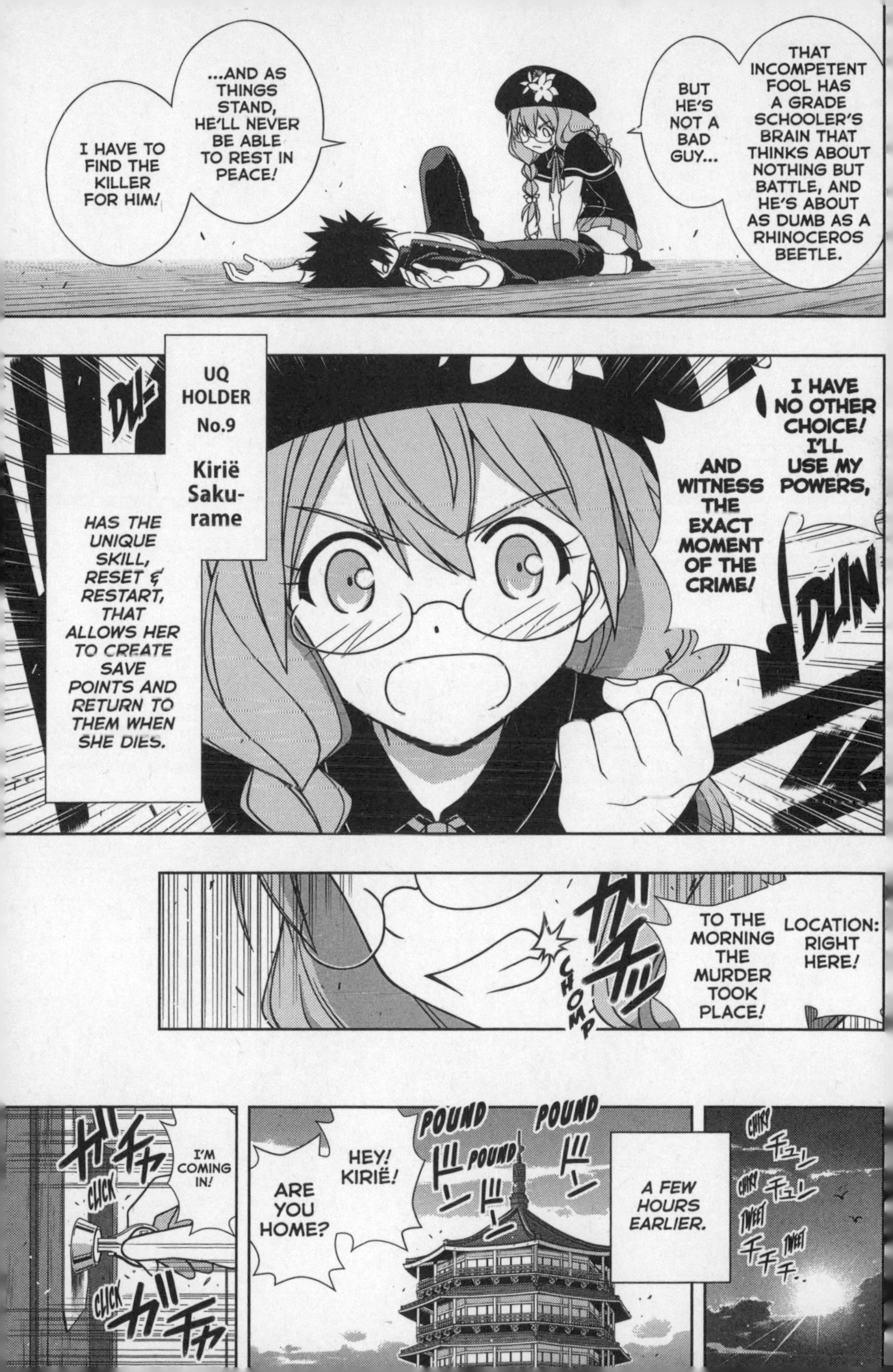
THAT INCOMPETENT FOOL HAS A GRADE SCHOOLER'S BRAIN THAT THINKS ABOUT NOTHING BUT BATTLE, AND HE'S ABOUT AS DUMB AS A RHINOCEROS BEETLE.
BUT HE'S NOT A BAD GUY...
...AND AS THINGS STAND, HE'LL NEVER BE ABLE TO REST IN PEACE!
I HAVE TO FIND THE KILLER FOR HIM!
DUN
I HAVE NO OTHER CHOICE! I'LL USE MY POWERS,
AND WITNESS THE EXACT MOMENT OF THE CRIME!
DU-
UQ HOLDER No.9 Kirië Sakurame
HAS THE UNIQUE SKILL, RESET & RESTART, THAT ALLOWS HER TO CREATE SAVE POINTS AND RETURN TO THEM WHEN SHE DIES.
LOCATION: RIGHT HERE!
TO THE MORNING THE MURDER TOOK PLACE!
CHOMP
CHIRP
CHIRP
TWEET
TWEET
A FEW HOURS EARLIER.
POUND
POUND
POUND
HEY! KIRIË!
ARE YOU HOME?
I'M COMING IN!
CLICK
CLICK

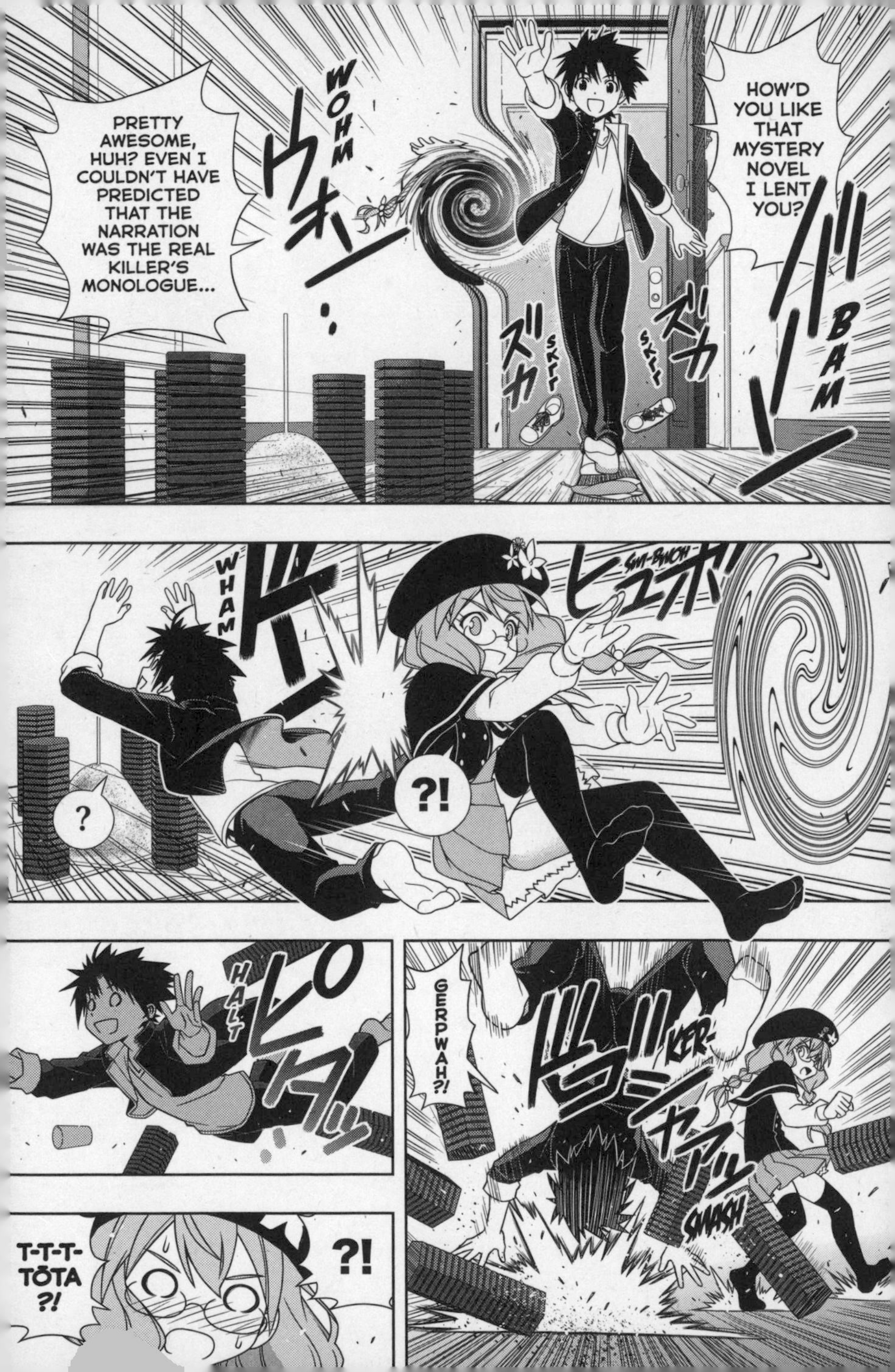
HOW'D YOU LIKE THAT MYSTERY NOVEL I LENT YOU?
BAM
SKFF
SKFF
WOHM
PRETTY AWESOME, HUH? EVEN I COULDN'T HAVE PREDICTED THAT THE NARRATION WAS THE REAL KILLER'S MONOLOGUE...
WHAM
?!
?
KER-SMASH
GERPWAH?!
HALT
?!
T-T-T-TŌTA ?!

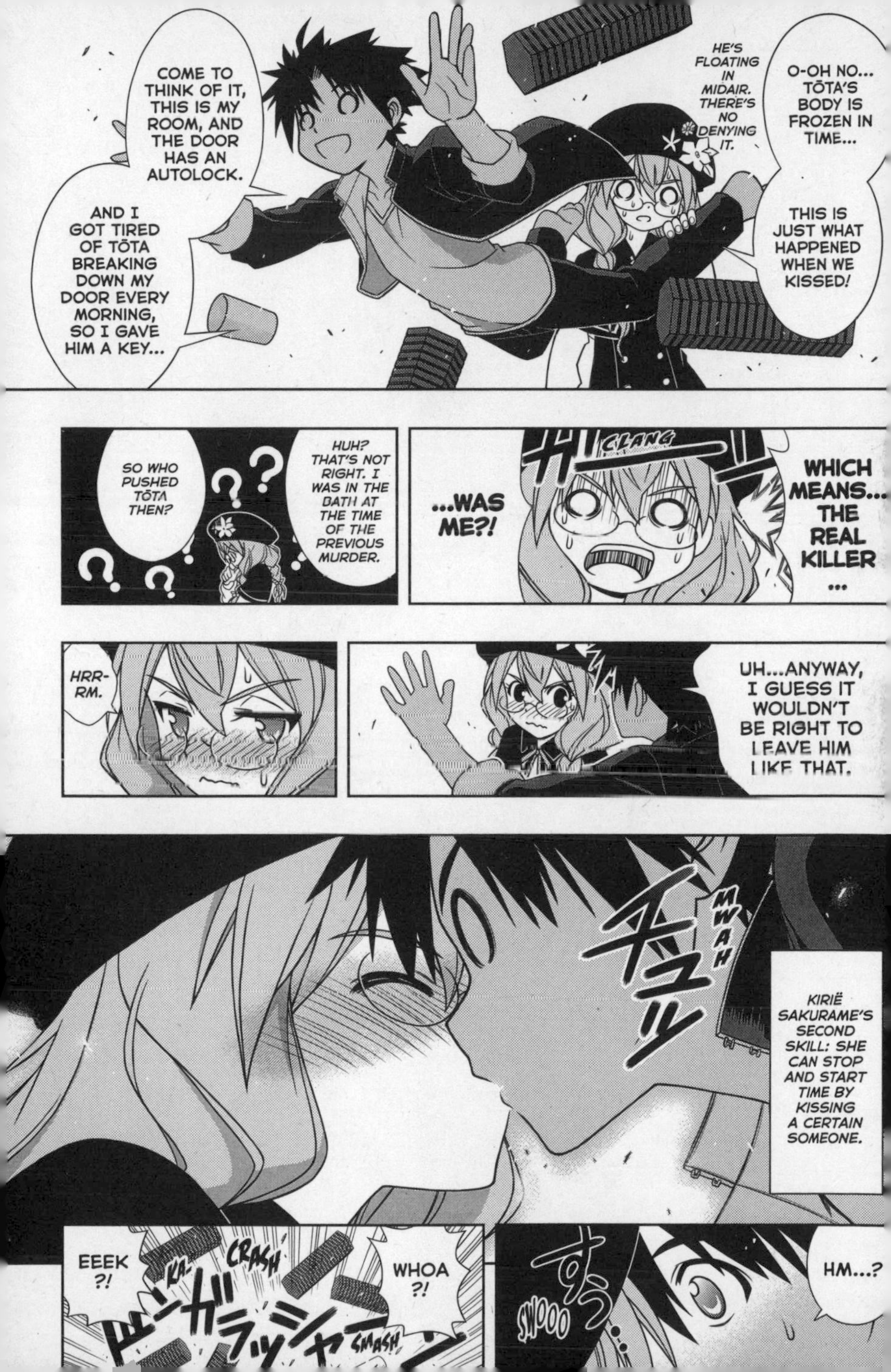
O-OH NO... TŌTA'S BODY IS FROZEN IN TIME...
HE'S FLOATING IN MIDAIR. THERE'S NO DENYING IT.
THIS IS JUST WHAT HAPPENED WHEN WE KISSED!
COME TO THINK OF IT, THIS IS MY ROOM, AND THE DOOR HAS AN AUTOLOCK.
AND I GOT TIRED OF TŌTA BREAKING DOWN MY DOOR EVERY MORNING, SO I GAVE HIM A KEY...
WHICH MEANS... THE REAL KILLER ...
CLANG
...WAS ME?!
HUH? THAT'S NOT RIGHT. I WAS IN THE BATH AT THE TIME OF THE PREVIOUS MURDER.
SO WHO PUSHED TŌTA THEN?
UH...ANYWAY, I GUESS IT WOULDN'T BE RIGHT TO LEAVE HIM LIKE THAT.
HRR-RM.
KIRIË SAKURAME'S SECOND SKILL: SHE CAN STOP AND START TIME BY KISSING A CERTAIN SOMEONE.
MWAH
HM...?
SWOOO
WHOA ?!
CRASH
KA-
SMASH
EEEK ?!

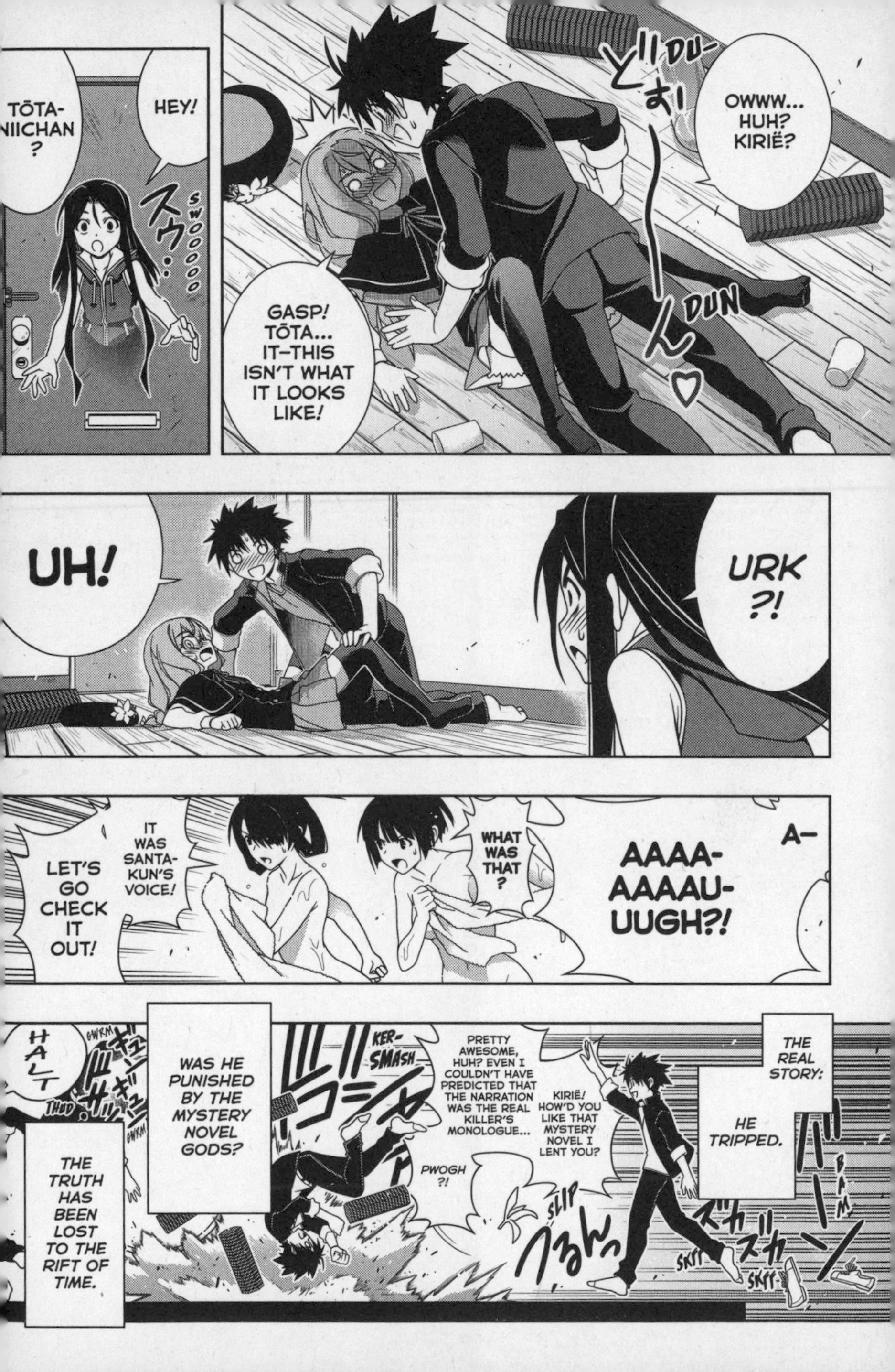
DU-
OWWW... HUH? KIRIË?
DUN
GASP! TŌTA... IT—THIS ISN'T WHAT IT LOOKS LIKE!
HEY!
TŌTA-NIICHAN?
SWOOOOOO
URK ?!
UH!
A—
AAAA-AAAAU-UUGH?!
WHAT WAS THAT?
IT WAS SANTA-KUN'S VOICE!
LET'S GO CHECK IT OUT!
THE REAL STORY:
HE TRIPPED.
BAM
SKTT
SKTT
KIRIË! HOW'D YOU LIKE THAT MYSTERY NOVEL I LENT YOU?
PRETTY AWESOME, HUH? EVEN I COULDN'T HAVE PREDICTED THAT THE NARRATION WAS THE REAL KILLER'S MONOLOGUE...
SLIP
PWOGH ?!
KER-SMASH
WAS HE PUNISHED BY THE MYSTERY NOVEL GODS?
GWRM
HALT
GWRM
THUD
THE TRUTH HAS BEEN LOST TO THE RIFT OF TIME.

UQ HOLDER!

STAFF

Ken Akamatsu
Takashi Takemoto
Kenichi Nakamura
Keiichi Yamashita
Yuri Sasaki
Madoka Akanuma

Thanks to Ran Ayanaga

A new series from the creator of *Soul Eater*, the megahit manga and anime seen on Toonami!

"Fun and lively... a great start!"
-Adventures in Poor Taste

FIRE FORCE

By Atsushi Ohkubo

The city of Tokyo is plagued by a deadly phenomenon: spontaneous human combustion! Luckily, a special team is there to quench the inferno: The Fire Force! The fire soldiers at Special Fire Cathedral 8 are about to get a unique addition. Enter Shinra, a boy who possesses the power to run at the speed of a rocket, leaving behind the famous "devil's footprints" (and destroying his shoes in the process). Can Shinra and his colleagues discover the source of this strange epidemic before the city burns to ashes?

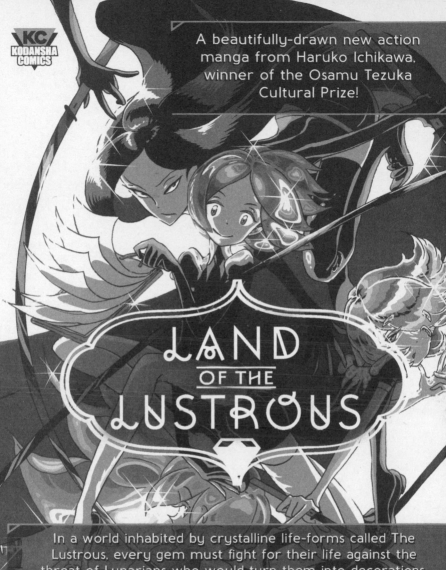

A beautifully-drawn new action manga from Haruko Ichikawa, winner of the Osamu Tezuka Cultural Prize!

LAND
OF THE
LUSTROUS

In a world inhabited by crystalline life-forms called The Lustrous, every gem must fight for their life against the threat of Lunarians who would turn them into decorations. Phosphophyllite, the most fragile and brittle of gems, longs to join the battle, so when Phos is instead assigned to complete a natural history of their world, it sounds like a dull and pointless task. But this new job brings Phos into contact with Cinnabar, a gem forced to live in isolation. Can Phos's seemingly mundane assignment lead both Phos and Cinnabar to the fulfillment they desire?

ANIME COMING OUT SUMMER 2018!

Mikami's middle age hasn't gone as he planned: He never found a girlfriend, he got stuck in a dead-end job, and he was abruptly stabbed to death in the street at 37. So when he wakes up in a new world straight out of a fantasy RPG, he's disappointed, but not exactly surprised to find that he's facing down a dragon, not as a knight or a wizard, but as a blind slime monster. But there are chances for even a slime to become a hero...

"A fun adventure that fantasy readers will relate to and enjoy."
— AiPT!

THAT TIME I GOT REINCARNATED AS A SLIME

A new series from Yoshitoki Oima, creator of The New York Times
bestselling manga and Eisner Award nominee *A Silent Voice*!

An intimate,
emotional drama
and an epic story
spanning time and
space...

TO YOUR ETERNITY

An orb was cast unto the earth. After metamorphosing
into a wolf, It joins a boy on his bleak journey to find
his tribe. Ever learning, It transcends death, even when
those around It cannot...

UQ HOLDER! VOLUME 16 IS A WORK OF FICTION. NAMES, CHARACTERS, PLACES, AND INCIDENTS ARE THE PRODUCTS OF THE AUTHOR'S IMAGINATION OR ARE USED FICTITIOUSLY. ANY RESEMBLANCE TO ACTUAL EVENTS, LOCALES, OR PERSONS, LIVING OR DEAD, IS ENTIRELY COINCIDENTAL.

A KODANSHA COMICS TRADE PAPERBACK ORIGINAL

PUBLISHED IN THE UNITED STATES BY KODANSHA COMICS, AN IMPRINT OF KODANSHA USA PUBLISHING, LLC, NEW YORK.

PUBLICATION RIGHTS FOR THIS ENGLISH EDITION ARRANGED THROUGH KODANSHA LTD., TOKYO.

FIRST PUBLISHED IN JAPAN IN 2018 BY KODANSHA LTD., TOKYO.

ISBN 978-1-63236-737-2

PRINTED IN THE UNITED STATES OF AMERICA.

WWW.KODANSHACOMICS.COM

9 8 7 6 5 4 3 2 1

TRANSLATION: ALETHEA NIBLEY AND ATHENA NIBLEY
LETTERING: JAMES DASHIELL
KODANSHA COMICS EDITION COVER DESIGN: PHIL BALSMAN